NORDIC GENRE FILM

Traditions in World Cinema

General Editors
Linda Badley (Middle Tennessee State University)
R. Barton Palmer (Clemson University)

Founding Editor
Steven Jay Schneider (New York University)

Titles in the series include:
Traditions in World Cinema
by Linda Badley, R. Barton Palmer and Steven Jay Schneider (eds)
Japanese Horror Cinema
by Jay McRoy (ed.)
New Punk Cinema
by Nicholas Rombes (ed.)
African Filmmaking
by Roy Armes
Palestinian Cinema
by Nurith Gertz and George Khleifi
Chinese Martial Arts Cinema
by Stephen Teo
Czech and Slovak Cinema
by Peter Hames
The New Neapolitan Cinema
by Alex Marlow-Mann
American Smart Cinema
by Claire Perkins
The International Film Musical
by Corey Creekmur and Linda Mokdad (eds)

Italian Neorealist Cinema
by Torunn Haaland
Magic Realist Cinema in East Central Europe
by Aga Skrodzka
Italian Post-Neorealist Cinema
by Luca Barattoni
Spanish Horror Film
by Antonio Lázaro-Reboll
Post-beur Cinema
by Will Higbee
New Taiwanese Cinema in Focus
by Flannery Wilson
International Noir
by Homer B. Pettey and R. Barton Palmer (eds)
Films on Ice
by Scott MacKenzie and Anna Westerståhl Stenport (eds)
Nordic Genre Film
by Tommy Gustafsson and Pietari Kääpä (eds)
Contemporary Japanese Cinema Since Hana-Bi
by Adam Bingham
Chinese Martial Arts Cinema
by Stephen Teo

www.euppublishing.com/series/tiwc

NORDIC GENRE FILM

Small Nation Film Cultures in the Global Marketplace

Edited by Tommy Gustafsson and Pietari Kääpä

EDINBURGH
University Press

© editorial matter and organisation Tommy Gustafsson and Pietari Kääpä, 2015
© the chapters their several authors, 2015

Edinburgh University Press Ltd
The Tun – Holyrood Road
12 (2f) Jackson's Entry
Edinburgh EH8 8PJ
www.euppublishing.com

Typeset in 10/12.5 pt Sabon by
Servis Filmsetting Ltd, Stockport, Cheshire

A CIP record for this book is available from the British Library

ISBN 978 0 7486 9318 4 (hardback)
ISBN 978 0 7486 9319 1 (webready PDF)
ISBN 978 0 7486 9320 7 (epub)

The right of Tommy Gustafsson and Pietari Kääpä to be identified as editors of this work has been asserted in accordance with the Copyright, Designs and Patents Act 1988, and the Copyright and Related Rights Regulations 2003 (SI No. 2498).

CONTENTS

List of Illustrations	viii
List of Contributors	x
Traditions in World Cinema	xii
Introduction: Nordic Genre Film and Institutional History *Tommy Gustafsson and Pietari Kääpä*	1

PART I. HERITAGE CINEMA AND NATIONAL NARRATIVES

1. *Sibelius* and the Re-emergence of the Great Man Biopic   21
   Kimmo Laine

2. Whose Repressed Memories? *Max Manus: Man of War* and *Flame & Citron* (from a Swede's Point of View)   33
   Erik Hedling

3. Voices from the Past – Recent Nordic Historical Films   47
   Gunnar Iversen

PART II. CRIME AND DETECTIVE NARRATIVES

4. Crime Up North: The Case of Norway, Finland and Iceland   61
   Björn Ægir Norðfjörð

CONTENTS

5. The Thrill of the Nordic Kill: The Manhunt Movie in the Nordic Thriller
   Rikke Schubart — 76

6. Bridges and Tunnels: Negotiating the National in Transnational Television Drama
   Anders Wilhelm Åberg — 91

7. Stockholm Noir: Neoliberalism and Gangsterism in *Easy Money*
   Michael Tapper — 104

8. The Private Life of the Prime Minister? Politics, Drama and Documentary in *Pääministeri* and *Palme*
   Anneli Lehtisalo — 119

PART III. NORDIC OPTIMISM: ROAD MOVIES, COMEDIES AND MUSICALS

9. Fathers and Sons Reunited: Road Movies as Stories of Generational Continuity
   Tommi Römpötti — 133

10. The Nordic 'Quirky Feel-Good'
    Ellen Rees — 147

11. Contesting Marriage: The Finnish Unromantic Comedy
    Jaakko Seppälä — 159

12. Powered by Music: Contemporary Film Musicals, Nordic Style
    Ann-Kristin Wallengren — 173

PART IV. NORDIC HORRORS

13. Slasher in the Snow: The Rise of the Low-Budget Nordic Horror Film
    Tommy Gustafsson — 189

14. Nordic Vampires: Stories of Social Exclusion in Nordic Welfare States
    Outi Hakola — 203

PART V. GENRE BENDERS

15. A National/Transnational Genre: Pornography in Transition
    Mariah Larsson — 217

16. Going Hollywood: Nordic Directors in American Cinema 230
    Arne Lunde

17. A Culture of Reciprocity: The Politics of Cultural Exchange in
    Contemporary Nordic Genre Film 244
    Pietari Kääpä

    Index 262

ILLUSTRATIONS

2.1 *Max Manus*: An idyllic image of the Stockholm City Hall showing that Sweden is also prepared for war. 37

2.2 *Flame & Citron*: The old town in Stockholm with the German church towering in the middle. Image courtesy of Nimbus Film Productions. 39

4.1 *Insomnia*: A Swedish police detective (Stellan Skarsgård) bewildered and out of his element in northern Norway. Image courtesy of Norsk Film. 62

4.2 *Headhunters*: A cosmopolitan employment recruiter (Aksel Hennie) very much at home in the nondescript world of global capitalism. Image courtesy of Friland. 62

4.3 *Priest of Evil*: A police detective (Peter Franzén) seeking revenge in a noir-inspired Helsinki cityscape. Image courtesy of Matila Röhr Productions. 66

4.4 *City State*: A corrupt police officer (Sigurður Sigurjónsson) faces 'interrogation' by Serbian gang members at the outskirts of Reykjavík. Image courtesy of Poppoli Pictures. 70

5.1 The protagonist Lucas (Mads Mikkelsen) is a deer hunter in the start of Thomas Vinterberg's *The Hunt* (Jagten, 2012). Zentropa. 85

5.2 Lucas, wrongly accused of sexually assaulting a little girl, becomes a target of the community's aggression and is beaten up by the local butcher. *The Hunt*, 2012, Zentropa. 85

5.3   At the end of the film former big-game hunter Lucas helps Klara over the stripes on the floor. He now no longer hunts. *The Hunt*, 2012, Zentropa. 85

9.1 and 9.2   Timo absorbed in his thoughts in *Road North*. Images courtesy of Marianna Films Oy. 136

9.3 and 9.4   Kai's subjective point of view in *Finnish Blood Swedish Heart*. Images courtesy of Hysteria Film AB/Klaffi Productions. 138

11.1   There is little upon which the protagonists could build a lasting relationship in *The Storage*. Image courtesy of Kinosto Oy. 160

11.2   Traditional gender roles are reversed in *21 Ways to Ruin a Marriage*. Image courtesy of Dionysos Films Oy. 163

11.3   Stigu's parents are happily married in *The Body Fat Index of Love*. Image courtesy of MRP Matila Röhr Productions Oy. 166

13.1   The Nordic version of the final girl. The resourceful and sexually experienced Jannicke (Ingrid Bolsø Berdal) finishes off the male monster in *Cold Prey* (2006). Image courtesy of Fantefilm. 190

13.2   Extreme violence in *Wither* (2013), a gruesome and well-crafted gore extravaganza loosely based on Nordic folklore of the Vittra. Image courtesy of Stockholm Syndrome Film. 195

15.1   'Bad swedish but still Swedish': National designations are very much alive as a part of the tagging of film clips. 221

17.1   Action in the fjords: *Norwegian Ninja* (Thomas Cappelen Malling, 2011). Image courtesy of Torden Films. 245

CONTRIBUTORS

Anders Wilhelm Åberg is Senior Lecturer of Film Studies at Linnaeus University, Sweden

Tommy Gustafsson is Associate Professor in Film Studies at Linnaeus University, Sweden

Outi Hakola is a lecturer in Area and Cultural Studies at the University of Helsinki

Erik Hedling is Professor of Film Studies at Lund University, Sweden

Gunnar Iversen is Professor of Film Studies in the Department of Art and Media Studies at the Norwegian University of Science and Technology

Pietari Kääpä is Lecturer in Media and Communications at the University of Stirling

Kimmo Laine is a collegium researcher at the Turku Institute for Advanced Studies (TIAS)

Mariah Larsson is Research Fellow at the department of Media Studies at Stockholm University, and Associate Professor at Malmö University, section of Sexology and Sexuality Studies

CONTRIBUTORS

Anneli Lehtisalo is a post-doctoral researcher in a three-year research project at the Academy of Finland

Arne Lunde is Associate Professor in the Scandinavian Section and in Cinema and Media Studies at UCLA

Björn Ægir Norðfjörð is Associate Professor and Director of Film Studies at the University of Iceland

Ellen Rees is Associate Professor at the University of Oslo's Centre for Ibsen Studies

Tommi Römpötti is University Lecturer of Media Studies at the University of Turku

Rikke Schubart is Associate Professor at the University of Southern Denmark

Jaakko Seppälä is a postdoctoral researcher at the University of Helsinki

Michael Tapper is film critic for the Swedish daily *Sydsvenska Dagbladet* and has a PhD in Film Studies from Lund University, Sweden

Ann-Kristin Wallengren is Professor in Film Studies, Lund University, Sweden

TRADITIONS IN WORLD CINEMA

General editors: **Linda Badley and R. Barton Palmer**
Founding editor: **Steven Jay Schneider**

Traditions in World Cinema is a series of textbooks and monographs devoted to the analysis of currently popular and previously underexamined or undervalued film movements from around the globe. Also intended for general interest readers, the textbooks in this series offer undergraduate- and graduate-level film students accessible and comprehensive introductions to diverse traditions in world cinema. The monographs open up for advanced academic study more specialised groups of films, including those that require theoretically oriented approaches. Both textbooks and monographs provide thorough examinations of the industrial, cultural, and socio-historical conditions of production and reception.

The flagship textbook for the series includes chapters by noted scholars on traditions of acknowledged importance (the French New Wave, German Expressionism), recent and emergent traditions (New Iranian, post-Cinema Novo), and those whose rightful claim to recognition has yet to be established (the Israeli persecution film, global found footage cinema). Other volumes concentrate on individual national, regional or global cinema traditions. As the introductory chapter to each volume makes clear, the films under discussion form a coherent group on the basis of substantive and relatively transparent, if not always obvious, commonalities. These commonalities may be formal, stylistic or thematic, and the groupings may, although they need not, be popularly identified as genres, cycles or movements (Japanese horror, Chinese martial arts cinema, Italian Neorealism). Indeed, in cases in which a group of films is not already commonly identified as a tradition, one purpose of the volume is to establish its claim to importance and make it visible (East Central European Magical Realist cinema, Palestinian cinema).

Textbooks and monographs include:

- An introduction that clarifies the rationale for the grouping of films under examination
- A concise history of the regional, national, or transnational cinema in question
- A summary of previous published work on the tradition
- Contextual analysis of industrial, cultural and socio-historical conditions of production and reception
- Textual analysis of specific and notable films, with clear and judicious application of relevant film theoretical approaches
- Bibliography(ies)/filmography(ies)

Monographs may additionally include:

- Discussion of the dynamics of cross-cultural exchange in light of current research and thinking about cultural imperialism and globalisation, as well as issues of regional/national cinema or political/aesthetic movements (such as new waves, postmodernism, or identity politics)
- Interview(s) with key filmmakers working within the tradition.

INTRODUCTION: NORDIC GENRE FILM AND INSTITUTIONAL HISTORY

Tommy Gustafsson and Pietari Kääpä

The demand for all areas of Nordic film and television culture outside the borders of the Nordic countries may come as no surprise. The popularity of television shows such as *The Killing* (*Forbrydelsen*, 2007) and *The Bridge* (*Bron|Broen*, 2011) both domestically and internationally have increased the profile of Nordic media while the crime novels of Henning Mankell and Stieg Larsson have penetrated the American market – the barometer for global commercial 'relevance'. *The Guardian* in the UK has published several articles on the craze, noting how the protagonist of the original Danish version of *The Killing*, detective Sarah Lund, has become an unlikely fashion icon with her knitted sweaters. While a certain type of Nordic film – the existential artistry of a Dreyer, a Bergman or a Kaurismäki – has existed at the periphery of this global consciousness, such perceptions are clearly shifting as the contemporary situation seems to be more characterised by Nordic contributions to global popular culture instead of the more traditional frameworks of artistic or experimental relevance. How did we get to this situation? In short, how did the media products of this small region of the world become part of global popular culture?

In order to understand the international emergence of the Nordic media of the twenty-first century, we must turn to the 'revival' of the Nordic film industries in the late 1990s and early 2000s. Specifically, we must focus on the history of the Nordic genre film and its relationship with governmental support and film institutes. Previous international scholarship on Nordic cinemas has been carried out through a dense focus of art house cinema, often with a small number of auteur films with international distribution as its preferred examples (see, for example, Hardy 1952; Cowie 1992; Thomson 2006). This institutionalised history is largely based on the concept of film as a national art cinema, a concept that relies on a sharp contrast with Hollywood's fordianesque output of genre films. The notion of the national art film is so prevalent that a historical dictionary on Scandinavian cinema published in 2012 states as fact that 'the production of genre film was sparse and, instead, a production of art house films and social problem films was favored' during the period from 1960 to 1990 (Sundholm et al. 2012: 3). However, a look at the actual output of Nordic films before, during and after the period mentioned reveals that the productions of genre films have always surpassed the productions of art house films by a wide margin. On the whole comedies have without competition been the prevalent genre in all Nordic countries with films like the Finnish musical comedies starring Tauno Palo and Ansa Ikonen, the Swedish smash hit *Love Mates* (*Änglar, finn dom?*, Lars-Magnus Lindgren, 1961), Icelandic *101 Reykjavík* (Baltasar Kormákur, 2000), Danish *Olsen Gang* films (*Olsen Banden*, 1968–98) and the Norwegian *The Man Who Could Not Laugh* (*Mannen som ikke kunne le*, Bo Hermansson, 1968), closely followed by the popular countryside melodrama, children's films, and war films like the Finnish *The Winter War* (*Talvisota*, Pekka Parikka, 1989).

The confusion between Sundholm et al.'s assertion and the realities of cinematic output seems to arise from what exactly is meant by the term 'genre'. Indeed, the term is contested within the body of scholarship on genre. For example, Jane Feuer considers genre as ultimately 'an abstract conception rather than something that exists empirically in the world' (1992: 144). For David Buckingham, genre is a culturally flexible term as 'it is in a constant process of negotiation and change' (1993: 137). If we were to define genre in the Hollywood sense of a marketable commodity with preset advertising conventions and audience demographics, often considered to consist of horror, action, science fiction, the western or the like, it would certainly be the case that Nordic productions are sparse. While it is true that the horror genre, for one, is a distinct rarity in Nordic film culture pre-2000s (see below for more discussion of this), it is also clearly overstating the case to argue that genre – as both a set of cinematic conventions and an industrial strategy – has not held a key place in Nordic film cultures.

Historically, genre films like the two Danish international sensations *The White Slave Trade* (*Den hvide slavehandel*, August Blom, 1910) and *The Abyss* (*Afgrunden*, Urban Gad, 1910) were the first Nordic films that entered the international film market. Nordisk Films Kompagni, the leading Danish film company at the time, specialised in entertaining thrillers and melodramas, often with equivoque elements. In Danish and international film history the period between 1910 and 1917 has also been dubbed a Golden Age (see, for example, Soila, Söderbergh Widding and Iversen 1998: 7–9). Likewise,

INTRODUCTION

Sweden had a Golden Age, usually placed between 1917 and 1924, when Swedish films successfully were exported to all known countries in the world. In retrospect this Golden Age has been linked to some twenty high-budget 'art films' that were typically based on a recognised novel and where the filmmakers every so often exploited Nordic nature in the narrative. Then again, this vast export of films, mainly due to the demand for film programming that the First World War had created, did in reality mostly consist of straightforward genre films, like the comedy *Love and Journalism* (*Kärlek och journalistik*, Mauritz Stiller, 1916) or the crime thriller *The Death Kiss* (*Dödskyssen*, Victor Sjöström, 1916). The biggest export success of all during these years was not a canonised film like *The Phantom Chariot* (*Körkarlen*, Victor Sjöström, 1921) but instead the immensely popular animations of *Captain Grogg* (Gustafsson 2007: 23–5). Finland, Norway and Iceland did not have similar periods of export success although Finland and Norway have had their own domestic Golden Ages, both in the 1930s and 1940s (Solia, Söderbergh Widding and Iversen 1998: 42–8, 110–13).

Genre film has not only dominated Nordic film production; genre films have also, with few exceptions like *The Silence* (*Tystnaden*, Ingmar Bergman, 1963), been the most successful ones at the domestic box offices year after year. In Sweden, for example, only one out of the thirteen films that have topped the annual box office list since 2001 (SFI 2014) can be labelled as an art film, or at least as a medium-concept film according to Andrew Nestingen's definition of films that linger between the genre and the art house (Nestingen 2008). That film was *As It Is in Heaven* (*Så som i himmelen*, Kay Follak, 2004), which became a huge art house hit in Europe with 3.5 million tickets sold (Lumiere 2014). Yet that pales in comparison with the success of the genre film *The Girl with the Dragon Tattoo* (*Män som hatar kvinnor*, Niels Arden Oplev, 2009) with a ticket sale that exceeded 10 million worldwide (Hedling 2014: 94), not to mention the American $90 million remake, *The Girl with the Dragon Tattoo* (David Fincher, 2011).

However, up until the turn of the new millennium domestic genre films were generally not exported. There were only a few exceptions, including the wave of Danish and Swedish sexploitations films in the 1960s and 1970s (see Stevenson 2010) and the production of direct-to-VHS genre films in the 1980s. Instead, beginning during the silent age and continuing up until today, the Nordic countries started to 'export' film talent to Hollywood, and the list of actors, actresses, directors and technical personnel is extensive with names like Ingrid Bergman, Renny Harlin, Nicolas Winding Refn and Swedish sound editor Paul N. J. Ottosson. This phenomenon is further discussed by Arne Lunde in this collection (see also Lunde 2010).

What was exported from the mid-1950s and onwards were films meant for the worldwide art house cinema circuit, which poorly reflects the actual film production in the Nordic countries. It was mainly Swedish and Danish films that got this international attention but art house films were exported among the Nordic countries. This development came about as a result of the difficulties that the Nordic film industries faced from competition with the introduction of television in the mid-1950s and early 60s. In order to save their national film industries, Nordic governments offered support in various forms, most commonly with the creation of influential film institutes that steered parts of film production towards the production of 'valuable' films, that is, art house films and social problem films (Soila 2005: 3). This is significant as Nordic countries make for small nation cinemas that have had to rely more and more extensively on governmental support because the small size of the domestic audiences makes financial success purely based on domestic returns very unlikely. Several studies have discussed the implications of domestic institutional structures for the type of cinema produced in these countries, and this has also consolidated the strong notion that cinema became a predominantly artistic endeavour which prioritised experimental or stodgy national histories over more commercially minded productions (see, for example, Cowie 1992; Solia, Söderbergh Widding and Iversen 1998; Thomson 2006).

This type of national film politics persisted until the late 1980s in the case of Sweden, Norway, Denmark and Finland, with Iceland only finding its film industrial bearing in the late 1980s. Changes started to take place in these politics as the organisations adopted more lenient views towards commercial production, with the film institute in Finland, for example, granting funding for the populist *Uuno Turhapuro* films (1973–2004) in 1987. Norway increased its investment in feature films, and in 2001 the Norwegian Film Institute was replaced by Norsk Filmfond. This new governmental body introduced a support structure that asserted that if the film producers could find private funding for 50 per cent of the budget then Norsk Filmfond would automatically cover the remaining 50 per cent (Iversen 2011: 293–4), a model also implemented by the Finnish Film Foundation in 2011. And in Sweden the creation of a number of regional film centres, with support from the European Union, broke and eventually changed the Swedish Film Institute's supremacy over film production (Hedling 2008: 8–17). A significant adoption of these new politics can be seen by the early 2000s as genre productions of a range of varieties became mainstream in all the Nordic countries. If art house, social problems or historical films were the norm before, nowadays it would not be overstating the case to suggest that domestic productions more often than not follow competitive genre strategies, successfully catering to domestic viewers as well as gaining a measure of international recognition, both on the film festival circuit and commercially. As several chapters in this collection emphasise, the restructuring of the Nordic film institutes plays a key role in the emergence of the new Nordic genre film.

INTRODUCTION

Comedy and Nordic Cultural Closeness

The Nordic countries are often lumped together as Scandinavia or the 'Norden', and in correspondence with this perception, the film industries are often considered as one homogeneous film culture. Considering this 'cultural closeness', the export and import of genre films within the region ought to be more frequent than they actually are. However, almost mechanistically, it is claimed that films do not travel between the Nordic countries, but this is a truth that has to be modified. First, historically, the export scene has been rather lively even though the flow of films has been in certain directions. For example, both Denmark and Sweden have been able to export considerably more films to the other Nordic countries than Denmark and Sweden have imported from those other countries (Soila, Söderbergh Widding and Iversen 1998: 236).

The films that have been exported usually belong to Nestingen's medium-concept category where the notion of valuable cinema has operated as a decisive factor in decisions to import a film from one of the neighbouring Nordic countries. That is, these are the same type of films that would have the chance to be exported to countries outside the Nordic region as well, often playing on the international art house cinema circuit. However, according to the statistics of the Swedish Film Institute, Swedish distributors brought in no fewer than 111 Danish films, 71 Norwegian films, 71 Finnish films and 13 Icelandic films between 2001 and 2014 (SFI 2014). Several of these films are co-productions such as the Norwegian/Swedish animated children's film *Hokus Pokus Alfons Åberg* (Torill Kove, 2013), and the majority can be characterised as medium-concept films like the Oscar-winning Danish film *In a Better World* (*Hævnen*, Susanne Bier, 2010). But also represented are straightforward popular genre films like the Norwegian horror vehicle *Dead Snow* (*Død snø*, Tommy Wirkola, 2013) and Finnish sci-fi *Iron Sky* (Timo Vuorensola, 2012).

Undoubtedly, it is not difficult to observe significant export patterns within the Nordic region, and the discrepancy between the statistics and the persistent notion that few films are exported must therefore be examined. When considering these 266 Nordic films that were screened at Swedish cinemas, the most obvious observation is the fact that only a handful of these films can be labelled as commercial successes. If one draws a tentative line at 100,000 visitors as a mark of success, only 6 out of the 266 films meet that criterion.[1] In fact the average number of tickets sold per film is 9,563. That means that Swedish distributors imported many of these films even though they probably knew by experience that they were not going to have a runaway success on their hands. Accordingly, a majority of the distributors that imported Nordic films catered mainly to the alternative Swedish cinema circuit, that is, to cinemas outside of Svensk Filmindustri's near-monopoly (SFI 2014). Thus, although there is clear evidence of a higher export/import rate than the general perception suggests, these films still have a hard time finding paying audiences in their neighbouring countries.

This especially goes for the popular genre films that often gain international recognition on different levels (at film festivals/artistically/commercially), but that nonetheless bomb at the box office in their neighbouring countries. As discussed by Tommy Gustafsson in his chapter on the Nordic horror film in this collection, well-made genre productions like the Norwegian *Cold Prey* (*Fritt Vilt*, Roar Uthaug, 2006), the Swedish *Wither* (*Vittra*, Sonny Laguna, Tommy Wiklund, 2013) or the Finish *Rare Exports* (Jalmari Helander, 2010) have been noticed internationally but are often not even exported to the other Nordic countries. A paradox is that the most popular genre, that is, the comedy film in its many different forms and subgenres, also is the most problematic when it comes to export. Jaakko Seppälä's chapter on the 'unromantic comedy' in this collection is a case in point. In order to discuss the question of why popular genre films have had such problems travelling within the Nordic region we will explore two comedy films in relation to national/transnational implications of genre formations and preferences. Significant here are the ways genre acts as a sort of battleground (or alternatively, a more productive soil) for developing domestic film culture as a dynamic part of an international system of cinema.

We start with an exception to the rule, the Oscar-nominated Norwegian film *Elling* (aka *Me, My Friend and I*, Petter Næss, 2001), a film that managed to cross borders and attract large audiences in all Nordic countries. *Elling* is a comedy about two men who try to cope with life in Oslo after a long period of institutionalisation. In Norway the film became one of the most widely viewed ever with 769,923 tickets sold (Kino 2014), and in Sweden, Denmark, Finland and Iceland it received respectable ticket sales of 91,178, 37,236, 18,819 and 10,657 respectively (SFI 2014; DFI 2014; Lumiere 2014). *Elling* was an adaptation of Norwegian author Ingvar Ambjørnsen's novel *Brødre i blodet* (1996), and although this book was subsequently translated into several languages, Ambjørnsen is more known internationally as a writer of children's books. Hence, *Brødre i blodet*, being the third part in a series of four books, could not be used as a selling point for the film version in the other Nordic countries and the main character, Elling, was unknown to people outside Norway.

Although reviews do not represent public opinion they are nevertheless important, not least in introducing new films that do not easily fit within the spectrum of domestic productions or Hollywood imports. When reading reviews for *Elling*, different national sentiments and points of friction, which are closely connected to historic neighbour relations, become quite apparent. In Norway *Elling* was, not surprisingly, hailed as a 'beautiful' and 'funny' film, and one reviewer started his review by declaring: 'Just rejoice: we have a Norwegian audience winner at the movies!' (Selås 2001). In Denmark the reviews had a more condescending tone, perhaps due to historic big–little brother relations as Norway had been a part of the Danish kingdom for several hundred years until 1814. In *Politiken*, one of Denmark's biggest daily newspapers, *Elling* was presented in negative terms: 'you can hardly call this Norwegian cinema success a work of art', but the same reviewer nevertheless used typical art house cinema vocabulary when referring to *Elling* as a 'chamber play' and comparing the film with iconographic artworks such John Steinbeck's novel *Of Mice and Men* (1937) and Milos Forman's film *One Flew Over the Cuckoo's Nest* (1975) (Skotte 2002). In Sweden, on the other hand, *Elling* got rave reviews and was considered to be an 'intelligent comedy' and a film that 'represents the best of the new European comedy: saucy, non-trivializing in an easy way, visually distinctive and particularly well played' (Gentele 2001). However, the Swedish reviews were surprised that Norway even could produce such a film: 'They not only have oil and lusekofter, those Norwegians, now they also show that they have humor. And who could have believed that?' (Hördin 2001), and in *Aftonbladet* the reviewer tried to explain to its Swedish readers that *Elling* 'made you happy' despite the fact that it was made in Norway (Peterson 2001).

While the Norwegian reviews focused on the national pride of an actual Norwegian genre hit in competition with films like that year's *Harry Potter and the Philosopher's Stone* (Chris Columbus, 2001) and *Bridget Jones's Diary* (Sharon Maguire, 2001), both the reviews in *Politiken* and *Aftonbladet* firmly position *Elling* as a medium-concept film that just happens to be a comedy. That is, this genre film transformed into an art film of sorts when it left the Norwegian national sphere. This is also in line with how Ellen Rees analyses *Elling* in her chapter on the Nordic 'quirky feel-good' genre included in this collection.

In an anthology on contemporary Nordic cinema, Nestingen and Elkington ask why the concept of national cinema seems to be more resilient in the Nordic countries than elsewhere, and summarise the reasons for the national concept very widely as a 'tradition of production and audience taste, institutionalized support for national cinema, and critical and scholarly cinema discourse' (Nestingen and Elkington 2005: 10). Yet we would like to propose that *Elling*, and especially the reception of the film, first and foremost is a result of fifty years of institutionalised film politics where national film institutes have sustained a strong emphasis on the qualities and centrality of the idea of 'valuable' national cinema on the one hand, and on the other created a distance that has undermined any perceivable cultural, geographical and historical closeness between the Nordic film cultures.

However, this cultural closeness is complicated and as Soila, Söderbergh Widding and Iversen assert, '[i]deas, novels and the like can be brought from a neighboring country, but they must be subjected to national decoding and be given specific national characteristics' (1998: 236). The second example where the national complicates the transnational genre ingredients is the most popular series of films that has been produced in Denmark, namely the fourteen instalments of the *Olsen Gang* series (*Olsen-banden*) made between 1968 and 1998. The Olsen Gang is a fictional criminal gang led by the 'genius' and habitual offender Egon Olsen with his accomplices Benny and Kjeld. The film series portrays the gang's criminal activities, which often fail, in a harmless and humorous way that appeal to family audiences. For example, three out of the eleven films that have had more than 1 million viewers in Denmark since 1976 have been *Olsen-banden* films: *Olsen-banden ser rødt* (Erik Balling, 1976), *Olsen-banden deruda'* (Erik Balling, 1977) and *Olsen-banden går i krig* (Erik Balling, 1978) (DFI 2014).

Despite this overwhelming success these films proved impossible to export to the other Nordic countries, even on VHS or DVD.[2] The first Danish instalment, *Olsen-banden* (Erik Balling, 1968), was exported to Norway where it failed miserably. This, however, inspired Norwegian director Knut Bohwim to make a Norwegian version, *Olsen-Banden* (1969), that became a huge success and it was followed by thirteen sequels made between 1970 and 1999. The Norwegian versions closely followed the Danish originals story-wise, even though they were not released in the same order. As film scholar Gunnar Iversen points out, the Norwegian *Olsen Gang* films 'became more Norwegian over time', which created vital nationally coded differences, including perceptions that the Norwegian versions were less sentimental than their Danish counterparts, that the jokes were not as rough, and that there were fewer sexual encounters and more scenes that revolved around jokes about alcohol. Accordingly the Norwegian *Olsen Gang* films became increasingly child-friendly over the years (Iversen 2011: 223–4).

Eventually the Olsen Gang emerged in a Swedish version as the Jönsson League in *Varning för Jönssonligan* (Jonas Cornell, 1981), which was followed by a further seven hugely popular instalments between 1982 and 2000. The first three Swedish films are adaptations of the Danish originals, while the latter are based on Swedish original stories, for example in *Jönssonligan dyker upp igen* (Mikael Ekman, 1986), where the Jönsson League tries to conduct a heist at IKEA with an elaborate plan. The Swedish versions are even more child- and family-friendly than the Norwegian ones. Alcohol jokes are kept down to a minimum and sexual encounters are absent. Instead, mainly through the acrobatic work of comedy actor Gösta Ekman, the Swedish versions concentrate more on inoffensive slapstick and word-play jokes.

Interestingly enough, in Sweden a series of four spin-off children's films, starting with *Lilla Jönssonligan och cornflakeskuppen* (Christjan Wegner, 1996), were produced between 1996 and 2006. Here, the main characters from the Jönsson League are portrayed as criminal kids who, in turn, had a spin-off television series (2001) and no fewer than six popular children's films (2003–10) in Norway called *Olsenbanden jr.* (Olsen Gang Jr). And to come all the way to the starting point, this in turn inspired a Danish children's film version, *Olsen Banden Junior* (Peter Flinth, 2001), which had moderate success compared with the original films. And to take it even further around the block, a Swedish reboot is in production, *Den perfekta stöten* (Alain Darborg, 2014), where the story is updated from a comedy to a thriller, and where the criminal characters' traits are changed to balance altering global and social stratifications, both ethnically and also gender-wise, as the exclusively white male constitution of the gang is now challenged by the inclusion of black and female characters. These genre adjustments are in line with those that Michael Tapper discusses in connection with the *Easy Money* trilogy (*Snabba cash*-trilogin 2010–13) in this collection, that is, that the ethnic 'Nordic' homogeneity has been transformed into a transnational heterogeneity. The step from comedy to the thriller/gangster genre does, although perhaps unintentionally in this case, also enhance this film's odds in the international film market, possibly even in the neighbouring Nordic countries – even though it seems more likely that history repeats itself with another round of Danish and Norwegian remakes of this darker version of the Olsen Gang.

THE CONTEXT FOR GENRE: EXPERIMENTAL EXAMPLES

While certain types of genre films have been the lifeblood of the Nordic film industries, genre has also provided the space of contestation for other forms of cultural politics. The role of popular genres – including horror or science fiction films – has proven especially problematic. Certainly, successful cases of popular Nordic genre productions can be traced back to the silent era. Others, such as the Finnish film *The White Reindeer* (*Valkoinen peura*, Erik Blomberg, 1954) combined rudimentary ethnographic filmmaking with horror film conventions and went on to considerable accolades at the Cannes Film Festival, amongst others. *The White Reindeer*, in theme and reception, is a rare example of early popular Nordic genre film due to the fact that it was a critical and commercial success. Had such genre productions been more common during the era, it may not have maintained such an imposing reputation, despite the fact that the film is undoubtedly a very impressive, atmospheric contribution to the genre. Even so, it was often discussed, at least up until the 2000s, as precisely the first of its kind, rather than for its unique qualities as part of a wider corpus of similar genre productions.

This success did not, however, set a pattern for other Finnish or Nordic filmmakers to follow, even though sporadic attempts at horror were made. Of these, the Norwegian *Lake of the Dead* (*De dødes tjern*, Kåre Bergstrøm,

1958) combines conventions from the psychological thriller and horror film to atmospheric effect. Drawing in large part on the whodunit genre, but peppering the film with well-chosen 'fantasy' sequences, *Lake of the Dead* has maintained an imposing presence even in the contemporary Nordic film scene, evoking homage in more recent horror films such as *Wilderness* (*Villmark*, Pål Öie, 2002). While horror does permeate some of the more artistic works of Ingmar Bergman (the surreal atmosphere of *Hour of the Wolf/Vargtimmen* (1968) most famously), and Finland saw its first science fiction film with *Time of Roses* (*Ruusujen aika*, 1968), the role of such popular genre conventions largely mirrored film politics of the 1960s, the era of the establishment of the film foundation structure. During this era, the emphasis was squarely on valuable cinema: finding room for popular genre forms predominantly came in ways where experimentations with these forms made them 'artistic' and disassociated them from any popular cultural connections.

While a range of popular genre emulations continued to be produced in the 1970s and 1980s, we have only seen intermittent attempts at producing popular genre cinema, from the Icelandic adaptations of the Norse Sagas as revenge narratives to Norwegian attempts at conspiracy thrillers (*Orion's Belt/Orions Belte*, Ola Solum, 1985) or Finnish emulations of the slasher (*The Moonlight Sonata/Kuutamosonaatti*, Olli Soinio, 1988). Underlying the production of these films was an attempt to connect with international trends and compete at the domestic box office. Genre was thus seen as a marketing strategy that would be useful for strengthening the status of domestic film. For example, *The Moonlight Sonata* took its shape from well-known horror films such as *The Texas Chain Saw Massacre* (Tobe Hooper, 1974) and the concurrently popular slasher genre. For many of its Finnish critics, it was to be commended for its attempts to ground these conventions in Finnish confines, with some even calling it 'fundamentally Finnish' (Lumirae 1988). The snowy landscapes and a pervasive sense of the rural gothic were undoubtedly key to achieving this effect even as it was commended for its ability to play with genre conventions. Somewhat surprisingly, half of the film's 4 million Finnish mark production budget came from the Finnish Film Foundation and the producers went on to receive quality bursaries from the same source. It was not however a major success domestically, with only 37,217 viewers, yet the institutional support enabled a sequel – *The Moonlight Sonata II: Street Sweepers* (*Kuutamosonaatti 2: Kadunlakaisijat*, Olli Soinio, 1991), a film with even more input from institutional sources but considerably fewer paying customers as the ticket sales stopped at 12,211.

The Moonlight Sonata II: Street Sweepers is emblematic of the circumstances of Nordic popular genre in this period of institutional transformation. While occasionally such popular genre productions did get off the ground in more or less all the Nordic countries, overall, the institutions have been hesitant in supporting these sorts of films. This is especially the case when compared to heritage epics – or the so called 'valuable' genre productions. While domestic audiences have had a tendency to frequently support both heritage films and popular comedies, imported counterparts of these popular domestic genre productions clearly both dominate the markets and provide a more or less uneven level of competition for them. The problems come from two main areas – the realities of small nation film cultures, operating with small budgets, and the persistent negative reputation accompanying attempts that dare to 'emulate' popular genre forms from the confines of domestic production.

Action Film in the Global North

To explain the difficulties of creating domestic popular genre films capable of competing with imported productions head on, as well as the repeated arguments that films from small nation film cultures ought to reflect their own unique qualities, we turn to two examples of the action film produced in the mid-1980s: the Swedish martial art film *The Ninja Mission* (Mats Helge, 1984) and the Finnish exploitation film *Arctic Heat* (Renny Harlin, 1985). They are very consciously moulded from their international counterparts, including the use of action film iconography and violence in ways that were largely perceived as culturally alien in the Nordic countries at the time of production. *The Ninja Mission* illustrates this well with its somewhat nonsensical narrative focusing on a band of CIA-trained Ninjas who rescue a scientist from the clutches of the KGB. The film is dubbed in English and has in later years been a topic of much fascination on the cult film circuit, receiving VHS releases in several international markets. And certainly it is a product of its time, ironically in the sense that it succeeds well in emulating the standards of popular Cannon fare, down to the sleaze that was often a key ingredient in their success. At the time, though, *The Ninja Mission* became a hit on the international VHS market that had expanded rapidly from the early 1980s, and Mats Helge directed another eight direct-to-VHS action films in the following years without support from the Swedish Film Institute. Yet, it did not prove to be much of a success at the domestic cinemas, and typically the Swedish Censorship Board made no fewer than ten cuts in the film.

Arctic Heat also takes as its theme the contemporaneously popular Cold War tensions between the US and the USSR – a theme that was especially popular with films produced in the US. Produced by the duo of Markus Selin and Renny Harlin, the film's narrative focuses on three Americans who must break out from a Soviet prison after accidentally crossing over the border from Finland. As an approximation of the currently popular one-man's-war action genre, exemplified by productions such as *Rambo: First Blood Part II* (George

P. Cosmatos, 1985), *Arctic Heat* provides a prominent showcase for its director's skills, combining over-the-top action spectacle with a clear sense of the snowy milieu. It is not surprising that Harlin went on to have a lucrative career in directing such snowbound blockbusters as *Die Hard 2: Die Harder* (1990) and *Cliffhanger* (1993).

Yet, the (in)significance of these productions in their domestic context signals the difficulty of producing such pure genre films in small nation contexts. Importantly, they were produced independently of the key institutional organisations of their respective nations – the Swedish and Finnish film institutes. While *Arctic Heat* would have its most important significance in initiating the path of the Nordic director going on to comparative success in Hollywood (see also Arne Lunde's chapter in this book), it ran into problems with the media as well as domestic censorship. The problems with the latter are especially intriguing as the fragile balance of the contemporaneous Cold War politics in Finland did not mesh well with the film's unabashedly anti-USSR arguments. The film was initially banned for its delicate political message, but later was released in truncated form, edited for its violent content. Ultimately, it is a sort of premature attempt to construct a Finnish blockbuster, a notion made apparent by the refusal of the Finnish Film Foundation to finance the film, its problems with censorship in the domestic market, its relative commercial success internationally, and its lack of real impact on the domestic industry.

Synergies of Art and Genre

The commercial and institutional problems of *The Ninja Mission* and *Arctic Heat* are significant for patterns of development within the Nordic film industries. In many ways, these experiments emphasised the difficulties facing producers interested in more explicitly commercial genre production. Markus Selin, the producer of *Arctic Heat*, for example, faced bankruptcy because of the losses he experienced in the domestic market. Considering all these difficulties, it is no wonder that the role of such genre productions remains on the sidelines for what is considered valuable cinema. These problems have also led to the dominance of the medium concept as a distinctly pragmatic approach to producing genre-ish films. Of course, the work of such 'auteurs' as Aki Kaurismäki, Lars von Trier, Thomas Vinterberg, Bent Hamer and others combine genre patterns with experimental characteristics and result in films that lie somewhere between commercial–experimental hybrid and deconstructions of mainstream cinema (see, for example, Ann-Kristin Wallengren's chapter in this collection). In many ways, such inventive uses of genre continue to structure the ways contemporary filmmakers approach genre, but Nestingen sees the medium concept as something that combines genre patterns from the 'high concept' films produced in Hollywood, for example, with relevant and specific social and political themes endemic to the Nordic countries (Nestingen, 2008). He lists a wide range of films in his study of the phenomenon, ranging from the Danish gangster trilogy, *Pusher* (Nicholas Winding Refn, 1996–2004), to the Finnish romantic war film *Ambush* (*Rukajärven tie*, Olli Saarela, 1998). What characterises all these films is the dialogue they construct between imported genre formulas and local material in ways that allow them to be simultaneously relevant for the various institutes that provide them with the official seal of approval, as well as a substantial part of their production capital, even as they promise to deliver something new to the domestic theatres.

The dominance of the medium concept is reflected in the chapters included in this collection. They range from ones focusing on the road movie (Römpötti) to horror (Hakola, Gustafsson), from Nordic noir (Norðfjörð, Åberg, Schubart and Tapper) to comedies (Seppälä), docudramas (Lehtisalo) and even the porn industry (Larsson). Underlying all these very different perspectives is the notion that Nordic genre productions combine the politics of the welfare state in transition with thematic areas familiar from international counterparts. In doing so, they work in between art and the popular in ways that set them apart internationally. Such comparisons with international patterns are relevant for understanding the particular contributions Nordic productions bring to developments of film culture on a global scale, and we will return to these debates in the concluding chapter.

For now, it may be enough to suggest that the role of Nordic film culture is in a state of flux. Even as more traditional genre productions continue to be extremely popular at the domestic box offices (witness discussion in chapters by Iversen, Laine and Hedling), especially historical and comedic films, it would not be too out of place to suggest that the contemporary scene in the Nordic countries is dominated by the medium concept. Yet the dynamic between art and commerce continues to transform as international-style popular genre productions challenge the role of genre in the Nordic media industries. In the past five years or so, productions that could be characterised as 'pure' genre films or ones that flaunt and subvert genre consciously have become ever more visible. These range from spy thrillers such as the Swedish *Hamilton* (*Hamilton: I nationens intresse*, Kathrine Windfeld, 2012) to science fiction films like Denmark's *The Substitute* (*Vikaren*, Ole Bornedal, 2007). While the specificities of their respective domestic contexts are inevitably a significant part of these films, the aesthetic and narrative choices they take rarely fit in with the type of sociopolitical commitment seen and preferred in the medium-concept films. For example, whereas in other science fiction, such as the Finnish *Lipton Cockton in the Shadows of Sodoma* (Jari Halonen, 1995), where the fate of the protagonist, a sort of facsimile of Deckard of *Blade Runner* (Ridley Scott, 1982), is to inexplicably self-combust whilst lying in bed dressed up as Marilyn

Monroe, *The Substitute* has a band of teenage kids defeating the alien menace in a very 'Spielbergian' manner. Similarly, Hamilton's semi-fascist take on protecting his country reminds one more of the antics of *24*'s Jack Bauer than the contemplative detectives that characterise much of Nordic noir. Yet, as both of these productions were successful at the domestic box office, their clear genre roots do indicate an increased acceptance of films with unabashed genre aspirations by the domestic finance institutions, but to a much lesser extent by the audiences.

A particularly innovative aspect of contemporary genre production has been their international networking (this is addressed in more depth in Kääpä's chapter on *Iron Sky*, Timo Vuorensola 2012, and *Norwegian Ninja/ Kommander Trehjolt og ninjatroppen*, Thomas Cappelen Malling, 2010). The strategies involved are multifaceted. They may be to do with individual producers constructing thinktanks and online platforms for collaboration, or with financing organisations such as the Nordic Film and Television Fund who support integration between the different countries. Often, these areas act in support of one another with the Finnish Film Foundation and the Norsk Filmfond respectively providing support for the producers precisely on the basis of their capabilities in pushing domestic cinema in new directions. Infrastructural transformations are key to understanding the uses of genre as both a domestic marketing strategy and a way for international networking. Indeed, a film like *Iron Sky*, with little in the way of direct thematic material connecting it to Finland, its context of production, can operate as a vital part of national cinema rhetoric precisely because it shows Finland as a hive of technological and formative innovation. Here, genre provides a platform from which to demonstrate such innovation, as large-scale computerised visual spectacle is ideal for providing a rationale for such shows of talent. What is for sure is that Nordic genre film has conclusively attained such diversity that old delineations between the valuable and the popular genres do not match its complexity.

Small Nation Film Cultures in the Global Marketplace

In Cannes 2013, a group of Nordic producers headed by Finland's Tero Kaukomaa (Blind Spot Pictures) and Norway's Kjetil Omberg (Tappeluft Pictures) publicised a co-production venture called Nordic Genre Invasion. In practice, this was a marketing venture designed to utilise the increasing profile of popular genre in the Nordic countries. Drawing on such international successes as *Iron Sky* and *Dead Snow*, the venture was a one-stop shop for Nordic networking. Combining Tappeluft Pictures and Blind Spot with Finland's Fisher King Production, Sweden's LittleBig Productions, Germany's 27 Films Productions and effects company Troll Vfx, the Nordic Genre Invasion venture would be a source for international distributors and production companies to participate in such wide-ranging undertakings as the TV series *Iron Sky: Houston, We Have a Problem* and *Dead Snow 2* (*Død snø 2*, Tommy Wirkola, 2014). By using the reputations generated by their previous successes, as well as the interests of the production houses participating in the venture to produce popular genre film, this venture suggests that Nordicness has now attained a marketable aspect in addition to providing a way to pool production resources from the region. This venture, in all, is one particularly visible aspect of the region's international aspirations.

As Nordic film production becomes more diversified, it is an increasingly obvious fact that the need for a critical collection exploring Nordic genre film and television from a multitude of angles is pressing. Hardly anything is written in English on contemporary Nordic film culture, and even less on popular genre films. Previous scholarship often consists of historical recollections that concentrate on art house films, that is, on 'valuable' films. To challenge the canon of literature on Nordic film, this is the first collection to focus on contemporary popular genres. In addition, as we suggested above, Nordic film production and distribution is increasingly based on transnational flow, necessitating that we challenge the focus of much of the Nordic film literature on specific national film cultures. To these ends, *Nordic Genre Film* explores the five small Nordic cinemas through a transnational perspective.

Accordingly, each chapter of the book contains comparisons between the Nordic countries in terms of, for example, style, themes, production, reception, international distribution and intra-Nordic export (or lack thereof). The purpose of this structure is to expand the existing theoretical and methodical use of the space between the local and the regional as well as the international and the transnational. By discussing the transnational circulation of cultural influences and creative industrial frameworks, the chapters take a range of approaches to genre in the Nordic context, from analysing the textual features of individual films to exploring industrial tactics in capitalising on cultural reputations by way of analysing the production, distribution and reception of contemporary genre films.

Another aim is to make use of and expand the scope of genre theory, and especially how 'genre' can be connected to the regional/transnational implication of genre formations and preferences – a notion of importance considering the transnational scope of collaborative projects such as Nordic Genre Invasion. Significant here are the ways genre acts as an arena within the international system of cinema, and how domestic film cultures adapt to and interact with this forever elaborate genre system, whether the outcomes are medium-concept films or popular genre films. The notion and the recognition of genre, so often downplayed within the Nordic film cultures, are therefore vital for the understanding of how the media products of a small region of the world became part of global popular culture. As Nordic film cultures are reaching an increasing level of global recognition, their popular dimensions need critical interrogation in the English language aimed at a wide readership beyond the region – indeed Nordic Genre Invasion is just one particularly visible example of these international dimensions. In addition, Nordic film industries can offer academic film studies an alternative model for understanding globalisation from a small nation perspective. The necessity to take into account this context and its audience/industrial realities allows our discussion to remain relevant even beyond the Nordic countries as they contribute to the ongoing dialogue on the complex flows of cultural circulation and globalisation.

Notes

1. Four of these films were Danish: *Italian for Beginners* (*Italiensk for begyndere*, 2000) with 212,349 tickets sold; *In a Better World* (*Hævnen*, 2010) 194,037; *After the Wedding* (*Efter brylluppet*, 2006) 158,439; *Day and Night* (*Dag og nat*, 2004) 134,175. One was a Finnish/Swedish co-production, *Mother of Mine* (*Äideistä parhain*, 2005) 141,179, while the last one was the Norwegian/Swedish co-production *Hokus Pokus Alfons Åberg* (2013) 114,012.
2. The Danish *Olsen Gang* films, however, became big successes in Eastern Europe during the 1970s and 1980s, especially in East Germany.

References

Buckingham, David (1993), *Children Talking Television: The Making of Television Literacy*, London: Falmer Press.
Cowie, Peter (1992), *Scandinavian Cinema: A Survey of the Films and Film-Makers of Denmark, Finland, Iceland, Norway, and Sweden*, London: Tantivy Press.
DFI (2014), The Danish Film Institute, <http://www.dfi.dk/Tal-og-fakta/Billetsalg.aspx>, accessed 23 March 2014.
Feuer, Jane (1992), 'Genre Study and Television'. In Robert C. Allen (ed.), *Channels of Discourse, Reassembled: Television and Contemporary Criticism*, London: Routledge, pp. 138–59.
Gentele, Jeanette (2001), 'Intelligent norsk komedi', *Svenska Dagbladet*, 14 December.
Gustafsson, Tommy (2007), *En fiende till civilisationen: Manlighet, genusrelationer, sexualitet och rasstereotyper i svensk filmkultur under 1920-talet*, Lund: Sekel bokförlag.
Hardy, Forsyth (1952), *Scandinavian Film*, London: The Falcon Press.
Hedling, Olof (2008), 'A New Deal in European Film? Notes on the Swedish Regional Production Turn', *Film International* 6 (5): 8–17.
Hedling, Olof (2014), 'Storleken har betydelse. Om det svenska produktionslandskapet i Millenniums tidevarv'. In Erik Hedling and Ann-Kristin Wallengren (eds), *Den nya svenska filmen: Kultur, kriminalitet & kakafoni*, Stockholm: Atlantis bokförlag, pp. 93–110.
Hördin, Peter (2001), 'Norge inte bara lusekoftor och olja', *Helsingborgs Dagblad*, 14 December.
Iversen, Gunnar (2011), *Norsk filmhistorie: Spillefilmen 1911–2011*, Oslo: Universitetsforlaget.

Kino (2014), *Film & Kino: Årboknummer 2001*, <http://www.kino.no/migration_catalog/article963498.ece/binary/%C3%85rbok2001>, accessed 23 March 2014.
Lumiere (2014), <http://lumiere.obs.coe.int/web/film_info/?id=17453>, accessed 23 March 2014.
Lumirae, Pertti (1988), 'Kuutamosonaatti', *Demari*, 4 November.
Lunde, Arne (2010), *Nordic Exposures: Scandinavian Identities in Classical Hollywood Cinema*, Seattle: University of Washington Press.
Nestingen, Andrew (2008), *Crime and Fantasy in Scandinavia: Fiction, Film, and Social Change*, Seattle: University of Washington Press.
Nestingen, Andrew and Trevor G. Elkington (2005), 'Introduction: Transnational Nordic Cinema'. In Andrew Nestingen and Trevor G. Elkington (eds), *Transnational Cinema in a Global North: Nordic Cinema in Transition*, Detroit: Wayne State University Press, pp. 1–28.
Peterson, Jens (2001), 'Elling', *Aftonbladet*, 14 December.
Selås, Jon (2001), 'Ellings evangelium', *Verdens gang*, 16 March.
SFI (2014), The Swedish Film Institute, <http://www.sfi.se/sv/statistik/>, accessed 21 March 2014.
Skotte, Kim (2002), 'Elling', *Politiken*, 4 January.
Solia, Tytti (2005), 'Introduction'. In Tytti Solia (ed.), *The Cinema of Scandinavia*, London and New York: Wallflower Press.
Soila, Tytti, Astrid Söderbergh Widding and Gunnar Iversen (1998), *Nordic National Cinemas*, London and New York: Routledge.
Stevenson, Jack (2010), *Scandinavian Blue: The Erotic Cinema of Sweden and Denmark in the 1960s and 1970s*, Jefferson: McFarland.
Sundholm, John, Isak Thorsen, Lars Gustaf Andersson, Olof Hedling, Gunnar Iversen and Birgir Thor Møller (2012), *Historical Dictionary of Scandinavian Cinema*, Lanham and Toronto: The Scarecrow Press.
Thomson, C. Claire (ed.) (2006), *Northern Constellations: New Readings in Nordic Cinema*, Norwich: Norvik Press.

PART I

HERITAGE CINEMA AND NATIONAL NARRATIVES

1. *SIBELIUS* AND THE RE-EMERGENCE OF THE GREAT MAN BIOPIC

Kimmo Laine

The popular Finnish biopic film *Sibelius* (Timo Koivusalo, 2003) about the composer Jean Sibelius (1865–1957) is a textbook example of a biopic – so obvious, in fact, that there is a touch of banality involved. There seems to be very little in the film we do not already know – 'we' referring here primarily to Finnish audiences or experts on biographies of classical composers. Despite the fact that parts of the film were shot in Latvia and Italy, the film is quite clearly targeted at domestic markets, as it relies on a nationally oriented and nationally limited knowledge of the past. Every element we may expect to be in the film is there: every character involved in cultural life around the fin de siècle, every piece of music, every political event.

Up to a point, this is typical of many historical films. In her book *Cinematic Uses of the Past* Marcia Landy (1996: 19) stresses the element of foreseeability in the genre: 'Melodrama and history feed on familiarity, ritualization, repetition, and overvaluation of the past to produce a déjà vu sense of "Yes, that is the way it was and is".' Further, we might see here a connection to the notion of banal nationalism as introduced by Michael Billig (1995), nationalism as conscious and unconscious everyday practices and habitual patterns of social life that likewise rely on familiarity and unending repetition.

And yet, in all its banality *Sibelius* does tell us about the past and it does resonate with what we think about certain aspects of Finnish, Russian and European history. The aim of this chapter is to consider *Sibelius* as a popular historical narrative, discussing it in relation to the mechanisms of historical explanation as well as the mode of argument and address used in the film. As reference points I shall discuss certain other Nordic biopics made during the last few years. Biopic seems to be one of the prominent genres in Scandinavia in the 2000s. *Monica Z* (2013), for example, has been a huge success in Sweden, and *Kon-Tiki* (2012) – on the Norwegian explorer Thor Heyerdahl – broke into international markets and became a Norwegian Academy Award nominee.

As a genre, biopic seems to be both culturally specific and universal at the same time. While addressing a predominantly national audience, *Sibelius* also shares many, if not most, of the generic characteristics analysed by George F. Custen (1992) in his classic study of the genre, even if Custen is talking about Hollywood films. And indeed, Hollywood has also produced countless biopics about non-Americans, including Scandinavians like the author *Hans Christian Andersen* (1952) or the composer Edvard Grieg (*Song of Norway*, 1970).

Return of the Great Man

Sibelius premiered in 2003, in the middle of what has been considered a high tide of Finnish film production. After a low point in the early and mid-1990s, there was a dramatic turning point at the end of the decade. By 1999, the top 10 list in Finland was dominated by domestic films. While in 1996 the market share for domestic films was less than 4 per cent, in 1999 the figure was 25 per cent, and has stayed relatively high ever since (Finnish Film Foundation 2014). The reasons for this rise are complex and have been widely discussed in Finland. For now, I shall only mention the strong investment in marketing and positive publicity, audience research and audience targeting – all of which were virtually non-existent in public film policy during the previous decades (see Salmi 2003 and Pantti 2005).

One notable characteristic of the film boom of the late 1990s and early 2000s was that a remarkable share of the films either took place in the past or reworked traditional domestic film genres like the lumberjack film (*Kuningasjätkä/A Summer by the River*, 1998), the 'rillumarei'-film (*Kulkuri ja Joutsen/The Swan and the Wanderer*, 1999) or the 'häjy'-film (*Häjyt/The Tough Ones*, 1999).[1] The boom of domestic films was thus also a boom of historical films and genres.

Not only did the turn of the millennium witness a rise in historical films at the expense of films handling contemporary issues, but also the number of biopics grew higher than ever. While the tradition of Finnish biopics originated in the studio era, the output was never very high: Anneli Lehtisalo's study on biopics lists a mere thirteen feature films made between 1937 and 1955 (Lehtisalo 2011a), and a handful of others were produced during the following decades. In the period between 1999 and 2010 the number of biopics was fourteen. Many of the recent biopics have also been among the highest grossing films of their production years.

The increase of interest in the past was not only a cinematic concern. One might argue that around the millennium there was a general rise of attraction to phenomena that historians have referred to as historical culture, public history or heritage industry, in Finland as well as in other parts of Scandinavia and Europe. In Finland this phenomenon has manifested itself in popular history books, historical novels, television series (both fiction and fact), countless debates in newspapers and journals, and on television and Internet sites – involving not only professional historians – over issues like the Finnish civil war of 1918, Finland's alliance with Germany during the Second World War, or the pro-Soviet politics of the 1970s.

Of special interest with regard to biopics is the Great Finns vote that was held in 2004 and surrounded by huge publicity (YLE 2014), arousing a lot of debate. As in the Great Britons vote (2002) that served as a model for the Finnish variant as well as many others, the top of the list was dominated by political and/or military persons like Carl Gustaf Emil Mannerheim (commander-in-chief during the Second World War and later president) and Risto Ryti (president during the Second World War). Sibelius was number 8, making him the highest-ranking artist on the list.

If we take a look at recent biopics, there is a remarkable parallel with the results of the Great Finns vote. Apart from Sibelius, many others on the 'top 100' list have been portrayed in recent biopics, among them the author Aleksis Kivi (*Aleksis Kiven elämä/The Life of Aleksis Kivi*, 2002), the ski jumper Matti Nykänen (*Matti*, 2006), the singer-songwriter Irwin Goodman (*Rentun ruusu/ The Rose of the Rascal*, 2001), the author Kalle Päätalo (*Päätalo*, 2008) and singers Tapio Rautavaara, Reino Helismaa and Olavi Virta (*The Swan and the Wanderer*, 1999). Several historical minor characters in the *Sibelius* film, like the author Eino Leino and the fine artist Akseli Gallen-Kallela, were also high on the list.

Besides correlating with the Great Finns vote, there are some common themes in most of the recent biopics. First, they are predominantly not only about Great Finns but also about Great Men, which of course is nothing new.[2] The protagonists of the biopics produced during the Finnish studio era were invariably men, reflecting an imbalance in Hollywood too: two thirds of the American biopics surveyed by Custen (1992: 103) are about men. Further, many of the recent biopics (for example *The Swan and the Wanderer*, *The Rose of the Rascal*, *Badding*, 2000) concentrate on profound friendships between the protagonist and his male friends, rather than on the heterosexual romance typical of the studio era biopic. A few notable exceptions have been produced lately, however, including *Hella W* (2011), a biography of the playwright Hella Wuolijoki, and *Putoavia Enkeleitä/Falling*

Angels (2008), a joint biography of the authors Aila Meriluoto and Lauri Viita.

Second, most Finnish biopics, as well as most other historical films made since the late 1990s, take place in the relatively recent past, usually in the post-Second World War decades and sometimes up to the 1980s or 1990s. Therefore, in the terms used by Andrew Higson (2003) in his *English Heritage, English Cinema*, they would count as period films, historical films or costume dramas, even if classifying them as heritage films would not be as easy: they do not take place among the upper or middle classes, and the issues of national past are not as central to these films as they are to heritage films 'proper'. In that sense, *Sibelius* and *The Life of Aleksis Kivi* are exceptions, the main characters being born around the mid-1800s, and the films being very much about the building of national culture.

A third common characteristic is that, in the terminology used by Leo Lowenthal (2006) in his classic study on biographies in American magazines in the early decades of the twentieth century, recent Finnish biopics do not take place in the sphere of political life, nor in the sphere of business and professions, but rather in the sphere of entertainment – that is, they focus on consumption rather than production. Once again, there seems to be a parallel between these films and Hollywood biopics. Custen (1992: 84–5) observes that whereas Hollywood biopics made before the Second World War are dominated by figures from politics, royalty, science and so on, after the war the emphasis shifts to entertainment. In Steve Neale's (2000: 61) words, 'the pre-war biopic tends to address its spectators as citizens whereas the post-war biopic tends to address its spectators as consumers of popular culture.' A similar shift emerged in Finland in the post-war era (Lehtisalo 2011a: 242), but around the millennium the emphasis on entertainment was stronger than ever. *Sibelius* is arguably a borderline case in this sense. In Lowenthal's (2006: 127) terms, Sibelius can be characterised an entertainer, even if he hailed from the serious arts rather than the mass entertainment industry. Also, the film addresses its spectators both as consumers (Sibelius was a celebrity with many of his compositions growing very popular in Finland) and as citizens (the film frames Sibelius's life conventionally in the context of the nineteenth-century national awakening).

An emphasis on arts and entertainment can also be seen in recent biopics made in Denmark and Sweden. Besides the idiosyncratic series of biopics by the Swedish veteran director Jan Troell – *Hamsun* (1996; about the controversial Norwegian author Knut Hamsun), *Maria Larssons eviga ögonblick/Everlasting Moments* (2008; about a little-known pioneering photographer), *Dom över död man/The Last Sentence* (2012; about the journalist Torgny Segerstedt fighting against Nazism) – some of the most notable Nordic biopics have focused on entertainment. *Cornelis* (2010) and *Monica Z* are about iconic

Swedish popular singers Cornelis Vreeswijk and Monica Zetterlund, respectively, both blurring the boundaries between high and low culture. *Dirch/A Funny Man* (2011) is a biopic of the popular Danish stage and film comedian Dirch Passer – who in a noteworthy sequence fails when trying to become a serious actor in a stage adaptation of John Steinbeck's *Of Mice and Men*. All of these films share many generic characteristics with *Sibelius*, as we shall see.

SIBELIUS AS A BIOPIC

Sibelius fits perfectly in many of the contemporary trends: it is a historical film and a heritage film, more so, in fact, than most other Finnish historical films of the period; it touches upon issues from the national past, of the 'origins' of Finnish cultural life; it is a biopic about the best-known Finnish composer of all; and finally, Sibelius is probably the best-known Finnish *person* ever, globally. Whether it was because of or in spite of its conventionality, *Sibelius* turned out to be a success: with its almost 300,000 spectators in cinemas it can be considered a domestic hit.

Further, as a biopic *Sibelius* is in many ways like a prototype of the genre. I would argue that the main difference between *Sibelius* and the other recent Nordic biopics mentioned above is that while the latter tend to pick one or two narrative threads as their dominant theme, *Sibelius* tries to cover all the conventional storylines of the genre. One of these is the importance of the family as a source of either support or opposition (Custen 1992: 152–6). As for Jean Sibelius, his childhood family offers opposition, wanting him to pursue the bourgeois career of a lawyer instead of becoming a musician. On the other hand, once he establishes a family and a career in music, his wife Aino turns out to be a faithful muse. In *Monica Z* the role of the family is clearly the most important source of narrative tension: the unsupportive attitude of Monica's father is presented as the major hindrance to her rise to the top, and the culmination comes only when the father finally admits that his daughter has an unusual talent.

The role of old friends in a biopic is often as dualistic as that of the family (Custen 1992: 161–5). A case in point is Jean's colleague Robert Kajanus who is at the same time a good friend and an envious fellow composer, ready and willing to manoeuvre himself into a teaching job at the university, yet knowing well enough that Jean would deserve it better than him. In *A Funny Man* this is highlighted, arguably, as the dominant theme of the film: the professional as well as personal relationship between Dirch Passer and his fellow comedian Kjeld Petersen is often quarrelsome and filled with envy, but all the same, it is presented as the crucial factor behind Dirch's success as a comic. Further tensions in a biopic typically emerge between the protagonist and members of a given community (Custen 1992: 72–4). In *Cornelis* these are the structuring elements of the narrative: Cornelis Vreeswijk is nonconformist not only as a songwriter but also in his private life, and his impulsive behaviour and heavy drinking lead him into constant conflict with many people, including the authorities. In *Sibelius* such tensions involve Jean's teachers who have trouble accepting Jean's radical musical ideas – this of course is familiar from *Amadeus* (1984) and many other biopics about artists. Since an important theme involves the national awakening of the late nineteenth and early twentieth century, antagonistic relations also rise between the nationally minded artists and Russian officials representing the tsarist power. In a key scene an orchestra plays Jean's composition *Finlandia*, which his compatriots recognise as a highly political nationalistic hymn, while the Russian officials are led to believe it is an innocent piece called 'Fantasy'.

On a more personal level, the film follows the generic convention of 'normalizing genius' (Custen 1992: 121–8). Besides being exceptional, a person above his contemporaries in his talent and his foresight, Jean is also depicted as a passionate and caring family man. Finally, as Custen (1992: 75–6) reminds us, in a biopic it is customary that with an unusual gift comes unusual suffering. According to a press release 'Sibelius's life contains not only success, but also crushing losses and misfortunes.' Jean encounters money and drinking problems, and he also suffers for his country, first under Russian suppression and later divided by a bloody civil war. The death of his little daughter drives him to despair, and his final tragedy stems from the loss of inspiration and the ability to write music. In addition the film uses cinematic devices typical of biopics, and central among these are flashback structures and montage sequences (see Custen 1992: 182–6). The latter are usually quite short – most often a sequence that condenses a certain event like Jean and Aino's wedding into a few shots, backed by Sibelius's music – but flashback is a central structuring element of the whole narrative, as we shall see in a moment.

There are, however, other features in the film that are less obvious for a biopic of a classical composer. The most notable is probably an extra-cinematic one: the background of the auteur, the director/writer/producer of the film, Timo Koivusalo. He started his public career as an entertainer, a popular songwriter, a television show host and a lowbrow comedian whose childlike character Pekko Aikamiespoika (Pekko the Bachelor) starred both in a television sitcom and a series of five films (1993–7). As a film director he is entirely self-taught: having started out directing his own Pekko comedies he gradually made his way to biopics and other more highbrow genres around the turn of the millennium. From biopics about post-war popular singers (*The Swan and the Wanderer* and *The Rose of the Rascal*) he moved on to *Sibelius* and a two-part adaptation of Väinö Linna's epic novel *Täällä Pohjantähden alla*/*Here, Beneath the North Star* (2009–10), but his cultural status still remains somewhat ambiguous. With all the public talk about the blurring boundaries between high and low cultures, the in-between ground often seems to be the most difficult to deal with. Thus, the reviewers' sentiment towards Koivusalo remains close to Dwight Macdonald's (1983: 37) classic denouncement of 'Midcult' as something that 'pretends to respect the standards of High Culture while in fact it waters them down and vulgarizes them'. Accordingly, some reviewers felt that Koivusalo would be better to focus on what he knows best and leave classical music be (see Suomen kansallisfilmografia 2014).

Another less obvious feature of the film is that, as many reviewers complained, there seems to be a lack of drama in the film: there are a few dramatic conflicts, but no such central conflict that would give the film the cohesive structure expected by critics. whereas a typical biopic centres on a turning point in the hero's life, like the moment of breakthrough (Custen 1992: 206–8), *Sibelius* tries to cover the whole life of the composer, who died at the age of 91. As a result, the structure of the film is fragmentary, even for a biopic – at least more fragmentary than the structure of a well-made mainstream film is supposed to be.

Explanation and Argument

All of these characteristics of the film – the overall obviousness, the loose structure of the film, the ambiguous position between high and low culture – are relevant when we look at *Sibelius* as a historical film. As such, *Sibelius* is undeniably a part of the heritage industry, and it does affect the way we think about the past, about national culture, about social classes, about high and low, and so on. Therefore, it is worth attempting to formulate a way to analyse the film as historical narration.

To start with its fragmentary form: what is it that ties the fragments into a story or historical narrative? A fragmented historical account is often referred to as a 'chronicle'. In *Metahistory* Hayden White (1990: 5–7) sees the chronicle as something which precedes historical narratives. A chronicle is simply an arrangement of events in the temporal order they happened. When this series of events is shaped into something with a beginning, a middle and an end, and when some of the events are characterised by different kinds of motifs, we are involved with a story. This, however, does not yet constitute historical narration. A story becomes historical writing only when it is provided with the different forms of explanation.

Bearing in mind that, according to the reviewers, one of the problems with *Sibelius* was that the narrative was fragmented, we might say in White's terminology that *Sibelius* is not really a historical film but merely a chronicle or – at most – a story film with a beginning, a middle and an end. In this case its mode of argument would be extremely simple: basically a series of separate and unique events put together. But in fact, the film is not quite as fragmented as that: there are several narrative and cinematic devices that work in the opposite direction and do provide this film with a slightly more solid form. One of these is the flashback structure, which can be seen as the dominant narrative technique of *Sibelius*.

The film begins with black and white images from a documentary short film made of Sibelius's funeral with thousands of people honouring the ceremony. The concluding image of this introductory sequence turns into colour, showing the ageing Aino and Jean – played by actors – watch a wedge of cranes fly south. With a quick dissolve we see Jean as a child, also watching cranes fly by. This is, once again, a fairly conventional transition in biopics: the protagonist as an adult pays attention to something allegedly meaningful or metaphorical that brings back memories from an earlier period of his or her life. A strikingly similar transition can be seen in *Cornelis*, which starts with the protagonist introducing a song about a boy and his parents over the opening credits. We hear the sound of a siren, followed by a flashback that opens with the young Cornelis looking at German bombers flying over his head in the wartime Holland of his childhood.

After the introduction, *Sibelius* is organised as a series of flashbacks. Every now and then we go back to the aged Aino and Jean, living an assumedly harmonious life in their home Ainola, darkened only by Jean's loss of musical inspiration. The film ends with Aino and Jean once again watching the cranes. One of the cranes breaks away from the wedge and then fades into the blue sky, while the camera tilts down and shows Ainola with the national flag at half-mast as a sign of Jean's passing away. The image turns into black and white, thus closing the narrative circle, as well as marking the documentary, 'true-to-history' quality of the framing shots. These last images are accompanied by Sibelius's *Finlandia*, as if to reassert that the fates of the nation and its most celebrated artist are eternally connected.

Flashbacks not only organise the narrative structure of a biopic but also affect the modes of argumentation and explanation of the film. Hannu Salmi (1993: 231–2) sees flashback as a most 'suitable' device for a historical film. As with historical research, we start with a known result, ask a question, and then with flashbacks explore the historical processes that lead to the result. On the other hand, as Marcia Landy (1996: 20–1) stresses, 'flashbacks, especially in biopics, often serve to create an organic sense of unfolding events and especially a sense of inevitability.' While the former mechanism – the historical process of questioning, exploring and answering – is definitely there in *Sibelius*, I would argue that it is overpowered by the latter. The sense of familiarity is, again, so strong that the historical questions asked by the film are token rather than real, and the overarching flashback structure underlines the goal-oriented, teleological and nationalistic mode of argument (see White 1990: 11–21): the initial flashback scene ends with Jean as a child running after the cranes and then almost bumping into a troop of marching Russian soldiers, which reminds the spectator of the fact that Finland was still part of the Russian Empire. The circular structure of the film closes not only the composer's life but also the seemingly inevitable trajectory of the nation into an independent state.

Another central means of giving form to the fragments is the strong reliance on intertextuality. The most obvious functions of intertextuality in *Sibelius* relate to recognition, repetition and ritualisation. We are supposed to recognise, at least up to a point, the different elements referred to: the music, the paintings, the photographs, the characters and so on. In some instances recognition is vital for a basic understanding of the narrative – for example, it might be difficult to comprehend the role of the painter Gallen-Kallela without any preconception of him – but in other cases the basic functions of recognition are about creating verisimilitude on the one hand, and providing the spectator with the pleasure of recognition on the other (see Lehtisalo 2011b). Such pleasure is on offer in other biopics too: typical for the genre is a party scene in *Monica Z*, where the protagonist, on the verge of rising to stardom, is introduced to the crème de la crème of Swedish cultural life of the sixties, one by one.

In terms of intertextuality, the film relies, first, narratively on the commonsense assumptions of history. As Pierre Sorlin (1980: 20) writes:

> The cultural heritage of every country and every community includes dates, events and characters known to all members of that community. This common basis is what we might call the group's 'historical capital', and it is enough to select a few details from this for the audience to know that it is watching an historical film and to place it, at least approximately.

In *Sibelius* the audience is expected to realise that the civil war has broken out, for example, from the front page of a newspaper that dates from January 1918 and from images of marching men with red armbands. It is this relatively strong dependence on the historical capital of the spectators that makes *Sibelius* next to inexportable.

Second, aurally the film relies on the familiarity and the connotations of Sibelius's music. The obviousness of the film is further accentuated by a strong emphasis on foreshadowing events, especially with music: many of Sibelius's compositions are strongly coded in the national consciousness, and when we hear this or that music starting to play on the track, we already know what is bound to happen in the next scene. A case in point is the song *Jääkärin marssi* ('The Jaeger March') that for a Finnish spectator immediately connotes the events of 1917 and 1918: the declaration of independence and the civil war.

The third form of intertextuality is visual. Stylistically *Sibelius* can be instantly recognised as a European historical film, since it strictly follows the visual conventions of the genre, relying on what Andrew Higson (2003) has termed 'mise-en-scène of the modern past'. The colour scheme of the film, for example, tends to emphasise the warmish browns, yellows and reds as a contrast to the blues and greys that often connote the technologised modern society. Another visual intertextual point of reference is the film's reliance on well-known photographs and paintings. To take just one example, the film dramatises, almost in a tableau-vivant style, the famous painting *Symposion* (1894) by Akseli Gallen-Kallela, showing Sibelius, Kajanus, the author Adolf Paul[3] and the painter himself, boozing up in the restaurant Kämp.

The frequent use of paintings and photographs gives the film a specific sense of history as a series of tableux. However, these tableaux are not static and immovable. On the contrary, there is a lot of movement involved: the camera moves almost constantly. There are countless tracking shots, crane shots, pans and tilts in the film that seem to be taking us near the characters or away from them, sweeping the skies or displaying the surroundings. Often a scene begins with a close-up, and then the camera pulls back and reveals a wider view of the site of action. Conversely, a scene might open with an establishing shot that is followed by closer framings, more often within a long shot and a moving camera than by classical decoupage. In terms of historical argumentation, by oscillating between details and wide views, as well as supposedly subjective and objective views, such camera movements tend to emphasise the relation between what is particular and what is general (see Salmi 1993: 225–9). A typical example in *Sibelius* is a scene where Jean, having just had his family's blessing to become a musician, passionately plays music with his brother and sister in the tower room of his family's house. Within one long crane shot the camera pulls out of the window and starts descending, until it shows the tower from a low angle against the sky, once again implying that Jean's music is more than just ordinary compositions, that is has an almost divine quality.

To sum up, together with certain cinematic devices like flashbacks and montage sequences, these intertextual relations provide *Sibelius* – the first impression of which is unusually fragmented – with a certain form: relying on the historical capital of the audience and the visual imagery and music supposedly familiar from different sources not only ties the scenes together, but also foreshadows the upcoming events. At the same time these intertextual relations also affect, if not actually create, the mode of historical argument employed in the film, however obvious and banal it is in its tendency to rely on what we think we already know.

Conclusion: This Is How It Was

Historical films constitute not only different modes of explanation but also different modes of address, for example, enquiring ('what was it like?'), challenging ('is this really how it was?') or counterfactual ('what if it had been different?'). In the case of *Sibelius*, and arguably most other mainstream biopics, the mode would rather be between affirming-educational ('this is how it was') and affirming-entertaining ('this is how it felt').

Yet, however limited the scale of most of the contemporary biopics is, there is something conspicuous in the film industry's and filmmaker's obsession with the past. Compared with the period from the 1960s until the early 1990s, a much larger proportion of Finnish films have been period films of some kind. This change has been widely noted, and critics have explained this turn to the past in different ways. Most often it has been seen as a counter-reaction to large issues like globalisation, Finland joining the European Union in 1995, the collapse of Soviet Union in 1991, millennium anxieties and so on (see Hietala 2003 and Nestingen 2003). All of these phenomena, it is argued, have increased the need to turn back to the issues of national past, national and local identities, and longing for some kind of nostalgic contemplation.

I believe that all of these are valid explanations. Certainly, it is easy to agree that history in these films is, in the words of Pierre Sorlin (1980: 208), 'a useful device to speak of the present time'. However, these explanations are partial, at the most. While a boom of period films definitely seems to exist, the emergence of such a boom is too complex a phenomenon to be reduced to simple cause–effect chains. For now, for the purpose of this chapter, I would like to rephrase the explanation in different terms: all of the aforementioned contextual factors – the growing market orientation of film funding and production, the flourishing of heritage industry and different forms of public history, the large-scale changes in national and international politics and economics – have created an atmosphere in which turning to the past is both easy and likely, and in which the filmmakers are more or less encouraged to turn their interest from contemporary issues to those of the preceding decades.

Notes

1. 'Rillumarei' refers to a cycle of films – as well as popular songs – from the 1950s that featured down-to-earth hobos and gold-diggers and that displayed populist and anti-urban sentiments. 'Häjy'-films were historical films that took place in the Ostrobothnia region in the late nineteenth century, focusing on conflicts between farmers, officials and outlaws – not unlike westerns.
2. It is worth noticing too that three-quarters of those on the Great Finns list were men.
3. In the painting – or paintings: there are actually two somewhat different versions – the fourth person is usually thought to be the composer Oskar Merikanto instead of Paul.

References

Billig, Michael (1995), *Banal Nationalism*, London: Sage.
Custen, George F. (1992), *Bio/Pics: How Hollywood Constructed Public History*, New Brunswick, NJ: Rutgers University Press.
Finnish Film Foundation (2014), 'Kotimaisella elokuvalla jälleen hieno vuosi', <http://ses.fi/ajankohtaista/ajankohtainen/?tx_ttnews[tt_news]595&=cHash=e7f4e837af21d52d7cd4f7b3cc726fe2>, accessed 5 July 2014.
Hietala, Veijo (2003), 'Romantiikkaa ja Rukajärven häjyjä: suomalaisen elokuvan ihmevuosi 1999'. In Kimmo Ahonen, Janne Rosenqvist, Juha Rosenqvist and Päivi Valotie (eds), *Taju kankaalle: uutta suomalaista elokuvaa paikantamassa*, Turku: Kirja-Aurora, pp. 23–9.
Higson, Andrew (2003), *English Heritage, English Cinema: Costume Drama since 1980*, Oxford: Oxford University Press.
Landy, Marcia (1996), *Cinematic Uses of the Past*, Minneapolis and London: University of Minneapolis Press.
Lehtisalo, Anneli (2011a), *Kuin elävinä edessämme: suomalaiset elämäkertaelokuvat populaarina historiakulttuurina 1937–1955*, Helsinki: Suomalaisen Kirjallisuuden Seura.
Lehtisalo, Anneli (2011b), 'As If Alive Before Us: The Pleasures of Verisimilitude in Biographical Fiction Films', *New Readings* 11: 100–17.
Lowenthal, Leo (2006), 'The Triumph of Mass Idols'. In P. David Marshall (ed.), *The Celebrity Culture Reader*, New York and London: Routledge, pp. 124–52 (first published 1961).
Macdonald, Dwight (1983), *Against the American Grain*, New York: Da Capo Press (first published 1962).
Neale, Steve (2000), *Genre and Hollywood*, London and New York: Routledge.
Nestingen, Andrew (2003), 'Nostalgias and their Publics: The Finnish Film Boom, 1999–2001', *Scandinavian Studies* 75 (4): 539–66.
Pantti, Mervi (2005), 'Art or Industry? Battles over Finnish Cinema During the 1990s'. In Andrew Nestingen and Trevor G. Elkington (eds), *Transnational Cinema in a Global North: Nordic Cinema in Transition*, Detroit: Wayne State University Press, pp. 165–90.
Salmi, Hannu (1993), *Elokuva ja historia*, Helsinki: Painatuskeskus and Suomen elokuva-arkisto.
Salmi, Hannu (2003), 'Nousukausi: katse kotimaisen elokuvan menestyksen tekijöihin'. In Kimmo Ahonen, Janne Rosenqvist, Juha Rosenqvist and Päivi Valotie (eds), *Taju kankaalle: uutta suomalaista elokuvaa paikantamassa*, Turku: Kirja-Aurora, pp. 13–21.
Sorlin, Pierre (1980), *The Film in History: Restaging the Past*, Oxford: Basil Blackwell.
Suomen kansallisfilmografia (2014), 'Sibelius', <http://www.elonet.fi/fi/elokuva/1198046>, accessed 5 July 2014.
White, Hayden (1990), *Metahistory: The Historical Imagination in Nineteenth-Century Europe*, Baltimore and London: The Johns Hopkins University Press (first published 1973).
YLE (2014), 'Suuret suomalaiset', <http://yle.fi/vintti/yle.fi/suuretsuomalaiset/in_english/index.html>, accessed 5 July 2014.

2. WHOSE REPRESSED MEMORIES? *MAX MANUS: MAN OF WAR* AND *FLAME & CITRON* (FROM A SWEDE'S POINT OF VIEW)

Erik Hedling

In 2008, both Norway and Denmark delivered major contributions to the cinematic genre of the 'occupation drama' (Norwegian), or 'occupation film' (Danish): the Norwegian film was *Max Manus: Man of War* (*Max Manus*, Joachim Rønning and Espen Sandberg, 2008) and the Danish *Flame & Citron* (*Flammen og citronen*, Ole Christian Madsen, 2008). In Scandinavia, these generic markers refer to many films set during the Second World War and depicting the fates of Danes and Norwegians in the years 1940–5, when their respective countries were occupied by Nazi Germany. Thus, both Norway and Denmark eventually came to be on the victorious allied side of the war.

The other Nordic countries had different obligations. Finland was between 1941 and 1944 fighting on the side of Nazi Germany in a savage war against the Soviet Union. This struggle was bound to be lost, and Finland came to switch sides in 1944, making peace with the Soviets and agreeing to evict a German army in northern Finland by military force.[1] Sweden, most importantly in the present context, was neutral and kept its independence throughout the war. This chapter will study how *Max Manus: Man of War* and *Flame & Citron* can be understood in a Swedish context, referring to Swedish history during the war, textual analyses of mainly the scenes from Sweden in the films, and the reception of the films in Sweden. That is, I analyse Norwegian and Danish perceptions of Sweden during the war, but strictly from a Swede's point of view.

It should be noted that films about the occupation of Norway and Denmark have been very common particularly in Norway, where the occupation drama has flourished and evolved in the cinema since 1946, including classics like the docudrama *Kampen om tungtvannet* (Titus Vibe-Müller and Jean Dréville, 1948) and the artistically refined *Kalde spor* (Arne Skouen, 1962) (Iversen 2011: 145–55). In Denmark, the first occupation film, *Den usynlige hær* (Johan Jacobsen, 1945) came shortly after the liberation, and the genre peaked in the early 1990s, with films like *Drengene fra Sankt Petri* (Søren Kragh-Jacobsen, 1991) (Schepelern, 2001: 136, 327). Few films, however, can match the domestic successes of *Max Manus: Man of War* or *Flame & Citron*.

Sweden's Relations with Norway and Denmark during the War

Research on Swedish actions during the Second World War has become more accessible lately due to several modern scholarly projects being summarised in a single volume written by Swedish historian Klas Åmark; the title of the book can be translated as 'To Be Neighbour with Evil: Sweden's Relationship to Nazism, Nazi Germany and the Holocaust' (Åmark 2011). This chapter will need some recounting of history, and here this will be based on Åmark's insights.

On 9 April 1940 Denmark and Norway were attacked and occupied by Nazi Germany in Operation Weserübung. The aim was to seal off Scandinavia, particularly the northern Swedish iron ore fields, on which the German war effort at this stage was dependent, and especially the sea route from the ice-free shipping harbour at Narvik, from where the iron ore was shipped to Germany in the winter season. Denmark capitulated more or less immediately; Norway resisted for a while, particularly in the sensitive Narvik area, where the Norwegians were aided by the British fleet as well as by allied ground troops.

Operation Weserübung caused shock not only in Norway and Denmark, but also in Sweden. Since Narvik was inaccessible by land from inside Norway, and the British navy blockaded the harbour from the sea, the best way to send German reinforcements was by train through Sweden. The Germans demanded three political concessions from the Swedish government: not to organise a corps of Swedish volunteers to go to Norway to fight against the Germans (as the Swedes had done to help the Finns against the Soviets in 1939), not to mobilise its armed forces, and to allow for German transits by Swedish rail to Norway.

Sweden conceded, but not entirely. The army was indeed partly mobilised and Sweden also challenged the idea of transiting German soldiers to Norway while there was still fighting going on. In the end Germany did send war materials and soldiers to the battle zone, disguised as 'humanitarian aid'. When the Germans had successfully concluded the fighting in June 1940, and Norway was fully occupied, regular transit traffic of soldiers on leave from Norway through Sweden, where the Germans kept more than 400,000 men, became the norm. This traffic was to last until the autumn of 1943, when Sweden stopped it (that is, in the wake of the German defeats against the allies at Kursk and in Sicily).

Obviously, the transit traffic was in breach of international conventions regarding neutrality, but the Swedes also tried to give the Norwegians some assistance, receiving more refugees from Norway than from any other country. And the Norwegian Legation at Stockholm was the very centre of coordination between the Norwegian government in exile in London and the resistance movement. But here Åmark notes:

> The Norwegian resistance movement in Sweden also cooperated with the British Special Operations Executive, SOE. But Swedish police closely monitored this activity. During the war years nearly four hundred Norwegians were convicted of spying or of illegal intelligence gathering because of their providing information to the British about the state in Norway ... The general pattern is obvious. At the beginning of the war, the government [of Sweden] was quite harsh when dealing with Norwegian activities on Swedish soil aimed against Nazi Germany. Eventually, the resistance movement became stronger, bolder and more efficient. (Åmark 2011: 578–9)

In some cases, however, Sweden played a more positive role regarding both Norway and Denmark. This pertained to the Jews, where Sweden had had a very restrictive immigration policy up until 1943 (hardly any Jews had had the opportunity to enter Sweden after the outbreak of war in September 1939). In the autumn of 1942, the Germans started the round-up of Norwegian Jews and 770 were sent to Auschwitz for extermination; however, 1,100 escaped to Sweden. Åmark states that: 'The major rescue mission was performed on the Norwegian side by the Home Front and other Norwegians who helped Jews cross the border to Sweden' (2011: 536). In Denmark, the rumours of the mass arrest of Jews in October 1943 leaked out before the arrests were implemented, making it possible for about 7,900 Jews to escape across the strait from Denmark to Sweden.[2]

Finally, one might add that Sweden, after 1943, when many politicians realised German collapse was imminent, set up and trained special police forces consisting of Norwegians and Danes, ready to keep order after the German defeat. They also established the White Buses in the spring of 1945, a Scandinavian help scheme fronted by Swedish diplomat Count Folke Bernadotte, a relative of the Swedish king, to get Scandinavian prisoners out of the concentration camp system (prisoners of many other nationalities also made it to Sweden on the buses). In general, though, Åmark in his final chapter – called 'The Moral Dilemma of Neutrality' ('Neutralitetens moraliska dilemma') – stresses the generally ambiguous stance of the Swedish government in the war years: it had not much stamina against the Germans up to the turn of the tide in 1943, but it did gradually take a stand afterwards (Åmark 2011: 641–74).

Max's Holidays in Sweden

Max Manus: Man of War, which opened in Norway on 18 December 2008, is a classically narrated war film, an occupation drama and a biopic based on historical events, depicting the actions of real Norwegian war hero Max Manus between 1940 and 1945. The second two-thirds of the film show Max's successful sabotage actions against the Germans after 1943. The beginning portrays how Max sees action on the Salla front in Finland in March 1940, having volunteered to fight the Soviet invaders, as did several other people from the Nordic countries. The rest of the film depicts him as a victim of post-traumatic stress disorder, which is further complicated by the deaths of several of his co-fighters – the so called 'Oslogjengen' – in the Norwegian resistance against the German occupation. Max turns gradually to drink in order to relieve his pains and the information supplied at the end of the film tells us that he suffered from alcoholism and problems with his nerves for the rest of his life.

Max Manus has been much discussed primarily in Norway where the film, according to Norwegian film historians Gunnar Iversen and Ove Solum, had been seen by nearly 1.2 million people by the spring of 2009, one of the highest audience figures for a domestic film ever in Norway, and it was also an overwhelming success on DVD (Iversen and Solum 2010: 299). One needs to take into consideration Norway's 5 million population in order to appreciate the film's enormous popularity. Iversen and Solum also provide the most thorough close reading of the film, emphasising the film as masculinity spectacle, a boys' adventure (not least in the shape of main actor Aksel Hennie's adolescent looks) and as a provider of a strong sense of national identity; *Max Manus* is a didactic presentation of Norway's role as one of the victors of the Second World War (Iversen and Solum 2010: 309–14).

But Iversen and Solum also address the more problematic aspects of the film as a representation of history: for instance, the lack of representation of ordinary Norwegian people and their lives under the occupation (Iversen and Solum 2010: 304–5). Many, many Norwegians were even collaborators, but in *Max Manus*, they are only hinted at, most strikingly in the character of Solveig Johnsrud (Victoria Winge), who becomes the mistress of the villain of the film, SS-Hauptsturmführer Siegfried Fehmer (at least partly sympathetically played by German actor Ken Duken), the head of the Gestapo in Oslo.[3] What could have happened to a girl who hobnobbed with the Gestapo after the war? No answer is provided in the film where she is just left out at the end.[4] In his review in *Sight & Sound*, Guy Westwell sums up the general strategy in *Max Manus*:

WHOSE REPRESSED MEMORIES?

Figure 2.1 *Max Manus*: An idyllic image of the Stockholm City Hall showing that Sweden is also prepared for war.

'Norway has produced a pasteurised, thoroughly conventional war movie that offers the audience the easy pleasures of individual heroism, personal redemption and nationalist reassurance' (Westwell, 2009: 72). One of the obviously repressed dimensions that Westwell emphasises is the fact that the freighter *Donau* that Max and his compatriots sabotage was the very ship in which a substantial part of the Norwegian Jews were sent to their destruction in the concentration camps. There is no mention whatsoever in the film of this event, or any general reference to the fact that one of the most striking aspects of Nazism was its murderous anti-Semitism. The persecution of Jews could indeed, as stated, be seen also in Norway during the war.

My primary interest here, however, is the references to Sweden in the film. Max visits Stockholm no less than four times in the film and several minutes of precious screen time are spent there, in fact more than 14 out of a total 117. The first time is after the completion of Operation Mardonius in Oslo harbour on 27 April 1943, where Max and his compatriots blow up several German ships. Realistically, they are afterwards depicted as walking over the Norwegian–Swedish border, and they then presumably take a train to Stockholm. The entrance into Sweden is somewhat romantically highlighted when Max tells his colleague, 'That, my friend, is Sweden', as they pass a pathway among birch trees.

The first image of Stockholm is iconic: the City Hall in bright sunlight with the south side of the town in the background; a tram passes the bridge which also contains a platoon of Swedish soldiers, signalling that Sweden was also mobilised at the time. At the British Consulate, Tikken (Agnes Kittelsen), who eventually becomes Max's lover and his future wife, supplies them with various items of military equipment, but also with whiskey and cigarettes. Later, they go to a restaurant where they drink red wine; the table is adorned with a yellow rose (one part of the Swedish blue and yellow colours – the blue is provided by the tram at the beginning of the sequence). All this is important, since wartime Stockholm is described as a beautiful haven. This idyllic depiction reappears in Max's further visits (or refuges from the Oslo heat). Max, Ticken and Max's co-fighter Gregers Gram (Nicolai Cleve Broch), who is later killed in action in Norway, visit another restaurant where they drink champagne and cognac; the yellow rose is there once again, and the blue tram can be seen in the beautiful establishing shot of Nybroplan (just in front of an invisible Royal Dramatic Theatre). Later, they end up in a smart apartment with a chandelier, drinking and dancing into the small hours. Stockholm is the site of relief from the terrible burdens of a resistance fighter, even providing lavish hospital care after Max later accidentally shoots himself in Oslo. 'You can be safe here', Tikken reassures Max, trying to prevent him from returning to Norway prematurely.

The stylish Stockholm imagery in *Max Manus: Man of War* is dramatically at odds with the sordid depiction of the Swedish capital at the time by Swedish author Ola Larsmo, who specialises in historical narratives, in the recent novel *Förrädare* – in English 'Traitors' (Larsmo 2012). Larsmo here tells the story of the work of the Swedish military intelligence during the war, like the country at large deeply divided in its moral stance against the belligerents. Several of the officers had been volunteers in the struggle against communism in the Finnish civil war of 1918, and they are shown as sympathisers of Nazi Germany, betraying Norwegian resistance fighters seeking refuge in Sweden to the Germans; in some cases the Norwegians end up on the guillotine in Hamburg. Larsmo tells about Max Manus's first visit to Stockholm in April 1941, which is not shown in the film. The Swedish authorities were indeed interested in Max Manus, who had then escaped from a hospital in Oslo, after having been arrested by the Gestapo. Larsmo has located an authentic memo written to the police by a civil servant at the National Board of Health and Welfare, the authority handling all foreign refugees in Sweden at the time, in which it was stated:

> The Norwegian citizen Max Manus ... has applied for a visa ... According to the Norwegian Police Bulletin ... Manus is wanted under A-2 as being a dangerous person, who might employ armed weapons if he is arrested. He is wanted for several crimes, among them violent assault ... Close surveillance is requested and an eventual arrest should be reported to the Head of the State Police in Oslo ... Manus's emergency visa and applications are enclosed and are expected back along with due investigation. (Larsmo 2012: 281)

A report to the Norwegian police at the time was of course the same as reporting to the Gestapo. Even if the Swedish authorities to a certain extent must have permitted the Norwegian resistance to operate on Swedish soil, the sheer bliss of the visits to Stockholm in *Max Manus: Man of War* is under all circumstances somewhat exaggerated, or at least biased. Indeed, there were strong forces in Sweden who disagreed with what the Norwegian resistance fighters were doing. A striking example of this is that the Commander-in-Chief of the Swedish armed forces, General Olof Thörnell, forcefully advocated an active Swedish intervention on the side of the Finns against the Soviet Union: that is, on the side of Nazi Germany (Åmark 2011: 125).

Bent and Jørgen under Surveillance in Sweden

Flame & Citron had its premiere in Denmark on 28 March 2008. Generically this film is similar to *Max Manus: Man of War* – war film, occupation film, biopic – but it is narrated in a different mode, derived from the ambiguities typical of European art cinema. In her review of the film in *Sight & Sound*, Kate Stables characteristically refers to the influence from French director Jean-Pierre Melville, whose *Army of Shadows* (*L'armée des ombres*, 1969) is one of the classics of the genre (Stables 2009: 57).

Bent Farschou-Hviid (Flame, played by Thure Lindhardt) and Jørgen Haagen Schmidt (Citron, Mads Mikkelsen) are two-real life hitmen, working for the resistance group Holger Danske, assassinating various collaborators and informants during the war. Like Max Manus, they are depicted as victims of their trade, suffering severe psychological strains. Their boss is the prosecutor Aksel Winther (Peter Mygind; Winther's real name was Vilhelm

Figure 2.2   *Flame & Citron*: The old town in Stockholm with the German church towering in the middle. Image courtesy of Nimbus Film Productions.

Leifer), who provides them with their murderous missions. Gradually Bent and Jørgen becomes entangled in a haze of mystery regarding why they are asked to assassinate certain people – are those people really guilty of collaboration, or is Winther following a trajectory of personal revenge? The film does not provide clear answers to all our questions and in the end the two protagonists die as a result of betrayal by the mysterious Ketty Selmer (Stine Stengade). She is paid the reward money by one of her lovers, the head of Copenhagen Gestapo, SS-Sturmbannführer Karl Heinz Hoffmann. He is another sympathetic German murderer, covering the bodies of Bent and Jørgen as the other German policemen desecrate the corpses when they are brought back to headquarters after having been killed; interestingly, Hoffmann is played by German actor Christian Berkel who was also the good Nazi – the SS doctor Ernst-Günther Schenk – in Oliver Hirschbiegel's controversial *Downfall* (*Der Untergang*, 2004), and one of the heroic conspirators, Colonel Mertz von Quirnheim, against Hitler in *Valkyrie* (Bryan Singer, 2008).[5]

Controversy also hit *Flame & Citron*, Denmark's most expensive film ever, but according to official Danish statistics it attracted 673,764 people to the cinemas, and was thus a smash hit in the domestic market. The debate regarding the film was massive, however, and a major reason, I suspect, why there is as yet no thorough academic study of the film (which would have to take into consideration a huge amount of newspaper articles). In short, the debate concerned the usual question of historical accuracy: for instance, whether Ketty Selmer really was a double agent and whether she, as indicated in the film, framed Flame, causing his death, and whether Winther really ordered the murders of innocent people (Fredensborg 2008). But generally, *Flame & Citron* is a film that problematises history, and of course it would cause some consternation since it depicts two posthumously highly-decorated war heroes performing – possibly – more or less meaningless deeds in the struggle against the German occupier. The film is also less ethnocentric than *Max Manus: Man of War* in that it portrays the nasty Danish collaborators, the so-called Schalburg Corps, used as auxiliary police by the Germans. It also refers explicitly to the Holocaust, in that Flame's motive for becoming a man of the resistance, as Swedish historian Ulf Zander has pointed out, has to do with his personal experience of the persecution of Jews in Germany (Zander 2011: 218).

Like Max Manus, Flame and Citron travel to Stockholm in the film, even twice, and in the final scene we see Ketty Selmer arriving at the Stockholm central station, ambiguously meeting with one of the heads of Danish military intelligence. In all, more than ten and a half minutes (of a total of 130) are set in Stockholm. This time the journey is not to hide out in a haven, however, but to receive orders from various superiors, including the shady Winther. As in *Max Manus: Man of War*, Stockholm is introduced by a touristy and sunlit establishing shot of the old town (here created by digital means). We can clearly discern the German church 'Tyska kyrkan', maybe coincidental, but to me a sign of German–Swedish connections. Flame, Citron and their superiors meet in restaurants, not the cosy ones in *Max Manus: Man of War*, but rather a large room with a single table and several waiters (far more than needed) walking around. I am not sure whether I read this as a realistically staged scene. Rather the many people constantly walking about seem to make for a theatrically inspired symbol for Stockholm as meeting point of various national interests (which it was, with all its embassies and legations). The fare served, however, is particularly lavish: white wine, pineapple, strawberries and crayfish, the latter being a Swedish speciality, signifying the luxuriousness of keeping out of the war, of being neutral.

One scene in Stockholm is particularly striking. By a hotel room window, Flame spots three men in long coats on the street. Winther informs him that they are Swedish security police and that they are scared of Flame, and that they fear that Flame will shoot somebody on Swedish soil. 'They don't want problems with their German friends', Winther adds laconically, thus explicitly expressing his opinion of the Swedes as German fellow travellers. Even if, as Larsmo indicated, it is realistic that Swedish security forces closely guarded resistance fighters when they were in Sweden, it is a bit late – the scene takes place in 1944 – to accuse the Swedes of harbouring such blatant pro-Nazi sentiments. The tide had in reality turned.

The most significant connection to Stockholm in the film, however, is the presumed traitor Ketty Selmer. She is married to a Swede, travels back and forth between Sweden and Copenhagen, and in the end is seen arriving one final time in Stockholm, after selling out Flame to the Gestapo. We have, then, quite a different portrayal of Sweden in *Flame & Citron* from that in *Max Manus: Man of War*. Whereas in the latter film it was reassuring and soothing, in the former it is treacherous and evasive.

Bleak Swedish Receptions

Max Manus: Man of War was certainly no hit in Sweden, as it had been in Norway. According to the Lumiere database, only 7,923 tickets were sold at the Swedish box office when the film was released in May 2009. Obviously, the Swedish audience was not interested in a film about Norway during the war. Taking the extremely modest box office returns of the film in Sweden, it feels particularly ironic that Aksel Hennie, the actor playing Max, gave an interview to the Swedish press just before the premiere. Here, he expressed his great expectations:

> If Sweden had not been neutral they [the Norwegian men of the resistance] would not have been able to sabotage. Sweden was of vital significance

to the resistance fighters. Trikken was in Sweden. That is where they found their love and it was thanks to Sweden that it survived. To me it is really something that Max Manus will be shown in Sweden. To me, Sweden provides an inspirational model regarding cinema. (Gentele 2009)

The Swedes did not appear to share his enthusiasm.

The film did however receive a lot of press coverage, although very little offered any comments regarding the depiction of Sweden in the film. One critic refers to a theory that *Max Manus: Man of War* probably opened in Sweden because of its connection to Swedish history (Engström 2009). Critics, however, were as lukewarm as the general audience. The highly experienced Jan Aghed in *Sydsvenska Dagbladet* compared the film to a series of great occupation dramas, like Roberto Rossellini's *Rome, Open City* (*Roma, città aperta*, 1945), Andrzej Wajda's *Kanal* (1957) and Melville's *Army of Shadows*, adding ironically: 'Only a blinded Norwegian patriot would get the idea to put the film in the earlier mentioned company' (Aghed 2009). And in the Stockholm major *Dagens Nyheter*, Eva af Geijerstam is mildly affirmative, although she complains about the need for jingoistic stories in Norway; Max and his friends will, however, she adds, come as a surprise to Swedish youth (Geijerstam 2009). The other Stockholm daily, *Svenska Dagbladet*, dismissed the film as an over-the-top generic mix (Janson 2009).

The most comprehensive part of the reception of *Max Manus: Man of War* in Sweden consists of two scholarly essays written by the earlier mentioned Ulf Zander, who has addressed the film in a comparative analysis along with *Flame & Citron* (Zander 2011: 207–25, Karlsson and Zander 2012: 173–86). Zander does mention the cool reception of *Max Manus* in Sweden, and puts emphasis on the very different apprehensions of the Second World War in the Nordic countries. Sweden, he claims, adopted neutrality after 1945 as a 'state of mind' (quoting Swedish historian Alf W. Johansson) (Zander, 2011: 215), that is, as I understand it, neutrality as something of an inherently superior stance. Zander also refers to the vivid public debates regarding neutrality during the war in Sweden in the 1990s, concluding that: 'The fact that the Swedes once and for all have dealt with injustices of the past has been an invitation to revive the notion of Sweden as a moral example' (Karlsson and Zander 2012: 183). This might have something to do with the lack of interest in Norwegians fighting during the war.

The only Swedish text that I have found that deals explicitly with the depiction of Sweden in *Max Manus: Man of War* is a teaching guide published by the Swedish Film Institute (Lagerström 2009: 4–5). Here, Sweden's role of provider is emphasised – it was because of the Swedish willingness to submit neutral ground for the Norwegian Legation and the British Consulate that espionage and intelligence work could be pursued (Lagerström 2009: 4). Also,

Lagerström underlines the fact that Swedish people along the border helped the Norwegians, often risking their own lives. But she does also problematise Swedish concessions to Nazi Germany: the transit trains, the submission of air and water space, and the export of iron ore. One can conclude that *Max Manus: Man of War* at least had some kind of reception in Sweden, in the sense that it was quite widely written about in spite of its poor performance at the Swedish box office.

Flame & Citron did not manage at all. The film was never distributed in Swedish cinemas, and accordingly was not even reviewed in the press. It was, however, shown on television in three episodes. The reason for not distributing *Flame & Citron*, besides a general disinterest in our fellow Danes' ordeal, had, I think, to do with its art cinema traits. The narration of the film is certainly convoluted, a fact that could have frightened off potential distributors. I have not seen any references to the negative depiction of Sweden in the film, just a very brief mention about the production that parts of the film were set in Stockholm (Anon. 2006).

Still, it is somewhat odd, taking the film's lavish production values into consideration. As most film scholars in Scandinavia should know, Nordic films, even domestically successful ones, do not generally perform well in the other Nordic countries. An exception here concerns certain Danish art films, like the films of Susanne Bier, which can be highly appreciated in Sweden, sometimes reaching an audience of 100,000. Very little was written in the press on the matter. One critic openly complained about Swedish distributors choosing not to release the film (Malmberg 2009). Another critic has obviously misunderstood the mode of art cinema narration in a very short review of the film as it was shown at a festival, complaining about superficiality as well as lack of motivation in the protagonists (Domellöf-Wik 2009). The most sympathetic writing on *Flame & Citron* in Sweden, besides the analyses by Zander, is a very short review of the television mini-series by historian Fredrik Persson. Here, Persson applauds the strategy of questioning the resistance in the film, and the challenge it poses to the dominant heroic tale in Denmark (Persson 2010).

There is actually not much more to find about the film in Sweden, except for a few interviews and some basic background to the film (like Oscarsson 2009). But, as stated, the film did not perform at all in the Swedish cinema market.

Some Concluding Remarks

Why, then, this monumental disinterest in Sweden for the fate of our Scandinavian neighbours, especially as this concerns two films that from a reasonably objective point of view must be regarded as proficient in terms of technical prowess, acting and scripting? My personal favourite is *Flame &*

Citron precisely because of its ambiguity and its superb actors. Beside the realistic motivation for the inclusion of Stockholm in the films, this also displayed a commercial pretention: with Sweden being used as a setting, Swedes could possibly be attracted to the films, which is particularly obvious in *Max Manus: Man of War*, with its idyllic representation of the Swedish capital. But in this case it did not work.

The fact that *Max Manus: Man of War* and not *Flame & Citron* was shown in the cinemas also reveals that Sweden is more concerned with Norway than with Denmark, which could have to do with the fact that Norway was governed by Sweden between 1814 and 1905. Also, Norway is closer to the Swedish capital than Denmark (this would not be true for southern Sweden, though, as it has had close cultural affinities with Denmark ever since Sweden conquered it in 1658). And presumably contacts between the countries during the Second World War were more intense between Sweden and Norway, as is also indicated by Åmark's book.

But as Zander claimed, there might also be a feeling of moral superiority in Sweden, a sense that neutrality was the only way when the big powers clashed during the Second World War. In this regard, some very interesting remarks on the two films were published a short time ago by highly lauded Swedish author Elisabeth Åsbrink in *Dagens Nyheter*, Sweden's largest morning newspaper. Åsbrink has achieved fame by unveiling Swedish capitalist Ingvar Kamprad (the creator of Swedish furniture giant IKEA) as a former Nazi. Åsbrink dismisses these two films out of hand as propaganda for two seemingly victorious countries, when, as she claims, in reality neither Norway nor Denmark put up any serious resistance to the German invader. Regarding *Flame & Citron* she maintains that it appealed strongly to an idealistic Danish self-image and that the Danish audience 'responded with love and ticket purchases' (Åsbrink 2012). This remark makes me conclude that she has not seen the latter film. And in the case of Norway, why did the Germans keep an occupation army of 400,000 men – towards the end of the war, troops badly needed elsewhere – if there was no resistance?

Even if Åsbrink generally displays a highly critical approach also to Sweden, she is clearly on dangerous ground moralising about Norway and Denmark with historical hindsight. One really needs to try to imagine what all those people really thought before they acted more than seventy years ago before jumping to conclusions. But she definitely illustrates a Swedish stance, perhaps even an image of moral superiority, as if Norway and Denmark had a choice. Obviously, we Swedes do not want to hear much about Norway and Denmark during the war, even if we are duly invited by our neighbours including scenes from our country in their films about the war. I am not sure that we are that keen to hear about ourselves either, even if the debate about Sweden's role during the Second World War is still ongoing. So if *Max Manus: Man of War* and *Flame & Citron* somehow represent repressed memories of the war, these are also memories integral to Sweden.

Notes

1. Finland also makes films about this period but they are obviously not occupation dramas, rather war films, some of them quite remarkable ones like *Ambush* (*Rukajärven tie*, Olli Saarela, 1999).
2. Here, however, a well-established theory claims that SS-Obergruppenführer Dr Werner Best, Plenipotentiary of the Nazi regime in occupied Denmark, consciously made this mass escape possible in order to improve German relations with the Danes (Åmark 2011: 538).
3. Fehmer is according to contemporary conventions depicted as a charming, friendly but still deadly person, particularly keen on Norwegian women, as was reputedly the case with the real-life Fehmer, eventually executed for war crimes in 1948 in Oslo. Regarding the contemporary conventions, I am here thinking of films like *Conspiracy* (Frank Pierson, 2001), where Kenneth Branagh convincingly portrays SS-Obergruppenführer Reinhard Heydrich as a man whose malicious power clearly derives from his highly developed social skills, even when condemning millions to death, as he did at the Wannsee meeting in 1942. Another example of this type of outwardly sympathetic Nazi is Sebastian Koch as SS-Hauptsturmführer Ludwig Müntze in the Dutch occupation drama *Black Book* (*Zwartboek*, Paul Verhoeven, 2006). Depicting Nazis as thugs, which has been the cinematic code, is often a bit too facile.
4. An article on the Internet about a Norwegian woman called Anne Marie Breien describes her as both Fehmer's mistress and as a hero of the resistance. According to her story, she had a long affair with Fehmer in order, first, to get her father, a man of the resistance, out of the Gestapo's claws. She continued to provide information to the resistance, but was nevertheless charged with treason after the war. Even if she was never condemned, she apparently had to live with rumours of her treachery, in spite of resistance people vouching for her innocence. See <http://www.side3.no/article3340091.ece#>, accessed 20 December 2013.
5. It could be added that the real-life Hoffmann was condemned to death in Copenhagen after the war; the death sentence, however, was commuted to a prison sentence.

References

Aghed, Jan (2009), 'Max Manus', *Sydsvenska Dagbladet*, 5 June.
Åmark, Klas (2011), *Att bo granne med ondskan: Sveriges förhållande till nazismen, Nazityskland och Förintelsen*, Stockholm: Albert Bonniers förlag.
Anon. (2006), 'Dansk storfilm i svensk miljö', *Svenska Dagbladet*, 16 October.
Åsbrink, Elisabeth (2012), 'Vårt behov av Raoul Wallenberg', *Dagens Nyheter*, 9 August.
Domellöf-Wik, Maria (2009), 'Flamman & Citronen', *Göteborgs-Posten*, 27 January.
Engström, Emma (2009), 'Max Manus', *Göteborgs-Posten*, 14 May.
Fredensborg, René (2008), 'Historikere advarer om att tro på Flammen og Citronen-film', *Avisen.dk*, 8 April.
Geijerstam, Eva af (2009), 'Max Manus', *Dagens Nyheter*, 20 March.
Gentele, Jeanette (2009), 'Max Manus liv innehöll allt', *Svenska Dagbladet*, 11 May.
Iversen, Gunnar (2011), *Norsk filmhistorie. Spillefilmen 1911–2011*, Oslo: Universitetsforlaget.

Iversen, Gunnar and Ove Solum (2010), *Den norske filmbølgen: Fra Orions belte till Max Manus*, Oslo: Universitetsforlaget.
Janson, Malena (2009), 'Krigsdrama utan fokus', *Svenska Dagbladet*, 14 May.
Karlsson, Klas-Göran and Ulf Zander (2012), 'Historien – livets dubbla läromästare'. In Trond Solhaug, Kjetil Børhaug, Ola Svein Stugu and Ove Kr. Haugaløkken (eds), *Skolen, nasjonen og medborgaren*, Trondheim: Tapir Akademisk Forlag, pp. 173–86.
Lagerström, Louise (2009), *Max Manus*, Filmhandledning utgiven av Svenska Filminstitutet, Stockholm: Svenska Filminstitutet, pp. 1–7.
Larsmo, Ola (2012), *Förrädare*, Stockholm: Bonniers.
Malmberg, Johan (2009), 'Flamman & Citronen', *Helsingborgs Dagblad*, 25 February.
Oscarsson, Mattias (2009), 'Laddat ämne för danskarna', *Sydsvenska Dagbladet*, 4 March.
Persson, Fredrik (2010), 'En annan sida av saken', *Sydsvenska Dagbladet*, 15 September.
Schepelern, Peter (2001), *100 Års Dansk Film*, København: Rosinante.
Stables, Kate (2009), 'Flame & Citron', *Sight & Sound* 19 (3): 57–8.
Westwell, Guy (2009), 'Max Manus: Man of War', *Sight & Sound* 19 (7): 72.
Zander, Ulf (2011), 'World War II at 24 Frames a Second – Scandinavian Examples'. In Helle Bjerg, Claudia Lenz and Erik Thorstensen (eds), *Historicizing the Uses of the Past: Scandinavian Perspectives on History Culture, Historical Consciousness and Didactics Related to World War II*, Bielefeld: Transcript Verlag, pp. 207–25.

3. VOICES FROM THE PAST – RECENT NORDIC HISTORICAL FILMS

Gunnar Iversen

Nordic cinema since the 2000s has turned to history to a greater degree than before, employing historical subject matter and settings to entertain, show off costumes and tell stories, but also to contribute with images and sounds to what historian Robert A. Rosenstone calls 'that larger History ... that web of connections to the past that holds a culture together, that tells us not only where we have been but also suggests where we are going' (Rosenstone 1995: 23).

This chapter discusses the connections to the past made by the genre of the historical film. By historical film I mean films that create stories that take place in the past and not the present. The main questions are: How do Nordic filmmakers interpret and construct Nordic history? How do Nordic filmmakers engage with the past? And, what constitutes history for current filmmakers in the Nordic countries?

I discuss four different feature films, from four different countries, in order to show the scope of the new Nordic historical film and different varieties of engagement with the past. The films are not necessarily typical of their countries, but they represent important aspects of the national film industries as well as important aspects of the historical film genre in the Nordic countries. In all of the Nordic countries, the study of history is important, and the publication of numerous history books as well as historical fictions is proof that history not only fascinates a large audience in itself, but plays a role in the construction of contemporary national identities. Even though the genre deals with the past, the historical film will always reflect its time of production, and most Nordic historical dramas use the past for the purposes of the present.

Nordic Historical Film

Compared to contemporary dramas relatively few films produced in the Nordic countries have been consciously historical in their subject matter or attempted to represent the past. Although some Nordic national cinemas, especially Finnish cinema, have relied on historical representations throughout their history, there are far fewer historical films than ones set in the present. The main reason lies in the small markets of Nordic cinema and the big budgets of most historical films. The extra cost of creating a believable historical past through costumes and settings, instead of filming a contemporary story, proved too expensive for many filmmakers and production companies. However, recent changes in the state film policies in the Nordic countries, with more emphasis on the production of popular genre films, and the goal of winning larger international audiences, have made it easier to finance historical films.

Even though most Nordic films deal with contemporary issues and their stories take place in the present, major exceptions have been historical dramas about the medieval period and the Second World War. Especially the medieval period seems to have had an attraction for many Nordic filmmakers. Films like *Witchcraft through the Ages* (*Häxan*, Benjamin Christensen, 1922), *Day of Wrath* (*Vredens dag*, Carl Th. Dreyer, 1943) and *The Seventh Seal* (*Det sjunde inseglet*, Ingmar Bergman, 1957), take place in the Middle Ages, and the medieval period has been an important exception to the dominance of contemporary films in the Nordic countries.

The neo-medieval wave that Umberto Eco described in several essays of the 1980s seems to persist (Eco 1985; Eco 1987). More people in the Nordic countries than ever appear to be fascinated by the Middle Ages, and filmmakers have responded to this in different ways. Eco interprets this ongoing fascination with the Middle Ages as something more than romance, exotica or fantasy. He writes:

> All the problems of the Western world emerged in the Middle Ages. The Middle Ages are the root of all our contemporary 'hot' problems, and it is not surprising that we go back to that period every time we ask ourselves about our origin. (Eco 1987: 64–5)

Eco describes the Middle Ages as an earlier stage in human development in his essay 'Dreaming of the Middle Ages', and consequently sees the medieval period as a key to understanding the modern world:

> Thus looking at the Middle Ages means looking at our infancy, in the same way that a doctor, to understand our present state of health, asks

us about our childhood, or in the same way that the psychoanalyst, to understand our present neuroses, makes a careful investigation of the primal scene. (Eco 1987: 65)

The same metaphor was used by Norwegian actor and director Liv Ullmann in the publicity material for her film *Kristin Lavransdatter* (1995). The press pamphlet begins with a question: 'The medieval period as a trend – perhaps the key to our whole existence?'[1] Then, Ullmann is quoted as to why she made the film: 'Reading about the medieval period in available sources, I felt the same way about the people of that time as I do about children: they know something I don't know, or something I have forgotten, some magic secret, a miracle that may be the key to our whole existence.'[2]

Kristin Lavransdatter is one of a number of films about the Middle Ages that have been made in Norway (Iversen 2000). In the other Nordic countries different medieval films have been made in recent years. One type of Nordic medieval drama is the Viking film. This trend started in Iceland in the early 1980s, with films like *Outlaw, The Saga of Gisli* (*Utlaginn*, Agust Gudmundsson, 1981) and *When the Raven Flies* (*Hrafninn flygur*, Hrafn Gunnlaugsson, 1984). Recent examples are the Danish *Valhalla Rising* (Nicolas Winding Refn, 2009) and the Icelandic *Beowulf & Grendel* (Sturla Gunnarsson, 2005). These later examples are more internationally oriented, and have bigger budgets and international stars. The medieval films range from romances and horror films to realist dramas that aim to create a more authentic portrayal of the harsh life of the medieval period. In the current period of growing multiculturalism and globalisation that has transformed the formerly homogeneous Nordic countries, some look to the Middle Ages as a key to understanding the modern world. Some films even propose solutions to modern problems by looking to the Middle Ages, such as the Swedish films about the Knight Templar Arn that will be discussed later in this chapter.

Another important exception to the dominance of contemporary plots in Nordic cinema is the large number of films produced in Denmark, Finland and Norway about the Second World War. War films and occupation dramas have been important, and the war plays a vital role in the identity of these countries. The war experience is a significant part of the way the Nordic countries are constantly recreated cinematically as nations. War films have gone through many changes since the mid-1940s, showing how the war experiences have been viewed in various ways through the prism of the present, and how the past has been moulded, interpreted, transformed and reworked for present uses.

In recent years new films about the Second World War have recreated the past for different purposes, and the popularity of these films are indications that the Second World War could also be seen as a key to understanding the modern

Nordic countries. The success in Denmark of *Flame & Citron* (*Flammen og Citronen*, Ole Christian Madsen, 2008) and *This Life* (*Hvidstengruppen*, Anne-Grethe Bjarup Riis, 2012) shows how important the war experience still is in Denmark. Both films deal with famous authentic episodes from the resistance against the German occupation forces, but they paint very different pictures of Denmark during the war years. In *This Life* a family of innkeepers and the people in a small town become involved in the resistance. Almost without a thought they just do their duty, and many end up dying heroically. *Flame & Citron* paints a very different picture of Denmark at war, and focuses on ethical grey zones and betrayal as well as heroism. In Norway, the film *Max Manus: Man of War* (*Max Manus*, Joachim Rønning and Espen Sandberg, 2008), a portrait of a famous resistance fighter, became a national success, and the film reformulated the Occupation drama by focusing on an individual, larger-than-life resistance hero (Iversen 2012).

Interesting also is the fact that Sweden has turned to making films about the war, reformulating the war experience of a neutral country. Neither *Beyond the Border* (*Gränsen*, Richard Holm, 2011) nor *An Enemy to Die For* (*En fiende att dö för*, Peter Dalle, 2011) became big successes. In contrast to the Danish and Norwegian films they were not based on actual events. Especially interesting is the historical fantasy *An Enemy to Die For*, where the war is depicted metaphorically through the story of a geological expedition to the arctic. The German and English members fight on a ship, and the Norwegian captain is on the side of the British, while a young Swedish geologist at the end saves the day – and the war – by blowing up the Germans. In this historical fantasy the passive and neutral Sweden becomes the real hero of the Second World War.

The films about the Second World War or the Middle Ages illustrate historian Warren I. Susman's four methodological points about the complex relationship between film and history. These films are products of wider historical events; they reflect their own production period and nation; they interpret history in a self-conscious way; and they *shape* history for the spectators of today (Susman 2012: 2–6). The same can be said for other recent Nordic historical dramas, which tell different stories from different periods, but all present powerful audiovisual arguments about Nordic history for the present.

ARN: THE MEDIEVAL MIRROR

One of the largest productions in the history of Swedish and Nordic cinema is the medieval epic *Arn: The Knight Templar* (*Arn: Tempelriddaren*, Peter Flinth, 2007) and *Arn: The Kingdom at Road's End* (*Arn: Riket vid vägens slut*, Peter Flinth, 2008). The films, and a television series made at the same time, were based on a book trilogy by Jan Guillou that had sold two million copies in Sweden. The budget for the two films was 210 million SEK, the biggest up until that time in Sweden. Even though the first film was a success, being seen by more than a million people in Sweden and more than 300,000 in the other Nordic countries, the film did not meet the expectations of the producers, and the critics were not impressed (Hedling and Wallengren 2013: 11–13).

The main character in the two films is Arn Magnusson (Joakim Nätterqvist). In the very beginning of the first film we meet Arn as a Knight Templar in the Holy Land in the year 1177, and the camera sweeps over a burning desert strewn with blackened bones. A male voiceover establishes the background of the epic tale of Arn, the fight between Christians and Muslims. In a prologue, Arn, named Al Ghouti by the Muslims, saves some Muslim traders from bandits in the desert. They pose a question, 'Why is he helping us?' This question is central to this medieval tale. Then, an intertitle takes us back many years earlier, when Arn is just a little boy.

Arn grows up in Västra Götaland, a small kingdom where three families fight over power. He survives an accident as a child, but his mother has asked God for help when he was injured, so Arn is sent to a monastery to please the Lord, and he grows up there. In the monastery he meets a Knight Templar who teaches him to fight. This comes in handy when he returns to his family as a young man and wins an important duel. However, politics becomes a problem for him when he meets young Cecilia (Sofia Helin). They fall in love, but her father cannot give her hand to Arn, because he is one of the king's enemies. When Cecilia's sister in a fit of jealousy tells her family about the secret meetings between the two lovers, both Cecilia and Arn are sent to different monasteries. Here they have to repent of their sins for twenty years.

As a blockbuster epic, the Arn saga is characterised by a typical Hollywood dual plot. On the one hand, it is the love story between Arn and Cecilia. This is a love that survives twenty years of separation, where Cecilia is tormented in her cell, and Arn sent to the Holy Land as a Knight Templar to fight the Muslims. On the other hand, it concerns the power politics of the small Swedish kingdom, and the larger battle for Jerusalem. In both films, the story switches back and forth between Arn in his exile in the Holy Land and the plot in Sweden.

As important as the love story is Arn's meeting with the Muslim military leader Saladin (Milind Soman). He is the one that Arn saves from bandits in the prologue of the first film, and they meet several times. Not a fictional character like Arn, Saladin led the Muslim opposition against the European Crusaders, and under his leadership the Muslim army defeated the Crusaders at the Battle of Hattin in 1187. Arn is captured by Saladin after this battle, but treated well, and after being nursed back to health he is sent home to Sweden. Here he is finally reunited with his beloved Cecilia.

The Arn epic ends with a big battle in Sweden, where a Muslim who is ordered by Saladin to accompany Arn helps Arn and his family to gain power. This successful battle fulfils Arn's dream of peace, and a final intertitle tells us that his son's son, Birger Jarl, is the person who, many years after Arn's death, unites the kingdom under the name Sweden. In this way, nation-building is explicitly thematised, and the war between Muslims and Christians is compared to the power politics in Sweden. The fight for power in Sweden is a small-scale version of the larger battle in the Holy Land.

The author Jan Guillou has written that his Arn novels were inspired by his work as a journalist, and how he saw CNN depicting Muslims as 'evil' and Christians as 'good' in their news stories. This led him to write the Arn epic as a medieval mirror, showing how current conflicts were similar to those of the Middle Ages. By establishing both contrasts and parallels between the present and the past, he hoped to call attention to how the distant past is linked to contemporary issues and battles and to change stereotypical conceptions of Muslims in the present (Renander 2007: 188–90).

The same can be said about the films, which explicitly work as history lessons that are meant to change contemporary minds for the future. By complicating the question of who the Swedes were, and their role in the Crusades, through the power politics that led to the creation of Sweden as a nation, the *Arn* epic creates a historical backdrop linked to questions of the Holy War as well as to Sweden's relationship with Muslims then and now. In particular, the sympathetic portrayal of Saladin is important in the films and their function as history lessons. In a very obvious way, the *Arn* films use history, hoping not only to entertain, but also to create new images of Muslims, Christians and Swedes. The *Arn* films do not represent a new direction in historical dramas, but rather follow established genre conventions.

Although most Nordic historical films could be seen as history lessons for the present, and many use the double plot structure of contrasting a love story to Big Historical Events, the Nordic films have different approaches to both love and history. In the *Arn* films an impersonal, male, third-person voiceover leads us through the story of Arn's life. In contrast, the Danish *A Royal Affair* represents a very different way of telling a story about the past.

A Royal Affair: Enlightenment and Erotics

A Royal Affair (*En kongelig affære*, Nikolaj Arcel, 2012) became a huge commercial and artistic success, winning prestigious prizes at film festivals, and getting a large audience in the Nordic countries. The film is based on real events and characters, and the story begins in England in 1766 when the young Caroline Mathilde (Alicia Vikander) is about to be sent to Denmark to become the new queen.

A Royal Affair tells the story of Queen Caroline Mathilde's troubled relationship with the mentally unstable King Christian VII (Mikkel Boe Følsgaard), whom she begins to hate, and how she falls in love with the king's personal physician Johan Struensee (Mads Mikkelsen). When she first meets Struensee she is not impressed, and dislikes him, but she discovers that he is a man of the Enlightenment, and that he has managed to smuggle books by Rousseau and Diderot past the Danish court censors. Later she falls in love with Struensee, and they become lovers. However, when she becomes pregnant, and the nobility and church leaders find out that the king is not the father of the child, she is sent away and Struensee is beheaded.

Nikolaj Arcel's film personalises the past through the erotic triangle of queen, king and personal physician, but the troubled and painful *ménage à trois* is pitted against a larger political backdrop. The film also explores how the nobility rules by oppression, supported by strong religious forces, and how the freethinkers try to reform the country. The young and beautiful queen is the main protagonist. She is also the one who tells the story, and she is the one who plants the idea in Struensee's head that he can use his influence with the king to change Danish society. For a short period Struensee, with the blessing of the weak and unstable king, rules Denmark by dissolving the state council. By passing hundreds of new, liberal laws, and restricting the power and income of the nobility, they make powerful enemies among the nobility, who in turn use the affair as the opportunity to get rid of both the liberal queen and Struensee.

A Royal Affair represents a very different way of personalising the past from the *Arn* films. The historical importance of a woman is underlined through the power of the voice, and how the past events are filtered through her memory and subjectivity. Her voiceover gives the past perspective. The queen, Caroline Mathilde, tells the story, but she is often seen from the back, as if she is faceless or unknown. However, her voice and her story give her back a face and a role in history. The voice links her story to oral history, creating an authentic but nearly forgotten woman's story. The film invests a female character with voice, visual agency and power.

Although Struensee might be the Enlightenment hero, the story of his actions and the erotic triangle between the queen, the king and him is framed by a letter that the queen writes to her children who have been taken away from her. This letter, the voiceover we hear throughout the film, is at the end revealed as the act that *really* changed Denmark, since it inspires her son Fredrik to seize power at the age of 16 and to reinstate Struensee's Enlightenment laws. Her son becomes the one who permanently changes Danish society. Aspects of Danish society other than court life are glimpsed only briefly, and become a backdrop for the erotic and political court drama, but the queen's letter and actions change the whole of Denmark.

A *Royal Affair* is a beautiful, eighteenth-century costume drama that thematises Enlightenment ideas and erotics. Both of these are important in the queen's search for love and freedom. As with most historical dramas, the historicity of the period that is represented is mixed with more 'eternal' existential ideas that speak easily to a contemporary audience. It engages with historical issues and portrays a specific historical period, but at the same time becomes a timeless existential drama.

KING OF DEVIL'S ISLAND: PAST AS PRISON

The Norwegian period drama *King of Devil's Island* (*Kongen av Bastøy*, Marius Holst, 2010) also blends historicity and timelessness. The story takes place in 1915, and is based on real events. A law in 1896 made it possible to send troublesome children to correction institutions, and between 1900 and 1953 boys from the southern part of Norway were sent to the prisonlike Bastøy on an island outside the capital Oslo. In 1915, a big insurrection took place on the island where the boys protested against their ill treatment, but the state responded with military troops. Although *King of Devil's Island* is based on real events, it is stripped of most of the surface elements of the historical genre. It is a story inspired by the specific events in Norway in 1915, but the timeless story of ill treatment and abuse could have happened earlier and later.

In the beginning of the film we are introduced to the two boys Erling (Benjamin Helstad) and Ivar (Magnus Langlete). Arriving on the island of Bastøy they are stripped of their personal identity and given numbers instead of names. They enter a harsh and brutal world ruled by the Manager (Stellan Skarsgård). Erling is a former sailor, and immediately rebels, while the weaker Ivar is sexually abused by the 'house-father' Bråthen (Kristoffer Joner). When Ivar cannot take the abuse any more, and kills himself, inspectors arrive on the island, but nothing happens. The ill treatment continues.

The Manager knows that Bråthen abuses the children, but cannot act because Bråthen knows that the Manager embezzles money that should have made life better for the young boys. Desperately, the boys attack the guards, nearly kill Bråthen, and burn down a house, before the military arrive and restore order. Erling has tried to escape earlier, and together with Olav (Trond Nilssen) he tries one more time to get away from the island. However, he is too heavy for the thin ice, and Olav watches his friend disappear in the water and drown. Years later Olav has become a sailor and his boat passes Bastøy, making him think about his friend and his years at the prison institution.

King of Devil's Island was among the most costly Norwegian films ever made, but most of all it is a chamber piece. It is a timeless story about cruelty and abuse, and how the young boys on the prison island are tortured by the Manager, Bråthen and the guards. The brutal story is enhanced by the austerity of the sets and the blue-grey winter light that casts a piercing coldness over the bleak story.

The past is a prison in Marius Holst's film, and no world exists outside the island and the brutal institution. The lack of a detailed surface historicity, through specific costumes or buildings, or manners and events, create a timeless atmosphere in the film. Even though everyone who saw the film in Norway knew that the film was based on real events, it was mostly received as a timeless metaphor on state brutality. The film spurred debates about how the state takes care of abused children and young criminals, and a number of newspaper articles focused on how the events in 1915 were only one example of state neglect of children, even in the present (Falch-Eriksen 2010; Nergård 2010).

King of Devil's Island was not meant as an explicit history lesson, or to start a bigger debate, but the timelessness of the story made it relevant to contemporary debates about state abuse and brutality, in Norway as well as elsewhere. The moving story of Erling, Ivar and Olav reveals double standards in the past and in the present, but also paints a strong portrait of youthful strength and rebelliousness.

SAUNA: HISTORY AS HORROR FANTASY

The Finnish film *Sauna* (Antti-Jussi Annila, 2008) is an example of a historical drama that ends as a fantastic horror fantasy. The story takes place on the border between Russia and Finland (technically Sweden at that time) in the year 1595. The two countries have been at war for many years, but after a peace treaty a new border is about to be drawn and established. The main characters are the brothers Eerik (Ville Virtanen) and Knut Spore (Tommi Eronen). For many years they have been soldiers in the war, but now they are the Finnish representatives in a joint border commision.

Early in the story, the older brother Eerik violently stabs an innocent man to death, while the younger Knut locks the man's young daughter up in a dirt cellar. They have to leave the area, to continue with the border work, and the girl is left to die in the dark underground cellar. This terrible deed starts to haunt Knut. The ghost of the young girl seems to follow him, and as he is haunted by his evil past he gets more and more confused and scared.

The border commision enters an unexplored area in a big marsh, and finds a small, mysterious community of people living there. The people living in the marshland say that they found the village empty while travelling through the area, and since they settled down, no one has died or been born. In the middle of the mysterious village is a strange rectangular building; a haunted sauna. As strange things start to happen, Knut becomes obsessed with the building, and entering it he sees the girl he left to die in the cellar with blood all over her head. The film ends with a mysterious vision of a faceless man murdering a child by a river.

The image of the past in *Sauna* derives more from other movies than from history proper. The same could be said about the *Arn* films as well as *A Royal Affair*, but in *Sauna* the references are not even to previous historical dramas, but to both horror films and art cinema. More important than the Russo-Swedish war between 1590 and 1595, and any real events of the sixteenth century, are fantasy films and Andrej Tarkovsky's film *Stalker* (1979). The many shots of water, mud and the grimy texture of the marshlands and detritus resemble Tarkovsky's existential science fiction film. There are also resemblances on the level of plot and story. *Sauna* is a historical fantasy, where the past is used to create atmosphere, but the past is a vague terrain of existential horror and despair.

Sauna is an example of a film that represents the past only at a superficial level. *Sauna* becomes a timeless evocation of violence, guilt and mystery. Although very different from Ingmar Bergman's *The Seventh Seal*, its representation of the past is similarly characterised by a lack of specific references to events, people or manners. Bergman's Middle Ages have been characterised by historian Arthur Lindley as 'less the 1340s of the plot premise than the sub-atomic early 1950s, with universal death looming out of the northern sky' (Lindley 1998). In the same way *Sauna* is rich in atmosphere, and may evoke a vague feeling of the sixteenth century, but has no real connection to historical events, no real historicity and no history lesson. It does not use the past for purposes other than atmosphere and as a background for 'eternal' existential themes.

Voices from the Past

Although the historical genre has not been dominant in the Nordic countries, because of its need for very big budgets and international exports and sales, a number of important Nordic historical genre films have been made, and in the last decade the number has increased. These films are most often part of ongoing identity work in the different Nordic countries, as by dealing with contemporary issues in period garb, they continue to shape and define the Nordic nations through stories about and representations of the past.

What constitutes the most important aspect of the genre is the combination of a surface historicity, through costumes, settings, manners and story elements, and more 'eternal' existential questions and themes. Another important aspect of the genre is its didactic element. In the *Arn* films, *A Royal Affair* and *King of Devil's Island*, the past mirrors contemporary issues and problems. These period dramas not only remind the viewers of past problems and events, but work as history lessons that can teach us about the present and the future.

Cinematic history is 'imagined' history, shared myths and stories from the past, but made for the present; either politicised contributions to contemporary debates, or almost empty signifiers for conveying arguments about the present.

All four examples in this chapter blend fiction and history, but in very different ways. In the *Arn* films some characters are fictitious, like the main characters Arn and Cecilia, but other characters and events are historically grounded. In *A Royal Affair* both main characters and events are based on what happened in eighteenth-century Denmark. In *King of Devil's Island* the main event, the rebellious insurrection, happened in Norway in 1915, but all the characters in the film are invented. And finally, *Sauna* has few ties to history proper, and uses the historical setting as a vague background for an exciting and mysterious horror story.

Most often historical films are big-budget epics and part of the prevailing blockbuster culture, even if the historical periods that are represented vary from the Middle Ages to the 1910s to the Second World War. Disseminating historical knowledge and facts about the past is not the main objectives of these films. Instead, they create historical worlds through stories, characters, feelings and atmosphere. They form a salient part of the Nordic countries' national identity, but what constitutes history for current filmmakers in the Nordic countries is a past that fits the traditions of the drama and the genre film. Thus, history is represented through drama, conflict, surface details and story elements.

Nordic historical films interpret and construct history as lessons for the present. Even the fantasy horror film *Sauna* is a discussion of guilt and violence born out of wartime experiences. Films like the *Arn* movies, *A Royal Affair*, *King of Devil's Island* and *Sauna* are history lessons conveyed with sounds and images. They do create an overall sense of the past. They also illustrate the desire of Nordic filmmakers to express the relationship of the present with the past, as well as the desire to use the past to explain or transform the present.

Notes

1. Publicity material for *Kristin Lavransdatter* (Oslo: Norsk Film A/S, 1995). No author indicated. The translation from Norwegian is my own.
2. Ibid.

References

Eco, Umberto (1985), *PS till Rosens namn*, Stockholm: Brombergs.
Eco, Umberto (1987), *Travels in Hyperreality*, London: Picador.
Falch-Eriksen, Asgeir (2010), 'De kriminelle barna', *Dagbladet*, 23 December.

Hedling, Erik and Ann-Kristin Wallengren (eds) (2013), *Den nya svenska filmen – kultur, kriminalitet & kakofoni*, Stockholm: Atlantis.

Iversen, Gunnar (2000), 'Clear, from a Distance: The Image of the Medieval Period in Recent Norwegian Film', *Scandinavica* 39 (1): 7–23.

Iversen, Gunnar (2012), 'From Trauma to Heroism: Cultural Memory and Remembrance in Norwegian Occupation dramas, 1946–2009', *Journal of Scandinavian Cinema* 2 (3): 237–48.

Lindley, Arthur (1998), 'The Ahistoricism of Medieval Film', *Screening the Past*, May, <http://www.latrobe.edu.au/www/screeningthepast/classics>.

Nergård, Halldis (2010), 'Stavne var mye verre enn Bastøy', *Adresseavisen*, 18 December.

Renander, Carina (2007), *Förförande fiction eller historieförmedling? – Arn-serien, historiemedvetande och historiedidaktik*, Malmö: Malmö Högskola.

Rosenstone, Robert A. (1995), *Visions of the Past: The Challenge of Film to Our Idea of History*, Cambridge, MA: Harvard University Press.

Susman, Warren I. (2012), 'Film and History: Artifact and Experience'. In J. E. Smyth (ed.), *Hollywood and The American Historical Film*, London: Palgrave Macmillan, pp. 1–10.

PART II

CRIME AND DETECTIVE NARRATIVES

4. CRIME UP NORTH: THE CASE OF NORWAY, FINLAND AND ICELAND

Björn Ægir Norðfjörð

Although the great local and global interest in Nordic noir bears witness to a remarkable change in the national cinemas of the Nordic countries, certain things remain the same: Norway, Finland and Iceland are overshadowed by Denmark and Sweden. With its roots in the police procedurals of writer-couple Maj Sjöwall and Per Wahlöö, a form later revitalised by Henning Mankell, not to mention the unparalleled success of Stieg Larsson's Millennium trilogy (a police procedural in journalism 'disguise'), Sweden was and remains the centre of Scandinavian crime fiction. Recently, however, Danish crime films and television series, including the influential police procedural *The Killing* (*Forbrydelsen*, Søren Sveistrup, 2007–12), have given adaptations of said Swedish crime series good competition for the primacy of Nordic noir. *The Bridge* (*Broen*/*Bron*, Hans Rosenfeldt, 2011–) could be said to consolidate their mutual supremacy as Danish and Swedish police officers (and television producers) join hands when a body is found exactly halfway across the Øresund bridge connecting the two countries – leaving the other Nordic countries watching from a distance. Norway, Finland and Iceland have, however, not remained out of it altogether and on occasion managed to grab the spotlight, as evidenced by films such as *Jar City* (*Mýrin*, Baltasar Kormákur, 2006) and *Headhunters* (*Hodejegerne*, Morten Tyldum, 2011), the latter based on a novel by the Norwegian Jo Nesbø (2011) – arguably Larsson's heir to the Scandinavian crime fiction crown.[1]

As these opening remarks suggest, it is impossible to discuss contemporary Nordic crime cinema and television without taking into account the

Figure 4.1 *Insomnia*: A Swedish police detective (Stellan Skarsgård) bewildered and out of his element in northern Norway. Image courtesy of Norsk Film.

Figure 4.2 *Headhunters*: A cosmopolitan employment recruiter (Aksel Hennie) very much at home in the nondescript world of global capitalism. Image courtesy of Friland.

ties to its literary counterpart – notably most of the films discussed in this chapter are adaptations. One of the benefits of the increasingly popular label Nordic Noir – English home video distributor Arrow Films even offers T-shirts marked thus for sale – is that it is not medium specific and perhaps even emphasises film due to its film noir connotations while 'fiction' (as in Scandinavian crime fiction) is conventionally limited to literature. Nordic noir is indeed a constellation of texts stemming from novels, television and cinema, tied together in various and often blurred ways. The coinage is, however, somewhat misleading.

Evidently 'noir' originates in France, where it was used to describe among other things American film adaptations of crime novels published with black covers in the series *Série noire* (Naremore 1998: 12–13). Central to it were private detective novels, for example by Raymond Chandler and Dashiell Hammett, and pessimistic and dark criminal accounts, such as those by Horace McCoy and Jim Thompson. Ever since, such narratives have constituted both roman noir, more commonly referred to as hard-boiled fiction, and film noir. Conversely, from its roots in Sjöwall and Wahlöö Scandinavian crime belongs primarily to the subgenre of the police procedural, which is most different both stylistically and ideologically from noir in its original and more narrowly defined meaning. There is no space here to provide a detailed comparison, but the antisocial critique of the roman noir, emphasised by the loner detective repeatedly running up against a suspicious police force, makes way in the police procedural for productive teamwork that encourages faith and trust in the state (Scaggs 2005: 85–104). Thus, from this perspective noir is critical while the procedural is complicit, notwithstanding many crime novelists' intention to use the form for social critique.[2]

This terminological confusion also hints at the problematics of the other half of the Nordic noir coinage, which suggests it to be something unique to the Nordic countries (as does much of its accompanying marketing material). Crime fiction, however, is an international genre with primarily English and American literary roots and shaped on-screen in particular by Hollywood and US/UK television, although France, Italy and Japan, for example, all have established traditions in this regard. While this goes for any regional demarcation of the genre it is worth asking if the specificity of Nordic noir has been overstated.

In this chapter I hope to account for the international (literary and filmic) origin of recent Norwegian, Finnish and Icelandic crime films and television series as well as their particular local specificity. I will thus not only be assessing them in relation to their Swedish and Danish counterparts, but also to what I will be simply referring to as the international crime film. It is a norm mostly associated with Hollywood (albeit not limited to it) that is, as regards style, form and narrative structure, for the most part devoid of regional or national specificities. My use of the word 'generic' is intended to emphasise this dual nature by referring both to the essentials of a particular genre (crime) and a broad universality. Of particular concern is whether one can pinpoint any particular trajectory in the development of contemporary Norwegian, Finnish and Icelandic crime films made with international aspirations during this dramatic rise of Nordic noir – that still shows no sign of abating.

Norway

Erik Skjoldbjærg's *Insomnia* (1997) was the first bona fide Nordic crime film made outside Sweden and Denmark to receive widespread international distribution and praise, and was ultimately remade in Hollywood under the same title (Christopher Nolan, 2002).[3] Notably it precedes the Nordic noir craze (Mankell's first novel was also translated into English in 1997 although it was translated earlier in the decade into German), and is made from an original script rather than adapted from a novel. The original Norwegian film was also received in terms most different from Nordic noir, although it is arguably much more deserving of that title than much of what is grouped under it. More than any other Nordic crime film, and one could spread the net much wider, *Insomnia* adheres to the subjective approach so strongly associated with noir generally and hard-boiled fiction in particular (Telotte 1989: 1–39). Despite shunning the more conspicuous first-person voice-over narration, the narrative perspective is limited to the central character, Swedish police detective Jonas Engström (Stellan Skarsgård), in his investigation of the murder of a teenage girl in Tromsø in Northern Norway. Not only is he ever present, nothing happens in the film unbeknownst to him save for the murder depicted in the opening credits scene, but the *mise-en-scène* is defined through his subjectivity, for example as deceased characters appear both to him and the audience. And although a police officer, Engström has little in common with his dedicated and honest literary colleagues, including fellow nationals Martin Beck and Kurt Wallander (the creations of Sjöwall and Wahlöö and Mankell respectively), who inform the police procedural tradition. The Scandinavian police detective may be anti-social, rude, out of shape, depressed and an alcoholic anti-hero but he is hardly ever unethical. Engström on the other hand works alone, keeps from his co-workers, and is morally suspect to say the least. After accidentally shooting his partner to death when in pursuit of the murderer, crime novelist Jon Holt (Bjørn Floberg), Engström not only covers up the shooting, but eventually teams up with Holt in framing a teenage boy for the murder. The thin line between good and evil is another central characteristic of noir, and *Insomnia* repeatedly draws attention to the numerous things Engström shares with Holt. Stylistically, *Insomnia* is also something akin to noir in reverse, as the traditional dark cityscape makes way for the bright outdoors and interiors of northern Norway, where the everlasting sun keeps the increasingly anxious Engström up at night, making his surroundings atmospheric and threatening. The light may not flow into the dark through the shades but the shades are there all right – just as bright as anything else.

The emphasis on style does not only tie *Insomnia* to noir – making it an ideal example of neo-noir in its displacement of its traditional stylistic register – but also art cinema. *Insomnia*'s form and style are clearly intended to emphasise

Engström's increasing anxiety and are thus very much a case of the psychological realism that is quintessential to art cinema. In his influential study 'The Art Cinema as a Mode of Film Practice', David Bordwell asserts: 'Most important, the art cinema uses 'realistic' – that is, psychologically complex – characters . . . The art cinema is less concerned with action than reaction; it is a cinema of psychological effects in search of their causes' (2008: 153). For a police investigator in a crime film Engström is in little control, readjusting and reacting to unforeseen situations, and his motives are much more mysterious than the murder case (that is solved rather early in the film). Ambiguity shapes all his actions – another quintessential feature of the art film according to Bordwell – and *Insomnia*'s concluding image of Engström's eyes staring in darkness leaves the audience puzzled: 'the ambiguity, the play of thematic interpretation, must not be halted at the film's close' (Bordwell 2008: 156). To its art film credentials one could also add *Insomnia*'s flaunted self-reflexivity, not least in making the murderer a crime novelist eager to try the 'real' thing, and, in combination with its noir heritage, the quoting of *The Third Man*'s (Carol Reed, 1949) famous underground tunnel scene.[4]

If the art cinema elements distinguish *Insomnia* from the films that were to follow in its wake (and incidentally its American remake), so also does its local specificity. The film's very first image depicts the victim opening a cabin door onto the bright exterior of a rocky beach – not your typical crime setting. More to the point, following the credits scene it is announced in an aeroplane carrying Engström to Tromsø that it is crossing the Arctic Circle and about to reach 'the land of the midnight sun'. A note has already been made of the film's omnipresent light, but additionally many scenes are set in the era's costal and mountain scenery, including the key scene in which Engström shoots his colleague in foggy surroundings by the coast. Thus *Insomnia*'s location does not merely provide picturesque landscape, but is interwoven into the plot at various levels.

It is instructive to compare *Insomnia* with Norway's other and much more recent international crime success *Headhunters*, as regards location, art cinema and noir. It is certainly an unusual crime film, where the police have at best a secondary role, while two criminals take turns playing cat and mouse. Norway's most successful employment recruiter Roger Brown (Aksel Hennie), and an art-thief in his spare time, meets his match in Clas Greve (Nikolaj Coster-Waldau), a brutal military operative turned business executive who is plotting to take over a business rival by tricking Brown into recruiting him. When Brown discovers Greve's sexual relationship with his wife Diana (Synnøve Macody Lund) he rejects the otherwise irresistible Greve, who responds by hunting him down as a human prey with cutting-edge GPS technology. After a long, extended and outlandish chase Brown ultimately manages to turn the tables on Greve and is happily reunited with his wife at the end of the film.

As this plot outline suggests, *Headhunters* has not much to say about Norway and could have been set pretty much anywhere. Despite the occasional reference to its Oslo setting, and its dialogue being in Norwegian and Danish, *Headhunters* is mostly located in the nondescript world of corporate business practices, modern architecture and technology – even its hero is named Roger Brown. Unlike *Insomnia* there is little locally specific about *Headhunters*. Similarly, the film's crime elements and stylistic affinities fit the generic mould of the international crime film. The opening credits scene of Brown listing the rules of his art-theft practice, captivating in their outlandishness and playful visuals, belong to a narrative strategy that should be familiar to most fans of the genre, as do many of the film's extraordinary events with their wacky humour. Overall *Headhunters* has a very professional and polished look – sleek and clean as the modern architecture it depicts – and at times its fast paced editing smoothly depicts important events from slightly differentiated perspectives. In this regard the form and the style are very much in tune with what might be more specifically referred to as the quirky or over-the-top crime film, and most different from the conventions of the art cinema mode.[5] Indeed, even though the narrative is mostly tied to Brown, style does not shape his psychology in the manner it does Engström's. *Headhunters* is altogether lacking the subjectivity that informs the narrative and style of *Insomnia*.

The confined narrative focus on Brown is inherited from Nesbø's original novel which is told in the first person by Brown himself, a strategy retained by his voiceover narration in the film, if mostly confined to its opening and conclusion. In addition to the first-person narration, the film retains important noir elements from the novel, including a morally suspect protagonist and hardly a sympathetic one (if not as disagreeable as the novel's Brown), devious femmes fatales and a focus on crime from the criminal's perspective. Brown

Figure 4.3 *Priest of Evil*: A police detective (Peter Franzén) seeking revenge in a noir-inspired Helsinki cityscape. Image courtesy of Matila Röhr Productions.

and the headhunters are, though, something of an anomaly for writer Nesbø who is best known for his third-person police procedurals focusing on officer Harry Hole.

The true Norwegian heir to the American noir tradition is writer Gunnar Staalesen whose novels on private detective Varg Veum have spawned a series of no fewer than a dozen feature-length film/television adaptations (2007–12). Told in the first person, and in a style reminiscent of Raymond Chandler (an early entry like *Yours until Death* (2010) is even filled with wisecracks and striking similes), Staalesen's novels delineate Veum's investigations while emphasising his sympathy and engagement with the parties involved. Notably many of the cases stem from hidden family secrets, with generational conflicts paramount, and in this regard he shares even more with Ross MacDonald, whose novels, as Leonard Cassuto points out, 'rely on complex family ties to spotlight social ills. In both family and society, human ties come undone' (2009: 159). Indeed, Veum was a social worker assisting children before making his grade as a private detective. However, the strong noir elements of the novels are somewhat dampened in the film/television series since there is no voiceover narration and actor Trond Espen Seims may be just a tad too handsome for a 'real' hard-boiled detective. It is also important to note that the partnership between Veum and police officer Jacob Hamre (Bjørn Floberg) – despite playful antagonism – would be out of place in classic noir and veers some of the series' entries towards the police procedural form. Nonetheless the Veum series is clearly different from the police procedurals that dominate Danish and Swedish (and British if one includes the BBC *Wallander* series) screens, and the rare Veum feature like *Buried Dogs* (*Begravde hunder*, Alexander Eik, 2008) will even question the motives of the police force and its complicit ties to suspect state policies.

FINLAND

Finland's most conspicuous film/television crime representative is also a private detective who has a lot in common with Veum – and quite a similar name. The creation of writer Reijo Mäki, Jussi Vares was first personified by Juha Veijonen in two films directed by Aleksi Mäkelä, *Vares: Private Eye* (*Vares: yksityisetsivä*, 2004) and *V2: Dead Angel* (*V2: Jäätynyt enkeli*, 2007), indebted to detective and gangster films in the Hollywood mould. More recently Mäki's work has been adapted in the form of a series of six film/television features (2011–12), starring Antti Reini as the detective. These share with the Veum series the feature-length structure and a location outside their respective national capitals – Veum in Bergen and Vares in Turku – and make use of similar introductory travelling overview shots, although it would be something of a stretch to describe either series as locally specific. While both certainly do touch upon national themes and stereotypes (the hard-drinking Finn a case in point), the crime plots are by and large generic in nature. Like Veum, Vares has a productive and mostly agreeable relationship with a police detective and relies on the help of a regular group of assistants/friends that functions in a similar manner to the procedural's police team. It is, though, a most different team, as it consists of a down-and-out former drug addict, an exploitative journalist, a stripper-cum-taxi driver, a discharged priest and a plagiarising crime novelist whose first novel saves Vares's life not once but twice by stopping bullets intended for him.

The Finnish series is, however, much closer to noir at heart than the Norwegian one. It makes extensive use of the first-person voiceover (although neither series limits itself to the detective's perspective) and has an overall darker appearance. Vares himself is rougher and tougher than Veum, drinks harder and is less scrupulous in his choice of assignments and handling of clients. In *Garter Snake* (*Vares – Sukkanauhakäärme*, Lauri Törhönen, 2011), for example, Vares accepts a dubious assignment from a wealthy businessman to follow his wife's foreign lover in the hope of finding information to deport him. When the lover is murdered, Vares gets caught up in a drug ring showdown, leaving him and his taxi driver/stripper assistant kidnapped and awaiting death, before a last minute rescue. Vares discovers not only that is the sole other private detective in Turku guilty of the murder, but that the businessman who hired him in the first place is running the drug ring. *Garter Snake* ends with Vares lamenting that 'the big boys always stay free', but although he cannot bring his client to justice, someone finds it fitting to shoot him in the head in the feature's concluding shot.

Another well-known figure of Finnish crime fiction has recently returned to the scene. Novelist Matti Yrjänä Joensuu's police detective Timo Harjunpää had been the hero of numerous television series (1983–2007) before Peter Franzén took on the role in the *Priest of Evil* (*Harjunpää ja pahan pappi*, Olli Saarela, 2010). Although the novel (Joensuu 2006) is very much a police procedural, the film adaptation veers much closer to noir territory, evoking such classics as *The Big Heat* (Fritz Lang, 1953), *Peeping Tom* (Michael Powell, 1960) and *Se7en* (David Fincher, 1995). After his teenage daughter is murdered, both Harjunpää's private and personal lives take a sudden downturn. The detective blames himself as he arrived too late to pick up his daughter the night she was murdered, and the situation is aggravated when her murderer is released after spending only two years in prison. While Harjunpää struggles with his desire to personally revenge his daughter's murder, a serial killer is stalking Helsinki, punishing violent people for their sins. In this way *Priest of Evil* clearly draws parallels between the punitive killer, who himself was abused by a violent father, and Harjunpää, who is only kept from shooting his daughter's murderer by a last-minute interference from a colleague. The emphasis on Harjunpää's own guilt and desire for revenge is straight out of noir and the film privileges his subjectivity in important ways if not fully confined to it. Conversely, in the novel there is no revenge plot, no harm has come to Harjunpää's daughter, and he himself plays an almost a secondary role among the novel's large gallery of characters. The film's *mise-en-scène* is also most noir-like as much of the action takes place in such desolate city scenes as subway or petrol stations. Harjunpää's home is contrasted with the warehouse-like dungeon of the serial killer and the police offices have that nondescript modern look – brightened by the light flowing in through the shades. Lighting is absolutely essential in delivering the film's dark cityscape – a generic universal noir city rather than the specific location of Helsinki.

The noir elements make *Priest of Evil* stand out somewhat among the Nordic police procedurals, but it does adhere all the more closely to the stylistic and narrational standards of the international crime film. And along the lines of Hollywood narrative closure, Harjunpää is redeemed in the end. After the killer rather uncharacteristically kidnaps his wife, Harjunpää arrives this time around just in time to save his loved one. He is reunited with his wife and it is suggested they can now put the ghosts of the past behind them.[6]

ICELAND

It used to be said that Iceland was too small and too innocent a location for crime fiction (with approximately two murders committed a year on average, considerably fewer than the other Nordic countries, themselves well below the average European homicide rate). While this notion has been proved spectacularly wrong with the success of Icelandic crime writers at home and abroad, with novelists Arnaldur Indriðason and Yrsa Sigurðardóttir central to Nordic noir, perhaps it could be said that Iceland is too small for private detectives. Certainly, they are hard to find among all the police officers and occasional journalists or lawyers at the forefront of Icelandic crime fiction. Since crime first made inroads into Icelandic television, the police procedural has also been the most conspicuous form, although the long-running series *Press* (*Pressa*, Óskar Jónasson, 2007–) focuses on a news reporting team.

The police procedural is also central to the first popular Icelandic crime film. Based on Indriðason's bestseller (Indriðason 2004), *Jar City* shows police detective Erlendur (Ingvar Sigurðsson) and his team unravelling a murder case with mysterious origins far in the past. Although the novel is very much indebted to the Swedish police procedural tradition, including its ancillary social critique, the film veers much closer to the international crime film, emphasising chases, prison escape, superhuman villains and femmes fatales while downplaying the novel's critical elements (Norðfjörð 2010: 46–7). Thus in terms of character types, style and form there is very little nationally specific about *Jar City*. The plot on the other hand is very much a local one, as it encourages throughout speculation on the national characteristics of Icelanders. When a middle-aged man is found murdered in his basement apartment the crime strikes Erlendur's partner Sigurói (Björn Hlynur Haraldsson) as a 'typical Icelandic murder. Messy and pointless. And with no attempt to conceal the evidence.' The murder turns out to be everything but typical, but in other ways an essentially Icelandic crime. Stricken by the loss of his daughter from a mysterious genetic disease, an employer at a biopharmaceutical firm succeeds in tracing its origin and ends up killing his biological father following a heated exchange at their first and last encounter. Unaware of having any descendants, the murder victim had bequeathed the disease that resulted in the death of his own grandchild. Emphasising the current and historical documenting of Icelandic genes, *Jar City* delineates a crime that could quite possibly only have taken place in Iceland. Notably the other crime film of 2006, *Cold Trail* (*Köld slóð*, Björn Br. Björnsson), with its natural wilderness setting, shared to a certain extent this national emphasis.

One of most striking things about the short history of Icelandic crime films is how quickly this national emphasis makes way for a global outlook: the apparent desire to make Icelandic crime appear like any other crime. Released only five years later, *City State* (*Borgríki*, Ólafur de Fleur, 2011) could be said to be the culmination of this process. Its multifarious interconnected narrative levels of crime, corruption and brutal violence give most Hollywood crime films a good run for their money. Icelandic gang members cheat Serb immigrant Sergej (Zlatko Krickic) out of his garage before beating him up along with his wife, who suffers a miscarriage as a consequence. Looking for revenge Sergej decides to take over the gang's 'business' with the help of some fellow nationals, well

Figure 4.4 *City State*: A corrupt police officer (Sigurður Sigurjónsson) faces 'interrogation' by Serbian gang members at the outskirts of Reykjavík. Image courtesy of Poppoli Pictures.

prepared from their participation in the Yugoslav Wars. Around the same time the gang's boss Gunnar (Ingvar Sigurðsson) has a health scare and decides to sell out, but British crime lord Jimmy (Jonathan Pryce) loses interest when Gunnar's holdings come under threat from the Serbs. To complicate matters still further police officers Rúnar (Björn Thors) and Andrea (Ágústa Eva Erlendsdóttir) begin an investigation into the gang's activities, but Gunnar and corrupt police chief Margeir (Sigurður Sigurjónsson) respond by having them roughed up. The 'lesson' leaves Rúnar paralysed but Andrea forms her own police militia gang and begins handing out the same treatment. Finally, Gunnar lays a trap for Sergej with the assistance of Margeir, but the Serb escapes capture and comes out on top against the Icelanders, and the film concludes with him and his wife finally coming to terms with the loss of their unborn child.

Remarkably, this complicated and stretched plot with its multiple important characters is delivered in a relatively short film (eighty-two minutes including final credits). In other words *City State* is characterised by a rapid pace, even surpassing the narrative speed of the Hollywood films whose norm it takes as a model. Scenes are short, and the film shifts back and forth in space and time, and editing relies heavily on the now common technique of fast cutting with little motivated changes in shot perspective: even the gobbling up of a hamburger has to be shot in a number of quick bursts from a variety of angles and distances. Other stylistic effects and plot elements familiar from the international crime film include shaky camera (even traditional shot/reverse shots are constantly fluctuating), intermittent shots depicting the city from above, stylised character name introductions (far into the film), extreme violence (e.g. cutting off a finger with big shears), eccentric crime bosses, stereotypical Eastern European criminals, unsavoury locations such as strip clubs and brothels along with the generic spaces of financial institutions, hotels, hospitals, harbours, multi-storey car parks, and so on. Save for the language, nothing in *City State* (note how its title also evokes the general rather than the specific) could be said to be particularly Icelandic.

Despite the presence of a police team, *City State* has little in common with the police procedural. The police officers do not work as a team but against one another, in fact they are either working with criminals or reverting to explicitly criminal methods (and privileging revenge over solving a crime). Despite the slippery line between criminals and police officers, the film also shares little with noir, for example lacking altogether in character subjectivity, and is instead primarily indebted to the gangster subgenre. Indeed, in recent Icelandic crime films the focus has for the most part been on the criminals, as both *Reykjavik Rotterdam* (Óskar Jónasson, 2008), remade in Hollywood as *Contraband* (Baltasar Kormákur, 2012), and *Black's Game* (*Svartur á leik*, Óskar Axelson, 2012) also confirm, while the police procedural has fallen by the wayside.

Conclusion

The trajectory of the Icelandic crime film also holds up broadly for Finland and Norway as more recent entries have gone for the general rather than the specific. The local specificity of earlier films has increasingly made way for the generic style of the international crime film, which has also completely swallowed up the art cinema credentials of the pioneering film *Insomnia*. Its strategy of distinguishing (Northern) Norway from the Scandinavian centre, or *Jar City*'s delineation of a specifically Icelandic crime, has not been maintained; instead the goal seems to be to blend in. No doubt it is the desire for international success – to ride the Nordic crime wave – that encourages adherence to either the international crime film (e.g. *Headhunters* and *City State*) or Danish and Swedish television series (the Veum and Vares series) or some mixture thereof. Thus rather than emphasise differences from Denmark and Sweden or international norms more generally, the crime films of Norway, Finland and Iceland emphasise similarity.

One striking difference can be pinpointed, though. While the police procedural is omnipresent in both Denmark and Sweden, it has only a minor presence on the screens of the other Nordic countries.[7] Instead they have privileged private detectives and criminals and when they do focus on policemen they are often morally ambiguous ones. In this the crime films and television series of Norway, Finland and to some extent Iceland live up to the name of Nordic noir much more than the Danish and Scandinavian police procedurals.

Notes

1. For a broad survey of Nordic noir, drawing on interviews with both authors and translators, see Barry Forshaw's *Death in a Cold Climate* (2012), while more analytical essays can be found in Paula Arvas and Andrew Nestingen's *Scandinavian Crime Fiction*, which also contains in its introduction a brief survey of Scandinavian crime fiction predating Sjöwall and Wahlöö (2011: 3–5).
2. It is worth emphasising the different critical perspectives here as, despite the procedural form the Scandinavian crime novel, and in particular its roots in the work of Sjöwall and Wahlöö, is typically seen to engage in social criticism. Rather than side with one view over the other I would suggest a reading that takes both perspectives into account, and thus emphasises the dual nature of Scandinavian crime fiction. In short, the bleak and critical view of Nordic society often depicted in the novels is undermined, balanced or countered by the solution of a crime by a dedicated police force fulfilling its role as a social guardian.

   Now if there is a risk in simplifying the diversity of shapes the procedural can take, it is all the greater when it comes to noir. In fact, among the noir classics one even finds the rare procedural like *The Naked City* (1948, Jules Dassin) or *Union Station* (1950, Rudolph Maté). The noir tradition that I am, however, concerned with is the one stemming from the roman noir/hard-boiled fiction. Overall it needs to be said that if film genres are broadly a slippery subject, the crime genre is especially so, and typically calls for a division into at least three subgenres. In his influential study of

Hollywood genres Steve Neale, for example, splits what he refers to as 'contemporary crime' into detective films, gangster films and suspense thrillers (2000: 65–78), while books focusing solely on the crime genre have added many more subcategories including lawyer films, prison films, erotic thrillers and crime comedies (Leitch 2002; Rafter 2006). It is, however, the detective film broadly defined that is the primary focus of this chapter, but the reader should keep in mind that these categories are always in some flux.

3. Conversely, the original Norwegian film draws somewhat on the American television series *Twin Peaks* (Mark Frost and David Lynch, 1990–1) and could be said to be something of a missing link between it and the Danish series *Forbrydelsen*, whose American remake *The Killing* (Veena Sud, 2011–) has completed the circle back to the state of Washington – the original setting of *Twin Peaks*. This national chain is quite suggestive of the varied transnational flows of contemporary crime cinema.

4. Although *Insomnia* certainly leaves the audience pondering the director's intentions, it is in the category of authorship where the film least fits Bordwell's analysis of the art cinema mode. And indeed I am not claiming that *Insomnia* is an outright art film but that it shares elements of both art cinema and generic crime films. Andrew Nestingen comes to a similar conclusion when analysing the film in relation to what he refers to as medium-concept cinema (2008: 73–4). Works by established auteurs such as Lars von Trier and Aki Kaurismäki that have had recourse to crime, including *The Element of Crime* (*Forbrydelsens element*, 1984) and *The Man Without a Past* (*Mies vailla menneisyyttä*, 2002), lie in this regard much closer to the art film mode. But, it is worth noting that in the United States *Insomnia* was released on home video by The Criterion Collection, which has released not only many films by both von Trier and Kaurismäki but also such stalwarts of Scandinavian art cinema as Ingmar Bergman and Carl Theodor Dreyer. Conversely, it would be hard to imagine the firm releasing the other films addressed in this chapter.

5. Although this version of the crime film is most strongly associated with the UK/USA, it is not unprecedented in Scandinavian cinema as evidenced by, for example, *In China They Eat Dogs* (*In Kina spiser de hunde*, Lasse Spang Olsen, 1999) and, verging on outright comedy, *Sound of Noise* (Ola Simonsson and Johannes Stjärne Nilsson, 2010).

6. I would like to thank Pietari Kääpä for invaluable help with the Finnish section of this chapter.

7. It is worth emphasising that this claim applies to television series and films with some international exposure – and broadly speaking at that, as exceptions can certainly be pinpointed – and not literature where the police procedural is in ample force and probably the most important crime subgenre in all the Nordic countries. And of course crime films of a different kind have also been made in Denmark and Sweden, like the *Pusher* (1996–2005) and *Easy Money* (*Snabba cash*, 2010–13) series, but they share more with outright gangster cinema than noir.

References

Arvas, Paula and Andrew Nestingen (2011), *Scandinavian Crime Fiction*. Cardiff: University of Wales Press.
Bordwell, David (2008), *Poetics of Cinema*, New York and London: Routledge.
Cassuto, Leonard (2009), *Hard-Boiled Sentimentality: The Secret History of American Crime Stories*, New York: Columbia University Press.

Forshaw, Barry (2012), *Death in a Cold Climate: A Guide to Scandinavian Crime Fiction*, London: Palgrave Macmillan.
Indriðason, Arnaldur (2004), *Jar City*, London: Vintage Books.
Joensuu, Matti Yrjänä (2006), *Priest of Evil*, London: Arcadia Books.
Leitch, Thomas (2002), *Crime Films*, Cambridge: Cambridge University Press.
Naremore, James (1998), *More than Night: Film Noir in Its Contexts*, Berkeley: University of California Press.
Neale, Steve (2000), *Genre and Hollywood*, New York and London: Routledge.
Nesbø, Jo (2011), *Headhunters*, New York: Vintage Books.
Nestingen, Andrew (2008), *Crime and Fantasy in Scandinavia: Fiction, Film, and Social Change*, Seattle: University of Washington Press.
Norðfjörð, Björn (2010), 'A Typical Icelandic Murder? The "Criminal" Adaptation of *Jar City*', *Journal of Scandinavian Cinema* 1 (1): 37–49.
Rafter, Nicole (2006), *Shots in the Mirror: Crime Films and Society*, Oxford: Oxford University Press.
Scaggs, John (2005), *Crime Fiction*, London and New York: Routledge.
Staalesen, Gunnar (2010), *Yours until Death*, London: Arcadia Books.
Telotte, J. P. (1989), *Voices in the Dark: The Narrative Patterns of 'Film Noir'*, Urbana and Chicago: University of Illinois Press.

Filmography

The Big Heat, directed by Fritz Lang. USA: Columbia Pictures, 1953.
Black's Game, directed by Óskar Axelson. Iceland: Zik Zak Filmworks, 2012.
The Bridge, created by Hans Rosenfeldt. Denmark/Sweden: Danmarks Radio og Sveriges Television, 2011–.
Buried Dogs, directed by Alexander Eik. Norway: SF Norge, 2008.
City State, directed by Ólafur de Fleur. Iceland: Poppoli Pictures, 2011.
Cold Trail, directed by Björn Br. Björnsson. Iceland: Saga Film, 2006.
Contraband, directed by Baltasar Kormákur. US: Universal Pictures, 2012.
The Element of Crime, directed by Lars von Trier. Denmark: Det Danske Filminstitut, 1984.
Garter Snake, directed by Lauri Törhönen. Finland: Solar Films, 2011.
Headhunters, directed by Morten Tyldum. Norway: Friland, 2011.
In China They Eat Dogs, directed by Lasse Spang Olsen. Denmark: Steen Herdel Filmproduktion, 1999.
Insomnia, directed by Erik Skjoldbjærg. Norway: Norsk Film, 1997.
Insomnia, directed by Christopher Nolan. USA: Warner Bros., 2002.
Jar City, directed by Baltasar Kormákur. Iceland: Blueeyes Productions, 2006.
The Killing, created by Søren Sveistrup. Denmark: Danmarks Radio, 2007–12.
The Killing, created by Veena Sud. USA: FOX Television Studios, 2011–.
The Man Without a Past, directed by Aki Kaurismäki. Finland: Sputnik, 2002.
The Naked City, directed by Jules Dassin. USA: Universal Studies, 1948.
Peeping Tom, directed by Michael Powell. UK: Anglo-Amalgamated Film Distributors, 1960.
Press, created by Óskar Jónasson and Sigurjón Kjartansson. Iceland: Saga Film, 2008–.
Priest of Evil, directed by Olli Saarela. Finland: Matila Röhr Productions, 2010.
Reykjavik Rotterdam, directed by Óskar Jónasson. Iceland: Blueeyes Productions, 2008.
Se7en, directed by David Fincher. USA: New Line Cinema, 1995.

Sound of Noise, directed by Ola Simonsson and Johannes Stjärne Nilsson. Sweden: Bliss, 2010.
The Third Man, directed by Carol Reed. UK: Carol Reed's Production, 1949.
Twin Peaks, created by Mark Frost and David Lynch. USA: Lynch/Frost Productions, 1990–1.
Union Station, directed by Rudolph Maté. USA: Paramount Pictures, 1950.
V2: Dead Angel, directed by Aleksi Mäkelä. Finland: Solar Films, 2007.
Vares: Private Eye, directed by Aleksi Mäkelä. Finland: Solar Films, 2004.

5. THE THRILL OF THE NORDIC KILL: THE MANHUNT MOVIE IN THE NORDIC THRILLER

Rikke Schubart

'This world's divided into two kinds of people: The hunter and the hunted,' big-game hunter Rainsford says in *The Most Dangerous Game* (1932) and self-assuredly continues, 'Luckily, I'm a hunter. Nothing can ever change that.' Well, he will discover that in the manhunt movie even the hunter can become prey. The manhunt movie is a subgenre of the Hollywood thriller which joins two elements: big-game sport hunting and hunting humans. Sport hunting stirs up themes of nature and culture, morals and ethics, masculinity, and, finally, civilisation. Here, we will ask what happens when the subgenre is used in the Nordic thriller.

The chapter has three aims. First, it establishes the central generic traits of the manhunt movie. Second, it sets up a theoretical framework of sociobiological and ecological theories with hunting as a reference point. And, third, it examines the Nordic version of the manhunt movie focusing on the themes of hunting, nature, social standing and civilisation. I look at the Danish drama *The Hunt* (Thomas Vinterberg, 2012), the Norwegian thriller-heist-comedy *Headhunters* (Morten Tyldum, 2011) and the Swedish thrillers *The Hunters* (*Jägarna*, 1996) and *False Trail* (*Jägarna 2*, 2011) by Kjell Sundvall.[1]

The Manhunt Movie

Since I cannot claim extensive knowledge of manhunt movies I will approach the subgenre with modesty. Some may claim that sport hunting of human game is not a genre but just a theme or a trope. I leave this discussion for others and will regard it a subgenre of the thriller and call it *the manhunt movie*.

The idea of combining sport hunting with hunting humans originates from Richard Connell's short story 'The Hounds of Zaroff' (1924) which was adapted as *The Most Dangerous Game* in 1932. Connell was inspired by big-game hunting in Africa, Asia and South America, which was popular among rich Americans in the 1920s.[2] In Connell's story the big-game hunter Rainsford falls off a yacht in the Caribbean and swims to an isolated island owned by a Russian aristocrat, general Zaroff. Zaroff is a big-game hunter who has bought an island where he hunts shipwrecked sailors. At first Zaroff thinks he can share his unique 'game' with this fellow hunter, but Rainsford declines. Zaroff then gives Rainsford the option: be killed or be prey. Rainsford gets a three-hour start and is free if he survives three days. During the hunt Rainsford sets three traps for Zaroff: a Malay man-catcher, a Burmese tiger pit and a Ugandan knife trap. When Rainsford jumps into the ocean, Zaroff thinks he has won and returns to his chateau. But Rainsford is hiding in the general's bedroom and the story ends with Rainsford sleeping in Zaroff's bed.

In *The Most Dangerous Game* by Irving Pichel and Ernest B. Schoedsack, Count Zaroff (Leslie Banks) already has shipwrecked visitors – Martin and his sister Eve – when Rainsford (Joel McCrea) arrives. After hunting and killing Martin, Zaroff offers Eve (Fay Wray) and Rainsford the game. Again, Rainsford sets three traps, jumps into the ocean, and returns to the chateau where he injures Zaroff and escapes with Eve. Zaroff falls from a window into the ocean. In the opening, one of the men on the yacht speculates: 'I was thinking of the inconsistency of civilization. The beast of the jungle killing just for his existence is called savage. The man, killing just for sport, is called civilized.' Rainsford answers about the tiger he killed on his last hunt: 'What makes you think it isn't just as much sport for the animal as it is for the man?' Rainsford regards his hunting as a competition between equal predators, but when he is himself hunted says, 'Those animals I cornered – now I know how they felt.' The film added a heroine and also a bow and a rifle to Zaroff's automatic pistol in Connell's story, and it showed human heads mounted as trophies in a trophy room.

Connell's story and its adaptation becomes founding material for the manhunt movie and the story was adapted again in 1945 and in 1956 with Zaroff as a Nazi. In 1987, the theme of big-game manhunting spread to action and science fiction, first with John McTiernan's *Predator*, where aliens use Earth as hunting territory and humans as big game. The film was followed by *Predator 2* (Stephen Hopkins, 1990) and *Predators* (Nimród Antal, 2010) and had an Alien-franchise, *AVP: Alien Versus Predator* (Paul W. S. Anderson, 2004) and *Alien Vs. Predators: Requiem* (Colin and Greg Strause, 2010), where Predators hunt Aliens on Earth. John Woo's thriller *Hard Target*

(1993) took manhunt to New Orleans where rich people hunt homeless veterans as big game. *Surviving the Game* (Ernest R. Dickerson, 1994) repeated the homeless-as-big-game formula. In 2000 the manhunt movie entered the Nordic cinema with Aage Rais-Nordentoft's Danish drama *Foreign Fields*, where a former mercenary soldier organises manhunts in Bosnia. Also in 2000, manhunt was used in the Japanese science fiction film *Battle Royale* (Kinji Fukasaku) where the government forces schoolchildren to hunt and kill each other on an island. Finally, in Suzanne Collins's bestselling book trilogy *The Hunger Games* (2008–10), children hunt each other as live television entertainment, adapted as *The Hunger Games* (Gary Ross, 2012) and *The Hunger Games: Catching Fire* (Francis Lawrence, 2013).

From 1924 to 2014 the manhunt movie develops from big-game hunting to live television entertainment. Among central characters are a good and an evil big-game hunter; location is typically a remote island or some wild nature far from civilisation; semiotic elements include hunting dogs, automatic pistol, bow, rifle, a chateau, a trophy room and the evil big-game hunter's taste in world cuisine and piano playing; and, as we will explore shortly, themes are sport hunting, culture versus nature, masculinity and civilisation.

Going 'Deep': Instincts and Universal Values

The appeal of the subgenre lies in hunting or, more precisely, sport hunting, since both good and evil hunters hunt professionally or for entertainment, but not for sustenance. Hunting is thus both a natural and a cultural phenomenon and a dramatic plot element. In the last two decades film studies have seen the development of a sociobiological approach which combines theories from the natural sciences with theories from the humanities. Some criticise this approach for ignoring the aesthetic and formal qualities of cinema; however, my aim here is to illuminate the appeal of the manhunt movie which I take to be primarily emotional. Since the thematic core of the genre is hunting, which is a highly sensory and emotional element, I will use neuropsychology and ecological philosophy to understand hunting as an innate behavior we share with other species as well as a cultural choice of leisure time that is uniquely human.

Emotionally speaking, hunting is a complex phenomenon. Whereas predators like lions and tigers have no natural enemies (except for humans), species like chimpanzees and humans have several enemies and are equipped with instincts to be both predator and prey. The innate fight-or-flight instinct (more precisely a fight-flight-freeze-or-fawn instinct) tells us how to react. Dependent on whether we are prey or predator, we either flee or hunt. But whether we belong to one or the other depends on our ability to master a situation and on our assessment of our own abilities.

Hunting also requires aggression. South African neuropsychologist Victor Nell (2006) argues that human cruelty has evolved from aggression and innate hunting instincts. He discusses three kinds of aggression: predatory aggression (hunting), territorial and sexual aggression, and defensive aggression which is the instinctive response to danger. The three are neuroanatomically distinct but easily invoke one another, and they connect to instinctive behaviours such as the seeking, rage and fear systems. The seeking system, says Nell, is 'a foraging, exploration, curiosity, and expectancy system' (2006: 214) used to stalk prey. The rage system is loud and spontaneously aggressive, and defensive aggression mixes rage with fear, the latter connected to our fight-or-flight response. A predator stalking its prey is in seeking mode, not rage or fear mode, whereas a prey is in fear mode. Unless, of course, the prey turns the tables on a hunter and becomes a hunter itself. Animals hunt instinctively. Humans, however, do sport hunting by choice. Sport hunting thus involves both instincts and conscious choice.

Let me briefly return to cruelty. Nell explains that hunting is hard work. Statistics show that most animal hunts end without a catch (2006: 217) and to compensate for empty stomachs, predation has to feel pleasant and rewarding to the animal. Therefore, to hunt feels extremely good even without a kill. '[P]redation is dopaminergic, affectively positive, and distinct from rage,' says Nell, '[it] is a powerfully rewarding experience even before satiation occurs' (ibid.: 212, 215). Hunting generates 'auditory, visual, olfactory, tactile, gustatory, and visceral stimuli' (ibid.: 213) that are extremely exciting and lead to behaviour we find cruel. Thus, the more a prey struggles, cries and bleeds, the more exciting for the predator. Where animals are predators by instinct and of necessity, humans can choose to hunt and only humans have the cognitive capacity to plan and intentionally inflict pain. Animals hunt when hungry; humans hunt for many reasons.

Hunting and sport hunting are related but have different motives. Philosopher Roger King defines sport hunting as 'the desire to kill a wild animal for sport under conditions in which such killing is not necessary for survival' (1991: 85). We still find substinence hunting today; however, in developed countries sport hunting is recreational, that is, for 'fun'. And sport hunting uses an instrumental terminology far from instincts: prey is called 'game' and game animals are 'stocks' that are 'managed' and 'harvested' (King et al. 2005: 392). Big game is hunted for trophies that can be displayed in a trophy room, where they signal man's mastery over nature.

Let us finish the framework with an eco-philosophical base. The expressions 'deep ecology' and ecosophy were coined by Norwegian philosopher Arne Næss. 'By an *ecosophy*,' writes Næss, 'I mean a philosophy of ecological harmony or equilibrium. A philosophy as a kind of *sophia* wisdom, is openly normative, it contains *both* norms, rules, postulates, value priority announcements *and* hypotheses concerning the state of affairs in our universe' (1973: 99, emphasis in original). To Næss, ecosophy is respect for the environment, nature and Earth. It places ecological balance before human desire or need. The difference between 'deep' and 'shallow' ecology is that the first seeks sustainable answers without prioritising humans over other species, and the latter settles for short-term solutions to environmental problems. Shallow ecology is instrumental and sees nature as a ressource to be harvested.

Næss argues for plurality, sustainability and respect. Human cognitive capacities have made it possible for us to exterminate other species and destroy the planet. Therefore, those same cognitive capacities bring a responsibility to care. To care means to have values, and this requires norms for living. An ecosophia demands a philosophy of values and of civilisation. As we shall see, those are at the heart of the manhunt movie.

The Nordic Manhunt Movie

American manhunt movies call up hunt and sport hunting in their titles: 'game' in *The Most Dangerous Game* and *Hunger Games* (playing on multiple meanings), 'target' in *Hard Target*, 'predator' in the *Predator* film series. So, too, does the Nordic manhunt movie with the Danish *The Hunt*, the Norwegian *Headhunters*, and the Swedish *The Hunters* and *False Trail*. We are warned that the stories involve hunting. However, where American manhunt movies explicitly place humans as big game at the centre of the plot, the Nordic manhunt movie uses this as part of its drama, as thematic subtext, and fuses these semiotic elements with other genres. Thus, *The Hunt* is a drama, *Headhunters* is a heist-comedy-thriller, and *The Hunters* and *False Trail* are thriller-crime-films. But in all four, variations of sport hunting and manhunts constitute the core emotional apppeal.

Hunting

Thomas Vinterberg's *The Hunt* opens with a group of men laughing and betting who will jump first into a November-cold lake. This is after a hunt and their joyful camaraderie springs from the shared experience of killing game. The film has three hunts: an initial hunt we do not see; a mid-way hunt where protagonist Lucas (Mads Mikkelsen) takes down a deer with a single shot; and the film ends with a hunt. The plot is about 42-year-old Lucas who has recently divorced and lost his job as a teacher. He now works in a kindergarten and has a teenage son, Marcus (Lasse Fogelstrøm). When 5-year-old Klara (Annika Wedderkopp) is upset because Lucas returns her pearl heart and says she ought to give it to her mother, she tells the head of the kindergarten, Grete (Susse Wold), that Lucas has 'a cock rigid like a stick', an expression she has heard her older brother use.

Lucas is now (wrongly) accused of molesting Klara and he shifts status from 'one of the guys' to an outcast: his house is attacked, his son rejected in the community, his dog Fanny shot and he is beaten up and kicked out of church on Christmas Eve. Klara is the daughter of Lucas's best friend Theo.

The two hunts – sport hunting and vigilante hunting – are paralleled. But what does it mean to hunt? We recall that hunting is stimulating for a predator and so, too, is sport hunting, which expresses man's domination of nature, his ability to kill and his possession of skills necessary for 'out-animaling . . . the animal', as British ethnographer Garry Marvin puts it (Marvin 2005: 22). In 'genuine' sport hunting, game is given fair warning and the hunter's weapons restricted to what is appropriate, that is, not machine guns or bombs. Only when sport hunting is a challenge does it generate the thrill of the hunt, which is the sensory and affective predator excitement. 'Concentration, alertness and awareness are fundamental to the hunter's mode of being,' says Marvin (ibid.: 22) and points to hunting as 'a contest and a competition between two sets of senses and sensing – the human and the animal' (ibid.: 18). A hunter is immersed in nature and fully absorbed in sensing his prey. Lucas is mild-mannered, wears glasses and works with children, but he is also the best hunter, silent, accurate and sensitive to game. In what Marvin calls 'justified' hunting, the hunter treats game with respect and eats its meat. When Klara asks Lucas what his favourite dish is, he replies deer, whereas Klara's favourite is fish fingers and at her house they eat pie and lasagne. The implication is that Lucas, by favouring unprocessed meat, is most immersed in hunting, attempting to be one with nature.

Sport hunting is also a social experience that is much more than recreational. As in Michael Cimino's *The Deer Hunter* (1978), sport hunting is the emotional glue that binds civilised men together, it is swimming in cold water and sharing life's experiences such as divorce and loss. We are in North Zealand, an upper-middle-class area north of the capital Copenhagen. The forest belongs to Bruun (Lars Ranthe) who has a chateau and hosts the post-hunt dinners. If the forest once echoed with aristocratic hunting, today's hunters are both commoners, such as the teacher Lucas and forest worker Theo (Thomas Bo Larsen), and the rich Bruun. Hunting is where hunters enjoy 'exercise, fresh air companionship/camaraderie, intimate personal contact with nature, and procurement of meat for the larder' (Causey 1989: 335). It is a male world of intimate emotions – Theo jokes 'there are no gays, only guns' in his home (a pun on 'bøsse', Danish slang for both 'gay' and 'rifle'), and Theo kisses Lucas on the mouth, later referring to him as 'dad's very, very, *very* best friend'.

And then, of course, hunting is a world with ethics. The film title refers both to Lucas as deer hunter and to the community's hunt when people think he is a sexual predator. What are the rules in sport hunting? A hunter invades the animal's 'home', nature, and makes it his 'game'. The game cannot negotiate with the hunter; it is the hunter who makes the rules and his ethics determine the nature of the hunt (its 'fairness'). In similar fashion, Lucas becomes 'game' when his intimate world is invaded by Grete, who phones his ex-wife and Marcus's school about the sexual assault, and when someone throws a stone through his window, kills Fanny and throws the body on his lawn, and when he is out shopping and is beaten by the shop employees. 'I have the right to shop here,' he objects and, when the butcher and the shop owner hit him, 'you cannot hit me, is this normal, to hit customers?' But in sport hunting, the game has no rights. The hunter decides the rules. In the community, people believe Klara, even when Klara recants her lie. 'I believe the children, I always do, they don't lie,' Grete tells Lucas and Theo says, 'I know my little daughter, she doesn't lie, she never did. So why would she lie now?'

So, in both natural hunting, sport hunting and the community's vigilante hunt of Lucas, we are asked to consider hunting ethics. What are they? Who decides if someone is game? Can we tell lie from truth? Can we trust our instincts? I shall return to values and ethics in the last section.

Nature

Nature is a central theme in the manhunt movie where it is both the external environment and dramatic setting (the remote island, the jungle, the mountains, the forest) and a question of innate nature, namely that of prey and predator (in manhunt movies the two are usually human). The two natures, external and internal, interact.

Rumle Hammerich's *Headhunters* is a comedy-thriller-heist film about the successful headhunter Roger (Aksel Hennie) who is also a successful art thief. He uses his information from interviews to steal art and support the extravagant lifestyle he thinks his trophy wife Diana desires. In voiceover Roger offers his reason for stealing: 'My name is Roger Brown. I am 1.68. And you don't need a psychologist to tell that that needs compensation for ... For someone like me to get what I want, there is only one way: Money. Lots of money.' He wants to be loved by Diana whom he sees as 'one of those tall, smart, beautiful people. Accustomed to be loved. Taking it for granted. There are plenty of men willing to give her love. And taller than 1.68.' Roger concludes, 'the only thing I have inherited are bad genes.' To compensate for deficient genes he has learnt to read people and to steal.

When Clas Greve (Nicolaj Coster-Waldau) applies for the position as head of Pathfinder, a Norwegian technology company, Roger discovers Clas has the priceless Rubens painting *The Caledonian Boar Hunt* in his apartment. Clas is former head of the GPS-tracking company Hote and also a former elite soldier specialised in tracking and winner of the European Military Pentathlon. In terms of hunting, Clas is pretty proficient, and he is cast in the role of former

Count Zaroff (his name Greve literally means 'count' in Norwegian). The Caledonian Boar Hunt is a classical myth recorded in Ovid's *Metamorphoses* about prince Meleager who kills a boar and presents its head as trophy to his beloved. Roger steals the painting and soon finds himself in position of the boar with Clas hunting him with a muscle dog, weapons and advanced nano-technology. When Roger accidently shoots and kills his partner in crime, he flees from the capital Oslo into the mountains.

'Hunting' now shifts from art to people and ground from civilisation to nature. Hiding from Clas and the dog, Roger ends up fully immersed in a faeces container to cover his scent. He manages to escape and kill the dog; however, Clas tracks him down and runs a car with Roger and two police officers inside off a cliff, sending it several hundred feet into a creek. Strapped in the passenger seat, Roger stares Clas in the eye without blinking, convincing Clas that he (that is, Roger) is dead. The scene is a point of no return where Roger faces his fears. He earlier got rid of his fancy city clothes and he now shaves off his long hair (realising the tracking device was smeared into his hair), bathes in the creek water and puts on one of the policemen's clothes. Roger emerges a new man and returns to Oslo.

In the manhunt movie, the question is never whether nature is good or bad, but how we use it. Ecological psychologist James J. Gibson has coined the term 'affordances' about an animal's use of nature. 'The affordances of the environment are what it offers animals, what it provides or furnishes, for good or ill' (1977: 68). Affordances are what the animal perceives and does with its environment. Thus, a fish can swim in water but a human can only swim if he or she has learnt to. Affordances are what we do with the environment using both our innate abilities and acquired learning. Gibson does not divide the environment into nature and culture. He thinks there is only one world and one environment, which holds various sets of affordances depending on who and where we are. The rules are the same: we can only work with what is here and what we can perceive. Roger cannot beat Clas in an environment where Clas has expert knowledge, but he can switch perspective from prey to predator and return to a hunting ground where Roger has expert knowledge, namely the city and the heist. Roger may be shorter, but height is unimportant when it comes to tricking Clas into drawing a gun with blanks. Roger then shoots and kills Clas.

Gibson invented the term 'affordances' to avoid the use of 'values' which is loaded with the philosophy of meaning. In Gibson's view, nature is neither good nor evil, whether we talk about the environment or our innate nature. The Norwegian mountains do not care if Roger lives or dies, nature is amoral and supports the good as well as the evil hunter. And, really, it is not important what the environment is but what it affords, be this mountains or cities. The same with innate nature; Roger may be shorter but he can out-heist Clas, and thus out-predator the predator. And he then finds that Diana doesn't care about money, she loves him and wants to have his child.

In civilisation, nature is a thing with fuzzy borders. We cultivate and adapt to nature, and this goes for the environment as well as our innate nature. What matters is not what nature is – city or wilderness, brains or muscles – but what it affords.

Social standing

When we compare the American and the Nordic manhunt movie we find they have different hunters who hunt for different reasons. In the American manhunt movie, the good big-game hunter is, mythologically speaking, a descendant of the frontier-hero Natty Bumppo we know from James Fenimore Cooper's *The Deerslayer* (1841).[3] This hunter is a self-contained and romantic hero who has no home or family because he belongs in the (moving) frontier. Nature is his home and he is essentially a defender of modern civilisation with one foot in the wilderness and one in civilisation. Hunting is his only way of living. The good hunter in the Nordic manhunt movie is a different character. He is a man planted in a community soil where he has social standing, and he has family and friends. He belongs.

If we return to Connell's story, Zaroff explains how he became a hunter: 'God makes some men poets. Some He makes kings, some beggars. Me He made a hunter.' Zaroff's whole life 'has been one prolonged hunt' (1924: n.p.). Rainsford is also presented as a natural-born hunter, as are also the antagonists and heroes in *Predator* and *Hard Target*. They are all examples of what philosopher Ann Causey calls the 'genuine' sport hunter who has an 'emotional commitment to the sport' (1989: 332). Causey differentiates between *sport hunters* and *shooters*. For the sport hunter, hunting is primary and the kill secondary. He treats game with respect and wants 'to be a link in the chain of nature, connected as predator to prey, and thus to participate directly in natural processes' (ibid.: 332). We see here a continuum between nature's predators and culture's sport hunter. The shooter, on the other hand, 'is not a hunter in the genuine sense', because his focus is not the hunt (ibid.: 333). 'It may be meat for the freezer, companionship with other hunters, male camaraderie, or exercise and fresh air . . .' (ibid.: 332). Shooters are 'the meat harvesters, the poachers, the "slob hunters," and the hunting jocks who are participating in a competition using game animals as foils for macho displays of strength and courage . . .' (ibid.: 333). A film like *Hard Target* triangulates its good/evil hunter dualism by adding the shooter, a 'slob hunter' customer who pays to go manhunting without possessing the proper skills.

What, then, characterises the Nordic hunter? In Kjell Sundvall's *The Hunters*, protagonist and police detective Erik (Rolf Lassgård) returns to his

Figure 5.1 The protagonist Lucas (Mads Mikkelsen) is a deer hunter in the start of Thomas Vinterberg's *The Hunt* (Jagten, 2012). Zentropa.

Figure 5.2 Lucas, wrongly accused of sexually assaulting a little girl, becomes a target of the community's aggression and is beaten up by the local butcher. *The Hunt*, 2012, Zentropa.

Figure 5.3 At the end of the film former big-game hunter Lucas helps Klara over the stripes on the floor. He now no longer hunts. *The Hunt*, 2012, Zentropa.

birthplace in northern Sweden after a divorce and out of frustration with life in the capital Stockholm. He has a brother, Leif (Lennart Jähkel), and a heritage (he returns for the father's funeral). When he was young, Erik escaped the abusive father and left his younger brother, who had a beautiful singing voice, behind. Erik 'got away' to Stockholm and now returns to Norrland to retrieve his roots. Leif is all that is left of those roots, and if Leif still sings beautifully in church, he now also heads poaching expeditions, abuses women and is borderline psychotic. His perverted reasoning is mirrored in his treatment of his dog Zorro, which he shoots when it doesn't obey. Leif buys a puppy that dies with him when he commits suicide after being exposed for his crimes.

In the relationship between the brothers Erik and Leif we do not find the same doubling as in the relationship of the good and evil hunter, since Erik is not a hunter. Erik goes fishing with Leif in The Hunters and with his nephew Peter in False Trail, and he can take down game (Erik goes hunting with Torsten (Peter Stormare), the big-game hunter and murderer in False Trail, and takes down an elk with a single shot). Rather, Erik is a hunter in the symbolic sense, a hunter of those who violate the rules of society. He is a truth-seeker, a detective-hero committed to upholding society's values. 'You will learn how we do things here,' the police chief tells him in The Hunters, but society cannot operate with two sets of values. The 'evil' big-game hunters in the two films – the five poachers headed by Leif in The Hunters and the unfaithful husband, policeman and big-game hunter Torsten in False Trail – are less evil than they are greedy and misguided. The poachers share organised poaching, four-wheel cars, homebrewed liquor and, eventually, killing people and raping women, but their motive is money for a consumer lifestyle. 'A reindeer is 3,000 Kronor, an elk is worth 10,000,' says a journalist at a town meeting about the now-public and therefore embarrasing poaching. 'I need 40,000 Kronor for payment on my new car,' one poacher protests when Leif suggests they lie low for a week. In this desire for a consumer lifestyle, they are no different from the rest of the men in the area, where everyone is a hunter and no one likes Erik with his high-headed ideas about ethics and policing. Erik finds that the local police ignore the poaching and the state willingly offers economic compensation to the Sami for their loss of stock without asking for a police investigation.

In the Nordic film, therefore, instead of a good/evil dualism we find a critique of consumerism and of a community's vigilante hunting. Hunting may be the only respectable masculine lifestyle, however, and at his funeral, Erik and Leif's father is remembered as 'a real asshole' by his friends in his livingroom, which is also a trophy room. The 'good' big-game hunter is a paradox and an impossible figure in the Nordic manhunt movie where 'good' means upholding social values and in a welfare state these do not include killing which is considered murder. Roger gets away with murder because *Headhunters* is a black comedy, but Lucas renounces his rifle and Erik – threatened point-blank three times in the two films – doesn't fire his gun at people. The good hunter in the Nordic manhunt movie renounces the thrill of the kill.

Civilisation

After discussing hunting, nature and the hunter's social standing, we will now take a broader look at the Nordic manhunt movie and ask what its values are. What values does the good hunter defend and what kind of civilisation does he represent? What is the ideology of the Nordic manhunt movie?

Asking for the meaning of hunting, we hit what philosopher Næss and biologist Ivar Mysterud call 'the rock bottom of philosophy and political ideology' (1987: 22). In an article on the Norwegian wolf, Næss and Mysterud discuss the rights of 5–10 wolves to live in a country with 3.2 million sheep and 4.1 million people, where inhabitants want to kill the wolves because they eat sheep. From an ecosophical perspective, Næss and Mysterud argue that no one has the right to decide this. Wolves are afraid of people and kill only sheep, and they suggest we conceive of a 'mixed community' including animals (sheep *and* wolves) as well as people, instead of a community existing solely of people who use animals as 'crops'. An ecosophia rejects speciesism and anthropocentric thinking. In other words, just because we have the means to make other species game or extinct, this does not give us the right to do so. All species have rights and are of value in themselves as part of Earth's ecological variation.

What does this have to do with sport hunting and the manhunt movie? Comparing the American and the Nordic manhunt movie, they have different hunting cultures. The American hunter is a hero by out-predatoring his predator. He proves himself equal at killing and better at hunting. To paraphrase Dirty Harry, there's nothing wrong with shooting as long as the right people get shot. The difference between the good and evil hunter is not the hunt, but game and motive. There is nothing wrong with hunting as long as the right game is killed. The evil hunter kills for egotistic reasons, the good hunter because it is his nature and he upholds social values. Hunting is a matter of instincts and beyond moral judgement. Thus Causey argues that:

> It is not morally wrong to take pleasure in killing game; nor is it morally right. It is simply not a moral issue at all, because the urge itself is an instinct, and instincts do not qualify for moral valuation, positive or negative. Thus, the urge to kill for sport is *amoral*, lying as it does outside the jurisdiction of morality. (1989: 338)

Hunting is differently presented in the Nordic manhunt movie. 'Hunting and the forest are his life. What happens if you take that away?' it is said about Tomme in *The Hunters* when Erik confiscates the poachers' rifles. 'What happens if I don't?' is Erik's reply. And in *False Trail* the community is furious when they must hand over their rifles to the police for calibre testing. The one complaining loudest is the murdered girl's father. A man's rifle is his being, his essence, we understand. But this is a delusion. In the Nordic version, sport hunting is not about instincts but is a culture with customs, rituals and an aggressive masculine lifestyle. In *The Hunt* this culture is seen in the eating and drinking and the organised dinners at each other's homes. Here we see a community's values acted out, values that are invisible as long as they are unchallenged. Thus, when Marcus comes to Theo's house to ask why Klara is lying, the families, who are there for a cosy dinner, kick him out and slap him. And when Lucas is in the grocery store he is kicked out, and when he is in church – where Lucas and Marcus read from the gospels – and tells Theo to stop harassing him, Lucas is again thrown out.

The Nordic manhunt movie replaces the ethics of individual hunters (good or evil) with the ethics of a community. What are the rules for inclusion or exclusion? What rights does a person – prey or predator – have? In an ecosophical perspective, values are balance, plurality, respect and sustainability, while shallow ecology values are consumer culture and capitalism. *The Hunters* portrays poaching as a repulsive slaughter executed with silencer and telescopic sight, yet accepted by local police and local people. *Headhunters* portrays Roger in the beginning as a scared and shallow person, more worried about appearances than about honest emotions. *The Hunt*, finally, reshuffles generic elements and plays them against expectations. Here, the rich chateau-owner and big-game hunter Bruun defends Lucas and believes he is innocent until proven guilty, while the kind head of kindergarten, Grete, leads the hunt. And when we think Lucas is helpless prey, he walks back into the grocery store, headbutts the butcher and demands his groceries, which he pays for at the counter in orderly fashion.

In the Nordic manhunt movie, sport hunting is portrayed as a male culture that lets aggression and greed take over reason. In nature, hunt is a matter of instincts. In society, however, sport hunting is a culture. What role we play is a choice, not an instinct. We can act like the butcher or like Bruun. In modern society it is hard to tell truth from lie. Civilisation is so complex that instincts only point us in the right direction if people are honest. We feel what is right and wrong, but 'instincts are no match for reason', as Zaroff says in Connell's story.

Conclusion: Deeper than Instincts

The good big-game hunter is a contradictory character in the Nordic thriller and the American frontier ideology is unacceptable in a Scandinavian welfare society. The Nordic subgenre goes beyond the dualism of good and evil. The problem is not with individuals, but with the conditions generating an aggressive hunting lifestyle. Civilisation builds on reason. Thus, although we share hunting instincts and aggression with other predator species, being human means to exist in a civilisation from which there is no return to a 'natural' order. Nature is amoral, but we are in the moral domain.

In *The Hunt*, Klara is afraid of straight lines. At the end of the film at a party at Bruun's chateau, Lucas lifts Klara up and carries her across the terrifying lines on a wall-to-wall carpet. The lines will not disappear. But one day Klara might learn to cross them. Until then she needs guidance. Similarly, the hunting culture is unchanged. In the very last scene, Lucas is shot at and is unable to see the shooter's face. He is unarmed because he has given his rifle to Marcus, who is old enough to join the hunt. But Lucas is armed with determination to remain standing. Although no longer a hunter, he cannot leave the hunting ground because there is only one world and we all live in it. Civilisation is the constant challenge to master instincts and uphold values that run deeper than instincts.

Hunting is exciting and intoxicating but in the Nordic manhunt movie the landscape is no mythic wilderness and the protagonist no frontier hero. The subgenre's values are the opposite of the Dirty Harry motto about shooting the right people. Instead, the Nordic manhunt movie expresses the ancient universal Golden Rule: Treat others as you want them to treat you.

Notes

1. In the Danish cinema, the dramas *Foreign Fields* (Aage Rais-Nordentoft, *På fremmed mark*, 2000) and *Headhunter* (Rumle Hammerich, 2009) are also relevant to this discussion; however, because of space I leave these out of this chapter.
2. Connell's short story was also adapted as *A Game of Death* (Robert Wise, 1945) and *Run for the Sun* (Roy Boulting, 1956) with the big-game hunter as an ex-Nazi officer.
3. For a discussion of the American frontier hero, see Richard Slotkin (2000).

References

Causey, Ann S. (1989), 'On the Morality of Hunting', *Environmental Ethics: An Interdisciplinary Journal Dedicated to the Philosophical Aspects of Environmental Problems* 11 (4): 327–43.
Connell, Richard (1924), 'The Hounds of Zaroff', <http://fiction.eserver.org/short/the_most_dangerous_game.html>, accessed 22 February 2014.

Gibson, James J. (1977), 'The Theory of Affordances'. In R. Shaw and J. Bransford (eds), *Perceiving, Acting, and Knowing: Toward an Ecological Psychology*, Hillsdale, NJ: Lawrence Erlbaum Associates, pp. 67–82.

King, Roger J. H. (1991), 'Environmental Ethics and the Case for Hunting', *Environmental Ethics* 13: 59–85.

King, Roger J. H., Fred Nelson, Ted Kerasote, Patrick Bateson, Heather E. Eves, Chrijstine M. Wolf and Scott C. Yaich (2005), 'The Ethics of Hunting', *Frontiers in Ecology and the Environment* 3 (7): 392–7.

Marvin, Garry (2005), 'Sensing Nature: Encountering the World in Hunting', *Etnofoor* 18 (1): 15–26.

Næss, Arne (1973), 'The Shallow and the Deep, Long-Range Ecology Movement: A Summary', *Inquiry: An Interdisciplinary Journal of Philosophy* 16: 95–100.

Næss, Arne and Ivar Mysterud (1987), 'Philosophy of Wolf Policies I: General Principles and Preliminary Exploration of Selected Norms', *Conservation Biology* 1 (1): 22–34.

Nell, Victor (2006), 'Cruelty's Rewards: The Gratifications of Perpetrators and Spectators', *Behavioral and Brain Sciences* 29: 211–57.

Slotkin, Richard (2000), *Regeneration Through Violence: The Mythology of the American Frontier, 1600–1860*, Norman, OK: University of Oklahoma Press.

6. BRIDGES AND TUNNELS: NEGOTIATING THE NATIONAL IN TRANSNATIONAL TELEVISION DRAMA

Anders Wilhelm Åberg

> As a global TV franchise, [*The Tunnel*] is pure gold: there's a US–Mexican version already screening and there are frontiers all over the world with tension and history dotted across the boundary. The South Korea–North Korea would be ace.
>
> Keith Watson (2012)

Introduction: Nations and Nationalisms in a 'Postnational' World

In a globalised world, the notions of neatly defined, homogeneous *ethnies* or national identities are difficult to sustain, especially if they are construed as organic features of social organisation and historical development. Instead, the present moment is characterised by hybridisation, multiculturalism and all manners of transnational movement, flux and entanglement. It has even been argued that we are now situated in a postnational condition, where the construction of supranationals, such as the European Union, and the transnational, 'deregulated', cross-border movement of capital, cultures and people is indicative of a decline of nations and traditional concepts of the national as key factors (Ezra and Rowden 2006: 1f.; see also Habermas 2001). Although the relation between the 'transnational' and the 'postnational' is not absolutely clear in this line of argument, the terms can be understood as connoting progressive stages in the decline of the national in the face of the challenges of globalisation (for example in Kääpä 2011: 14ff.). However, in the postnational condition more traditional or conservative ways of imagining the nation and national community simply will not make sense (Hedetoft and Hjort 2002). Modernist theories of nationalism hold that feelings of national belonging and community are constructed ('imagined') and sustained through mediated social communication (Deutsch 1966: 96–8 and 188; Gellner 1983: 127; Anderson 1991: 122). One implication of this for the contemporary postnational condition seems to be that national community remains a potent fiction; whereas postnational flux is the reality this fiction tries to disavow.

Indeed, on a political level, nations, conceptions of national specificity and nationalisms are still very real, and loom large in the mobilisation of various groups (conceived as, precisely, national, or ethnic, religious or otherwise designated) for political action (Juergensmeyer 2002: 3–8). Current development in Europe and elsewhere makes this abundantly clear. Rampant nationalist discourses are, as I write, central features in contemporary politics in China, Russia and the Ukraine. Nationalist parties – in some countries, like Hungary, even overtly fascist ones – play significant roles in several European parliaments. Catalonia has carried out an unofficial poll about national sovereignty for the region and separation from Spain, and Scottish nationalists only narrowly failed to achieve independence for Scotland in a referendum there. In Norway, Denmark, Finland and Sweden nationalist parties have entered the parliaments, and in Great Britain the UK Independence Party has recently become a major political force. In the USA 'illegal aliens' and immigration are increasingly being discussed as threats to American national identity (see for example Huntington 2004). Furthermore, even if globalisation has indeed challenged and changed the systemic nature of international relationships, nations are still 'subjects' in this system, which is one of the reasons that nationhood is desirable. These are but a few examples that show that even if the world may be, in some sense, postnational and globalised, it is by no means postnationalist.

In this chapter, I will discuss the Swedish/Danish television series *Bron|Broen* (*The Bridge*, 2011–) as a transnational media phenomenon, where conceptions of nation are thematised. I will argue, against the backdrop briefly introduced above, that the discourse of nation in *Bron|Broen* is a vital part of its adaptability.[1]

Bridges and Tunnels

Bron|Broen premiered as a ten-part television series in Sweden and Denmark in the autumn of 2011. It is a crime thriller set in the Øresund region, primarily the metropolitan area of Copenhagen in Denmark and Malmö in Sweden – divided by a strait, but connected by the Øresund Bridge of the title. It narrates the story of two police officers, Saga Norén (Swedish) and Martin Rohde (Danish), trying to catch a serial killer and presumed terrorist in a complicated international case. As will be explored further below, the relationship between Saga and Martin is presented as symbolic of the clash between the Swedish and the Danish, and the characters have traits that are readable as stereotypical for each national culture.

The series is a transnational packet deal in terms of financing, featuring production companies, including public service television companies, from Sweden, Denmark, Norway and Germany, as well as funding from public bodies such as Nordisk Film- och TV-fond and the European Union MEDIA programme. Creative personnel (directing, acting, cinematography, editing etc.) are almost exclusively Swedish or Danish, and the series is bilingual. The writing team is mixed as well, but the Swede Hans Rosenfeldt is credited as main author, and his fellow Swedes Måns Mårlind and Björn Stein are co-credited as creators ('Based on an idea by . . .'). Therefore, the series has been presented and discussed in the press and in fan discourse as a Swedish–Danish co-production, whereas Swedish media sometimes tend to emphasise the Swedish creative trio, treating it as a substantially Swedish feat as well as an object of national pride that resides in the fact that *Bron|Broen* has become a global success. Several sources reported in autumn 2013 that the first season had been sold to over 130 countries. It won a Prix Europa award in 2012 and was nominated for a BAFTA award in 2013, where it lost to Lena Dunham's *Girls* (2012–), in the respectable company of *Game of Thrones* (2011–) and *Homeland* (2011–). This level of achievement is outstanding, though not unprecedented, for a Nordic television production.

Bron|Broen has also spawned two spin-off adaptations to date: *The Bridge* (2013) and *The Tunnel* (2013). They are set in the metropolitan area of El Paso–Cuidad Juárez, and the regions of Folkestone and Calais near the Channel Tunnel. The set-up in both series is identical with that of *Bron|Broen*, featuring an odd couple of detectives, but substituting the Swedish/Danish national stereotyping with corresponding versions tapping prejudices and preconceptions pertaining to US–Mexican and Anglo-French relations respectively. *The Bridge* stands out as being produced exclusively by American companies. The creative personnel are of the American 'melting pot' variety, ethnically mixed, as it were, but only the cast has a significant portion of Mexican or Latino talent. Some of the crew from *Bron|Broen* are credited, among them Rosenfeldt, Mårlind and Stein (as creators) and Charlotte Seiling (director of one episode to date). That is: this is an Anglo-American (US) production, not a US–Mexican co-production. *The Tunnel*, by contrast, makes a publicity point of being an Anglo-French co-production, mainly produced by the two respective national distributors, Canal+ (France) and Sky Atlantic (UK). It is advertised, for example, as being the first bilingual television series (using subtitles) in either country. Creatively though, it is mainly a British production with an Anglo-French cast. Rosenfelt, Mårlind and Stein are credited as creators.

Thus, *Bron*/*Broen*, its mode of production, reception and (re)circulation stands out as a model case of transnationalism in the media. As Will Higbee and Song Whee Lim (2010) have observed, the move to conceptualise contemporary cinema in transnational, rather than national, terms has unpacked a set of questions concerning the types of phenomena and practices that may most productively be framed by the discourse of transnationalism. They discern three broad approaches, of which two are clearly applicable to *Bron*/*Broen*. First, *Bron*/*Broen* obviously transcends national borders in terms of production, distribution and reception to such a degree that any understanding of the series in national terms alone would be severely limiting, even impossible (see also Higson 2009: 67–9). Second, from the vantage point of the world outside the Nordic countries, *Bron*/*Broen* is an exemplar of 'Nordic' crime, that is, a production marked by a supranational, however shared, cultural heritage. Higbee and Lim (2010: 10) also note that 'the national continues to exert the force of its presence even within transnational film-making practices', and the ability to capture and analyse this essential dynamic in *Bron*/*Broen* is what makes the discourse of transnationalism productive in this particular case.

Branding and Nation: Nordic Noir

Clearly, origin matters in the fan discourse and marketing of commercially viable literature, film and television. In fact, *Bron*/*Broen* has been riding the wave of Scandinavian crime fiction, 'Scandi-crime' or 'Nordic noir', that became a very visible, publicised and commercially important concept in the wake of the global success of, especially, Stieg Larsson's Millennium trilogy of novels, and the Danish television series *The Killing* (*Forbrydelsen*, 2007–, remade in the US as *The Killing*, 2011–).[2] There had been important precursors, dating back to the novels of Maj Sjöwall and Per Wahlöö in the 1960s and 1970s, considered by scholars and fan sites alike as the benchmark of modern Swedish (or Nordic) crime fiction (Tapper 2011: 17 and passim; *Scandinavian Crime Fiction* 2014). Henning Mankell's novels about the small-town detective Kurt Wallander continue the tradition of Sjöwall and Wahlöö, and have reached a substantial international readership since the 1990s.

However, the massive global impact and coverage of this brand of crime fiction is a fairly recent phenomenon. The present commercial appeal of Scandinavian crime fiction is significant. The Swedish press, for example, reported that an international survey of the bestselling authors globally in 2009 placed Stieg Larsson second and Henning Mankell in tenth place (*Dagens nyheter* 2009). *The Guardian* recently reported that Stieg Larsson's trilogy had sold more than 75 million copies worldwide as of December 2013 (*The Guardian* 2013). Great Britain is a booming market for Scandinavian crime fiction. The British company Arrow Films, for example, hosts the sub-label Nordic Noir that promotes Scandinavian films and television series, publishes the specialised *Nordic Noir Magazine* and organises the Nordicana Expo (since 2013).

A key aspect of franchising Nordic Noir is the more or less stereotypical distinctiveness of the Nordic countries in terms of national characteristics and temper, landscape and climate, and various cultural associations or markers. One representative example is found in Laura Miller's (2010) introductory piece on Nordic crime fiction in the *Wall Street Journal*:

> What's the appeal of all this blood on the snow, police boots crunching over frozen grass and detectives whose every utterance comes in a puff of visible breath against a background of interminable night? Many of us do seem to be having an Ingmar Bergman moment right now. We love to slouch on our IKEA sofas watching the characters in 'Mad Men' as they ruminate on the loneliness and impotence of their life while staring silently off into darkened rooms filled with Danish modern furniture. (Could the scene from 'Mad Men' in which a traumatized Sally Draper watches the televised self-immolation of a Vietnamese monk be a reference to Liv Ullman watching the same footage during a nervous breakdown in Mr. Bergman's masterpiece, 'Persona'?)

These types of associations may be understood as supranational rather than strictly national, especially since national differences *between* the Nordic countries have tended to go unnoticed in transnational reception (Elkington and Nestingen 2005: 4f.). It is unclear, for example, whether Miller consciously throws Norway into the mix by referencing Liv Ullmann, or whether she figures as a 'Nordic actress'? However, the growing interest in Nordic noir seems to foster an ever-keener awareness of national specificity. The quote above does in fact specify some national distinctions, and as a matter of course specialised websites such as *Scandinavian Crime Fiction* (2014) carefully note the nationality of all featured authors.

Much of this attention to national/cultural distinctiveness seems to feed into a fetishising discourse of 'exotic' difference and nationally defined – or tagged – elements of style, such as the Danish furniture and Bergmanesque aesthetics of *angst* in the quote above. Particularly interesting instances of this tendency are the British Mankell adaptations featuring Kenneth Branagh as Kurt Wallander from 2008 to 2010. The films are in English, featuring a British cast, but shot on location in Sweden. As film scholar Ingrid Stigsdotter (2010: 245) has observed, this creates 'a visual semiotics of Swedishness', and the films provide the audience with a touristic experience that expands their geographic and cultural imagination of Sweden.

When *Bron|Broen* was introduced in Great Britain, issues of national specificity were paramount, since the story calls for a specific audience understanding of Denmark and Sweden as two distinct nations with cultural and linguistic differences. For example, Vicky Frost (2012) in *The Guardian* pedagogically illustrated differences between the Danish and the Swedish by way of a 'Sweden versus Denmark' fact sheet. Facts include cultural stereotypes: 'Swedes are depicted as rich and arrogant and loving order and rules. Danes are depicted as being beer-drinking, happy-go-lucky and disorganised.' There are also contrastive examples of presumably well-known cultural markers designed to convey subtle difference between seemingly similar entities, such as 'Abba vs Aqua' and 'Smorgasbord vs Smørrebrød'. There is no doubt that in the discourse on Nordic noir, and specifically concerning *Bron/Broen*, nationhood and aspects of national culture are constantly highlighted and thematised, both as a form of necessary pre-understanding and as an object of fascination.

THEMES OF NATION IN *BRON/BROEN*

The film scholar Mette Hjort (2009) has made a set of useful distinctions concerning the theme of nation in the cinema. She argues that 'nation' is a topical theme, as opposed to a perennial theme like 'love'. The topical theme of nation is specific, bound by historical contingency, and invested in the current ideologies and self-representation of a particular nation, usually the one where the film is set and/or produced. For example, the perennial theme of 'community' can be articulated in terms of nation, thereby topically thematising, let's say, a certain historical formation of 'the Swedish'. As Hjort underlines, this explains why: 'most film-makers would reject outright the idea that they are committed first and foremostly to the making of films that contribute to the thematics of nation' (Hjort 2009: 107).

Almost every realistic film – in this context, this means a film set in 'our world', as opposed to, for example, Mordor – has a recognisable setting that is, in a sense, national. Elements like language, fashion, historical events and landmark buildings may be obviously Swedish, for example. Does that mean that the film is about Sweden, the nation? Hjort calls this 'banal aboutness', with reference to Michael Billig's notion of 'banal nationalism', and distinguishes between such films and films that clearly direct focal attention to signifiers of nation, thereby truly thematising the nation in question. This distinction is not clear-cut in theory, but highlights that some amount of consistent foregrounding (iconographic, narrative, dialogue-wise etc.) is necessary to distinguish 'banal aboutness' from thematisation. Furthermore, Hjort distinguishes monocultural thematisations of nation – focusing on one specific national culture – from intercultural thematisations, that use 'contrastive cultural elements to foreground and direct attention toward specifically national elements' (Hjort 2009: 113).

In the Vicky Frost article quoted above, Anders Lindström, one of the producers working with *Bron/Broen*, voices this reluctance to work explicitly with themes of nation. Commenting on the fact that some people have understood Saga and Martin's relationship as 'shorthand for the way the nations see each other', Lindström claims that this is 'purely coincidental'. Intentionality will not be discussed in detail here; suffice it to say that this is very difficult to believe. In fact, the situation that sets the story in motion seems meticulously constructed to foreground an intercultural thematisation of nation.

The Øresund Bridge joins the cities of Copenhagen and Malmö. *Bron/Broen* starts with the discovery of a woman's corpse on the bridge. On closer inspection, it turns out that the corpse is placed on the border, half of it in Sweden, half of it in Denmark. Furthermore, it is actually two dead bodies. The lower part – we learn later – belonged to a Danish prostitute, and the upper part is a local Swedish politician. This complex set-up necessitates a joint Swedish–Danish police operation, but of course, it also focuses our attention on convoluted issues of nationality, boundaries and the transgression of boundaries in the transnational metropolitan area of Copenhagen–Malmö. This theme is immediately picked up in the characterisation of Saga Norén and Martin Rohde, who meet on the crime scene. They do, indeed, conform to popular stereotypes held by Swedes and Danes. Saga is pathologically bent on following rules and procedure, and she is distant and socially inept – she does seem to be somewhere on the autism spectrum. At the same time, she is intellectually superior and forcible. This reflects the most common popular views (or 'myths') about Swedes in Denmark: compulsive followers of rules, however capable and efficient (Sanders 2006: 10–15). Saga's last name, Norén, probably alludes to the notoriously dark and pessimistic Swedish playwright Lars Norén, thereby capturing a stereotypical aspect of Swedishness otherwise associated with Ingmar Bergman outside and within Sweden: gloom, catastrophically miserable interpersonal relationships and ultimately suicide. Martin, on the other hand, is laid back and socially gifted, though a bit sloppy and prone to give in to temptation when it comes to food or sex. He is a lover and a romantic, which is actually a vital part of the Danish self-perception, as opposed to the Danish perception of Swedes, stiff and set on efficiency and development (Linde-Laursen 1995: 145–52). Martin initially seems to embody the Danish *hygge* (roughly: 'cosiness'), which *VisitDenmark* (2014) tries to define as follows:

> Hygge is as Danish as pork roast and cold beer and it goes far in illuminating the Danish soul. In essence, hygge means creating a nice, warm atmosphere and enjoying the good things in life with good people around you. The warm glow of candlelight is hygge. Friends and family – that's hygge too. And let's not forget the eating and drinking – preferably sitting

around the table for hours on end discussing the big and small things in life.

Later in the series, Martin's jovial appearance crumbles. In a dramatic logic of mirroring and reversals Saga, correspondingly, takes Martin's cues on social behaviour and tries to act more 'human'. So, I would contend that this Swedish–Danish complex, as it were, is obviously privileged in the series' overture. Hjort stresses that thematisation of nation requires some degree of consistent foregrounding; a single instance is not enough. In *Bron|Broen*, the spectator is primed by the set-up to observe contrast and difference, as well as similarity or sameness – or perhaps: enmeshment – and frame this within a cultural logic of Swedishness versus Danishness. This national theme is, more subtly, rearticulated several times, especially in the earlier part of the series. As noted, much of this centres around the contrasting characters of Saga and Martin. Saga's obsessiveness continues to be explored. She almost always works; instead of going home she puts on fresh deodorant and takes a new t-shirt out of her office drawer; she reports Martin for misconduct; she interviews shocked relatives of victims in a deadpan, harsh manner; she is a loner. Martin, on the other hand, makes friends with his new Swedish colleagues; he chats with the police clerks and offers them Danish pastries; his domestic life is full of kids and a loving wife; his appetites and tendency to cut corners at work and in love prove to be fateful as the plot unfolds. Another element of contrast regards their respective police departments: the Swedish one appears effective and at the same time nurturing – Saga's boss, for example, tries to help her overcome her social difficulties – whereas the Danish department seems more byzantine and corrupt. Far from exuding the Danish *hygge*, this motif appeals to Swedish associations of Copenhagen as a place 'south of the border', desirable but potentially dangerous, which naïve Swedes can have difficulties navigating (Löfgren 2002: 260–2).

The clearest instance of formalised repetition of the theme of nation is found in the credit sequence. The series' logo features the Swedish and Danish words for 'the bridge' separated by a line: *Bron|Broen*. The play of similarity and difference is introduced here on a graphic and linguistic level that runs through the credit sequence. The bridge itself is introduced first in the sequence, shot from a moving vehicle, suggesting movement and passage. Then follows a montage of, mostly, extreme long shots of urban cityscapes at night. The perspective is a bit warped, which, along with the darkness, makes it difficult to pinpoint the exact location of each shot even if one has some familiarity with the cities. This treatment underpins the perception of the Copenhagen–Malmö area as a unified cityscape. However, interspersed are shots of landmark sites that virtually no Dane or Swede would misplace, for example the skyscraper Turning Torso in Malmö and the last shot of the statue of the Little Mermaid in Copenhagen. The credit sequence thus combines a powerful sense of duality with the nocturnal sprawl of a transnational cityscape, thereby signalling the differences and enmeshments of Danish and Swedish that the series explores.

SWEDE–DANE RELATIONSHIPS AND THE MAKING OF A TRANSNATIONAL METROPOLIS

Two things should be clarified at this point. First, the differences explored by *Bron*|*Broen* by way of an intercultural thematisation of nation reflect a historically and culturally specific formation of mutual (mis)understandings. Had this been a story about a Swedish and a Finnish detective, there would have been a different set of expectations and stereotypes in play, for example. Second, the invention of the Øresund region as a transnational hub is a longstanding political effort, with the opening of the bridge in the year 2000 as a sort of enabling culmination. *Bron*|*Broen* can be seen both as a result of this development and as a fictionalised commentary of it.

The reiteration in *Bron*|*Broen* of the Swede–Dane relationship – which is antagonistic and symbolically incestuous, evoking notions of kinship and sibling rivalry – as well as the references to transnational enmeshment implied by the construction of a 'borderless' region must be understood in terms of historical processes that have shaped the self-perception of the two nation states. The present border between Sweden and Denmark was decided after the peace treaties at Roskilde in 1658 and in Copenhagen in 1660. The formerly Danish regions of Skåne, Halland and Blekinge thereby became Swedish territories. Locating the new national border in Øresund had geopolitical significance, since this placed control over the passage between the Baltic and the North Sea in two different nations, and it was therefore supported internationally. In the national narratives constructed in Sweden and Denmark in the nineteenth and early twentieth centuries, Øresund was perceived as a 'natural' border between culturally distinct nations. Øresund was thus transformed from a link between regions within Denmark, to a 'dividing ditch' between two countries (Linde-Laursen 1995: 11–26). In this process, the geographically close neighbours were mutually defined in terms of crucial differences in temperament and culture. For example, Gustav Sundbärg (1911) made frequent contrastive use of Swedish and Danish properties in his hugely influential essay on Swedish public temper.

Plans to cross the Øresund with a bridge or a tunnel date back to the late nineteenth century, culminating in the 1960s in the vision of the Øre City (Ørestad), a futuristic metropolis surrounding Øresund (Berg and Löfgren 2000: 10). In the 1980s and 1990s a discourse of regionalisation within the EU spawned interest among a wide range of private and public organisations to reinvigorate the idea of the Øresund region. The developments leading up to the building of the Øresund Bridge were embedded in a heated and optimistic discourse on local development – Ørespeak – focusing on merging, mobility and transcendence, and evidence of a virtual cult of the prefix 'trans':

> 'Trans-' carries a powerful aura of both bridging and changing. It focuses not only on that which is transportable, but also on that which can be translated, transplanted, and transformed across national borders. This, among other things, accounts for the great EU interest in the project – the Øresund Bridge becomes part of the positive narrative of globalization and European integration in the breaking down of traditional national barriers. (Löfgren 2000: 38)

In the fictional universe of *Bron|Broen*, the 'trans-' is primarily articulated in terms of mobility. The case takes Saga and Martin as well as the spectator back and forth between Malmö and Copenhagen. Although it is almost always possible to determine where a scene is set, the emphasis tends, with a few exceptions, to be on geographical similarity – or oneness – rather than contrast, which would have been a possible aesthetic choice. The travelling – frequently by car, using the Øresund Bridge as setting – is almost never pictured as cumbersome. In reality, the trip by car between the city centres is about forty kilometres, and takes around forty-five minutes depending on traffic conditions and exact destination. In the fiction, the sense of proximity is emphasised. Establishing the Malmö–Copenhagen area as an integrated place does feed into and vitalise the branding of the Øresund region as a transnational hub. However, as discussed above, the thematisation of nation introduces a counter-narrative that reflects the fact that at least two centuries of mutually contrastive nation-building is not easily dismissed. Nationalism lingers in the transnational development of the region, and *Bron|Broen* is an opportunity to process this in fictionalised form.

Conclusion: Remapping National Otherness

Nationalism is a paradigm and therefore – somewhat paradoxically – a transnational phenomenon. That is, even if the relationship between, say, Sweden and Denmark is historically and culturally specific, it is paradigmatically similar to other international relationships. That, I would suggest, is one of the reasons that, as Keith Watson noted, the concept in *Bron|Broen* is 'pure gold'. *The Bridge* and *The Tunnel* do in fact both thematise nation in a similar way, and this is evidence that the national/transnational problematic is a presumably attractive aspect of *Bron|Broen* as a commodity in the transnational television market. It does not seem to have been remade on the strength of its serial killer plot alone.

The first episodes of *The Bridge* and *The Tunnel* respectively are fairly similar to the original series. The intercultural thematisation of nation also follows the same pattern, but adapts the specific signifiers of nation and national difference. Hence, detectives Sonia Cross and Marco Ruiz in *The Bridge* personify the US–Mexican relationship. The first few scenes introduce the motifs of illegal immigration, poverty versus wealth and proper procedure versus laxness, or even corruption. The tone is quite sombre, whereas in *The Tunnel*, perhaps characteristically, the Anglo-French relationship is treated more playfully. The British detective Karl Roebuck jokingly tries to comment on the icy demeanour of his French colleague Elise Wasserman by referencing the Hundred Years War and Jeanne d'Arc: 'Steady on Joan, I'm not looking for a war over it!' Here, in the first few scenes nation is thematised by reference to food, language (including the bilingual song in the credit sequence), history and temperament, interestingly reversing the north–south dynamic of *Bron/Broen* and *The Bridge*.

Comments in the press suggest that the theme of nation was clearly perceived (but variously valued) as an integral part of *The Bridge* and *The Tunnel* alike. Chuck Bowen (2013) in *Slant Magazine*, for example, remarked about *The Bridge*: 'Positing the U.S.'s relationship with Mexico as a manifestation of a dysfunctional relationship writ globally, the creators present a series of American/Mexican pairs that parallel and parody one another.' Making a corresponding observation about *The Tunnel*, Gerard O'Donovan (2013) of *The Telegraph* writes:

> A co-production with the French TV station Canal+, The Tunnel's English vs French rivalries were worked up to entertaining but largely superficial effect – such as Wasserman's observations on the deficiencies of English humour (she can talk), or Roebuck's failed efforts to ingratiate himself with French colleagues by means of a bag of cheap croissants.

The depth and sincerity of the confirmation of nationalist sentiments in popular entertainment can of course be questioned. But there can be little doubt that the transnational appeal of *Bron/Broen* is largely due to two characteristics, analysed above: (1) That it works through and exploits issues of national identity by way of a consistently foregrounded intercultural thematisation of nation. (2) That it exploits a recent upsurge in the demand for Nordic in crime fiction, which entails a keen attention to national/cultural distinctiveness that feeds into a fetishising discourse of 'exotic' difference. Thus, the national is an essential ingredient in this pre-eminently transnational enterprise, and its success is indicative of a need to process transnational developments and the meaning of national specificity and difference within these developments.

Notes

1. I wish to thank the students at the Film and Nation course at Linnaeus University for their vivid discussions and input, and especially Tomas Söderlind who brought *Bron|Broen* to my attention.
2. Scandinavia consists of Denmark, Norway and Sweden. The Nordic countries are Denmark, Norway, Iceland, Sweden and Finland, and the territories Åland Islands, Faroe Islands, Greenland, Svalbard and Jan Mayen. The difference (and overlap) between Scandinavia and the Nordic countries is seldom consistently observed in the English-language use of the terms. Therefore, the adjectives 'Scandinavian' and 'Nordic' are often used as synonyms or with a vague denotation.

References

Anderson, Benedict (1991 [1983]), *Imagined Communities: Reflections on the Origin and Spread of Nationalism*, 2nd edn, London: Verso.

Berg, Per Olof and Orvar Löfgren (2000), 'Studying the Birth of a Transnational Region'. In Per Olof Berg, Anders Linde-Laursen and Orvar Löfgren (eds), *Invoking a Transnational Metropolis: The Making of the Øresund Region*, Lund: Studentlitteratur, pp. 7–26.

Bowen, Chuck (2013), 'The Bridge: Season One', 6 July <http://www.slantmagazine.com/tv/review/the-bridge-season-one>, last accessed 30 January 2014.

Dagens nyheter (no author, 2009), 'Stieg Larsson tvåa i VM i försäljning', <http://www.dn.se/dnbok/stieg-larsson-tvaa-i-vm-i-forsaljning/>, last accessed 30 January 2014.

Deutsch, Karl W. (1966 [1953]), *Nationalism and Social Communication: An Inquiry into the Foundations of Nationalism*, 2nd edn, Cambridge, MA: MIT Press.

Elkington, Trevor G. and Andrew Nestingen (2005), 'Introduction'. In Andrew Nestingen and Trevor G. Elkington (eds), *Transnational Cinema in a Global North: Nordic Cinema in Transition*, Detroit: Wayne State University Press, pp. 1–28.

Ezra, Elisabet and Terry Rowden (2006), 'General Introduction: What is Transnational Cinema?'. In Elisabeth Ezra and Terry Rowden (eds), *Transnational Cinema: The Film Reader*, London: Routledge, pp. 1–12.

Frost, Vicky (2012), 'The Bridge may make a killing with fans wanting Wallander or longing for Lund', *The Guardian*, 20 April, <http://www.theguardian.com/tv-and-radio/2012/apr/20/bridge-killing-wallander-lund>, last accessed 30 January 2014.

Gellner, Ernest (1983), *Nations and Nationalism*, Oxford: Blackwell.

Habermas, Jürgen (2001), *The Postnational Constellation: Political Essays*, Cambridge, MA: MIT Press.

Hedetoft, Ulf and Mette Hjort (2002), 'Introduction'. In Ulf Hedetoft and Mette Hjort (eds), *The Postnational Self: Belonging and Identity*, Minneapolis and London: University of Minnesota Press, pp. vii–xxxii.

Higbee, Will and Song Whee Lim (2010), 'Concepts of Transnational Cinema: Towards a Critical Transnationalism in Film Studies', *Transnational Cinemas* 1 (1): 7–21.

Higson, Andrew (2009 [2000]), 'The Limiting Imagination of National Cinema'. In Mette Hjort and Scott MacKenzie (eds), *Cinema and Nation*, London and New York: Routledge, pp. 63–74.

Hjort, Mette (2009 [2000]), 'Themes of nation'. In Mette Hjort and Scott MacKenzie (eds), *Cinema and Nation*, London and New York: Routledge, pp. 103–17.

Huntington, Samuel P. (2004), *Who are We? The Challenges to America's National Identity*, New York: Simon & Schuster.

Juergensmeyer, Mark (2002), 'The Paradox of Nationalism in a Global World'. In Ulf Hedetoft and Mette Hjort (eds), *The Postnational Self: Belonging and Identity*, Minneapolis and London: University of Minnesota Press, pp. 3–17.

Kääpä, Pietari (2011), *The Cinema of Mika Kaurismäki: Transvergent Cinemascapes, Emergent Identities*, Bristol and Chicago: Intellect.

Linde-Laursen, Anders (1995), *Det nationales natur: Studier i dansk-svenske relationer*, Copenhagen: Nordisk ministerråd.

Löfgren, Orvar (2000), 'Moving Metaphors'. In Per Olof Berg, Anders Linde-Laursen and Orvar Löfgren (eds), *Invoking a Transnational Metropolis: The Making of the Øresund Region*, Lund: Studentlitteratur, pp. 27–53.

Löfgren, Orvar (2002), 'The Nationalization of Anxiety: A History of Border Crossings'. In Ulf Hedetoft and Mette Hjort (eds), *The Postnational Self: Belonging and Identity*, Minneapolis and London: University of Minnesota Press, pp. 250–74.

Miller, Laura (2010), 'The Strange Case of the Nordic Detectives', *The Wall Street Journal*, 15 January, <http://online.wsj.com/news/articles/SB10001424052748703657604575004961184066300>, last accessed 30 January 2014.

O'Donovan, Gerard (2013), 'The Tunnel, Sky Atlantic', *The Telegraph*, 16 October, <http://www.telegraph.co.uk/culture/tvandradio/10384157/The-Tunnel-Sky-Atlantic.html>, last accessed 30 January 2014).

Sanders, Hanne (2006), *Nyfiken på Danmark – klokare på Sverige*, Göteborg and Stockholm: Makadam.

Scandinavian Crime Fiction (no author, 2014), <http://www.scandinaviancrimefiction.com/Sjowall_Wahloo.htm>, last accessed 30 January 2014.

Stigsdotter, Ingrid (2010), 'Crime Scene Skåne: Guilty Landscapes and Cracks in the Functionalist Façade in *Sidetracked, Firewall* and *One Step Behind*'. In Erik Hedling, Olof Hedling and Mats Jönsson (eds), *Regional Aesthetics: Locating Swedish Media*, Stockholm: National Library of Sweden, pp. 243–62.

Sundbärg, Gustav (1911), *Det svenska folklynnet: Aforismer*, Stockholm: P. A. Norstedt & söners förlag.

Tapper, Michael (2011), *Snuten i skymningslandet: Svenska polisberättelser i roman och film 1965–2010*, Lund: Nordic Academic Press.

The Guardian (no author, 2013), 'Sequel announced to Stieg Larsson's Girl With the Dragon Tattoo trilogy', 17 December, <http://www.theguardian.com/books/2013/dec/17/stieg-larsson-girl-with-dragon-tattoo-sequel>, last accessed 30 January 2014.

VisitDenmark (no author, 2014), 'The Art of Danish Hygge', <http://www.visitdenmark.com/en-us/denmark/culture/art-danish-hygge>, last accessed 30 January 2014.

Watson, Keith (2012), 'The Tunnel was The Bridge in anything but theme music', *Metro*, 16 October, <http://metro.co.uk/2013/10/16/the-tunnel-was-the-bridge-in-everything-but-theme-music-4149170/>, last accessed 30 January 2014.

7. STOCKHOLM NOIR: NEOLIBERALISM AND GANGSTERISM IN *EASY MONEY*

Michael Tapper

Every man is enemy to every man.
Thomas Hobbes *Leviathan* (1651/2004, p. 77)
Adios losers.
Jorge in Jens Lapidus's *Easy Money* (*Snabba cash*, 2006/2008, p. 467)

Young punks go from rags to riches, enjoy a brief time in the sun before their downfall in a hail storm of bullets. So goes the classical dark tale of gangsters such as Rico in *Little Caesar* (novel 1929, film 1931). The American motion picture code's specification that there should be no sympathy for the criminals suggested that there was a dangerous aspect in the attraction to these films (Black 1994: 108). It could very well be that the Motion Picture Producers and Distributors of America (MPPDA) president Will H. Hayes was averse from seeing the harsh social realities of the 1930s Depression depicted on the screen, including a corrupt legal system, but a danger of the gangster film was also its disturbing allegory on the daring entrepreneur that capitalism held up as a social ideal.

In essence, the gangster story is a warped Horatio Alger tale. Carl Freedman notes in his book *Versions of Hollywood Crime Cinema* (2013: 15–45) that it connects to the mystery of the origins of capitalism in what Karl Marx called 'primitive accumulation', the consciously repressed history about how common lands and natural resources were privatised and how companies, backed up by national armed forces, plundered non-European continents of their riches. The greedy and ruthless gangster's rise to social success is but a small-scale reflection of the genocides and the violent redistribution of wealth that gave birth to modern-day capitalism.

Gangsterism is also the ultimate expression of what the German sociologist Ferdinand Tönnies called *Gesellschaft*. While his other key concept *Gemeinschaft* describes the 'natural' personal relations and values often found in rural communities, *Gesellschaft* stands for the 'constructed' impersonal relations through business and formal interaction that characterise life in the urban capitalist era (Asplund 1991: 63–90). As national identity became a central issue in twentieth-century Europe – Fascism being the most extreme ideological project – gangsters and other social, legal and moral transgressors were often defined in popular culture as an alien intrusion of an otherwise idyllic *Gemeinschaft*.

Gangsters as Alien Invaders

Portraying crime as an issue of ethnicity and nationality diverted attention from the allegory of gangsterism and capitalism. In Swedish popular culture the alien criminal before the Second World War was either a foreign spy or an ethnic Other: Romani, Traveller, Jew and so on.[1] Then, as post-war Sweden came under American influence, the criminal became a juvenile delinquent led astray by the spell of wild jazz, even wilder rock and roll and a Hollywood fandom for gangsters on the silver screen.[2] In the film *Gangsterfilmen* ('The Gangster Film', 1974), crime as 'alien invasion' even becomes literal, as some American gangsters, led by the iconic actor Clu Gulager, terrorise a small Swedish village. The Vietnam War allegory is rather obvious.

The 1990s saw a new wave of juvenile delinquents on film. In films such as *Sökarna* ('The Searchers', 1993), *Nattbuss 807* ('Night Bus 807', 1997) and *9 millimeter* (1997), the children of the segregated immigrants and Swedish punks 'gone native' – that is, adopting the clothes, attributes, jargon and attitudes of the ethnic Other – come from the concrete suburbs to terrorise the inner cities. The hip-hop soundtrack, the *Scarface* (1983) film poster over the bed at some protagonist's apartment, the drugs and more caring sex and violence might have looked new, but they were essentially just props in the same old story of young savages speeding down the highway to hell.

The link between nationality/ethnicity and criminality also made a comeback in cop novels and films in the 1990s. Ystad in Henning Mankell's Wallander novels is frequently invaded by killers, drug smugglers and traffickers from the former Soviet empire, including Eastern Europe. Cop film series like *Beck* (1997–2010) and *Johan Falk* (1999–2013) had an abundance of immigrant and/or foreign criminals threatening an idyllic Sweden in narratives close to the political agenda of right-wing extremists (Tapper 2014: 205–63, 290–310).

One notable difference, though, was the complete absence of reform as a way out of crime. Relatives and friends were portrayed as helpless or resigned, and society was only discernible through its repressive institutions: the police force and the prison system. The lack of hope was a sign of the neoliberal era that had begun in the mid-1970s, when the liberal–conservative coalition took power in Sweden after more than forty years of Labour government and changed the course of crime politics back to the classical penal system. Sweden was by no means alone in this respect. The trend was an international one, and no matter which political colour the governments had, the backlash course was set (Jenkins 2006: 41–5, 236–42).

The Neoliberal Challenge

The war on crime that began in the United States in the 1960s spread throughout Europe with the rise of the neoliberal right in the 1970s and 80s. In crime politics, the criminal was again reduced from a citizen in need of reform to a risk factor or, worse, a deranged terrorist who had to be eliminated. Theories of the incorrigible bad seed as modern monster were backed up by the serial killer craze in popular culture and crime journalism. In Sweden, we got our very own serial killer in the infamous 1990s case of Thomas Quick, recently acquitted of all crimes due to two investigative journalists revealing the scandalous police investigations that led to his convictions.[3]

Dismantling the reformist penal code and correctional care has continued under governments of all stripes for the last few decades (Tham 1999: 98). Criminologists saw this return to the criminal policies of the pre-welfare state era as the end of an era permeated by progressive optimism (Andersson 2002: 8). It was also part of the neoliberal strategy of rolling back the welfare state, restoring old class barriers while eliminating the very notion of class in the political discourse. What began as a call for a counter-revolution in Henri Lepage's 1978 anti-Keynes manifesto *Tomorrow Capitalism* (Lepage 1980) became the new hegemony bible with Francis Fukuyama's 1992 *The End of History and the Last Man*. Echoing Margaret Thatcher more than a decade before, in 1990 Swedish Conservative Party chairman Carl Bildt declared capitalism triumphant and the neoliberal dismantling of the welfare state as 'the only political way'.

Since the early 1990s, Sweden has been socially transformed like no other nation in the Western world. A 2011 report from the Organisation for Economic Co-operation and Development (OECD) on inequality stated: 'The growth in inequality between 1985 and the late 2000s was the largest among all OECD countries, increasing by one third.' As indicated by the 2013 summer riots of Husby and other Stockholm suburbs, Sweden had become a nation segregated by class and ethnicity just like any other Western country.

It is a cliché to see the international success story of Swedish crime fiction as a fascination with the downfall of the Third Way, but with the neoliberal makeover Sweden has been brought down to an average social level in the EU. Therefore, it is more likely that audiences see Swedish crime as a mirror of their own societies, perhaps with a whiff of Nordic exoticism. The welfare system that used to be only lingers as a distant memory.

A Criminal Perspective

Criminal lawyer Jens Lapidus's choice to write crime fiction from the criminal's worm's-eye perspective is rather new in Sweden. The juvenile delinquent films had been all but moralist studies in the downfall of society's black sheep, and the detective novel that dominated crime literature until the mid-1960s had hardly evolved from the 1920s puzzle formula. As an international brand, Swedish crime fiction, from Sjöwall and Wahlöö's debut novel *Roseanna* in 1965 to the success of Henning Mankell in the 1990s, has been synonymous with cop protagonists looking for something rotten in the state of Sweden from a Marxist–Leninist point of view.[4]

In the 1970s, Kenneth Ahl – pen name of author Christer Dahl and ex-convict Lasse Strömstedt – had a brief success with tragicomic novels *Grundbulten* ('The Cornerstone', 1974) and *Lyftet* ('The Boost', 1976; filmed in 1978) about the life of small-time crooks and drug abusers. There was also the occasional autobiographical book written by celebrity jailbirds such as Olle Möller and Clark Olofsson. Still, no one could challenge the cop narrative until journalist Gellert Tamas published his bestselling documentary novel *Lasermannen – en berättelse om Sverige* ('The Laser Man – A Story About Sweden', 2002). In the book, Tamas portrays the racist sniper John Ausonius, named 'The Laser Man' by the media due to his use of a laser sight when shooting immigrants or Swedes of foreign origin in the winter of 1991–2. The book is a parallel narrative between the police investigation as the official story and Ausonius's own story, revealing the truth behind the crimes.

This contrasting of perspectives with a social context of the crimes became the model for the internationally successful author duo Roslund and Hellström – journalist Anders Roslund and ex-convict Börge Hellström – whose books have elaborated on Tamas's narrative structure. In novels such as *The Beast* (*Odjuret*, 2004) and *Box 21* (2005) they contrast the official story of the crime investigation, as seen from Inspector Ewert Grens's perspective, with the revelation of what really happened, as witnessed by the criminals under investigation. Jens Lapidus took it a step further and eliminated the cop perspective, focusing entirely on criminals in the Stockholm underworld.

By poetic coincidence, the first title *Easy Money* (*Snabba cash*) was published in 2006, the year of the election that put a liberal–conservative coalition in power, stepping up the neoliberal makeover into a more tangible change of the social system. The book is a portrait of criminality both as an integral part of capitalist economy and as a metaphor for its cynical narcissism and banal materialism. These two worlds of black and white economy connect in the neo-yuppie nightlife at Stureplan square in downtown Stockholm.

Easy Money, the Novel: Sons of Gordon Gekko

The novel and the film adaptation both open with a parallel narrative introducing the three protagonists. Johan 'JW' Westerlund is an economics student of humble small-town origins who pretends to be an upper-class insider in the reckless gang of wealthy young brats he hangs out with in Stockholm. The two others are Jorge Salinas Barrio, son of Chilean immigrants, an expert cocaine pusher, and Mrado Slovovic, a brutal henchman of the Serbian mafia. While the latter two are traditional ethnic outsiders who survive by their own individual wits, JW is the blind follower of neoliberal hegemony, a social careerist enamoured with the ideas of self-serving individualism and meritocracy. He strives to rise to the social elite by means of his entrepreneurial talent, but the very set-up of his social charade reveals that deep down he understands that breeding, rather than intellectual and creative merits, holds the keys to success.

In the novel he fully embraces the brats' nihilist credo, articulated by their favourite party rock song blurting out the lyrics on the stereo: 'They say I don't give a shit about anything, but I don't give a shit about that.' He approves, thinking: 'That's right. Why care about what a bunch of socialists think?' (Lapidus 2006/2008: 24–5).[5] The only object of reverence in his circle of acquaintances – calling them friends would be a misnomer – is Gordon Gekko and his 'greed is good' mantra in Oliver Stone's *Wall Street* (1987). However, they have left behind his 'lunch is for wimps' workaholism and money fetish.

As the sons of the Gekko generation, their life is one long holiday in the sun, indulging in consumerist pleasures with distinction, that is, flaunting products of exclusive brands as fetishes. Some pages are so packed with brand names that it looks more like a catalogue of merchandise than a novel. 'Brand', both as a noun and as a verb, is one of the key words in the corporate bullshit lingo of the brats.[6] Their brattish sociolect is a parallel to the creolised 'Rinkeby Swedish' of Jorge and Mrado, highlighting the two worlds as separate subcultures.[7] The concept of Swedishness as an ethnically unified normality is challenged, and the dividing line in society is class.

Easy Money portrays a Marxian world, populated by Hobbesian men.[8] Alienation and reification, commodity fetishism and the objectification of persons have created a wealthy breed of *homo economicus*, who makes choices detached from all concerns other than maximising his – male, white, heterosexual – profit.[9] Love and solidarity are flaws that victimise and ultimately kill the weak in the dog-eat-dog competition that, according to Thomas Hobbes, is in the fundamental nature of human relations. Consequently, JW's circle of narcissistic hedonists has no interest in other humans. Their only interest is looking out for Number One and the auto-erotic consumerist pleasures in which objects and humans are interchangeable.

To JW, this is, at first, a blessing in disguise, since it means that his true identity as an ordinary working-class 'loser' stays under the radar until he can fully transform himself into a believable brat who lives the deluxe lifestyle of his dreams. During a business trip to London with drug kingpin Abdulkarim this seems to finally come true. In between the negotiations for a major drug delivery, JW enjoys a shopping craze that the author describes like a sexual frenzy. Almost four pages is dedicated to a writing-in-tongues babble about the luxury brands that makes JW's hormones go bananas. In order to prolong the orgiastic joy for the rest of his life, JW finds a tax haven in the Isle of Man. There he registers a number of companies to turn the black drug money into a snow-white fortune and to keep it out of reach of the Swedish Tax Agency.

Like the classical gangster stories, everything seems to run smoothly until personal feelings – read: human weaknesses – interfere with the *Gesellschaft* that is brutal and impersonal crime. Rico's downfall in *Little Caesar* is caused by his homoerotic attachment to close friend Joe. Tony in *Scarface* (1932; even more pronounced in the 1983 remake) is destroyed because of his incestuous desire for his sister. In *Easy Money*, the road to ruin for the three protagonists during the arrival of the big drug shipment from England is also personal: revenge. Though they end up on opposite sides, both Jorge and Mrado are both motivated by their hatred for Serbian mafia boss Radovan, who has betrayed and degraded them. But ultimately, it is JW's act of revenge for his beloved and murdered sister Camilla, whose disappearance he investigates throughout the novel, which finally botches the job.

Easy Money, the Movie: Capitalism Hangover

Between the novel's publication in 2006 and the premiere of the film version in 2010 something happened that would affect the adaptation: the financial crash of 2008, soon deepening into a depression on the scale of the 1930s. Neoliberal guru Milton Friedman, whose reputation had been largely unchallenged since the late 1970s – not even during the 1990s financial crisis – came under attack from several respected names. They argued for a resurgence of John Maynard Keynes, the very economist Friedman wanted to kill off with his neoliberal monetarist model.

Economy professor James K. Galbraith, son of John Kenneth Galbraith, ironically used the 25th Annual Milton Friedman Distinguished Lecture in March 2008 to attack the hegemony based on Friedman's monetarist ideas that had ruled since the late 1970s.[10] Soon others followed, including Friedman's fellow laureate of the Nobel Memorial Prize in Economic Sciences, Paul Krugman, with a book and a series of columns in the *New York Times* beginning in January 2009.[11] The ideological climate was changing during the production of *Easy Money*, the movie.

In the film, JW (Joel Kinnaman) is no longer a missionary man for neoliberalism, but an outsider, observing and registering the shallow and sometimes mean-spirited games of the social elite as a camera, acting as if in a well-rehearsed play. We get no real insight into his true views and feelings, and it is suggested that he is a social chameleon, learning the rules but remaining noncommittal, distant and elusive. Self-consciously staging his character. The gap between his real life and the all-night party escapades with the brats is repeatedly stressed in the film.

He is introduced in a montage from a typical Saturday night fever with champagne, cocaine, a stripper-for-hire and a visit to some fancy downtown clubs. The morning after he sits naked on his bed in his small and sparsely furnished student room, brooding over the fact that he has only a small sum left in his bank account. Cue the film title. Later we watch him make the best out of his poverty by replacing the buttons on a shirt to make it look like a more expensive brand.

The scenes are not based on the novel, and neither are the many clips from his unglamorous work as an unregistered taxi driver, trying to avoid bumping into his brat friends when driving downtown. Furthermore, JW's success as a cocaine dealer is downplayed, and gone are both the shop-till-you-drop trip to London and the visit to the Isle of Man for the tax shelter scheme. JW the social trickster is downsized to JW the proletarian 'loser' seeking success before his downfall in crime. All in an act of desperation for social acceptance rather than cold and calculated greed.

If the JW in the novel could comment on the JW in the film, he would say that his celluloid alter ego is not dedicated to his task but a defeatist. The 2006 social careerist is utterly convinced about the unlimited possibilities of becoming a self-made Master of the Universe, but the 2010 insecure wannabe jet-setter is only anxious to go for the next fistful of money so he can keep up an act he really does not believe in. Consequently, the ideological beliefs JW articulates in the novel are in the film uttered by his upper-class friends and acquaintances. This adds to the film's destabilising of JW's ambitions and identity, making his position in the brat circle insecure and his world-views undecided.

This is highlighted in two scenes. The first one shows him talking mockingly to some aristocratic family portraits during a party at a mansion, trying out a social fantasy that he both longs for but also despises. The second scene follows a disastrous dinner with his upper-class girlfriend Sophie's parents, during which his web of lies about his background starts to crumble, much to his dismay. Afterwards, he breaks down and cries out to Sophie (Lisa Henni) in self-contempt, asking her why her parents or, indeed she, would care about him when they clearly want a brat of prime cut to fit with the family tradition. Only one in the brat circle seems to know the truth about his social status, and that is Niklas 'Nippe' Creuz (Joel Spira), who shamelessly exploits it. After a lecture at the university we see him pay JW for completing an exam assignment on his behalf. This foreshadows Nippe's theft and betrayal of JW in the sequel *Easy Money II* (*Snabba cash II*, 2012).

In the final showdown at the drug delivery (this time from Germany), not only JW but everybody is acting out of social desperation. The novel has Mrado (Dragomir Mrsic) degraded by his Serbian mob boss Radovan Kranjic (Dejan Cukic), and in seizing the drug shipment his plan is to get the sufficient financial muscle for a hostile takeover of the mob organisation. In the film, however, Kranjic attempts to kill Mrado, who therefore has no choice but to seize the drug shipment to finance a new life back in Serbia. He also has to consider his daughter, left in his care when her drug-addicted mother is deemed unfit by the social services.[12]

Likewise, Jorge in the novel is acting out of pure greed, lusting for the same high-society life that JW enjoys. In the film, Jorge (Matias Varela) has no such desires whatsoever. Instead, he seeks to secure money for his impoverished and pregnant sister, who has been abandoned by her boyfriend and now has to face taking care of their elderly mother as well as her soon-to-be-born baby all on her own. Even drug kingpin Abdulkarim (Mahmut Suvakci) gambles his entire remaining resources in a desperate act to rebuild his crime syndicate after his office is destroyed by Kranjic's hitmen.

All in all the novel is a 500-page colourful joyride of neoliberal hedonism, written as a hard-boiled gangster novel spiced with black comedy, social comment and a dark final twist. In contrast, the film is an all-bleak, sometimes grim, thriller, portraying crime in a gritty social context that updates the political subtext of the novel and pushes it to the foreground. Director Daniel Espinosa adapts the musicality of Jens Lapidus's James Ellroyish laconic telegram prose in his moderate use of intensified continuity and hand-held-camera (shaky-cam), sometimes inserting short flashback and flash forward cuts and moments heightened by subjective sound or a musical score.[13] Although it largely follows the novel's narrative, the film version is a radical departure, an adaptation that reinterprets the gangster story for a new social and political landscape.

There are no illusions in the film about JW's abilities to cross the class barriers or to make the big score, except perhaps initially in his own mind. If not earlier, the turning point seems to be Mrado's surprise first visit to JW. Looking back at his experience as a gangster, Mrado reflects on gangsterism in terms that fit perfectly with the neoliberal philosophy of JW's brat circle. It is, of course, all about greed, how it cuts the ties between friends and partners, turning the possibility of shared wealth into a cut-throat game of getting it all for yourself.

He envisions how everybody in the drug-smuggling operation starts to go behind each other's back, lie and betray and eventually fight each other to the death. In this business, he says, 'everybody takes care of themselves and the money first.' His monologue has an authentic ring to it through the fact that Dragomir Mrsic, who plays Mrado, was a bank-robber before going into acting.[14] Jorge continues on the subject in a later scene: 'Everyone is a son of a whore, no one gives a shit about anybody else.' The finale will prove them right. Well, almost. Ultimately, JW decides to help Jorge escape from the crime scene, thereby ending up in prison himself.

The Shape of Neoliberalism to Come

Easy Money fits Andrew Nestingen's (2008: 71–8) 'medium-concept' model in which art cinema and genre film mix while keeping the excess of style in high concept at bay, here a moderate intensified continuity. Perhaps more than any other crime film in the last two decades from the Nordic countries, it expressively displays the struggle between the values of solidarity, collective social bonds and equality from the twentieth-century welfare state with the self-interest, individualism and competitiveness of the neoliberal era in the new millennium. When compared to other Nordic gangster films, such as Nicolas Winding Refn's *Pusher* trilogy (1996, 2004, 2005), the social analysis of crime and entrepreneurialism is much deeper in *Easy Money*, connecting not only legal and illegal capitalism, but also how the two classes reflect each other.

The strong element of deception in the film heightens the staged qualities of the performances, inviting a *verfremdungseffekt* when looking at the social rituals of the bourgeois brat circle and the criminal precariat. Through JW's social status as outsider in both worlds we become aware of *Gesellschaft*: the formal, almost theatrical construction of the relations, relying on master suppression techniques and latent violence respectively. They are two extremes of the social Darwinist society that is the effect of the neoliberal project, and JW's tragedy is his ambition to comply. In following the ideological dichotomy of 'winners' and 'losers', he therefore must reject his love for Sophie, since she can never love a 'loser', and deceive his only friend Jorge since he is even lower on the 'loser' scale.

More clearly than Lapidus's novel, the film *Easy Money* illustrates the dystopian prophesies sketched by cultural historian Christopher Lasch in his seminal book *The Culture of Narcissism* (1979/1981: 218–36). The new bourgeoisie break away from the old one's education, discipline, work ethic and social responsibilities to a culture of stupidity, leisure, hedonism and self-realisation, much like the classical gangster. At the same time, financial capitalism is established and with it a new Klondyke of accumulating money disconnected from labour and production. In the film, one of the brats comes up with what he thinks is a great business idea at a party. He propose that they should start a company, but not to produce or sell anything, only to use for buying consumer products without having to pay VAT. Also, the only brat-parent we see at work is a man who runs an investment bank willing to go into business with the shady drug smugglers that JW represents. Thus, the title *Easy Money* becomes a metaphor not only for crime in the traditional sense but for crime as the very fabric of a society that promotes nihilism.

A Tale of Two Trilogies

JW, as the working-class chameleon with access to capitalism on both sides of the law, is clearly the key to the success of *Easy Money*. Without his social transgressions the connection between neoliberalism and gangsterism is gone, and with it the innovative thriller element that made the film a topical hit. That is unfortunately what happens in the later instalments of the two trilogies.

Lapidus's two following titles in what was eventually called his Stockholm Noir trilogy, *Never Fuck Up* (*Aldrig fucka upp*, 2008) and *Life Deluxe* (*Livet deluxe*, 2011), had nothing to do with the plot of the original novel and were only loosely related to the cast of characters in *Easy Money*. In *Never Fuck Up* we are introduced to three new characters in parallel narratives: drug-peddler Mahmud, ex-mercenary Niklas and volatile undercover cop Hägerström. They come together in a hit against Serbian mob boss Radovan Kranjic's *Eyes Wide Shut*-style brothel for the social elite.

Life Deluxe is a bit closer to *Easy Money*, combining two classic gangster genre scenarios: Jorge doing a 'last big job' while the smooth financial operator JW is getting involved with the Serbian mafia through a dangerous love affair with the heiress to mobster boss Radovan Kranjic, his daughter Natalie. In between novels two and three, Lapidus also wrote the graphic novel *Gängkrig 145* ('Gang War 145', 2009), illustrated by Peter Bergting, about Mahmud's brutal revenge on a gang that raped his sister.

Titled *Easy Money II*, the second instalment of the film series tried to stay on the course set by the original film. This is emphasised stylistically by director Babak Najafi, who kept the intensified continuity, handheld camera and inserted cuts of flashbacks and flash forwards from Daniel Espinosa's film. Even the lighting, colour schemes and parts of the film music are the same.

However, the criticism of the neoliberal project is lost, save for a subplot in which the wealthy Nippe steals a financial management computer program that JW has invented and sells it for a substantial profit under his own name. When JW confronts Nippe, the issue of class is out in the open. Tauntingly, Nippe argues the logic of his crime based on his superior standing in society, perhaps even superior genes. Moments later, JW strikes him down and decides to live his life as an outlaw.

The rest of the film – a remix of bits and pieces from all three novels – is a somewhat conventional thriller about the hunt for mobster boss Radovan Kranjic's ten millions lost to Jorge in a scam. Superficially, the story looks rather like a Quentin Tarantino or Guy Ritchie romp, in which hard-boiled macho crooks are caught in a black comedy of petty criminal mastermind schemes all gone wrong, ending in a laughable and bloody mess. However, playing it straight and emphasising the devastating consequences of crime on just about everybody and their families maintains a social criticism, if yet of a smaller scope.

Crime is never a glamorous subculture of cool poseurs in *Easy Money I* and *II*, only a no-win game for social desperados who delude themselves into thinking they can get a quick fix to upper-class heaven. Here, everybody ends up dead or traumatised for life. No one climbs the social ladder, nor are we inclined to believe that they could ever make such a journey.

That fuels Jorge's escapist dreams in the third film, *Easy Money – Life Deluxe* (*Snabba cash – Livet deluxe*, 2013), of starting a new life at some Garden of Eden much like the fairy-tale ending of *Fast Five* (2011), the fifth instalment of the *Fast and Furious* film series. *Easy Money*, part three, consists of two loosely connected plots. One follows Jorge's attempt of making 'the last big job', inspired by the spectacular Helicopter Robbery against G4S Cash Services' safe depot in Västberga, south of Stockholm, on 23 September 2009.[15] The other follows the novel's *Godfather* pastiche, portraying the struggle of Natalie Kranjic (Malin Buska) to keep control of the Serbian mafia when her father Radovan is murdered.

In some scattered clips we also see JW's efforts to find out the truth about his sister in Los Angeles, a subplot obviously constructed to fit actor Joel Kinnaman's busy Hollywood schedule. The sloppy plotting substitutes JW with undercover cop Martin (Martin Wallström), whose function as the object of Natalie's affections is contrived to say the least, and there are numerous logical mishaps and continuity errors. Director Jens Jonsson also abandons the style of the previous instalments for a conventional narrative and a dull style. It all ends in a montage of short scenes that stitches the loose ends together with no intellectual logic nor any emotional impact. The features that made the first and second instalment of the trilogy engaging and topical as comments on Sweden as a neoliberal society are now diluted into a quaint old-fashioned crime spectacle.

Cultural Impact

Easy Money was an economic and critical success, both as a novel and as a film adaptation. It was well received when it came out in 2006, but the success took a new spin when it was published in a paperback edition in 2008, the year after the outbreak of the financial crisis. By 2010 it had sold 600,000 copies in Sweden alone, and it was subsequently translated and distributed in thirty more countries.[16] Together with Stieg Larsson's Millennium trilogy, Jens Lapidus's Stockholm Noir trilogy represented the apex of Swedish crime fiction as both a national and international cultural phenomenon.

The original novel turned into a cultural phenomenon that shifted the genre's focus from cops to criminals. For instance, Roslund and Hellström's later novels – *Three Seconds* (*Tre sekunder*, 2009) and *Two Soldiers* (*Två soldater*, 2012) – move cop protagonist Ewert Grens almost to the margins of stories about criminals victimised and abandoned by society, told from their points of view. A series of best-selling true-crime books related to gangland violence in Sweden also followed, most popular being journalists Lasse Wierup and Matti Larsson's *Svensk Maffia* ('Swedish Mafia', 2007; a second volume was published in 2010), which mapped organised crime.

The 2010 film adaptation was also a success, perhaps an even bigger hit than the novel. Not only did it sell more than 600,000 tickets in Sweden, which is exceptional for a film rated for viewers of age 15 or above, it was also shown to great acclaim at several film festivals and was commercially released in sixteen other countries.[17] Add to that the revenues from the TV and Blu-ray/DVD market.

Coinciding with the premiere of the film was the introduction of a new magazine called *Skurk* ('Crook'), writing about crime from the criminal's perspective, and the premiere of a new hit TV show dedicated to crime journalism, *Veckans brott* ('Crime Weekly'), attracting more than a million viewers per programme.[18] Thus, crime had become a mainstream attraction as entertainment and infotainment from the perspectives of both cop and criminal. There were even some indications of criminals embracing the trend. Lapidus, who lectures on law at police seminars, claimed that many officers shared the experience of finding a 1983 *Scarface* poster, a copy of *Easy Money* and one of *Svensk Maffia* whenever they entered the home of a young suspect.[19]

Easy Money connected crime with capitalism, gangsterism with the neoliberal project, in a narrative that captivated the audience at a time of crisis in the monetary system. Although the literary follow-ups and the movie sequels were of a lesser quality, the original novel and film had a profound impact on the genre in Sweden.

Notes

1. For a more elaborate treatment of the crime genre's evolution in Sweden during and after the Second World War, see Tapper 2014: 46–59.
2. A special history of the Swedish post-war juvenile delinquency film 1942–62 is Bengtsson 1998.
3. Råstam 2012/2013 and Josefsson 2013 (to be published in English, title as yet

unknown). The books are the source of a British documentary on the Thomas Quick case currently being made by Brian Hill; see Tagesson 2014.
4. For a history of the Swedish cop novel and film, see Tapper 2014.
5. My translation. In the original text he says *sossar*, which can be interpreted as socialists in general but is often used specifically as a derogatory term for social democrats and their egalitarian politics.
6. Lars Melin, associate professor in Swedish at Stockholm University, mapped in a book what he called corporate bullshit as part of a sociolect spoken mostly in downtown Stockholm by economists and the financial elite. It came out the very same year as *Easy Money* and could be used as a grammar and dictionary of Lapidus's novel. See Melin 2006.
7. Rinkeby is a name of a Stockholm suburb in which almost 100 per cent of the population are immigrants or Swedish citizens of immigrant descent. Several studies of multi-ethnic or creolised Swedish have taken place there, as well as in many other suburbs with a significant share of the population of immigrant descent. 'Rinkeby Swedish' is also called 'Shobree Swedish' after a common creolised expression.
8. Freedman 2013: 55–67. Robin 2009.
9. Reification, see Lukács 1923/1967.
10. Galbraith 2008.
11. Krugman 2008 and 2009.
12. In the novel the drug shipment is secretly financed by Radovan through his employee Nenad, who in turn controls drug kingpin Abdulkarim. However, at the drug delivery for Abdulkarim, Nenad has decided to join forces with Mrado. The film has a different scenario, with Abdulkarim as a competitor to Radovan.
13. Intensified continuity, see Bordwell 2002.
14. Wiman 2010.
15. Stengård and Håkansson 2009.
16. Natt och Dag 2011.
17. According to the Swedish Film Database, administered by the Swedish Film Institute, *Easy Money* sold 608,371 cinema tickets in Sweden. Among previous successes for crime movies rated 15, only Bo Widerberg's *Man on the Roof* (*Mannen på taket*, 1976) and Kjell Sundvall's *Jägarna* ('The Hunters', 1996) had surpassed *Easy Money*, with more than 700,000 tickets sold. See <http://www.sfi.e/sv/statistik/> (accessed 1 February 2014). For data about the film being released in other countries, see the International Movie Database (IMDb) at <http://www.imdb.com/title/tt1291652/releaseinfo?ref_=tt_ql_9> (accessed 1 February 2014).
18. See Mediemätning i Skandinavien's (MMS) web site at <http://www.mms.se/#> (accessed 1 February 2014).
19. Natt och Dag 2011.

References

Andersson, Robert (2002), *Kriminalpolitikens väsen*, Stockholm: Kriminologiska institutionen.
Asplund, Johan (1991), *Essä om Gemeinschaft och Gesellschaft*, Göteborg: Korpen.
Bengtsson, Bengt (1998), *Ungdom i fara*, Uppsala: Stockholms Universitet.
Black, Gregory D. (1994), *Hollywood Censored: Morality Codes, Catholics, and the Movies*, Cambridge: Cambridge University Press.
Bordwell, David (2002), 'Intensified Continuity: Visual Style in Contemporary American

Film', *Film Quarterly* 55 (3): 16–28, <http://academic.csuohio.edu/kneuendorf/frames/editing/Bordwell02.pdf>, accessed 5 October 2014.

Freedman, Carl (2013), *Versions of Hollywood Crime Cinema: Studies in Ford, Wilder, Coppola, Scorsese, and Others*, Bristol: Intellect/Chicago: The University of Chicago Press.

Fukuyama, Francis (1992), *Historiens slut och den sista människan*, original title: *The End of History and the Last Man*, Swedish translation: Staffan Andræ, Stockholm: Norstedts.

Galbraith, James K. (2008), 'The Collapse of Monetarism and the Irrelevance of the New Monetary Consensus', lecture at Marietta College in Marietta, Ohio, retrieved on PDF from the University of Texas at <http://utip.gov.utexas.edu/papers/CollapseofMonetarismdelivered.pdf>, 29 January 2014.

Hobbes, Thomas (1651/2004), *Leviathan Or The Matter, Forme & Power of a Commonwealth Ecclesiasticall and Civill*, New York: Barnes & Noble.

Krugman, Paul (2008), *The Return of Depression Economics and the Crisis of 2008*, New York: W. W. Norton.

Krugman, Paul (2009) 'Fighting Off Depression', *The New York Times*, 5 January, <http://www.nytimes.com/2009/01/05/opinion/05krugman.html>, accessed 28 January 2014.

Jenkins, Philip (2006), *Decade of Nightmares: The End of the Sixties and the Making of Eighties America*, Oxford: Oxford University Press.

Josefsson, Dan (2013), *Mannen som slutade ljuga*, Stockholm: Lind & Co.

Lapidus, Jens (2006/2008), *Snabba cash*, (*Easy Money*), paperback edn, Stockholm: Månpocket.

Lapidus, Jens (2008), *Aldrig fucka upp*, (*Never Fuck Up*), paperback edn 2013, Stockholm: Månpocket.

Lapidus, Jens (2011), *Livet deluxe*, (*Life Deluxe*), paperback edn 2012, Stockholm: Månpocket.

Lapidus, Jens and Peter Bergting (2009), *Gängkrig 145*, Stockholm: Wahlström & Widstrand.

Lasch, Crisopher (1979), *The Culture of Narcissism: American Life in an Age of Diminishing Expectations*, New York: W. W. Norton.

Lepage, Henri (1980), *I morgon capitalism*, original title: *Demain le capitalism* (1978), English title: *Tomorrow Capitalism*, Swedish translation: Hans Granqvist, Stockholm: Ratio.

OECD (2011), 'Divided We Stand: Why Inequality Keeps Rising. Country Note: Sweden', <http://www.oecd.org/sweden/49564868.pdf>, accessed 21 January 2014.

Lukács, Georg (1923/1967), 'Reification and the Consciousness of the Proletariat', *History and Class Consciousness*, London: Merlin Press, 1967, published on the web at <http://www.marxists.org/archive/lukacs/works/history/hcc05.htm>, accessed 24 January 2014.

Melin, Lars (2006), *Corporate Bullshit: Om språket mitt i city*, updated edn, Stockholm: Schibsted.

Natt och Dag, Niklas (2011), 'Jens Lapidus', *King*, Spring, <http://www.kingmagazine.se/bloggar/kulturkrock/20120816/jens-lapidus/>, accessed 25 January 2014.

Nestingen, Andrew (2008), *Crime and Fantasy in Scandinavia: Fiction, Film, and Social Change*, Seattle: University of Washington Press.

Råstam, Hannes (2012/2013), *Thomas Quick: The Making of a Serial Killer*, originaltitel: *Fallet Thomas Quick: Att skapa en seriemördare* (2012), Edinburgh: Canongate Books.

Robin, Corey (2009), 'The First Counter-Revolutionary', *The Nation*, 19 October, <http://www.thenation.com/article/first-counter-revolutionary?page=0,0>, accessed 31 January 2014.

Stengård, Mikael and Catarina Håkansson (2009), 'Här närmar sig polishelikoptern den rånade värdedepån i Västberga, men en dag för sent', *Aftonbladet*, 24 September, <http://www.aftonbladet.se/nyheter/article12009759.ab>, accessed 30 January 2014.

Tagesson, Eric (2014), 'Quick-skandalen blir film', *Aftonbladet*, 14 January.

Tapper, Michael (2014), *Swedish Cops: From Sjöwall & Wahlöö to Stieg Larsson*, Bristol: Intellect.

Tham, Henrik (1999), 'Lag och ordning som vänsterprojekt: Socialdemokratins kriminalpolitik'. In Anne-Marie Begler (ed.), *8 reflektioner om kriminalpolitik*, (BRÅ-rapport 1999: 9), Stockholm: BRÅ, pp. 97–117.

Wiman, Erik (2010), 'Stjärnan dömd för grovt rån', *Aftonbladet*, 23 January, <http://www.aftonbladet.se/nojesbladet/article12116805.ab>, accessed 30 January 2014.

8. THE PRIVATE LIFE OF THE PRIME MINISTER? POLITICS, DRAMA AND DOCUMENTARY IN *PÄÄMINISTERI* AND *PALME*

Anneli Lehtisalo

In spring 2003, Finland's first female Prime Minister was inaugurated. The leader of the Centre Party, Anneli Jäätteenmäki, led her party to an electoral victory by challenging the ruling Social Democratic Party and its leader, Paavo Lipponen. In election debates, Jäätteenmäki accused Lipponen of pulling Finland into the US-led alliance against Iraq, basing her information on the so-called Iraq memorandum compiled by the Ministry for Foreign Affairs. However, it was revealed that the Iraq memorandum was a classified report. The advisor of the President, Martti Manninen, who had faxed the information to Jäätteenmäki, was accused of violating official secrets. Manninen was dismissed from his post, and, only a couple of months into her appointment, Jäätteenmäki was forced to resign from the premiership. After six years, this political scandal re-emerged in public when the Finnish Broadcast Company (YLE) screened a dramatised account of the incident, *Pääministeri* ('The Prime Minister', Finland, 2009). Although the drama did not further inflame political disputes, it attracted the public's attention. It was estimated that the drama reached nearly 700,000 viewers, which is a substantial figure in Finland (Anonymous 2009).

In autumn 2012, an even more dramatic true story was screened in cinemas throughout Sweden. The documentary *Palme* (Sweden, 2012) tells the life story of the famous Swedish politician and former Prime Minister Olof Palme. The film deals with the traumatic national memories that have lingered in Sweden since the assassination of Palme in the winter of 1986. The assassination shocked Swedish society and is still an unsolved crime Interest in Palme may partly explain why the film *Palme* attracted an unusually large audience for a documentary – over 240,000 cinema admissions in autumn 2012 (Swedish Film Institute 2013: 7, 9).[1]

Palme and *Pääministeri* can be considered exceptional films in their respective national contexts. Politics and public figures have not been a typical subject for contemporary feature films in Sweden or in Finland, although similar topics have thrived in Anglo-American media culture. Films like *The Deal* (UK, 2003), *Looking for Fidel* (USA, Brazil, 2004), *The Queen* (UK, France, Italy, 2006) and *Margaret* (UK, 2009) have depicted the political past and present by portraying the experiences or actions of known politicians in different generic modes, such as documentary dramas, documentaries and fictional biographical films. In Sweden, a few examples include documentaries *H:r Landshövding* (Sweden, 2008), *Ebbe – The Movie* (Sweden, 2009), *Facing Genocide – Khieu Samphan and Pol Pot* (Sweden, 2010) and *Palme*. The film *Palme* differentiates itself in the Swedish context with its extremely controversial main character and sensitive topic. In Finland, as well, politicians have rarely been depicted in recent years. The documentaries *Eden Pastora – Commandant 'Zero'* (Finland, 2006), *Within the Limits* (Finland, 2009), *In the Shadow of Doubt* (Finland, 2009), *Rouva Presidentti* (Finland, 2012) and the documentary drama *Pääministeri* exemplify such Finnish films. Although the docudramatic mode was not unprecedented in Finland (e.g. *Piru ja peijooni*, Finland, 2008), *Pääministeri* exemplified a new, international trend in television production by depicting a dramatised account of a living person and a relatively recent political incident. The scriptwriters of *Pääministeri*, Timo Harakka and Antti Karumo, also admitted that they aimed to adopt the model of present British documentary drama – in line with *The Deal* or *The Queen* – in Finnish television (Wessman 2009).

Pääministeri and *Palme* seem to stem from different generic traditions. The former follows the conventions of a documentary drama (docudrama) as it portrays a real event by using actors and mixes facts with fictitious episodes (on docudrama see Paget 2011: 94, 120–1). The latter is a documentary which uses conventional materials for a documentary, such as archive film, news footage, photographs, interviews and voiceover narration, to tell an evidenced life story encompassing nearly sixty years (on the conventions see Nichols 2010: 7–8, 14). However, by attempting to tell a true story about the past, the films exemplify how the generic lines between documentary and docudrama are becoming increasingly blurred (e.g. Paget 2011: 3–5; Nichols 2010: 15–16).

Brian Winston (2013a: 8; see also Paget 2011: 3–4) employs the idea of a continuum to define documentary and, at the same time, to describe how audiovisual texts are related to real subjects and events. One end of the continuum is unambiguously factual without any intervention by filmmakers, including, for instance, footage from surveillance cameras. The other end of the continuum is fiction featuring actors and invented events. A continuum is a good way of comprehending the heterogeneous audiovisual modes which depict the real world. One can place different non-fiction texts on the continuum: documentaries with 'permitted interventions', that is, arrangements or direction from filmmakers; documentaries based on research or acquired evidence, such as historical documentaries; and docudramas with actors and invented scenes. According to Winston (2013a: 8), the crucial element which marks the place of a text on the continuum is a witness, because a witness, be it the witness of the camera, a filmmaker or an interviewee, demonstrates that there is a claim on the real in the text. Thus, a witness is the essential element of a documentary (see also Nichols 2010: 8, 12). As the number of unwitnessed and completely imaginative elements in the text grows, it comes increasingly closer to fiction.

One should not imagine the continuum as a straight line; rather, it is fragmented. Winston finds the following two problematic non-fiction types: filming 'the possible', in other words, 'typical actions by non-actors without the authority of witness'; and reality television, which depicts 'previously unwitnessed situations created by film makers' (Winston 2013a: 8). I suggest that the place of non-fiction texts on the continuum is fluctuating according to how witnessed elements are included in a film and how they are combined with unwitnessed or imaginative elements. This applies particularly to the genre of docudrama, which comprises different combinations, including documented reconstructions and based-on-the-true-story films with invented storylines (Paget 2011: 94–5, 120–1). Nonetheless, the place of the documentary is fluctuating as well. The style and narration in a documentary can, of course, be understood as essential parts of a documentary genre (Winston 2013b: 95; Nichols 2010: 12, 14). However, stylistic and narrative solutions can entail unwitnessed meanings and excess of meanings which are not documented. Circulating structural patterns, motifs and narrative modes, in particular, may bring a documentary closer to docudrama.

The similarities between the films *Pääministeri* and *Palme* illuminate this point. Unlike *Pääministeri*, there are no actors, reconstructed events or fictitious elements in *Palme*, but the construction of the main character follows a similar narrative pattern in both films. In addition, both films recycle narrative modes typical of fictitious stories, that is, melodramatic and tragic modes. Hence, as noted by some Swedish film critics (Engström 2012; Eklund 2012; Lindblad 2012), *Palme* is akin to fictitious drama with its affective plot and skilfully characterised protagonist. *Palme* can be productively considered what Paget calls a 'dramatic documentary' (Paget 2011: 134), which tells a coherent, dramatised story about a person, and could thus be placed on the continuum next to docudrama. The understated style of *Pääministeri*, in turn, makes the film appear more like a matter-of-fact historical reconstruction in a television documentary than a theatrical film with high production values such as *The Queen*. Eventually, however, a film's place on the generic continuum is determined by public framing and the film's reception (see also Winston 2013a: 9).

Hence, it is a challenging task to fix the place of *Pääministeri* or *Palme* on the continuum. At the same time, it raises interesting questions regarding how these multifaceted audiovisual texts depict the political past and present, how narrative patterns and modes are used to create an account of a known political figure, and how different generic means may affect the accounts. I will discuss these questions in detail below.

The Dramatised Past

Both *Pääministeri* and *Palme* rely on the assumption that the audience is familiar with the story. As such, the films face the challenge of transforming known facts into an interesting whole in order to appeal to viewers. The political events in the spring of 2003 in Finland and the life of Palme have to be narrativised. The coherence in the films is created by using conventional modes of narration, which is not uncommon in stories based on real events (Lehtisalo 2011: 156; Taylor 2002: 114–15). Steven N. Lipkin (2002: 5–11) suggests that the basic mode in an Anglo-American docudrama is melodrama. Typically there is a victim, suffering, pathos and confrontations between the good and the bad (on American melodrama see Williams 2001: 19, 28–41). The melodramatic mode entails a moral judgement, which is also the main argument of a docudrama (Lipkin 2002: 4–5).

One can find a melodramatic structure in *Pääministeri* as well. Pathos is mainly suppressed in the film, as are all emotions, but Anneli Jäätteenmäki (Jonna Järnefelt) is presented as a suffering victim. Jäätteenmäki is like an ambitious 'good girl' who wants to succeed in everything. This is expressed through a metaphoric fictitious subplot in which Jäätteenmäki makes friends with a waitress Satu and her daughter. The daughter does apparatus gymnastics and is desperate to be number one – a figure who parallels Jäätteenmäki whose ambition is explained as originating in her upbringing.

The plot sets a group of male politicians as Jäätteenmäki's opponents. They form a suspicious, secret clique which even includes Jäätteenmäki's own party member, the long-time politician Mauri Pekkarinen (Pertti Koivula), as well as the unseen, acting Prime Minister Lipponen. The male politicians comply with the politics of the USA, which is about to attack Iraq. Jäätteenmäki – among other women figures in the film – opposes a war alliance with the USA. The melodramatic confrontation was probably invented, since the real Pekkarinen strongly and publicly opposed the film's depiction of these events (Nordman 2009). In the film, the clique eventually wins, as all attention is focused on

Jäätteenmäki's malpractices, not on Lipponen's unauthorised promises to the USA. According to *Pääministeri*, Jäätteenmäki is a victim of both her own ambition and the clique, and she must suffer the shame of resignation even though she was right in her claims about the secret pact with the USA and in opposing the war in Iraq. This is underlined by ending the film with news footage of violent actions in Iraq.

Palme, in turn, recycles the narrative mode of tragedy (on modern tragedy, see Felski 2008). Palme's life is portrayed in chronological order starting from his birth and ending with his funeral. As such, it is a tragic story about the public career of a magnanimous upper-class man who sets out to make the world a better place but who ends up making excuses for the malpractices of elite politicians and the Swedish Social Democratic Party. In parallel, the story of the rise and the decline of the Swedish welfare state unfolds. The film portrays how Sweden developed into a modern welfare state during the 1950s and 1960s under the leadership of the Swedish Social Democratic Party: living standards rose and there were advances in equality issues and social welfare. Young Palme is introduced as a protégé and successor of the long-time Prime Minister Tage Erlander. Together with his young male colleagues, 'Palme's boys', he pushed reforms through. Palme is depicted as a leading figure in the peace and anti-racism movements, who enhanced Sweden's fame as a modern model state in the world – although Palme's critical statements about the Vietnam War broke diplomatic relations with the USA for several years.

However, as one of Palme's colleagues, Anders Ferm, tells in an interview in the film, Palme together with his party were guilty of hubris: everything had gone so well for Sweden for so long that they lost their sense of reality. Palme himself is portrayed as being arrogant and aggressive towards his political opponents. With his superb rhetorical skills he could offend them publicly because he enjoyed performing in public and wanted to win. Yet, according to the film, his worst offence was making excuses and lying for his colleagues and for his party when different kinds of malpractices were revealed by the media.

The plot of *Palme* is constructed in such a way that it forms a tragic line from Palme's success to his fall, from the successful days of his career, to his political miscalculations and the increasing hatred towards him, and, eventually, to his death. Obviously Palme must have experienced some difficulties in his early career, but problems and obstacles are introduced only later in the plot. Although Palme is portrayed as an active agent in history, it seems that he could not escape his fate. His destiny is implied several times in the plot, starting from the beginning when Palme is asked in an interview how he would like to be remembered after his death. Later, Palme is compared with President John F. Kennedy. The tragedy of Palme is reiterated in the story of the welfare state, as history seems to unfold inevitably from the golden years of the boom to the era of unemployment, xenophobia and the harsh values of neoliberalism in the 1980s.

Both films make a pessimistic argument about politics. Although the films portray active agents in history, the results seem frustrating. Palme's era of reforms ended up in stagnation, while Jäätteenmäki compromised her morals while trying to win the elections. The narrative modes of the films effectively underline the argument that the political system is somehow defective. The melodramatic mode in *Pääministeri* shows how real political issues were superseded by scheming and how an enthusiastic politician became the victim of such scheming. The tragic history depicted in *Palme* demonstrates the fall of the sublime cause, the sad end of Palme's life as well as the Swedish welfare state.

Creating the Mystery

In both films the story is built on the main character, and as such, their characterisations sustain the plots. The characterisations create suspense in the plots – as the end of each story is already well known, there would not be much suspense otherwise. In *Palme*, a mystery is introduced: who was Olof Palme, actually? In *Pääministeri*, the gradually forming characterisation of Anneli Jäätteenmäki reveals the motives underlying her actions.

The central question in *Palme* is why this brilliant young man from a rich upper-class family joined the Social Democratic Party. Was he an opportunist who only wanted to make a career? Was his ambition best realised by following the victorious party and its popular leader Erlander? The question is never really answered in the film, because the narration does not offer any information about Palme's innermost thoughts and feelings. Only Palme's publicly known ideas are presented, as the film usually allows Palme to speak for himself. In his eloquent and affective speeches, he talks about democracy, social and racial equality and solidarity. Yet, doubts about his motives remain. The doubt is further sustained by Palme's friend, Lars Edelstam, who speculates in an interview that Palme would have been happier in a right-wing government.

The unresolved mystery sustains the tension in the main character which makes the character fascinating. Otherwise the viewer is offered plenty of information about Palme the politician. He is characterised through his own words in past interviews, by the voiceover narrator, by his family, friends, colleagues and by political opponents. Palme's sons and wife share a few anecdotes and peculiarities about Palme's private life. The film also includes home movies from the 1950s and 1960s. However, viewers never find out whether Palme had other interests besides politics. Despite a round and interesting characterisation, Palme remains remote to viewers. Because there are only insinuations of Palme's private thoughts or feelings, viewers never really get to know Olof Palme, the person behind his public persona.

Pääministeri employs the means of docudrama in the characterisation of the protagonist, that is, invented scenes and actors' performances. In the film, Anneli Jäätteenmäki is also marked by tension. An outside tension is caused by her gender. Jäätteenmäki is seen in a party meeting arguing with her male colleagues. They want her to use 'feminine softness' in the election campaign, but Jäätteenmäki is more interested in hard topics such as foreign policy because she sees it as a way to challenge the ruling party, the Social Democrats. Pekkarinen denigrates Jäätteenmäki's skills in foreign policy. According to Pekkarinen, an agreement was made with the opponents that such topics would be left out of the election debates. The patronising Matti Vanhanen (Mikko Reitala) wants to protect and support Jäätteenmäki, but she refuses his help, stating that she is the leader of the party and thus is responsible.

In addition to external pressures, there is an inner tension in her character as well. Jäätteenmäki is portrayed as a kind of dual personality. On the one hand, she is a strong-willed and ambitious party leader, who unscrupulously presses Manninen (Markku Huhtamo) to reveal the classified documents to her. On the other hand, she is actually worried about the war in Iraq and feels guilty about her suspicious actions. She is even too timid to exchange a few words with Kofi Annan when President Tarja Halonen (Pirkko Saisio) offers her mobile phone to Jäätteenmäki in the middle of her conversation. This duality is underlined by the use of mirrors in the visual composition, a motif which recurs three times in the film.

Although *Palme*'s portrayal relies on documented material and interviews, whereas more artistic licence is used in *Pääministeri*, it is interesting to note that the characterisation in both films is constructed on the pattern of tension in the main character. It is common for fictional biopics to feature a pattern in which tension manifests due to the contradiction between the private and the public role of a protagonist (e.g. Lehtisalo 2011: 26-9, 392-3). Such tension aims to explain – while also simultaneously adding to – the myth of a famous person, including how she or he is extraordinary and ordinary at the same time. In addition, the depiction of a private life is considered as an attraction which is expected to appeal to audiences (Lehtisalo 2011: 391-2). *Pääministeri* and *Palme* both eschew the questions of private life. Jäätteenmäki and Palme are portrayed as having family lives that do not cause any problems or affect their public roles. The focus in both films is on the public person. The tensions which sustain the characterisations and the plots stem from society, as Palme's challenge in the film is his 'suspicious' class status, and Jäätteenmäki – in addition to her inner contradictions – is plagued by the expectations of her gender role.

The generic conventions employed in the films generate different relations between a viewer and the protagonist. In *Pääministeri*, with the help of the invented scenes and the actor Jonna Järnefelt's performance, viewers are able to feel close to and sympathise with Jäätteenmäki. The camera closely follows the actor Jonna Järnefelt who subtly expresses the inner tensions, private feelings and thoughts. Palme, in turn, remains a remote figure, but the interrogative structure in *Palme* makes him the centre of all attention. The narrator asks the elementary question about Palme and the plot offers different answers witnessed by the interviewees and archive films: all the interviewees talk about him, and there is no action without him. Palme in *Palme* is reminiscent of the national heroes in George F. Custen's study on classical biopics from the studio era, as Palme is like the remote sun around which other characters, the narrator, and viewers as well, revolve (Custen 1992: 159). Nevertheless, the ways in which viewers are positioned in relation to the protagonists in the films entail a curiously similar argument regarding political agency. Political power seems to be out of reach of viewers, in the hands of a distant, but charismatic leader like Palme, or steered by the secret clique who make important decisions and leave Jäätteenmäki, and the viewers along with her, aside.

Engaging the Audience

As films based on real events and persons, both *Pääministeri* and *Palme* face the challenge of transforming familiar facts into an attractive story. Known facts are, however, not only a challenge, they can also be utilised to address the audience. To begin with, the interest in a public figure can be considered as a starting point for films depicting known politicians. Yet it is notable that, in contrast to much-used conventions of docudrama, *Pääministeri* does not turn known events into an emotional story with affective engagement with characters, but appeals to the political interest and curiosity of the audience. The documentary *Palme*, instead, exploits emotions and the known past in order to engage the audience.

Palme offers the viewer an affective engagement with the past by evoking the viewer's own memories – or the memories of recycled visual images of past events. In fact, viewers who lived through those times are invited to identify with their past self. For those too young to have experienced the events first-hand, the audiovisual story, which skilfully compiles news and document footage, affective music and voiceover narration, enables the viewer to experience the portrayed events. *Palme* is full of emotion, and according to the film reviews this emotional address worked. *Palme* was hailed by reviewers as a touching film as well as a good documentary about the recent history of Sweden (e.g. Engström 2012; Lindblad 2012; Söderbergh-Widding 2012; Tapper 2012).

In *Pääministeri* as well, the presumed memory of the audience is utilised, albeit to a different end. Publicly known facts and real public figures are part of an economically told story, as there is no need to devote time to introducing the main characters, familiar Finnish politicians or the political situation in Finland. The film does not appeal to viewers' emotional experiences, nor does it offer them one. Despite the actor Jonna Järnefelt's emotional performance, it is difficult to engage emotionally with any character, because the atmosphere in the film is dominated by matter-of-factness. The style of the film is realistic, even minimalistic – for example, the film features a very exiguous soundscape, only a few extras and just a few strictly framed locations. This creates a distancing effect in the film. The stylistic decisions in *Pääministeri* are interesting, because – as Paget (2011: 111–16) and Lipkin (2002: 37–9) respectively note – a central feature in docudrama is considered to be its ability to offer an emotionally appealing account of real events. Although resources and production values may naturally explain the style in *Pääministeri*, one could ask whether the distribution channel, the public service television channel YLE1, influenced the tone of the film. Perhaps, the informative, non-emotional tone was used in order to introduce the film as a serious political drama that differs from more entertaining television dramas. As such, it seems that the filmmakers tried to appeal to the audience's political interest and curiosity. On the other hand, the reason for the style might be political caution, a need to avoid treating acting politicians with strong emotions.

One may wonder whether the public generic definitions of the films influenced the success of the address. In the reviews of *Pääministeri*, the film was not referred to as a docudrama, rather it was understood to be a political drama (e.g. Bamberg 2009; Moring 2009; Pitko 2009). The film was reviewed accordingly as a drama, and the result was generally considered uneven (however, see Kulmala 2011; Pitko 2009). It seems that the film's appeal to political interest was not very successful, as political issues were only incidentally referred to in the reviews (however, see Kulmala 2009). In *Palme*, the emotional address appeared to work just because the film was defined as a credible documentary (e.g. Engström 2012; Lindblad 2012; Tapper 2012). The supposedly plausible witness, that is, archive films and news footage in *Palme*, generates the atmosphere of authenticity, which in turn enhances the emotional charge in the film – it creates the feeling of the really experienced, shared past.

Historical Accounts, Circulating Narratives

Despite the popularity of Anglo-American docudramas and documentaries, as well as the personalisation of politics and in media culture, the topic of politics and real politicians is not very typical in Swedish or Finnish feature films.

Pääministeri and *Palme* are two examples of the few such films. As portrayals of famous people, they are decorous. The private life of the prime minister is left aside, the films focus instead on the public role of the protagonist. It is, perhaps, revealing of Finnish television culture that even the docudrama *Pääministeri* does not exploit its artistic licence in this respect, but adopts a matter-of-fact approach.

All in all, *Pääministeri* and *Palme* illustrate the blurriness of the generic borders between docudrama and documentary. There are differences, no doubt. As a docudrama with invented scenes and actor performances, *Pääministeri* offers a hypothetical account of past events and public figures. *Palme* as a documentary is considered to give a witnessed – and at the same time a very emotional – account of Palme and the Swedish welfare state. Accordingly, *Pääministeri* makes hypothetical claims about Jäätteenmäki's character and motives, and at the same time, dramatic devices enable viewers to follow closely the political actions and feelings of the imagined Jäätteenmäki. *Palme*, in turn, searches for the truth about Palme from documented materials and interviews. Although the film gives a rich characterisation of Palme, some questions are left unanswered, some questions not even asked. As the protagonist of the story, Palme remains remote to viewers.

Despite the differences, both *Pääministeri* and *Palme* recycle similar narrative modes and patterns. The pattern of tension in the character, the conventional structure in fictional biopics, is utilised in both films. It creates a dramatic suspension in the films, but in contrast to fictional biopics, in these films the pattern does not reiterate the old ideas of the contradiction between the private and the public role of the protagonist. Instead, it brings forward the questions of class, gender and political agency. In addition to the dramatic characterisation, the films turn the political past into a coherent, dramatised story by using the narrative modes of melodrama and tragedy. Unintentionally or not, the narrative modes circulate a pessimistic argument about political life: something is rotten in the Nordic welfare state.

Note

1. The film was also broadcast in three parts by Sveriges Television at the end of 2012. This chapter is based on the theatrical version of the documentary which is available in DVD-format.

References

Anonymous (2009), 'Pääministeri keräsi yli 660 000 katsojaa', *Kainuun Sanomat*, 22 October.

Bamberg, Rolf (2009), 'Menestystarina vai kujanjuoksu?', *Uutispäivä Demari*, 19 October.

Custen, George F. (1992), *Bio/Pics: How Hollywood Constructed Public History*, New Brunswick, NJ: Rutgers University Press.
Eklund, Bernt (2012), 'Palme', *Expressen*, 11 September.
Engström, Emma (2012), 'Recension: Palme', *Göteborgs-Posten*, 14 September.
Felski, Rita (2008), 'Introduction'. In Rita Felski (ed.), *Rethinking Tragedy*, Baltimore: The Johns Hopkins University Press, pp. 1–26.
Kulmala, Markku (2012), 'Irak-gaten upottama', *Ilkka*, 19 October.
Lehtisalo, Anneli (2011), *Kuin elävinä edessämme. Suomalaiset elämäkertaelokuvat populaarina historiakulttuurina 1937–1955*, doctoral dissertation, Helsinki: Finnish Literature Society.
Lindblad, Helena (2012), 'Hängörande film ger Olof Palme liv', *Dagens Nyheter*, 14 September.
Lipkin, Steven N. (2002), *Real Emotional Logic: Film and Television Docudrama as Persuasive Practice*, Carbondale and Edwardsville: Southern Illinois University Press.
Moring, Kirsikka (2009), 'Irak-gate näytti, miten elämä potkaisee takaisin', *Helsingin Sanomat*, 19 October.
Nichols, Bill (2010), *Introduction to Documentary*, 2nd edn, Bloomington and Indianapolis: Indiana University Press.
Nordman, Joonas (2009), 'Jäättenmäen kaataja', *Iltalehti*, 19 October.
Paget, Derek (2011), *No Other way to Tell It: Docudrama on Film and Television*, 2nd edn, Manchester and New York: Manchester University Press.
Pitko, Matti (2009), 'Politiikan intohimoa Irak-gaten aikaan', *Aamulehti*, 19 October.
Söderbergh-Widding, Astrid (2012), 'Stark Palmeporträtt', *Svenska Dagbladet*, 14 September.
Swedish Film Institute (2013), *Filmåret i siffror 2012/ Facts and figures 2012*, <http://www.sfi.se/sv/om-svenska-filminstitutet/Publikationer/Verksamhetsberattelser/>, Stockholm: Svenska Filminstitutet.
Tapper, Michael (2012), 'Nya pusselbitar av politiken', *Syd-Svenskan*, 14 September.
Taylor, Henry M. (2002), *Rolle des Lebens. Die Filmbiographie als narratives System* (Zürcher filmstudien 8), Marburg: Schüren.
Wessman, Lili (2009), 'Annelin arvoitus. Televisiodraama yrittää avata Suomen ensimmäisen naispääministerin tarinaa', *Satakunnan Kansa*, 13 September.
Williams, Linda (2001), *Playing the Race Card: Melodramas of Black and White from Uncle Tom to O. J. Simpson*, Princeton and Oxford: Princeton University Press.
Winston, Brian (2013a), 'Introduction: The Filmed Documentary'. In Brian Winston (ed.), *The Documentary Film Book*, London: British Film Institute, pp. 1–29.
Winston, Brian (2013b), 'Life as Narrativised'. In Brian Winston (ed.), *The Documentary Film Book*, London: British Film Institute, pp. 89–97.

Filmography

The Deal, television film, directed by Stephen Frears. UK: Granada Television, 2003.
Ebbe – The Movie, film, directed by Karin af Klintberg and Jane Magnusson. Sweden: Acne Film, 2009.
Eden Pastora – Commandant 'Zero', film, directed by Alvaro Pardo. Finland: Filmitakomo Oy, 2006.
Facing Genocide – Khieu Samphan and Pol Pot, film, directed by David Aronowitsch and Staffan Lindberg. Sweden: Filmregion Stockholm Mälardalen, Medieoperatørene, Story Ab, 2010.
H:r Landshövding, film, directed by Måns Månsson. Sweden: Anagram Production AB, 2008.

In the Shadow of Doubt, film, directed by Pekka Lehto. Finland: First Floor Productions, YLE, 2009.
Looking for Fidel, film, directed by Oliver Stone. USA, Brazil: HBO Documentary Films, Ixtlan Productions, Morena Films Ltda, 2004.
Margaret, television film, directed by James Kent. UK: Great Meadow Productions, 2009.
Pääministeri, television film, directed by Jyri Kähönen. Finland: YLE, 2009.
Palme, film, directed by Maud Nycander and Kristina Lindström. Sweden: B-Reel AB, 2012.
Piru ja peijooni, television series, directed by Atro Lahtela. Finland: YLE, 2008. 2012.
The Queen, film, directed by Stephen Frears. UK, France, Italy: Pathé Pictures International, Granada Film Productions, Pathé Renn Productions, BIM Distribuzione, France 3 Cinéma, Canal+, Future Films, Scott Rudin Productions, 2006.
Rouva Presidentti, film, directed by Aleksi Bardy. Finland: Helsinki-Filmi, Funny Films Oy,
Within the Limits, film, directed by Annika Grof. Finland: Illume Oy, YLE, 2009.

PART III

NORDIC OPTIMISM: ROAD MOVIES, COMEDIES AND MUSICALS

9. FATHERS AND SONS REUNITED: ROAD MOVIES AS STORIES OF GENERATIONAL CONTINUITY

Tommi Römpötti

Road movies are usually defined as stories of resistance and freedom. The road is seen as a space of possibility which, when moving away from certain place, gives the wanderer a sense of freedom and the opportunity to criticise what is left behind. As such, road movies can be understood as progressive, for they give rise to the possibility of reinterpreting societal conventions and boundaries. In Western societies, which cherish the notion of rationality and productivity, freedom reached on the road through aimless wandering means opposition. It is often coded as youthful rebellion, but the road genre has never been only confined to young people (e.g. Mills 2006: 20).

This chapter asks what happens to the conventions of the road movie, and in particular its ethos of resistance, when younger and older generations hit the road together in Nordic films of the 2000s. In raising this question I discuss the use of road movie conventions in two Finnish road movies, the fictional *Road North* (Mika Kaurismäki, 2012) and the documentary *Finnish Blood Swedish Heart* (Mika Ronkainen, 2012), which both feature stories of father–son pairings driving together towards a new kind of understanding of their roots. The films offer two ways to see how road movies, in essence, work between the national and the transnational. *Road North* depicts a road journey inside the borders of Finland. *Finnish Blood Swedish Heart*, in comparison, is profoundly transnational anyway in its subject matter of a father and son duo driving from Finland to their past in Sweden, but film was also financed as a Finnish–Swedish co-production and, before being awarded as the best Finnish documentary of the year, it received the Dragon award for the best Nordic documentary at the Gothenburg International Film Festival 2013.

It is often said that cinema cannot be understood as nationally isolated, for the boundaries between nations are crossed in several dimensions from financing and production to distribution and exhibition (e.g. Elkington and Nestingen 2005: 1–16). This is eminently true when talking about road movies. The road movie is the epitome of transnational cinema because of its circulating conventions and universal theme of struggle between individual and community. The road movie is arguably the most American of all genres historically (e.g. Kääpä 2011: 43), for its roots lie in the iconography and frontier mythology of westerns. Westerns provide a popular cultural frame to understand the motorised wanderings depicted in road movies (e.g. Cohan and Rae Hark 1997: 3; Laderman 2002: 23–4; Watson 1999: 22), but in Nordic road movies the societal context for road journeys is rather different from their American counterparts.

In road movies there are two main, often overlapping, narrative trajectories: the protagonists either have an urgent need to escape something or an existential compulsion to try to find out who they are (e.g. Stringer 1997: 165). The difference between stories of escape and those about identity quests lies in the way the concept of freedom is defined. In Nordic road movies the negative understanding of freedom, which is common to American road movies and which emphasises the individual's need to leave everything behind, is placed in negotiation with the definition of freedom as consensus between the individual and society. In the Nordic welfare state view, the individual is free only when acting as a part of the nation (cf. Eyerman and Löfgren 1995: 76). In this respect, freedom is not literally about individuality, but about cooperation based on the spiritual heritage and material conditions of these nations – in short, freedom is about continuity (Karkama 1989: 37, 50–1; Römpötti 2012: 85–6).

Keeping these specificities of the Nordic context in mind, I will examine *Road North* and *Finnish Blood Swedish Heart* by focusing on the role of the car and the functions of music, especially as they pertain to questions of memory and identity. I want to suggest that twenty-first-century road movies, instead of providing a space for rebelling individuals, offer an opportunity to find a lost connection for maintaining generational and societal continuity.

Accented Views

Conventionally road movies challenge the limits of societal continuity by sending the wanderers to the no man's land of the road, which provides a possibility to criticise the regulative nature of the national order. This is made clear already in the first scene of both films discussed here. The starting points for the journeys are different in the fictional *Road North* and the documentary *Finnish Blood Swedish Heart*, but both films begin by emphasising the constructed nature of national identity.

In *Road North* Timo (Samuli Edelmann) is a celebrated pianist, who takes his music extremely seriously. His wife (Irina Björklund) has moved with their daughter from Helsinki to Rovaniemi in Northern Finland, because Timo tends to practise during the night and their small baby cannot sleep. When Timo's father Leo (Vesa-Matti Loiri) arrives in Finland after having been away for thirty-five years, the threshold zone of the airport, a transitional and transnational non-place where 'the scrambled game of identity and relations is ceaselessly rewritten' (Augé 2008: 64), emphasises the types of interstitial identity familiar to protagonists of earlier Kaurismäki films (see Kääpä 2011: 15). Leo's relationship to his Finnish identity is shown as artificial in a concrete way, when he walks through customs with a false passport with the name of Paavo Nurmi, the 'Flying Finn', on it. In the same evening, after his successful concert, Timo finds Leo – 'some drunk' in a Hawaiian shirt, as he calls him – sleeping in the staircase in front of his door. Leo asks Timo to take a drive with him and because of the emptiness caused by the blow to his family life, Timo, who has acted as though everything was fine in his life, goes along with his father for a drive, which turns into a long convalescent journey to his silenced past.

With the concept of accented cinema Hamid Naficy (2001: 4) brings the questions of journeying, identity, liminality, displacement, historicity and nostalgia to the fore. In the movie, Leo's experience as an outsider in the changed homeland of his memories can be analysed from this perspective and connected to a wider critique of capitalism. Consider two examples. First, when Leo provides a vague hint of where they are going, he uses the Finnish word *susiraja*, with which he refers to the northern Finland as periphery, literally the frontier where wolves live. But for Timo, the younger generation, the word refers to the Ring Road number three surrounding the capital city area of Helsinki. Inside the Ring Road, the inhabitants have an elitist saying that the countryside begins beyond Ring Three. The different understanding of the word makes it possible to see the journey as a comment on geographical class formation in an economically polarised nation. They drive away from the core of capital-driven transnational Finland, but crossing the artificial frontier of capital does not change anything.

Second, Leo's memories clash with the changes caused by the flow of culture, or more precisely the flow of capitalism. Leo keeps on reminiscing about the Finland of his past, but global consumer culture has swept away the key objects of his past. He, for example, wants to take his son to the place where he lived as a child. They meet a man from Leo's past, who says 'it is a significant place nowadays', but when they approach the place, they drive to a vast parking area of a huge castle-like shopping centre. 'What kind of a place is this?' Leo asks. The place, The Village Shop Tuuri, built in Central Finland 'in the middle of nowhere' and known as a place of shopping tourism, is indeed significant, but only as a sign of capitalism and consumerised culture.

For Naficy (2001: 4–6), accented cinema is produced by transnational or 'diasporic and exilic subjects' and can be understood 'as a performance of its author's identity'. Although Mika Kaurismäki, the director of *Road North*, is not in the subaltern diasporic position, he can be seen as accented or at least a transnational filmmaker. Since the early 1990s Kaurismäki has lived in Brazil, which has offered him an insider–outsider, or an in-between, position, which also defines the characteristics of an accented filmmaker. While Kaurismäki's in-between position organises the documentaries he produced in Brazil (see Kääpä 2011: 110), *Road North* indicates that accented interstitiality is also present in his films produced in Finland.

To describe the world in Kaurismäki's films, Pietari Kääpä (2011: 17–18) uses architectural theorist Marcos Novak's concept of transvergence. Transvergent films show cultural transformations as leading to a state of constant instability and uncertainty – cultural transformation can be 'a relevant social condition in its own right'. Will Higbee (2007: 85), on the other hand, explains transvergence by comparing it to national ideology: where national ideology conceals the differences, transvergence is a state which keeps them visible. This

Figures 9.1 and 9.2   Timo absorbed in his thoughts in *Road North*. Images courtesy of Marianna Films Oy.

comparison is consistent with the conventional ideological difference between classical film genres and the road movie, which usually underlines the nature of national unity as imagined or impossible. In road movies transvergence is a central concern due to the significance of the road as a space between identities and open endings, which deny sustaining the continuity of the fixed hegemonic order.

Transvergent and accented both refer to a position between the national and the transnational, but an accented form of filmmaking practice differs from transvergent with its starting point, which is language, distinguishable speech and the filmmaking accent of those who for some reason live in a foreign country. The documentary *Finnish Blood Swedish Heart*, a journey of two generations of Swedish Finns, Kai and Tauno, who cross the national boundaries and language barriers while driving to their past in Sweden, foregrounds the feelings of its accented protagonists literally. *Finnish Blood Swedish Heart* is the story of Kai Latvalehto, a former guitar player with the famous Finnish rock group Aknestik, which hit its peak at the end of the 1990s with the nostalgia-driven song 'Suomirokkia' (Finnish rock). Kai struggles between his Finnish and Swedish identities, his present-day Oulu and his childhood years in Gothenburg. Immediately in the prologue of the film Kai is shown drifting between languages. An anxious Kai feels alienated and angry while playing Finnish rock on stage. His voiceover is heard in Finnish, but in the end of the prologue he states in Swedish: 'För jag är ju urpsprungligen inte en riktig Finne' ('Because originally I'm not a real Finn'). By playing 'Suomirokkia' Kai has helped to maintain the artificial construction of his Finnish identity, but during the opening credits we see him packing away his guitar.

The documentary depicts a conscious attempt to plug into both private and collective versions of the past. The private objective emerges for example in a radio interview (Länsi-Ruotsin Sisuradio/Sveriges radio, 29 January 2013), where Kai states: 'For me this documentary is about searching for my roots, and about my relationship with my father.' In one way the collective past can be described by following Mette Hjort's (2010: 16–17) typology of cinematic transnationalism. According to that typology, *Finnish Blood Swedish Heart* can be defined as a work of epiphanic transnationalism, which in the Nordic context refers to a conscious effort to increase public knowledge of 'the issue of transnational, Nordic belonging'. Hjort's example is the work of the Nordic Film and TV Fund (NFTF), which also co-financed *Finnish Blood Swedish Heart*.

The documentary's historical background is in the end of the 1950s and the 1960s, when fast urbanisation had a drastic effect on Finnish society. The unemployment rate rose particularly in the late 1960s, and Sweden's simultaneous economic boom drew Finns to immigrate to Sweden, where wages and living standards were at a radically higher level (Korkiasaari 2001: 13).

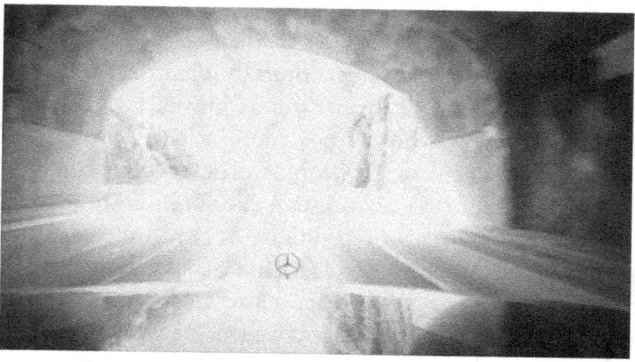

Figures 9.3 and 9.4   Kai's subjective point of view in *Finnish Blood Swedish Heart*. Images courtesy of Hysteria Film AB/Klaffi Productions.

In the 1960s and 1970s around 320,000 people, Kai's family among them, immigrated to Sweden as economic refugees (Institute of Migration, Finland). When Kai's parents left Finland he was 2 years old, and when they came back he was 13. This marked his identity profoundly, for in Sweden he felt he was considered a Finn and in Finland a Swede.[1] To understand why he feels alienated Kai decides to drive towards the past with his father.

Resisting Alienation by Car

In *Road North* and *Finnish Blood Swedish Heart* the journey in a car provides a connection between father and son who have previously had a distant relationship or no relationship at all. Their journeys have destinations, but it is the moving car that raises the questions and offers the answers about the past. It has been suggested that in almost every film some important piece of dialogue is situated in a car (Kolker 2000: 41). Historically, alongside cinema, the car is probably the most significant invention of the twentieth century, for it has profoundly changed the way we perceive the world today. This significance is not because of the car in its own right, but more precisely the community planning in favour of motorised movement (see Wollen 2002: 11).

The car has often been defined as a machine dictating human needs (e.g. Ross 1998: 55; Shove 1998: 10). But rather than see the car as opposite to human nature, anthropologist Daniel Miller (2001: 2–3) argues we should understand the car through its humanity. He uses the provoking expression 'humanity of the car', because the car is an inseparable 'part of the cultural environment within which we see ourselves as human'. It is notable that automobility is integral to everyone's understanding of being in the Western world. Nevertheless, as Miller (2001: 3) states, we should not see the car only as a force of alienation, but rather as a vehicle to resist alienation and empower enabling the search for one's identity.

On the level of narration, the main reason why the car is important in films is the possibility for drama: a car provides a small, closed, intimate space. In *Road North* Timo and Leo seem to be in constant conflict as the car space makes it possible and even compels them to communicate, stay close to each other and enter each other's private space. It would be a good space to depict people becoming closer, but even a peaceful moment may easily descend into conflict. For example a crucial scene in *Road North* illustrates this friction. After visiting Leo's mother in a retirement home, Timo asks about the colour of his mother's hair, but Leo gives the wrong answer. Timo realises he has not grown up with his biological mother, and their journey continues in silence.

One conventional road movie image is a two-shot seen from the bonnet through the windscreen. This shot is a conventional image of any Western feature film, for it frames the characters in the front seats travelling together. If the scene in the car turns into conflict, the unity of the space could be separated in narrative discourse by cutting the two-shot in half. The convention of separated close-ups as shot–reverse-shot cutting leads the spectator into the character's thoughts and can make the disagreement visually stronger than it actually is. The mother conversation scene consists of two-shots seen through the windscreen and closer ones shot from both sides inside the car. Immediately after Leo says he will not talk about Timo's biological mother before the time is right, the film cuts to a close-up of Timo's tearful face staring through the windscreen (Figure 9.1). The sad close-up is accompanied by melancholic non-diegetic electric guitar, which draws us into Timo's private thoughts. This change between objective and subjective points of view is a conventional technique in road movie narration, for the road movie's driving force is an existential conflict between the individual and the community.

In addition to two-shots, the framing and reflecting surfaces of windows and mirrors emphasise the act of looking. As David Laderman (2002: 16) writes, in the road movie, the reflection of the character's own face 'serves often as a literal projection of character onto the car, and into the space being traveled'. When driving towards the past through the landscape of the past, the frame compositions of the car are even more important. The car can be seen as a kind of time machine, for though the inner space of the car is situated in the present, it is still constantly communing with the future represented by the big screen of the windscreen, and the past represented by the reflection of rearview mirrors. As a time capsule, the car is a liminal space, and as such a proper vehicle for exploring volatile identities on the move. On the road Timo gradually begins to understand his roots. When his staring close-up dissolves together with the landscape they are passing (Figure 9.2), it is the landscape of his identity he is trying to map.

Music, Memory and Togetherness

In both *Road North* and *Finnish Blood Swedish Heart* the road is a space between identities. This is underlined in narration with the use of music as a sign of private or collective memory, or as a force able to create togetherness. In road movie narration music is used in two conventional ways; to create music-video-like driving sequences and to establish a connection to contemporary culture and society. In *Road North* and *Finnish Blood Swedish Heart* music plays an important role in their identity politics as in both films the sons are musicians. Music ties Timo from *Road North* and Kai from *Finnish Blood Swedish Heart* to places where they do not feel at home, but it also serves as a gateway to reminiscing. Through emotional sensibilities of the inner journey music leads Timo and Kai to gradually interrogating their past.

The significance of music in creating a subjective point of view is emphasised in *Finnish Blood, Swedish Heart* as Kai and Tauno approach Gothenburg. Kai talks about the times when his father was such a heavy drinker that he could have drunk himself to death. Motivated by his son's words, Tauno starts talking about how he quit drinking after having had a vision of his own coffin. He keeps on talking, but Kai is absorbed in thought just like Timo in *Road North*, and does not hear him any more. The gentle, echoing sound of a guitar and keyboards blankets the external world. At the same time cutting separates the generations, as we see Kai's glazed look in close-up through the windscreen. The reflections of trees hit the windscreen of the moving car like a flow of flashing memories Kai is not able to catch (Figure 9.3). The mind-floating music continues when, via the subjective perspective of the camera, we travel into a tunnel and to the sunny brightness on the other side of the tunnel (Figure 9.4). The subjective perspective highlights Kai's anxiety as he is getting closer to his childhood. In road movies it also underlines the possibility of interpreting various topographical border crossings as passages in getting closer to one's real identity. These affective images and sounds of individual experiences underline the road as a space for accented agency and, more generally, why it is possible to see road movies as encouragements of questioning (cf. Mills 2006: 20–1).

In *Finnish Blood Swedish Heart* music also forms a larger narrative for the journey depicted. The private memories and the drive through the Swedish landscape are juxtaposed with performances of nine 1970s immigrant songs shot live on location. The vintage songs performed by second-generation Swedish Finnish artists, such as Love Antell, Darya Pakarinen, Markus Fagervall and Anna Järvinen, form a historical context for private memories and raise questions concerning collective memory.

A good example of how private and collective history are joined together in narration is Kai's conversation with Harri Mänty, the former guitar player of the Swedish rock group Kent. They reminisce about the ways Swedish Finnish children were kept segregated in school from the native population. Despite the negative references to immigrants' position as a lower class, a longing echo characterises their words. The conversation is commented upon in the song that follows: Darya Pakarinen, dressed up in the colours of the Swedish flag, performs 'Suomalainen neekerilaulu' (The Finnish Nigger Song) in an autumnal garden. The lyrics of the song, for example 'a child of Finland has the same golden hair / and the same blue eyes as a child of Sweden has', cast an ironic, doubtful shadow to the feeling of nostalgia. From the accented position the documentary also casts a shadow on the road movie journey, which is often constructed as a possible nostalgia trip. Bryan S. Turner (1987: 150) has defined nostalgia as culturally constructed feelings of longing and alienation caused by the sense of loss and absence of personal wholeness. The longing spirit of *Finnish Blood Swedish Heart* is put across clearly in the Finnish name of the film, which literally means 'a song about homesickness'. The Finnish name refers to a 1970s immigration song by the same name.

Through narrative continuity between dialogue and songs performed live, private history is merged with the collective past of Swedish Finnishness. But the representations of the past as music-video-like performances are not unproblematic. The songs and the performances are touching nostalgic spectacles, just like the song 'Suomirokkia' which Kai performed on stage in the prologue and which keeps on haunting him even in Gothenburg. When walking in his old school yard, Kai runs into a Swedish Finnish cover band, which is right at that moment practising 'Suomirokkia'.

The songs performed provide a context for shared history, but as nostalgia-driven constructions they also suggest that it is impossible to reach a spectacle-free view of the history. The songs offer popular cultural explanations for accented Swedish–Finnish identity, which at the same time accentuate the fact that deep down being Swedish–Finnish is a private and much more complex matter than the songs are able to tell.[2] In narration this is emphasised clearly with quick shots and tram sounds as puzzling subjective glimpses of the past, at which Kai is seen marvelling in close-up when he reaches Gothenburg.

In *Road North* music is used to depict private longing, but it is also used to create metafictional spectacle. This is emphasised at a hotel, where Timo and Leo stop soon after Timo has found out that his biological mother has been kept secret from him. In the hotel they meet two women, mother (Elina Knihtilä) and daughter (Ada Kukkonen), who in the hotel's restaurant complain about the lack of music. Timo and Leo prove their capability as men by walking on stage and performing together 'Kuolleet lehdet', a Finnish version of 'Les Feuilles mortes'.[3] The stage moment highlights the film as a metafictional, national star vehicle, for in real life both actors are also famous recording artists. As one critic (Poussu 2012) stated, when on stage 'We do not see the father and son of the story anymore. Instead, we now recognize the multitalented performers Loiri and Edelmann.'[4]

After the star performance Timo and Leo are dancing with the women they have met, and later have sex with them. During the sex scene there are crosscuts between the two rooms, and Serge Gainsbourg's 'Je t'aime moi non plus' (1969), 'the pop equivalent of an Emmanuelle movie' (Spencer 2005) is heard. The nostalgia-driven songs and simultaneous sex acts mark a turning point in the male relationship. The father and son connect through music and their communion is strengthened later through dialogue and when they repeat the performance of 'Kuolleet lehdet' in the car. At the filling station they find out the women have robbed them. Timo wants to drive back to the hotel, but Leo says 'it was all worth it', and they laugh, high-fiving in their stolen Pontiac. The buddy-like ethos of male freedom is once more emphasised when Leo says laughingly: 'Father and son travelling the world.' The humorous one-liner confirms that *Road North* does not deter from the gender patterns of the earlier films of Kaurismäki (see Kääpä 2011: 35) and the convention of road movie as 'male escapist fantasy' (Cohan and Rae Hark 1997: 3). But the feeling of togetherness created cuts off the remains of the ethos of resistance and turns the journey towards generational and societal continuity, which is exceptional for Kaurismäki.

Continuity as Freedom

Conventionally road stories are about resistance and freedom. People hit the road because for some outer or inner reason they do not feel at home. Road stories are often coded as youthful rebellion, but in this chapter I have examined what happens to road movie conventions when younger and older generations hit the road together. I have concentrated on two Finnish road movies, the fictional *Road North* and the documentary *Finnish Blood Swedish Heart*. They are stories of identity quests, which lead sons closer to their fathers. In films like these freedom is not mainly about individuality, for hitting the road is not depicted as being wild and free, which is usually seen as the key road movie convention. The journeys of *Road North* and *Finnish Blood Swedish Heart* are adapted to the context of Nordic welfare societies where freedom is rather seen as cooperation in favour of continuity. The resistance depicted in the films does not fall upon society but stays on a more private level.

In *Road North* there is no proper object of resistance, since in the beginning the son is passive, resisting the whole idea of a journey. *Road North* concentrates on the father-and-son relationship with a few comments on contemporary transnational Finnish society. They drive away from the capital city of Helsinki towards their shared past in northern Finland. In *Road North* the road movie's movement-and-stop structure is more important than the geographical route. *Finnish Blood Swedish Heart* is more profoundly transnational, for its subject matter, the Swedish Finns' conscious accented journey to their haunting past in Sweden, challenges the idea of national borders and fixed national identity. Its resistance is existential; the son wants to get rid of his feelings of alienation. On their way from Oulu to Gothenburg, before their destination, Kai and Tauno spend some time in Stockholm, where they meet some Swedish Finnish people. The discussions with fellow immigrants are important for the historical theme of the film. The discussions help the spectator to understand societal contexts of Swedish–Finnishness, and at the same time Kai has a chance to understand the reasons for his feeling of alienation.

Both *Road North* and *Finnish Blood Swedish Heart* show that for self-exploration and questioning the limits of identity, the liminality of the road is a proper space. The movement on the road, symbolising hope and possibility for change, has a therapeutic or even convalescent potential. As movies featuring a father and son driving together towards their shared past, *Road North* and *Finnish Blood Swedish Heart* are clear examples of how the movement on the road in Nordic films of the 2000s serves to maintain continuity and makes the road movie's conventional ethos of resistance disappear. This is crystallised at the end of both movies.

Within a transnational road-genre framework, Kai of *Finnish Blood Swedish Heart* manages to trace his dual nationalities, and Timo of *Road North* reintegrates with his family. In their last day in Gothenburg Kai drives with his father to a hill, which provides a panorama over the city. On the hill Kai hugs his father and an emotional close-up testifies that generations have been reunited on the road. Kai's glimpses of memories have grown to the point where he has come to understand the meaning of history and continuity as a crucial aspect of his identity.

I have previously shown that Finnish road movies of the twentieth century favour the individual in their individual/community dichotomy (Römpötti

2012). According to *Road North* and *Finnish Blood Swedish Heart*, the twenty-first century is still about individuality, but more in favour of the community. When people are sent on the road to consider questions of identity, to connect with community and then return as changed persons, the conventional understanding of the road as a space of resistance is seized by the ideology of continuity. This is explicitly clear in *Road North*.

Road North ends with death, which is a frequent road movie convention, as Leo dies in the rundown log house where Timo was conceived. By getting there to die Leo manages to take his son to his roots and before that guide him back to his wife and daughter and introduce him to his half-sister, grandmother and, importantly, his biological mother. In the epilogue the film comes full circle; after Leo's death Timo is playing in a concert the same composition, Piano Sonata D 894 by Schubert, that he was rehearsing the night Leo appeared outside his door. In the beginning Timo's playing was interrupted by Leo, but in the end the composition is heard as a kind of farewell piece for the father he had a chance to connect with. The generational connection attained on the road reaches beyond death. The generational continuity is cemented in narration as the camera moves slowly in the concert audience to show a close-up of Timo's wife and daughter. His wife turns her head so that we also recognise Pirkko. Thus the journey has joined together three generations.

The end is the most important ideological aspect in road movies as it closes the narrative discourse and proposes a final statement on the events of the road. The in-between space of the road is conventionally seen as a space for resisting hegemonic order. These journeys have often led to an unhappy ending. But the deeply rooted convention of dead ends, which rises from the classical counterculture films of the 1960s and 1970s, particularly *Easy Rider* (1969), is misleading, for road movies do not always emphasise opposition (Römpötti 2012: 35–6). American road movies may suggest that the existential project on the road is doomed to fail, that there is nothing to be found but death or forced reintegration into the order first left behind (Stringer 1997: 165), but as *Road North* and *Finnish Blood Swedish Heart* indicate, in Nordic road movies of the 2000s there is a tendency towards generational understanding. In *Road North* and *Finnish Blood Swedish Heart* the protagonists return to the antecedent order. Conventionally that would indicate failure, but for drifting persons in these films generational continuity provides security in the changing Nordic society and an otherwise insecure world.

In the beginning of the journey Kai's father said, 'I've been wondering about the actual purpose of this trip,' and in the end of their journey he states: 'I guess we would never have talked about these issues if we had not taken this trip.' The question–statement pair indicates how and why the car as a space of conversation has led to a close connection between fathers and sons. The movement along the Nordic road in the humanity of the car has shown its convalescent potential as the space of mutual understanding. In their cars fathers and sons are already at their destination.

Notes

1. As a subject matter, immigration to Sweden from Finland is also referred to in a few other Finnish feature films, such as *Kesäkapina/Summer Rebellion* (Jaakko Pakkasvirta, 1970), *Yhden miehen sota/One Man's War* (Risto Jarva, 1973), *Ajolähtö/Gotta Run!* (Mikko Niskanen, 1982) and *Kivenpyörittäjän kylä/The Last Wedding* (Markku Pölönen, 1995). Swedish Finnishness is also a substantial subject in the Swedish film *Svinalängorna/Beyond* (2010) directed by Pernilla August.
2. This, of course, does not mean, that representations are not able to offer shared feelings and even experiences. I saw *Finnish Blood Swedish Heart* for the first time in Rauma Blue Sea Film Festival 2013. Kai Latvalehto was there as a guest. Before and after the screening some audience members with a similar background wanted to share their immigration experiences with Kai. The same thing has also happened in several other places.
3. The song 'Les Feuilles mortes' is based on Jacques Prévert's poem. It was originally recorded by Yves Montand (1945) and it is heard in Marcel Carné's film *Les Portes de la nuit* (1946).
4. The self-consciousness of the star vehicle is emphasised by the also well-known band Kaihon karavaani ('Nostalgic caravan', led by Tuure Kilpeläinen), which turns up from backstage to accompany the stars on stage.

References

Augé, Marc (2008/1992), *Non-Places. An Introduction to Supermodernity*, 2nd edn, trans. John Howe, London and New York: Verso.
Cohan, Steven and Ina Rae Hark (1997), 'Introduction'. In Steven Cohan and Ina Rae Hark (eds), *The Road Movie Book*, London and New York: Routledge, pp. 1–14.
Elkington, Trevor G. and Andrew Nestingen (2005), 'Introduction: Transnational Nordic Cinema'. In Andrew Nestingen and Trevor G. Elkington (eds), *Transnational Cinema in a Global North: Nordic Cinema in Transition*, Detroit: Wayne State University Press, pp. 1–28.
Eyerman, Ron and Orvar Löfgren (1995), 'Romancing the Road: Road Movies and Images of Mobility', *Theory, Culture & Society* 12 (1): 53–79.
Higbee, Will (2007), 'Beyond the (Trans)national: Towards a Cinema of Transvergence in Postcolonial and Diasporic Francophone Cinema(s), *Studies in French Cinema* 7 (2): 79–91.
Hjort, Mette (2010), 'On the Plurality of Cinematic Transnationalism'. In Nataša Ďurovičová and Kathleen Newman (eds), *World Cinemas, Transnational Perspectives*, New York and London: Routledge, pp. 12–33.
Institute of Migration (Finland), Statistics, *Emigration and immigration 1945–2010*, <http://www.migrationinstitute.fi/stat/index_e.php>, accessed 21 October 2013.
Kääpä, Pietari (2011), *The Cinema of Mika Kaurismäki: Transvergent Cinescapes, Emergent Identities*, Bristol and Chicago: Intellect.
Karkama, Pentti (1989), *J. V. Snellmanin kirjallisuuspolitiikka*, Helsinki: SKS.
Kolker, Philip (2000), *A Cinema of Loneliness*, 3rd edn, Oxford: Oxford University Press.

Korkiasaari, Jouni (2001), 'Suomalaisten Ruotsiin suuntautuneen siirtolaisuuden yhteiskunnalliset syyt 1900-luvulla', Turku: Institute of Migration, <http://www.migrationinstitute.fi/articles/005_Korkiasaari.pdf>, accessed 22 October 2013.

Laderman, David (2002), *Driving Visions: Exploring the Road Movie*, Austin: University of Texas Press.

Miller, Daniel (2001), 'Driven Societies'. In Daniel Miller (ed.), *Car Cultures*, Oxford and New York: Berg, pp. 1–33.

Mills, Katie (2006), *The Road Story and the Rebel: Moving Through Film, Fiction, and Television*, Carbondale: Southern Illinois University Press.

Naficy, Hamid (2001), *An Accented Cinema: Exilic and Diasporic Filmmaking*, Princeton: Princeton University Press.

Poussu, Tarmo (2012), 'Isä ja poika tien päällä', *Ilta-Sanomat*, 24 August.

Römpötti, Tommi (2012), 'Vieraana omassa maassa' – Suomalaiset road-elokuvat vapauden ja vastustuksen kertomuksina 1950-luvun lopusta 2000-luvulle (Nykykulttuurin tutkimuskeskuksen julkaisuja 109), Jyväskylä: Jyväskylän yliopisto.

Ross, Kristin (1998), *Fast Cars, Clean Bodies: Decolonization and the Reordering of French Culture*, Cambridge and London: The MIT Press.

Shove, Elizabeth (1998), 'Consuming Automobility: A Discussion Paper', *Project SceneSusTech Report* 1.3. (final), 10 December (SceneSusTech = Scenarios for a sustainable society: car transport systems and the sociology of embedded technologies), <http://www.tcd.ie/ERC/pastprojects/carsdownloads/Consuming%20Automobility.pdf>, accessed 1 February 2014.

Spencer, Neil (2005), 'The 10 Most X-Rated Records', in *The Observer Music Monthly*, 22 May, <http://observer.theguardian.com/omm/the10/story/0,,1487369,00.html>, accessed 3 February 2014.

Stringer, Julian (1997), 'Exposing Intimacy in Russ Meyer's *Motorpsycho!* and *Faster Pussycat! Kill! Kill!*'. In Steven Cohan and Ina Rae Hark (eds), *The Road Movie Book*, London and New York: Routledge, pp. 165–78.

Turner, Bryan S. (1987), 'A Note on Nostalgia', *Theory, Culture & Society* 4 (1): 147–56.

Watson, Stephanie (1999), 'From Riding to Driving: Once upon a Time in the West'. In Jack Sargeant and Stephanie Watson (eds), *Lost Highways: An Illustrated History of Road Movies*, London: Creation Books, pp. 21–37.

Wollen, Peter (2002), 'Introduction: Cars and Culture'. In Peter Wollen and Joe Kerr (eds), *Autopia: Cars and Culture*, London: Reaktion Books, pp. 10–20.

10. THE NORDIC 'QUIRKY FEEL-GOOD'

Ellen Rees

In this chapter I want to propose the 'quirky feel-good' as a particular Nordic film genre. What exactly is meant by the term 'feel-good' is poorly defined within film studies, and it is often used to dismiss superficial films that lack intellectual or emotional depth.[1] Yet as Mette Hjort suggests in her book-length study of Lone Scherfig's *Italiensk for begyndere* (*Italian for Beginners*, 2000) – itself perhaps the most widely recognised example of what I am calling the Nordic quirky feel-good – a film that makes its viewers feel good does not preclude it from having significant depth (Hjort 2010: 116–17). Hjort proposes the term 'ethical feel-good' as a genre delineation for *Italian for Beginners*, but I think such a term underplays the importance of humour. As I see it, generally speaking a 'feel-good' is a film that combines drama with comic effects in order to establish emotional connections between viewers and characters, and among characters, rather than simply to generate laughter or for the purposes of ridicule. A feel-good will thus by definition have an ethos that emphasises emotional connections. Understood in this way, there are clearly many, many feel-good films, both in the US film industry and around the world; films like Jean-Pierre Jeunet's *Amélie* (2001) and the works of Pedro Almodóvar are probably the most prominent quirky examples worldwide. The genre can also be said to encompass the romantic comedy, which is more narrowly focused thematically, privileging heterosexual romance over all other preoccupations as it most often does. Feel-goods more generally can and do concern themselves with a much broader spectrum of human relationships. They also straddle many more traditional categories, such as

147

the coming-of-age film, the road movie, the literary adaptation and even the documentary.

The choice of the modifier 'quirky' for the Nordic context is based on my sense that the film industries in the five Nordic countries have actively cultivated a kind of exoticism that is non-erotic; it is a foreignness in relation to the Anglo-American cultural context that emphasises what is perceived to be the strange but charming oddness of Scandinavia rather than the perceived seductive or threatening otherness of more culturally distant societies. This quirkiness has been used as a marketing strategy that targets the international film festival circuit. 'Quirky' as a word is of obscure origin; a quirk denotes a sudden turn, a trick, or a peculiarity, and something 'quirky' might be said to be unexpected or peculiar, but not in a negative way. It is something that piques one's curiosity and interest, but that is still safe and familiar enough not to be off-putting. At the same time, the preoccupation with the quirky allows 'feel-good' films to explore troubling thematic material (illness, death, alcoholism, abuse, loss etc.) in some depth. Quirkiness is often posited as a coping mechanism on the part of the characters in response to personal tragedy.

The term 'quirky' has received a certain amount of attention in relation to contemporary American 'Indie' cinema. James MacDowell has identified a number of conventions that characterise quirky independent cinema from the 1990s and 2000s, including the use of deadpan humour, comic book aesthetics and slapstick humour, as well as nostalgia towards childhood and a concomitant preoccupation with naïveté and innocence. MacDowell focuses on examples such as Wes Anderson's *The Royal Tenenbaums* (2001), Paul Thomas Anderson's *Punch-Drunk Love* (2002) and Michel Gondry's *Eternal Sunshine of the Spotless Mind* (2004), among many others, to demonstrate how the 'quirky' is 'a tone that exists on a knife-edge of judgment and empathy, detachment and engagement, irony and sincerity' (MacDowell 2010: 13). MacDowell argues against construing the quirky as a genre, in part because it (like *film noir*) 'is also consistently drawn to certain genres' (2010: 2). I am thus conjoining a similar (but by no means identical) quirky 'tone' or 'structure of feeling' with the 'feel-good' genre to posit a Nordic subgenre that I have called the 'quirky feel-good'.

Scandinavian 'quirkiness' is a familiar stereotype in British humour, made famous by the comedy ensemble Monty Python's Flying Circus, where references to the Nordic countries invariably suggested either sexual liberation (largely inspired by mid-twentieth-century Nordic pornography and films like Vilgot Sjöman's *Jag är nyfiken – en film i gult* (*I am Curious – Yellow*, 1967)) or eccentricity, or both. The famous 'Dead Parrot Sketch' from 1969 (in which Michael Palin's character identifies the parrot in question as a 'Norwegian blue' that is not dead but merely 'pining for the fjords') sets up a comic absurdity in the notion that there might be a Nordic variant of an exotic tropical bird.

The Nordic quirky feel-good genre as I see it, then, has its origins in the 1980s with the international breakthrough of what Andrew Nestingen calls medium-concept films such as Lasse Hallström's *Mitt liv som hund* (*My Life as a Dog*, 1985) and Gabriel Axel's *Babettes gæstebud* (*Babette's Feast*, 1987) leading the way for similar successes in, for example, Colin Nutley's *Änglagård* (*House of Angels*, 1992), Friðrik Þór Friðriksson's *Börn náttúrunar* (*Children of Nature*, 1991) and *Á köldum klaka* (*Cold Fever*, 1995). Lars von Trier's *Breaking the Waves* (1996; perhaps better described as a 'feel-bad'), Pål Sletaune's *Budbringeren* (*Junk Mail*, 1997), the previously mentioned *Italian for Beginners*, Josef Fares's *Jalla! Jalla!* (*The Best Man's Wedding*, 2000), Lukas Moodysson's *Tillsammans* (*Together*, 2000), Petter Næss's *Elling* (2001), Knut Erik Jensen's *Heftig og begeistret* (*Cool and Crazy*, 2001), Aki Kaurismäki's *Mies vailla menneisyyttä* (*The Man without a Past*, 2002) and Sara Johnsen's *Upperdog* (2009). As medium-concept cinema, these films distinguish themselves from their predecessors in that they borrow heavily from both the European art cinema and Hollywood traditions, combining these elements in new ways that distinguish them from other cinematic traditions.

If we think of genre as being defined by similarities in the form, function and content of a group of films, how might we delineate the quirky feel-good? In terms of *form*, they are mostly narrative fiction films. They combine elements from both drama and comedy and are essentially hybrid, striving on the one hand to represent the realities of human life as complex and nuanced, while on the other hand activating comedy and at times appearing unabashedly nostalgic and sentimental in relation to the groups and places represented. The mode is realist, with an intimate and subjective, but often wandering, point of view that encompasses the ensemble rather than the star. The layering of multiple perspectives is important. While it is not necessarily a defining criterion for the genre, many of the quirky feel-goods are based on original screenplays rather than adaptations of literary works.

In terms of *content*, quirky feel-goods focus on complex interpersonal relationships, integration into a community and a connection to place. There is a real effort to depict even minor characters as unique individuals, typically with humorous behavioral quirks, an odd sense of style, or as unwittingly retrograde in behaviour or style. Protagonists can be either adults or children, but they are usually thrust into a new environment or forced to confront some conflict from their past. While a focus on the 'quirky' can be seen in a number of Hollywood films as well (Tim Burton's *Edward Scissorhands* from 1990 and Robert Zemeckis's *Forrest Gump* from 1994 come to mind), typically it is limited to one eccentric character who then helps the people he is close to to see the error of their ways, while the rest of the community remains relentlessly conventional.² In the Nordic quirky feel-good, on the other hand, nearly everyone is quirky. This collective quirkiness signals the essential goodness of the community; despite their foolishness and oddity the characters' hearts are in the right place. Those who appear 'normal' in these films are almost without exception revealed to be psychologically damaged or in some way a threat to the community. Typically, a lot of attention is paid to interiors and clothing, which serve as outward signs of the characters' personality traits. Frequently outdated or retrograde objects are fetishised in these films through prominent display in the *mise-en-scène*, which taps into the collective nostalgia of the audience.

While there may be a romance that develops, it is typically not the main structuring element of the film, or if it is, there may be more than one relationship that develops, or it may be balanced by a parallel focus on other types of relationships (parent–child, for example). Merely ending the narrative with some kind of heteronormative union between the protagonists is not enough, and the ending will typically be complicated or made bittersweet by other relationships. Similarly, a 'quirky' road movie structured around the journey highlights and privileges the forging of emotional connections and community along the way over the fantasy of escape and freedom that is often the hallmark of the road movie.

The *function* of the quirky feel-good is twofold. On the one hand, the aim is to entertain. These are not art films, though they may at times borrow or reference elements from the European art cinema canon. On the other hand, they are more complex and demand more intellectual and aesthetic evaluation on the part of their audiences than formulaic blockbuster genre films. They thus fit into Nestingen's description of 'medium-concept' as a 'combination of art film and genre film aimed at mainstream national and regional audiences' (2008: 53). While they have strong affective content, they do not aim to produce the full emotional catharsis of drama or melodrama, nor are they so uproariously funny that they offer the audience the escapist release of pure comedy. Instead, I believe the real function of these films is to present idealised versions of the 'imagined communities' (following Benedict Anderson) of the Nordic welfare states, and to allow contemporary audiences to frame their societies as better, more tolerant and inclusive than they may actually be.

In what follows, I aim to sketch out a corpus of films from each of the five Nordic countries that exemplifies some parameters for the quirky feel-good genre. This is by no means a definitive or delimiting list; my intention is to discuss a cluster of tropes, ethical concerns, narratological preoccupations and (to a lesser extent) aesthetics that are shared to such an extent that we may indeed speak of a distinct genre. Finally, in the conclusion I want to touch on how the Nordic quirky feel-good taps into the flows of the global film-festival market.

THE NORDIC 'QUIRKY FEEL-GOOD'

A Village in Sweden has Embraced its Idiots

Lasse Hallström's *My Life as a Dog*, an adaptation of Reidar Jönsson's 1983 novel of the same name, sets the standard for the quirky feel-good. It presents rural Sweden in a nostalgic and humorous light, while at the same time activating a certain melancholia, which reserves it from being categorised as an outright comedy. There are a number of key characteristics: (1) in terms of plot, a sudden relocation to an idyllic rural setting occurs; (2) a sense of loss in relation to the family troubles the main character and creates a persistent undertone of melancholy in the film; (3) a relatively large cast of supporting characters with decidedly quirky habits and behaviours provides most of the comedic material for the film; (4) it concludes with a loosely happy ending, where most but not all of the characters' problems are at least partly resolved; and (5) it contains an overarching thematic focus on what might be called a national fantasy of social integration.

This fantasy of integration functions both within the community depicted in the film itself, as well as more generally as commentary upon the larger imagined community of the nation. Through the struggles the main character undergoes, and through the humour and inclusiveness he brings to his new community, the film creates a hopeful image of a warmer, more inclusive society. A number of times in the film's voiceover narrative, Ingemar (Anton Glanzelius) says that it is important to be able to compare; that one's own situation has to be understood in relation to those who find themselves in worse circumstances. This opens the way for a meta-filmic reading of the village as an allegory for Sweden. The 'outsider' main character overcomes the scepticism of the closed-minded small-town citizens, and teaches them how to be freer and more accepting of their own difference and oddity (but not necessarily of the difference of 'othered' groups). Though seemingly a pure fantasy of village life, the film needs to be understood as a response to specific social problems in an increasingly urbanised Scandinavia.

My Life as a Dog layers the young protagonist Ingemar's troubles at home, his adventures while staying at his uncle's house in a small Swedish village, and Swedish boxer Ingmar Johansson's world championship victory against Floyd Patterson in June of 1959. With a dying mother unable to care for him, Ingemar is left in the hands of the larger community. Contrary to expectation and despite adversity such as the loss of his beloved dog, separation from his brother, and the death of his mother, Ingemar becomes fully integrated into the village community.

The closing montage sequence of the film emphasises a positive resolution to Ingemar's struggles, and posits the village as a microcosm for the nation. Hallström depicts the villagers listening to the Johansson–Patterson fight on the radios in their various homes and places of work. As Johansson wins, we see people running out onto the dirt road from various houses and the local factory to celebrate, followed by an exterior shot of a Falun red house, and we hear Ingemar's uncle Gunnar (Tomas von Brömssen) shout 'Heja Sverige!' (Hurrah for Sweden). In the next shot we see Ingemar and his friend and adversary Saga (Melinda Kinnaman) asleep on the sofa with the radio on. This shot is loving and warm, suggesting that despite the loss of his family (mother, brother, dog), Ingemar has established new connections. It echoes an earlier shot of Berit (Ing-Marie Carlsson) sleeping while her boyfriend sits on the bed listening to the boxing match in silence. The whole village comes together as one – despite their differences – in their pride over the victory of not just Johansson, but all of Sweden.

Yet the final shot of the entire movie moves away from the joyous celebration to frame the house of Fransson (Magnus Rask), the quirkiest of the villagers. Fransson remains unperturbed despite the ruckus, and continues to hammer away at the shingles of his roof as he has throughout the entire film. The camera stays on Fransson's house as the credits roll, suggesting that it is Fransson's stubborn quirkiness and desire to be left alone to do his own thing that is the real heart of the movie rather than the budding romance between Ingemar and Saga. Fransson appears to be the only villager who wants nothing to do with anyone, which ironically makes him the object of intense scrutiny. When he climbs down from the roof to swim in the river in the middle of the winter, the entire town follows him from the bridge, despite his angry demands to be left in peace. At this point the movie vacillates in point of view; in this sequence the previously benign and charming villagers briefly appear threatening and mob-like as they hound Fransson. And indeed it is the plight of Fransson that jolts Ingemar out of his sorrow and reestablishes him as a member of the community. The film thus emphasises the necessity of the 'Othered' social outsider in the construction of Swedish (and perhaps all) identity.

Idiosyncratic Iceland

In the early 1990s, Friðrik Þór Friðriksson's *Children of Nature* and *Cold Fever* placed Iceland on the map cinematically speaking, and together with high-profile international pop star Björk – whose influence on the international conceptualisation of Nordic quirkiness cannot be overstated – consciously cultivated a sense of Iceland as magical and otherworldly. Unlike other more strictly realist directors considered here, Friðriksson activates and depicts the supernatural in these films. Both films are road movies, but they depict journeys that do not correspond with any map because the characters encounter the supernatural along the way, which the director represents through rather crude camera tricks, judged by today's standards.

Friðriksson's Academy Award-nominated *Children of Nature* is permeated with a domestically oriented nostalgia for both the Icelandic landscape and the recent past. Using old age and the notion of returning home as his primary themes, Friðriksson (together with acclaimed Icelandic author, Einar Már Guðmundsson, who wrote the screenplay) creates a parallel between quirky Icelandic cultural praxis and the uniqueness of the landscape in an idealised vision of the nation. In the film Þorgeir (Gísli Halldórsson) is forced by his family to leave his farm and move into a nursing home in Reykjavik. There he meets the sweetheart of his youth, Stella (Sigríður Hagalín), who has also been relocated. The two escape the home and embark on a supernaturally guided, cross-country road trip back to the remote area where they grew up. It is an allegory that suggests that Friðriksson's idealised vision of the Icelandic nation is in danger of dying out. We see this most clearly in the film after Stella's death both through the insertion of an extended sequence of archival documentary footage of life in the remote and depopulated Westfjords region of Iceland, and in the extended sequence that depicts the slow process of building a coffin by hand and the subsequent burial of Stella carried out by Þorgeir alone. The strikingly beautiful shot of Stella's corpse on the beach lapped by tidal water echoes the driftwood that was used to build homes in this largely deforested nation. Her desire to die at home in the western fjords becomes a kind of national allegory that memorialises a way of life that is dying out.

The film ends with a coda of sorts that takes it out of purely domestic national nostalgia, and creates connections to the rest of Europe through Þorgeir's 'pilgrimage' to a military installation abandoned after the Second World War. Here Friðriksson references Wim Wenders's *Der himmel über Berlin* (*Wings of Desire*, 1987) visually through the use of a very similarly depicted angel figure (a middle-aged man in a long overcoat with wings) as a way of suggesting Þorgeir's death without depicting it realistically. The ending is bittersweet; the viewer is relieved that Stella and Þorgeir have come home, but is sad at their passing. Þorgeir and Stella were sweethearts in their youth, but lived full lives as adults with other partners. Reunited in the film, their elderly romance in itself can be understood as quirky and off-beat compared to standard romantic comedy tropes, where the protagonists are young and sexually attractive. The film's frequent use of 'supernatural' solutions to the hindrances that confront Stella and Þorgeir on their last journey home, as well as details in the *mise-en-scène* such as Stella's sneakers or the dance concert they come across on their journey, all reinforce the quirkiness of the way Iceland is represented as a community that is unusual both in and of itself and because it is (ostensibly) infused with the supernatural.

Danish Dogme Lite

Perhaps surprisingly, given the intellectual and aesthetic roots of the movement, two of the first four Dogme 95 films fit the criteria of the quirky feel-good quite well. While Søren Kragh-Jacobsen's *Mifunes sidste sang* (released internationally as *Mifune*, 1999) and Lone Scherfig's *Italian for Beginners* conform to the technical requirements of Dogme 95 and thus mirror their 'feel-bad' Dogme 95 counterparts – respectively Thomas Vinterberg's *Festen* (*The Celebration*, 1998) and Lars von Trier's *Idioterne* (*The Idiots*, 1998) – in terms of content and emotional power they aim for an entirely different affective register.

Italian for Beginners contrasts the pressures of suburban life in Denmark with an idealised 'other' place, in this case Italy. In this film a group of social misfits come together in their dream of a more generous, more sensual and more authentic way of life, symbolised by Italy. As Hjort points out, *Italian for Beginners* is essentially a film about losers and their inferiority complexes; in the film we as viewers see that 'the effects of disappointment, loss, and socially accepted violence and bullying can ... be overcome ... through a genuine openness to the friendships and loves that fate and chance bring our way' (Hjort 2010: 107). While the film does end with a group pilgrimage to Venice, the real transformation has already taken place at home, in their interpersonal relationships. The longing for the 'other' is ultimately revealed to be a fantasy of the self. The only actual Italian in the group, Giulia (Sara Indrio Jensen), serves as a sort of emotional catalyst, teaching the quirky but repressed Danes how to embrace and express their emotions. The film is never really about Italy; instead it is about opening up Danish society to become more inclusive and loving.

Italian for Beginners presents essentially the same story and same ethos as Gabriel Axel's breakthrough hit, *Babettes gæstebud* (*Babette's Feast*, 1987), where the warmth and exoticism of an outsider from southern Europe provides what is perceived to be lacking in Danish society. Yet in these films it is important to note that the exotic other is carefully selected and contained. Each belongs to a privileged class of foreigners who have positive valence in the Danish cultural imagination, maintaining the conceit that Denmark just needs a little freshening up with carefully selected foreign elements. These films are thus ultimately not really about integration in the face of globalisation, but rather about individual self-realisation, and perhaps – by extension – the consolidation (rather than hybridisation) of national identity.

Norwegian Nutters

One of the notable common denominators of a significant subset of Norwegian quirky feel-good movies is the representation of the urban environment as a safe haven, a nest of sorts that brings the intimacy of village life to urban living. In Petter Næss's *Elling*, the viewer is encouraged to identify closely with psychologically disturbed characters who, by the end of the film, appear quite normal.[3] The journey taken by Elling (Per Christian Ellfsen) and Kjell Bjarne (Sven Nordin) in *Elling* is from institution to society. We meet them halfway to integration, as they are placed in an apartment under the regular supervision of the social worker Frank Åsli (Jørgen Langhelle). Their journey from the trauma of the mental institution to the idyll of the metropolis reverses in some respects that of hundreds of thousands of Norwegians historically, who have left the predictability and security of rural life to try their luck in Oslo. Elling and Kjell Bjarne are placed right in the middle of the trendy district of Majorstuen, which in the film becomes a kind of village of its own, populated by quirky and welcoming locals who accept the psychological problems with which Elling and Kjell Bjarne struggle without batting an eyelid.

The film is pure wish fulfilment, reaching an affective climax of sorts when the urbane waiter at an über-trendy café (Knud Dahl) joins Kjell Bjarne in celebrating the birth of his child with improbable joy and enthusiasm. Through the course of the film the two misfits find themselves; Elling becomes a poet and Kjell Bjarne becomes a loving partner and father. Despite psychological problems so severe that they have been institutionalised and require observation, the film presents them as ultimately no different from the rest of the community. This message was central in the film's popular reception. The words of actor Per Christian Ellefsen are typical: 'Det bor en Elling i oss alle' ('there is an Elling in all of us'; Olsen 2001: 38). This belies the real-world situation in Norway for groups like the mentally ill and people struggling with substance abuse, who continue to be marginalised and shunned, despite policy changes and consciousness-raising campaigns to de-stigmatise them.

Fetishising Finland

Aki Kaurismäki's *The Man Without a Past* is far more aesthetically stylised than the other quirky feel-good films considered so far, yet it still fits within the parameters of the genre. Like Elling, M (Markku Peltola) moves from the country to the city, where we find an anachronistic, warm and accepting quirky community of container-dwellers embedded in the otherwise hostile urban environment. The container village in *The Man Without a Past* becomes a refuge for M and for its other marginalised inhabitants. Kaurismäki plays much more self-consciously and ironically with the fetishisation of the past than most of the other Nordic directors considered here, and at the same time the film is quite political. Anu Koivunen explains that 'While operating with communitarian rhetoric and via tropes of nostalgia, *The Man without a Past* does not partake in the production of national sentimentality' (Koivunen

2006: 144). The indeterminate ironic complexity of Kaurismäki's work distinguishes it from many of the other films considered here, yet I still see *The Man Without a Past* as an important example of the quirky feel-good genre.

M and Salvation Army worker Irma (Kati Outinen) find each other in the end, but, in typical quirky feel-good fashion, this is not the main focus of the film's denouement. Instead, Kaurismäki shifts attention to the rest of the container community – and thus allegorically to all of Finland – through their defeat of a gang of thugs, and through the prominent position given to the Finnish 'Schlager' singer Annikki Tähti's rendition of the song 'Muistatko Monrepos'n' (Do you remember Monrepos?). Koivunen argues for an allegorical reading of the closing song that posits 'the whole film being about a loss of an ideal, be it the political project of the welfare state or the leftist revolutionary dreams' (Koivunen 2006: 142). Nestingen makes a similar argument, stating, 'The irony of Kaurismäki's films disrupts their ostensible nostalgia to put the emphasis on solidarity' (Nestingen 2008: 143). It is precisely the unresolved vacillation between humour and drama, nostalgia and social criticism, combined with a visual and thematic focus on oddity that makes up the quirky feel-good more generally as a genre, and it is thus no surprise that films that manage to combine these elements successfully have done well with the same international audiences that hail Kaurismäki as a cinematic genius. These audiences are largely to be found at the many film festivals that have sprung up around the globe.

Conclusion

It is reasonable to surmise that the development of the Nordic quirky feel-good as a genre coalesced at least in part in response to growth in the international film festival circuit. In the words of Bill Nichols, 'An encounter with the unfamiliar, the experience of something strange, the discovery of new voices and visions serve as a major incitement for the festival-goer' (Nichols 1994: 17). High production costs have for the most part precluded Nordic filmmakers from producing films that can compete with Hollywood blockbusters; directors with such ambitions typically relocate to Hollywood itself rather than try to recreate the Hollywood blockbuster in a Nordic context (Renny Harlin and Harald Zwart come to mind). Given such financial and logistical limitations the film-festival circuit has, at least until now, offered the best opportunity for Nordic filmmakers to reach an international audience.

Thomas Elsaesser documents the history of the European film-festival circuit, arguing that it has become perhaps the most powerful force in the international distribution and critical reception of small nation cinema (Elsaesser 2005: 83). Noting the essentially postnational nature of contemporary European cinema – where financing across national borders is now the norm – Elsaesser draws a parallel to a kind of postnational horizon of expectation among festival audiences as well:

> Films made in Europe . . . tend to display the markers of their provenance quite self-consciously. The emphasis on region, neighborhoods, and the local in recent successes . . . provides access points for the international and global markets, which includes the national audience, thoroughly internationalized through the films on offer in cineplexes and videotheques. (Elsaesser 2005: 82)

Given the market realities, it makes sense that filmmakers in the Nordic countries have responded by creating a recognisable 'brand' that meets the demands of festival audiences. From Björk's striking 'Swan Dress' at the 2001 Academy Awards ceremony, to Lars 'von' Trier's infamous Nazi comments that got him expelled from the 2011 Cannes Film Festival, Nordic filmmakers continue to invest in maintaining a profile of quirkiness in order to succeed in the intense competition for the cultural capital that festival success engenders.

It is typical in the scholarly literature on the film-festival phenomenon to describe it as an essentially neutral vehicle in which 'a small film from an obscure source is picked up by a succession of festivals and shown consecutively in various territories, thus getting true global exposure, even if this exposure does not translate into measurable financial gains' (Iordanova 2008). As Felicia Chan suggests, however, festival programmers and audiences alike exert pressure on filmmakers to meet expectations about what kinds of 'small' films are worthy of attention (Chan 2011). The film-festival circuit has had a profound impact on film production in the Nordic countries, to the extent that we can now speak of a festival genre with a set of identifiable aesthetic and content elements.

It may be that the film-festival successes of Hallström's *My Life as a Dog* (fifteen awards and four additional nominations), Scherfig's *Italian for Beginners* (twenty awards and twenty-two additional nominations), and Kaurismäki's *Man Without a Past* (twenty-two awards and an additional twenty-one nominations) have functioned – consciously or unconsciously – as the models for ways of framing and marketing Nordic narratives and Nordic experiences internationally.[4] As different as these three films are, they each incorporate the elements that I have identified as central to the quirky feel-good: there is a sudden relocation to an idyllic setting, a sense of loss that creates a persistent undertone of melancholy, a quirky cast of characters who provide comedic relief, a loosely happy ending, and – most importantly – an overarching thematic focus on what might be called a national fantasy of social integration. They create a sense of authenticity and sincerity for festival audiences that both confirms and in some cases challenges expectations and assumptions about the nature of contemporary life in the Nordic welfare states.

Notes

1. See Mette Hjort's *Lone Scherfig's 'Italian for Beginners'* for a discussion of the treatment of the term 'feel-good' in film studies (Hjort 2010: 122). Hjort lists a number of qualities that she uses to define 'standard' feel-good cinema, including: (1) happy endings, (2) make-believe and fantasy, (3) positive emotions and escapism, (4) superficiality (136–8). She makes no mention of humour.
2. There are, of course, many exceptions to this generalisation. It is, however, not coincidental that one of the American films that most closely fits the quirky feel-good genre, *What's Eating Gilbert Grape*, was directed by Swedish director Lasse Hallström. Woody Allen's *Hannah and Her Sisters* (1986), Rob Reiner's *When Harry Met Sally* (1989), Jeremiah S. Chechik's *Benny and Joon* (1993) and James L. Brooks's *As Good as it Gets* (1997) conform fairly closely to the Scandinavian quirky feel-good, and indeed popular television sitcoms like *Seinfeld* (1989–98), *Northern Exposure* (1990–3) and *Friends* (1994–2004) in part fit the model, despite the differences in medium and format.
3. *Elling* is an adaptation of Ingvar Ambjørnsen's series of four novels about the mentally disturbed Elling: *Utsikt til paradis* (1993), *Fugledansen* (1995), *Elsk meg i morgen* (1999) and *Brødre i blodet* (1996), the last of which is the primary source for Næss's adaptation. Subsequently two other film adaptations have been made: Eva Isaksen's *Mors Elling* (2003) based on *Fugledansen*, and Næss's *Elsk meg i morgen* (2005) based on the novel of the same name.
4. Figures taken from the International Movie Database.

References

Chan, Felicia (2011), 'The International Film Festival and the Making of a National Cinema', *Screen* 52 (2): 253–60.
Elsaesser, Thomas (2005), 'Film Festival Networks: The New Topographies of Cinema in Europe'. In Thomas Elsaesser (ed.), *European Cinema: Face to Face with Hollywood*, Amsterdam: Amsterdam University Press, pp. 82–107
Hjort, Mette (2010), *Lone Scherfig's 'Italian for Beginners'*, Seattle: University of Washington Press.
Iordanova, D (2008), Introduction: 'Genre Films and Festival Communities', *Film International* 6 (3): 4–7.
Koivunen, Anu (2006), 'Do You Remember Monrepos? Melancholia, Modernity and Working-Class Masculinity in *The Man Without a Past*.' In C. Claire Thomson (ed.), *Northern Constellations: New Readings in Nordic Cinema*, Norwich: Norvik Press, pp. 133–48.
MacDowell, James (2010), 'Notes on Quirky', *Movie: A Journal of Film Criticism* 1: 1–16
Nestingen, Andrew (2008), *Crime and Fantasy in Scandinavia: Fiction, Film, and Social Change*, Seattle: University of Washington Press.
Nichols, Bill (1994), 'Discovering Form, Inferring Meaning: New Cinemas and the Film Festival Circuit', *Film Quarterly* 47 (3): 16–30.
Olsen, Trygve Aas (2001), 'Derfor elsker vi Elling', *Dagblade*, 16 March, p. 38.

11. CONTESTING MARRIAGE: THE FINNISH UNROMANTIC COMEDY

Jaakko Seppälä

Mother-in-law: 'Are you going to get married?'
Karita: 'We don't know yet.'
Antero: 'No, we're not.'
Mother-in-law: 'That's good. It's easier to separate when the time comes. And it will come.'
Antero: 'Yes, it will.'
Mother-in-law: 'That's right.'

The conversation is taken from the Finnish romantic comedy *The Storage* (*Varasto*, 2011). The film is based on a gritty realist novel of the same name written by the late Arto Salminen (1998). In the scene in question Karita and Antero, a new and dysfunctional couple about to have a child, are visiting his future mother-in-law whose experiences of marriage are appalling to say the least. She has faced poverty, domestic violence and cheating before her husband committed suicide. Before that he tried to kill her. Now, because of her sexual needs, the mother-in-law lives in a common-law marriage with another man who is an overweight drunk who spends his days watching sports on television. The young couple find him disgusting, but the mother-in-law defends her choice: 'I like it when my lady neighbours are jealous when I'm out, happy and glowing with my man. And he doesn't beat me.' Clearly, she has learnt to lower her demands and expectations when it comes to relationships.

'(Un)romantic comedy' was the tagline with which *The Storage* was advertised. In the context of the romantic comedy genre this definition is a purposeful twist on the genre because romantic comedy, contrary to Salminen's novel, is regarded as escapist entertainment that fuses the romance and comedy genres (Mortimer 2010: 4). Readings and interpretations of the novel, which has been turned into a play that was performed at The Finnish National Theatre, have been pessimistic. Director Taru Mäkelä says that contrary to these interpretations she modelled her film on Howard Hawks's *Bringing Up Baby* (1938)[1] and other screwball comedies of Hollywood's golden era in order to heighten the comic aspects of Salminen's story (Laakso 2011). As *The Storage* combines conventions of the romantic comedy genre with Salminen's realism, (un) romantic comedy can be taken to mean realistic romantic comedy. This fusion of realism and conventions of the genre is emblematic of various contemporary Finnish romantic comedies. This is especially evident in the ways these films discuss underlying tensions that are present between sexuality and marriage.

'The happy couple', to use the phrase that Nicolas Pillai (2012) has at the centre of his study of classical Hollywood films, is becoming something of a rarity in contemporary Finnish cinema. Marriages portrayed in Finnish films, unlike those studied by Pillai, are only on the odd occasion happy and continuous. As Andrew Britton (1984/2003) states, there is 'implicit disharmony between sexual romanticism and the institution of marriage.' It seems that Finns on film are losing their faith in marriage. One reason for this state of affairs is the changed social reality. In 2011, the year when *The Storage* premiered, 13,468 Finnish marriages ended in divorce (Official Statistics of Finland 2013). This is a high figure considering that that year the number of

Figure 11.1 There is little upon which the protagonists could build a lasting relationship in *The Storage*. Image courtesy of Kinosto Oy.

contracted marriages was only 28,408. The numbers have remained about the same for the last ten years. Almost every other marriage ends in divorce and these statistics suggest that many Finnish couples are anything but happy. In the 2000s divorces have been relentlessly discussed in the Finnish media, especially in the tabloids, women's magazines and television shows (Maksimainen 2010: 10). Now romantic comedies are participating in the discussion. One reason for this is that for contemporary Finnish films set in present-day Finland to be believable, they need to acknowledge the state of marital affairs in some way. This is easy in art house films, but problematic in romantic comedies, an age-old convention of which is marriage as a happy ending (Mortimer 2010: 16 and passim), and in Finnish films too (Koivunen 1995: 214). But it is only by adapting to new historical circumstances that the genre overall can survive (Williams and Deleyto 1998: 1). Filmmakers are now questioning traditional ideas of marriage with the result that contemporary Finnish romantic comedy is more unromantic than before.

The genre of the romantic comedy was domesticated in the studio era of Finnish cinema that lasted from the early 1930s to late 1950s by filmmakers who admired Hollywood films, an example of whom would be Valentin Vaala (Alanen 2004: 74–6). This domestication was an easy process for the reason that romantic comedies are universal in tone, which means they can be set pretty much in any location, discuss context-specific problems related to relationships and be produced with the modest budgets of small nation cinemas. This has made the genre more than suited for Finnish cinema. The budget of *The Storage* was a mere €748,105, which is only half of the typical budget of a contemporary Finnish film (Finnish Film Foundation 2011). The film was nonetheless seen by roughly 200,000 viewers (Finnish Film Foundation 2013a), which means its mixture of genre conventions and realism was in accord with the tastes of contemporary Finnish audiences. Now other filmmakers are trying to repeat its success by discussing similar themes.

Another romantic comedy tackling the reality of the Finnish marriage, *21 Ways to Ruin a Marriage* (*21 tapaa pilata avioliitto*, 2012), was even more successful. Johanna Vuoksenmaa's film – which was advertised with the tagline 'is someone still married?' – was seen by a spectacular 400,000 viewers (Finnish Film Foundation 2013b).[2] More conventional romantic comedies like *The Body Fat Index of Love* (*Rakkauden rasvaprosentti*, 2012), which is the third film I am analysing in this chapter, have not been as popular. Mikko Kuparinen's film, produced in collaboration with The Family Federation of Finland, drew only 42,120 viewers (Finnish Film Foundation 2013b) even though it touches on similar issues to the other two. It seems to me that the popularity of *The Storage* and *21 Ways to Ruin a Marriage* was largely based on their satirical discussion of contemporary problems related to sex and marriage. Audiences probably found the films an effective aid in making sense of these issues. However, one might counter this by saying that their popularity resulted more from the comedians who had become national favourites in the sketch television show *Putous*. I do not want to deny the impact of these actors on the popularity of these films, but I want to point out that *No Thank You* (*Ei kiitos*, 2014), a romantic comedy – in which there are no actors from the show – that tells the story of a middle-aged woman who gets herself a lover in order to save her sexless marriage, drew over 25,000 viewers in its first weekend. The film is still playing in cinemas at the time of writing, but it is already predicted that it will draw more than 200,000 viewers (Halttunen 2014). We clearly need a better understanding of the ways in which these films discuss sex and marriage if we are to understand their national importance and popularity.

The Storage, *21 Ways to Ruin a Marriage* and *The Body Fat Index of Love* are all part of a corpus, a cycle of the contemporary Finnish romantic comedy that I term the Finnish unromantic comedy. These films, and the first two in particular, question what Peter Evans and Celestino Deleyto (1998: 3) call the 'relatively unchanged view of love, sexuality and marriage' of the genre. As Stanley Cavell (2005: 165–6) says, we should not assume that romantic comedies are popular commodities that simply serve to support the ideology of marriage. Here I am working with a notion of cycle that is based on Cavell's (1981: 146) definition of a genre 'that demands that a feature found in one of its members must be found in all, or some equivalent or compensation found in each'. There are two interrelated defining themes to the Finnish unromantic comedy. First, traditional genre roles (especially those of women but often those of men too) are radically transformed in comparison to earlier Finnish films. This shows especially in the ways in which these films openly discuss sex and female desire. Second, serious relationships (especially marriage) are contested. In many of these films the main characters, in most cases new kinds of modern women, are looking for sex without commitment.

Film reviewers discussed these films in relation to Hollywood's popular romantic comedies and their ilk[3] for the reason that these Finnish films make use of their established genre patterns. Nordic representatives of the genre – except other Finnish films – were not mentioned. Even though Finland has close film relations with Sweden and co-productions are common, contemporary Swedish films are largely unknown in the country. Contemporary Swedish romantic comedies like *Cockpit* (2012), *Once Upon a Time in Phuket* (*En gång i Phuket*, 2011) and *Midsummer of Love* (*Sommaren med Göran*, 2009) have not been shown in Finland. A comparison of these Swedish films to the films I am analysing here reveals some interesting similarities and differences. Swedish films, too, rely on international genre patterns and discuss contemporary societal issues, in the case of *Cockpit* gender roles and gender equality, but sexually active women are not at the centre. Both *Once Upon a*

Figure 11.2　Traditional gender roles are reversed in *21 Ways to Ruin a Marriage*. Image courtesy of Dionysos Films Oy.

Time in Phuket and *Midsummer of Love* star the actor Peter Magnusson, who has become a seminal actor in Swedish romantic comedies due to his popularity as protagonist in the Swedish sketch television show *Hey Baberiba*. And when women are at the centre, as in *Love and Lemons* (*Små citroner gula*, 2013), they are not portrayed as sexually active and the institution of marriage is not contested. The most radical of the mentioned films is *Cockpit* in which the protagonist faces a divorce. His wife then marries an elderly man for his fortune; and even though this can be seen as a satirical statement, the film does absolutely nothing to make the audience share her views on the importance of wealth and unimportance of love in marriage. Even though divorce rates are just as high in Sweden (Eurostat 2012), Swedish romantic comedies are less cynical and more optimistic about marriage than their Finnish counterparts. This serves to remind us that romantic comedies do not reflect society's marital reality in any straightforward way.

Before analysing the Finnish films in detail, I am going to provide a quick background exploration of Finnish romantic comedies of the studio era in order to show the transformation. The endings of even the most boundary-pushing of these, like Valentin Vaala's *Substitute Wife* (*Vaimoke*, 1936) and Matti Kassila's *Father's Old and New* (*Isän vanha ja uusi*, 1955), are conservative and conformist when it comes to questions of sex and marriage. *Substitute Wife* tells the story of a couple who get married not for love but for a bet and a will to embarrass each other. The marriage turns out to be a kind of a game that both enjoy playing to such an extent that they fall in love.[4] The film ends with a kiss that may be formulated with the words: 'They lived happily ever after.' In *Substitute Wife*, like in virtually all studio era romantic comedies, marriage comes first and sex follows. *Father's Old and New* tells the story of a man who has divorced and married a flighty woman[5] who is much younger than his first wife. The marriage turns out to be a disappointment. The man cannot stand his wife's constant partying and the wife is bored with her husband's wish to stay home and read. They both do their best to sabotage the marriage so that she can move away with her foreign lover and he can re-marry his first wife, whom he now understands he should not have divorced in the first place. Anu Koivunen (1995: 220–1) argues that there is much more to Finnish romantic comedies, or to 'modern comedies' as she calls them, of the studio era than mere conservatism and conformism. The reason for this is that the happy endings that preserve the sanctity of marriage cannot undo all the tensions and contradictions that the films (and their many contexts) create. Ambiguity and variety might even be part of the convention of the happy ending itself (MacDowell 2013: 192 and passim). These cracks in the happy endings, as I term them, some of which are intentional although others are not, are even more vivid in the Finnish unromantic comedy.

The Implausible Marriage

Film reviewers criticised *The Storage* for downplaying Arto Salminen's social criticism. The film culminates in what was regarded as 'a forced happy ending' (Poussu 2011). In this closure, which takes place 'a couple of years later', the young child of Karita and Antero tells in voiceover narration that her parents have not divorced and that her mother is planning a church wedding. During her speech we see photographs of Antero and Karita who are now a happy couple. 'The cute summary at the end functions as a banal and tawdry conclusion to the story,' Jussi Virratvuori (2011) claims. This suggests that viewers interested in the film's satirical discussion of societal issues found the ending unbelievable. In order to better understand these feelings we need to scrutinise how Antero and Karita's relationship is portrayed in the film.

In classic romantic comedies characters are likeable and the relationships they finally form ideal. 'What this pair does together is less important than the fact that they do whatever it is together, that they know how to spend time together, even that they would rather waste time together than do anything else,' Stanley Cavell (1981: 88) analyses the couple in *It Happened One Night* (1934). According to Wayne C. Booth (1988/2005: 204), films make us certain kinds of desirers. In *It Happened One Night* we desire to see the couple get married for the reason that they go so well together and we find it hard to believe that either of them could be happier alone or with someone else. The same could be said about the couple in *Substitute Wife* and the original couple in *Father's Old and New*, but certainly not of Antero and Karita. They work in the same paint shop and have sex nearly every weekend, as a result of which Karita is now pregnant. When Antero is informed about the future child he refuses to believe it is his for the reason that other men are sleeping with Karita as well. 'Even your neighbour's dogs are screwing you,' Antero protests in his highly dislikeable manner. Karita nonetheless believes that she and Antero could be happy. This is irrational, as is obvious from her comment: 'We make the perfect couple because your ascendant is in Taurus.' Clearly Karita's faith in their 'love' is comparable to superstition. Even so, when she learns that Antero has been stealing from the shop's storage she manages to blackmail him into moving in with her and starting a family. This is hardly a basis on which a happy marriage could be built, the reviewers must have thought.

Antero finds the idea of living with Karita so repulsive that he attempts to abort the baby by putting emergency contraception pills in her yoghurt. This plan, which fails, further illustrates Antero's immorality and implies that he does not recognise Karita as a fellow human with equal rights. He merely wants to take advantage of her sexuality, which does not make us, the viewers, like him. The dysfunctionality of this couple is best illustrated in a scene where Karita and Antero watch television shortly after moving in together. The programme they see is *The Singing Bee*, during an opening insert of which — in which there is nothing particularly funny — Karita cannot help laughing. Her laughter is reminiscent of Jayne Mansfield trademark 'ooo' in *Will Success Spoil Rock Hunter?* (1957), which heightens Karita's screwball character to which Antero (and presumably most viewers as well) finds it difficult to relate. When the host of the show makes a lame joke she becomes nearly hysterical. Antero cannot enjoy the show or her company. It is evident that there is absolutely nothing upon which these two could build a lasting relationship and it is hard to believe that their baby could undo these tensions and contradictions. In his study of Jane Austen's *Emma*, Booth (1983: 259) discusses the marriage, which he finds a complete and perfect resolution to the story. According to him 'this will be a happy marriage because there is simply nothing left to make it anything less than perfectly happy. It fulfils every value embodied in the world of the book.' When it comes to *The Storage*, in which the relationship is based on sex and taking advantage of the other, and in which the best hope for the couple comes from an astrological sign, we are guided to wish that Antero would treat Karita better, but we certainly do not desire a church wedding, as there is little that could make their marriage even relatively happy.

Unsatisfactory and Satisfactory Endings

The main female character of *The Body Fat Index of Love*, Ella, is interested in sex without commitments, unlike her friend who craves romance. When Ella meets Stigu in a restaurant she flirts with him and makes a direct suggestion: 'My place, Wednesday, 7 pm. 45 minutes, sex only.' Stigu is offered what Antero had but lost. The precision of the suggestion indicates that Ella is a rational person; she knows exactly what she wants and where her limits are.

For her, all kinds of relationships are off limits: 'I don't want to know anything about you or tell you anything about myself. No commitment, no soul searching. And certainly no Facebook friendship.' When Stigu comes to meet Ella the following Wednesday, he brings a bottle of wine. The bottle refers to the possibility of loosening one's rational judgement and spending a romantic evening together. Ella puts the bottle away and picks up an egg timer, as forty-five minutes of sex is all there is going to be. The timer, which refers to temporality and measurability, further enhances her rational nature and comes to characterise the relationship.

In this film, too, love is portrayed as an irrational force that could destroy the lives the protagonists want to lead. Ella and even Stigu, regardless of his romantic interest in her, are ambitious and care more about their careers than about each other. Ella dreams about her own vintage clothes shop, while Stigu makes commercials for an advertising agency. Such career commitments are typical problems that many young couples face today. At the turning point of the story, Stigu erases from Ella's calendar a meeting that he knows to be most important for her as her vintage shop depends on it. Stigu does this to save his own career, because he needs Ella's help on a commercial on that particular day. In other words, he knowingly, all things being equal, destroys Ella's career so that his can continue. The conventional happy ending where Ella and Stigu not only get together but also end up co-owning the vintage shop is hardly a resolution that can undo such tensions the story has touched on – there are severe cracks in the happy ending.

Film reviewer Rane Aunimo (2012) was disappointed with *The Body Fat Index of Love* because it discusses different kinds of relationships in a laid-back manner, but despite all its quasi-courage the main message is conservative. He

Figure 11.3 Stigu's parents are happily married in *The Body Fat Index of Love*. Image courtesy of MRP Matila Röhr Productions Oy.

implies that the film should have portrayed a new way of being a couple. Juha Rosenqvist (2012) says why he thinks the story is flawed: 'Ella would be every guy's dream woman, sex without necessary lovers' talk, but lovers' talk is what Stigu wants.' Soila Ojanen (2012) found the film's conventional plot twists that result in the happy ending formal to the extent that the film is not believable. These reviewers, and presumably many viewers as well, wanted to see a more unromantic ending. It seems that conventional happy endings, which may be suited to contemporary Hollywood films, are not suited to the Finnish unromantic comedy. The probable reason for this is that these films, due to their locality and discussion of contemporary societal issues, are more realistic to Finnish audiences than Hollywood films that are typically watched with different kinds of expectations. The same seems to be true when it comes to Finnish crime films (Seppälä 2013: 230).

Of the three films, only *21 Ways to Ruin a Marriage* was not criticised for its ending. In this film, as in the other two, the affair of the main couple is built on promiscuous sex. Unlike in the romantic comedies of the studio era, in these films sex unites couples and it is love that comes later, if it comes. The protagonist in *21 Ways to Ruin a Marriage* is Sanna, a PhD student who explores reasons why couples divorce. She conducts her study by filming and interviewing married people. Sanna believes she can predict divorces from certain signs in these videos. Her lengthy list of ways of ruining a marriage contains behaviour like 'be blind', 'be clingy' and 'treat your spouse like a child'. Sanna argues that 'divorce is a natural and probable consequence of falling in love'. She does not believe in love, probably because her own parents have divorced, and she satisfies her sexual needs by having next to anonymous sex. 'Sex happens separately and just once with everyone. It works well, and there is no emotional mess' – thus Sanna, who believes this is rational behaviour, explains her conduct.

The film guides us to see Sanna's friend's beliefs in love and marriage as irrational. Especially telling are scenes in which she tries to foretell her future love life and possibility of getting married by randomly listening to radio stations and interpreting what she hears. Love is also portrayed as irrational in the sequence in which Sanna is totally drunk, at her most irrational that is, and her list of ways of ruining a marriage is transformed in her mind into ways of creating a happy marriage: 'touch, listen, love, love, love'. Against her better judgement, she falls in love with Aleksi who is one of her recently divorced interviewees, a kind young man who looks after his two children and believes in marriage despite his bad experience.

'Whether it lasts one day or the rest of your life, being in love has its value,' Sanna says after seeing her gloomy father happy and glowing with a new woman with whom he has fallen in love. Sanna and Aleksi decide to give their relationship a chance. Falling in love might not be rational, but it should not be avoided, the film suggests. On the night they get together, Sanna and Aleksi go through the lengthy list of ways of ruining a marriage, ways that they should now avoid. 'I don't think anyone can avoid all of that,' Aleksi remarks and in so doing acknowledges his human weaknesses. 'I guess that's my point,' Sanna says. The film implies a marriage needs to be based on love, but there is no guarantee that it will last. 'Despite the happy ending there seems to be a fundamental distrust in love in this movie,' film critic Antti Alanen (2012) suggests. To be more precise, there is a fundamental distrust of marriage in the film. Sanna and Aleksi, like all Finnish couples who fall in love, hope that their relationship will last. This might be wishful thinking, but they have a chance, and considering that they acknowledge their weaknesses, it is probably much more than a chance. Yes, *21 Ways to Ruin a Marriage* has a happy ending, but this ending does not downplay the societal realities and therefore it does not feel unsatisfactory.

Young Couples and the Married Generation

The ending of *The Storage* is not actually as happy as the reviewers found it. The photographs of the happy couple and the child's voiceover narration that accompanies them follow a scene in which Antero has shown the child a storage worker's cotton canvas glove. In the eyes of the baby the grip dots of the glove transform to a starry night sky, across which two shooting stars race. As they say, when you see a shooting star, you can make a wish; and this is precisely what the child does! This means that her happy talk about Antero and Karita being together after couple of years and Karita making plans for a church wedding is mere wishful thinking. We have learnt that there is nothing but the child to keep the couple together. Besides, Antero has said that the average length of a relationship in their suburbs is about three years. That is probably as long as the child can hold them together as a family. This does not have to mean that the relationship could not be happy and last longer, as Karita and Antero also, have a chance, slim as it chance may be. The important point is that the ending of *The Storage* is open and not that dissimilar from that of *21 Ways to Ruin a Marriage*. Unlike the romantic comedies of the studio era, these endings do not guide viewers to make confidently optimistic predictions for the future of their couples.

So, the relationships I have discussed might last, but the question is, what form are they going to take and how happy are they going to be? All three films imply that their main couples probably need to find new ways of being happy, as there is no certainty that old models will work for them. The films create this sense by contrasting the young couples with older couples. In *The Body Fat Index of Love* Stigu's parents are a happy couple: they enjoy each other's company and have a continual relationship. In one scene they show

Stigu a video clip of the Wife-Carrying World Championships in which they participated. While watching the video, the parents sit close to each other, which marks their relationship with love and warmth. Stigu, who thinks he has lost his chances with Ella, is sitting on the other side of the table looking sad and lonely. The positioning of the actors and their expressions heighten the generational gap that exists between the characters. 'I was almost ready to quit but I thought to myself: It's not a shame to lose but it's a shame to give in,' Stigu's father says about his experience in the race. 'It's awesome,' Stigu says, referring to his parents' marriage and the video that represents it. In this video the couple seem to lose the race, but look happy nonetheless. After crossing the finish line the husband lowers his wife to her wheelchair and they embrace while spectators cheer in the background. Happy and ideal as this marriage may be, it is also marked as one that might not be possible for Ella and Stigu. This is because the parents are from a different time. They are old-fashioned or, maybe better put, traditional, and live in the countryside in Sonkajärvi. Their marriage has been built and maintained in circumstances that were vastly different from those in which the younger generation lives. Besides, what could this generation really learn from Stigu's father's words? The film suggests that they should be taken as an analogy of a marriage, but the way I see it, both losing and giving in result in the same thing and that thing is divorce.

Most marriages in *21 Ways to Ruin a Marriage* are anything but happy and will probably end badly. The only happy couple in this film are an elderly couple, even older than Stigu's parents in *The Body Fat Index of Love*. The couple live next door to Sanna, which enables her to watch their life, and she does this without fully understanding them. 'I want something like that,' says Sanna's friend who yearns to be happily married, and she points at the old woman who is giving her husband a haircut on a sunny yard. 'Now I know why he always has such a funny haircut,' Sanna says. 'She's almost blind and he can't hear anything.' Here too the happy couple are portrayed as a loving couple in which the husband and wife complement each other. In the most touching scene of the film Sanna sees an ambulance taking the woman away while the husband stands behind waving his hand. Clearly their love affair, which has lasted their whole life together (with its ups and downs, I am sure), is about to end. In other words, the only marriage in *21 Ways to Ruin a Marriage* that is happy and does not end in a divorce is one from another era and about to disappear from this world.

Conclusion

Social realities are satirically discussed in contemporary Finnish romantic comedies, as a result of which these films are more unromantic than before.

This tendency is most evident in the cycle I have termed the Finnish unromantic comedy. There are no happily married couples in *The Storage*. Only the mother-in-law and the overweight drunk who live together seem satisfied with their lives. Even though Karita and Antero find this couple disgusting, they can be seen as a new kind of happy couple. As James Wood (2009: 135) argues, following Leo Tolstoy, 'the only way to understand people properly is to see things from each person's point of view.' As I have suggested, this is a relationship that both participants find satisfactory. The mother-in-law gets sex and the drunk can watch television and drink beer in his solitude, just as he pleases. Their relationship might not last forever, but that does not have to mean that it could not make them happy. The crucial point is that this is their relationship and it is built from their needs and wishes. The lesson that the young couples could learn from the mother-in-law and her drunk is that they too have to find their own ways of being together, married or not. Marriage is nothing but a social institution, in a sense a coulisse, whereas the relationship is the content. Considering that *The Storage* and *The Body Fat Index of Love* were criticised for their endings, it seems that Finnish audiences are of the opinion that filmmakers who fuse social realism and conventions of the romantic comedy genre ought to find fresh endings, probably ones that portray new ways of being together. Actually, the first steps have already been taken, as the latest film in the cycle, *No Thank You*, ends with a scene in which the protagonist acknowledges that she does not always have to love her husband, as it is enough that they both love their daughter. Such an unromantic ending would have been unimaginable in a Finnish romantic comedy in the studio era.

Notes

1. Karita is a screwball lady who knows what she wants and has her way of getting it, much like Susan Vance, the fast-talking dame played by Katherine Hepburn in *Bringing Up Baby*.
2. *21 Ways to Ruin a Marriage* received the audience award at Jussi Gaala 2014, which is a further indication of its broad appeal. The Jussi Award is the Finnish equivalent of the Academy Award, an accolade recognising excellence in the Finnish film industry.
3. British romantic comedies of the 1990s and early 2000s were also mentioned, especially in reviews of *The Body Fat Index of Love*, which, according to its director Mikko Kuparinen (Paju, 2012), was modelled on films like *Love Actually* (2003).
4. This battle of the sexes theme is reminiscent of that in American screwball comedies where both the man and the woman are so extraordinary that they cannot be anywhere but together, even though they try.
5. The woman is more than reminiscent of Marilyn Monroe, which, among other things, implies that the film was modelled on American romantic comedies.

References

Alanen, Antti (2004), 'Nuoren Vaalan kansainvälisiä vaikutteita'. In Kimmo Laine, Matti Lukkarila and Juha Seitajärvi (eds), *Valentin Vaala*, Helsinki: SKS, pp. 65–77.
Alanen, Antti (2012), '21 tapaa pilata avioliitto/21 Ways to Ruin a Marriage', <http://anttialanenfilmdiary.blogspot.fi/2013/05/21-tapaa-pilata-avioliitto-21-ways-to.html>, accessed 24 January 2014.
Aunimo, Rane (2012), 'Usko ja patja koetuksella', *Demokraatti*, 21 December (clipping held in film files of the Finnish National Audiovisual Institute).
Booth, Wayne C. (1983), *The Rhetoric of Fiction*, Chicago: The University of Chicago Press.
Booth, Wayne C. (1988/2005), *The Company We Keep: An Ethics of Fiction*, Berkeley: University of California Press.
Britton, Andrew (1984/2003), *Katharine Hepburn: Star as Feminist*, New York: Columbia University Press.
Cavell, Stanley (1981), *Pursuits of Happiness: The Hollywood Comedy of Remarriage*, Cambridge, MA: Harvard University Press.
Cavell, Stanley (2005/1988), 'Two Cheers for Romance'. In William Rotham (ed.), *Cavell on Film*, New York: State University of New York Press, pp. 153–66.
Eurostat (2012), 'Marriage and Divorce Statistics', <http://epp.eurostat.ec.europa.eu/statistics_explained/index.php/Marriage_and_divorce_statistics>, accessed 4 October 2014.
Evans, Peter William and Celestino Deleyto (1998), 'Introduction: Surviving Love'. In Peter William Evans and Celestino Deleyto (eds), *Terms of Endearment: Hollywood Romantic Comedy of the 1980s and 1990s*, Edinburgh: Edinburgh University Press.
Finnish Film Foundation (2011), *Elokuvavuosi 2010 Facts & Figures*, Helsinki: Suomen elokuvasäätiö/Finnish Film Foundation.
Finnish Film Foundation (2013a), *Elokuvavuosi 2012 Facts & Figures*, Helsinki: Suomen elokuvasäätiö/Finnish Film Foundation.
Finnish Film Foundation (2013b), 'Admissions to Domestic Films 2013', <http://ses.fi/en/statistics/yearly-statistics/domestic-admissions-2013/>, accessed 24 January 2014.
Halttunen, Jukka (2014), 'Kyllä kiitos! Kotimainen romanttinen komedia tähtää huippulukemiin', *Episodi* 13 January 2014, <http://www.episodi.fi/uutiset/kylla-kiitos-kotimainen-romanttinen-komedia-tahtaa-huippulukemiin/>, accessed 24 January 2014.
Koivunen, Anu (1995), *Isänmaan moninaiset äidinkasvot*, Turku: Suomen elokuvatutkimuksen seura.
Laakso, Kimmo (2011), 'Arton kanssa varastossa', *Voima*, October (clipping held in film files of the Finnish National Audiovisual Institute).
MacDowell, James (2013), *Happy Endings in Hollywood Cinema: Cliché, Convention and the Final Couple*, Edinburgh: Edinburgh University Press.
Maksimainen, Jaana (2010), *Parisuhde ja ero: Sosiologinen analyysi terapeuttisesta ymmärryksestä*, Helsinki: Unigrafia and University of Helsinki.
Mortimer, Claire (2010), *Romantic Comedy*, Oxford and New York: Routledge.
Official Statistics of Finland (2013), *Changes in Marital Status*, Helsinki: Statistics Finland, <http://www.stat.fi/til/ssaaty/2012/ssaaty_2012_2013-04-19_tie_001_en.html>, accessed 24 January 2014.
Ojanen, Soila (2012), 'Kaavamaisesti kesäyössä', *Satakunnankansa*, 21 December (clipping held in film files of the Finnish National Audiovisual Institute).
Paju, Anna (2012), 'Elokuvantekijän kesä: Toppatakkeja ja aurinkorasvaa', *Kansan Uutiset Viikkolehti*, 28 December (clipping held in film files of the Finnish National Audiovisual Institute).

Pillai, Nicolas (2012), 'The Happy Couple: American Marriages in Hollywood Films 1934–1948', PhD thesis, University of Warwick.
Poussu, Tarmo (2011), 'Sukupuolten sissisotaa työpaikalla', *Ilta-Sanomat*, 30 December (clipping held in film files of the Finnish National Audiovisual Institute).
Rosenqvist, Juha (2012), 'Tylsä pariutumiskomedia', Film-O-Holic 21 December 2012, <http://www.film-o-holic.com/arvostelut/rakkauden-rasvaprosentti/>, accessed 24 January 2014.
Salminen, Arto (1998), *Varasto*, Helsinki: WSOY.
Seppälä, Jaakko (2013), 'Kiikaritähtäimessä tasavallan presidentti: Herraviha ja amerikkalainen väkivalta elokuvassa Jäähyväiset presidentille'. In Kalevi Koukkunen, Kimmo Laine and Juha Seitajävi (eds), *Elokuvat kertovat, Matti Kassila*, Helsinki: SKS, pp. 224–36.
Virratvuori, Jussi (2011), 'Köyhän taivas', *Karjalainen*, 30 December (clipping held in film files of the Finnish National Audiovisual Institute).
Wood, James (2009), *How Fiction Works*, London: Vintage Books.

12. POWERED BY MUSIC: CONTEMPORARY FILM MUSICALS, NORDIC STYLE

Ann-Kristin Wallengren

THE MUSICAL AS (AN AMERICAN) GENRE

When thinking about Nordic cinema, the musical is not the first genre to come to mind. This holds true for the global audiences as well as for Nordic ones, nowadays and in retrospect. The film musical, in some kind of down-to-earth classical generic sense, is for a Western audience most probably associated with Hollywood films from the 1930s and onwards, with an obvious decline after the successful productions *Mary Poppins* (1964) and *The Sound of Music* (1965). Some European musicals are probably also well-known to the non-specialist public, such as Jacques Demy's *Les Parapluies de Cherbourg* (*The Umbrellas of Cherbourg*, 1964) and *Les Demoiselles de Rochefort* (*The Young Girls of Rochefort*, 1967). Since then musicals have changed or transformed. Even if some characteristics usually connected with the genre are still in use, they are now often utilised in an excessive or transformed way (Altman 1987; Grant 2012).

It is not at all curious that audiences in general, at least Western audiences, link musicals primarily to Hollywood. After all, it was a very important genre for the American film industry as well as for the music industry. The films were a feast for the eye which attracted audiences globally, and songs and music from the musicals had worldwide appeal. Some of the most renowned scholars even write from the standpoint that, in a strict sense, only Hollywood musicals can be classified as musicals. In his essay in *The Oxford History of World Cinema*, Rick Altman argues that Hollywood is the only film industry that has produced films that match the genre. Consequently Altman asserts: 'To study the musical is thus primarily to analyze the history of Hollywood's 1,500 or so musical films' (Altman 1996: 294). Jane Feuer also, more or less without discussion, writes about musicals as a Hollywood phenomenon in her classical book *The Hollywood Musical* from 1993. And an overwhelming corpus of books about the musical, as genre and as history, has titles that directly state the musical to be an American or Hollywoodian cultural product.

To pin down the characteristics of the musical as a genre is not as simple as, say, those of the western genre, where iconography, settings and characters are usually clear-cut and rather easy to define. A musical can have practically any setting, characters and iconography (apart from backstage musicals that are often set in entertainment establishments), but the lowest common denominator is that music, songs and often dance permeate the narration; indeed music is the determining element for the organisation of the film, formally as well as narratively (Altman 1999; Feuer 1993; Grant 2012). In order to make it possible to include global variants of the genre, some scholars suggest a slight transformation of the terminology. Richard Dyer reminds us of the inclusive definition stated by John Russell Taylor, that a musical is 'a film which has its shape, its movement, its whole feeling dictated by music' (Dyer 2012: 145). Adrian Martin agrees, and in his aim to make the genre all-embracing he wants to discuss it in terms of the music-film which he defines as 'any film which feels as if it is *driven* by its music . . . where the guiding role of music in relation to image is especially foregrounded', and of which the musical is a sub-category (Martin 2001: 74).

Thus, if we agree with Martin, an overarching genre is the music-film which is defined as a film that is *driven* by music. A further notion is used by Barry Keith Grant (2012), who states that the music in a film musical has a more radical narrative importance and is organically connected to the characters, whereas the music in a musical film has a more outsider position:

> In George Lucas's nostalgic film about California high schoolers in the 1960s [*American Graffiti*], the music does comment on the characters and their situations, but does not emanate from them. This makes all the difference between a musical film and . . . the film musical. (Grant 2012: 1)

A musical, according to this broad definition, is thus a film where music *emanates* from the characters. I will use both notions in the following discussion, the music-film and the musical, and in the hierarchical positions proposed by Martin.

Disagreements concerning whether music-films from other parts of the world should be considered as musicals are consequently up for discussion.

For Martin, the genre must be considered to be global, and thus he makes the definition broader and proposes the music-film as designation because, as he states, genre elements modify when transferred to other geographies and cultures, and the 'over-restricted and over-prescriptive form constitutes, unknowingly, a kind of blockage in academic cinema studies' (Martin 2001: 74). Some genre elements are also tightly knit to the classical Hollywood musical and have no or little relevance in the new, or as Martin terms them, 'mutated' musicals. The genre has changed since the classical musicals of the 1960s. Not only has the music itself transformed decisively, its connection to youth culture and different identifications have given the music distinctly other connotations. Yet, the literature on the genre continues to debate whether the musical is an American or a global genre, as well as the importance of the genre in other parts of the world besides the US. This is actually a motif per se in one of the films in this article.

In this chapter I will discuss Nordic films where musical/music-films merge with other genres: melodrama, children's film, road movie, documentary, experimental film. Musicals are often combined with other genres and the criterion for selection here is that apart from being musicals or music-films, they show a variance in their secondary genres. The relation to the American musical will be highlighted, while I focus on my central question of what characterises the Nordic musical and how that relates to the music-film (where music is the driving force) and the musical (where music emanates from the characters). The films are also chosen according to shared motifs, and a characteristic of Nordic musicals during this study has turned out to be that they often centralise some sociopolitical themes such as migration and multiculturalism, and feature characters from the strata of the lower social classes. Other characteristics are that music often emanates from or is compounded by natural sounds, and, not least, that music is an empowering force not only for the narrative but also for the characters. All selected films have also received awards in national and international competitions and festivals.

DANCER IN THE DARK – GENRE CRITIQUE AND THE AMERICAN DREAM

To fuse art cinema and genre formulas is a phenomenon which, as Andrew Nestingen points out, has 'figured prominently in Scandinavian cinema from the 1990s onward' (2008: 48). It is also part of a globalisation strategy, at least a Danish one according to Ib Bondebjerg, in which European art film co-productions usually incorporate genre elements (Bondebjerg 2005: 132). *Dancer in the Dark* (2000) by Lars von Trier uses features from the melodramatic and musical genres in its story about the Czechoslovakian single mother Selma sacrificing herself to save her son from a genetic eye disease. Even as it uses genre material, it also transcends these genres.

Some writers have questioned whether *Dancer in the Dark* really is a musical, or whether it is not transgressing the rules to a degree that deconstructs the musical concept. Martin writes that it is 'a musical mutation so bold and brazen' that it is 'forcing people to ask themselves the question at least, "Just what is a musical, anyway?"' (2001: 75). Both Susan Smith and José Arroyo call it an anti-musical (Arroyo 2000; Smith 2005). Smith labels it as such because of the protagonist, who differs totally from the glamour we associate with musical stars, hence tacitly presupposing the centrality of the classical American musical. Selma is kind of 'ugly', wears glasses and dreary clothes, and sings differently. Arroyo agrees that the 'look' of the film contributes to its status as an anti-musical, as well as the absence of a 'true filmed choreography' of the dances, and, as Arroyo phrases it, songs that sound too much alike (2000: 15). The film shows much awareness of the musical as genre, Arroyo states, but seems to forget the element of pleasure also connected with the genre. And it is hard to argue that this film evokes pleasure in its tragic, deeply emotive narrative. Some critics have, indeed, drawn attention to this and other operatic elements, such as the overture or the 'death-aria', in the film (Austin-Smith 2006; Badley 2011; Bainbridge 2007).

It is true, as Arroyo states, that *Dancer in the Dark* shows knowingness about the musical as a genre. So much in fact, I would argue, that the film has as one of its motifs a negotiation of the musical, its status as an American genre, and how the Hollywood film/musical has influenced global audiences. And furthermore, all of this is connected to an overarching theme that on different levels discusses the relation between Europe and the US, not least from the perspective of migration. The film is a musical, but also a meta-musical, and a critique of the musical. The self-reflexivity which is characteristic of the classical musical, widely discussed by Jane Feuer and others, is here upgraded. In genre theory, self-reflexivity in connection to musicals usually concerns itself with how musicals narrate themselves in, for example, backstage musicals, or how they are an intertextual (postmodern) play where the musicals refer to each other. *Dancer in the Dark* also uses this common variant of self-reflexivity in, for example, the deployment of Catherine Deneuve (who plays Kathy/Cvalka) which evokes Demy's musicals, and Joel Grey, Master of Ceremonies in *Cabaret* (Bob Fosse, 1972), who plays the Czechoslovakian musical star Oldrich Novy (note that both these actors here refer to Europe in different ways), not to mention the rehearsals of the amateur production of the musical of musicals, *The Sound of Music*. Kathy and Selma also visit the cinema to watch Lloyd Bacon's *42nd Street* from 1933, a Busby Berkeley highlight, and there are numerous references to American musicals throughout the film (Schepelern 2000). But most of all, it is a self-reflexive theoretical discussion about the musical as a genre.

Despite the operatic qualities in the film, *Dancer in the Dark* should be considered a musical and the film presents many of the typical features connected with the genre, though most often in such an exaggerated and distorted way that it makes the film transcend the genre boundaries. The film is a multi-layered discussion about the genre, the US, and the American dream, all intertwined. Selma has immigrated to the US to get her son an eye operation, for which she saves money by working hard. Before she came to America, her ideas about the country were based on Hollywood musicals and films, a global phenomenon which is subject to critique as a form of American cultural imperialism. Selma is like so many other immigrants, historically and presently, a poor person who comes to the US to earn a living and to have her dreams fulfilled. This element of social critique permeates the film: the money is decisive in that people cannot get medical care without money, and because of that, money becomes the narrative factor that proves to be fatal. Selma has in a way been seduced to immigrate by Hollywood films; still, the love of musicals is so strong that they help her to survive mentally. This ideological ambivalence towards the genre is characteristic of the ambivalence towards the US and American culture that has permeated Nordic cultural and political discourses through the twentieth century (Wallengren 2008).

The dualism of America/Europe, or even capitalist/communist, can be said to influence how the narrative parts and the musical numbers are interrelated. The non-musical sequences are filmed in a Dogme-style, with discontinuous takes, showing us the grey and dull life Selma lives, 'the socialist-realist ambience', as Linda Badley puts it (2011: 95). The musical scenes contrast distinctly with this in their use of a hundred digital cameras, producing pictures that are edited in a rapid montage, shifting between excessive angles but without any camera movement, as light and colours are enhanced. The aesthetic is sometimes reminiscent of Busby Berkeley's choreographies from the 1930s. All the numbers are musical fantasies in Selma's mind, triggered by sounds in her surroundings, such as the factory noise or a train passing by, thus relating both to American and European traditions – for example *The Pajama Game* (Stanley Donen, George Abbott, 1957) which was set in a factory. But first and foremost Selma's fantasies are reminiscent of the Soviet musicals from the 1930s and 1940s, which 'turned physical labor into choreographed collective pleasure' (Badley 2011: 95). In the negotiation of the musical as an American genre, and in the narrative dualism between communist countries, where Selma comes from, and the US, von Trier thus mixes Danish dogme, American musical choreography and Soviet 'tractor' musicals. Selma uses the musical numbers in a psychological self-suggestion. She explicitly says that in musicals nothing bad can happen, and the rehearsal of *The Sound of Music* at the beginning of the film where Selma and others sing 'My Favourite Things' – a comforting song when you 'feel bad' – as well as Selma's heartbreaking attempt to bring this song to life in the prison, becomes a metonymy for this motif: in an American musical, a song can provide the antidote to evil.

Thus, the musical numbers blend aspects from different traditions while they twist them and add so many new ingredients – formally, stylistically and narratively – that something completely new arises. Even such a classical element as the romance duet, or the American courtship ritual as Rick Altman terms it, gets a bizarre expression in the number after the murder, where Bill resurrects from the dead to take part in Selma's fantasy. The use of fantasies or a dream world in musicals, mostly with the intention of finding realistic motivations for the musical numbers, was rather common from the 1940s and onwards, and von Trier uses this practice, not only for realistic motivation, but as part of a discussion about utopian elements in the musical as entertainment (Altman 1987; Grant 2012). In a famous essay Richard Dyer thoroughly discusses the utopian function of entertainment as 'the sense that things could be better, that something other than what is can be imagined and maybe realised' (1981: 177). Utopia in entertainment does not imply any 'models of utopian worlds' understood rationally, but rather it is 'contained in the feelings it embodies' (Dyer 1981: 177). In this sense *Dancer in the Dark* is almost an illustration of Dyer's famous article, but, again, it can also be regarded as utopian in a more literal sense, and that includes a reading of the film through the lens of Christianity.

Selma does actually play Maria, a nun, in *The Sound of Music*, the musical-within-the-musical, but Gilbert Yeoh argues convincingly that *Dancer in the Dark* as a whole has a 'crucial religious dimension' (Yeoh 2011: 1). Not only is sight – Selma becomes increasingly blind and sacrifices herself to give her son 'new eyes' – a well-known form of Christian symbolism, but also, Yeoh claims, the son's name *Gene* is a sign for inherited sin, here vision. Even more interesting, though, is how the genre itself is an important aspect of the allegory: 'how the film's musical world is von Trier's allegory for the realm of Christian divinity' (Yeoh 2011: 4). That is to say, the musical world as Selma constructs it is, if we accept this interpretation, a utopia of Christian divinity, and in that way von Trier has transformed Dyer's original notion of utopias in musicals into a literal and divine signification. But in the end, Selma, as I see it, is no longer able to evoke utopia. Throughout the film, we see the fantasies as they are enacted inside Selma. In prison however, almost devoid of sounds that can trigger her musical imagination, the utopia does not come to life – she is left without hope or redemption – and now we see, from outside Selma, how it looks and sounds when she is inside her fantasies: quiet, awkward singing and small pattering steps that are supposed to resemble a dance. In the face of death, she is no longer able to attain self-suggestion through musicals; they can no longer help her.

In different layers of the film, von Trier negotiates and challenges the concept of the musical as an American genre. He uses some of its classical elements but transforms, mutates, exceeds and criticises them. Some critics have read the film as an anti-American standpoint anticipating the 'USA: Land of Opportunities' trilogy, and of course, viewing the end as an austere commentary about the death penalty is unavoidable. It is also hard, from a genre perspective, to ignore the critique of Hollywood escapism, but at the same time, perhaps contradictorily, it is also impossible not to see the interest in, or even love of, (American) musicals. Some critics go so far as to assert 'that Hollywoodized illusions are partly to blame for her death' (Badley 2011: 94). However, Hollywoodised illusions can also be regarded as the reason for her endurance, even if the utopia finally does not help any more

Migration, Identity and Music as Redeemer

The theme of migration is vital in *Dancer in the Dark*, and themes of migration and ethnicity return in other Nordic films. The Swedish film *Förortsungar* (*Kidz in da Hood*, 2006) by Ylva Gustavsson and Catti Edfeldt, a remake of the *Rännstensungar* (*Guttersnipes*) films produced in 1944 and again in 1974, is labelled as musical and children's film in reviews and online. Both *Guttersnipes* films contained extensive music and singing, and the title song became quite famous in Swedish popular music discourse. However, *Kidz in da Hood* is less a musical than expected, but it is possible to regard this expectation of singing as part of the film's dramaturgy.

If the earlier versions of the film had a story that was about class in Swedish society, the remake has transferred this negotiation to ethnicity and migration (Bergström and Åberg 2012). The film's story is about Armina from a country which is never specified, who, when her grandfather dies, is taken care of by Johan, a budding rock musician. Armina waits for her residence permit, and also hopes that Johan will become her foster father with the help of the social worker Janet. During the wait she rehearses for a music show together with the children on the same block.

Because of Johan's aspirations to be a musician, and the children's show rehearsals, the film recalls the classic backstage musical. These narrative elements and short scenes, rhythmically edited to rap music or to rhythms made of everyday objects, give an impression that music in some way controls the narrative of the film. Music seems to be an element that wants to pop up all the time: not until about halfway through does the film present a real number with a duration of more than thirty seconds – all bursts of singing or music before that are very short. When the grandfather dies, we anticipate a song for emotional expression and relief but it never comes. That is to say – we *expect* music to start properly several times in the film, as well as for the story to unfold in expected directions. But it is as if the music is narratively confined to the same degree that the characters are emotionally and socially confined. Not until almost the end of the film, when Johan has decided to be a foster father to Armina, are they able to sing a whole song with a beginning, climax and ending (in Johan's case the number is performed on a table in exact resemblance to Milos Forman's *Hair* from 1979). Before that, only Janet is able to sing, partly because she is characterised as a confident person, and partly because the song can be considered as the first part of a romance number which Johan later completes. Hence, the music functions as an emotional and narrative agent in its *absence* for a considerable part of the film. The protagonists are not able to sing and music is not allowed to unfold until they are happy and complete persons. When they are, music is the sign of redemption.

Rap music is the style most used in the film besides rock, and of course these styles work as identity and cultural markers. In the film rap is used in a domesticated and watered down way, but still carries associations with black American subaltern youth culture. The children in the Stockholmian suburb thus are connected socially with this youth culture and the specific complex of problems it expresses. Two other song numbers in the film, performed by a Swedish woman as a lover of traditional rock 'n' roll and a Finnish man expressing his identity through Finnish tango, also serve as cultural (here above all from a class perspective) and national identity markers.

The last-mentioned type of music permeates another film that thematises migration experience and the feeling of being an outsider, namely Finnish *Laulu koti-ikävästä* (*Finnish Blood Swedish Heart*, 2012) directed by Mika Ronkainen. The film presents itself as a musical documentary, and in the film we follow a Finnish father and middle-aged son who visit Gothenburg in Sweden where they lived as labour immigrants in the 1960s and 1970s. The story is often and regularly interrupted by songs and music performed by an orchestra that play songs from the 1970s about the life of Finnish immigrants in Sweden. These songs are enacted as live performances in surroundings that thematise the trip and the memories – factory yards, a meadow with apartment blocks in the background, a green park. The lyrics are quite harsh and austere, and together with the harmonically beautiful and melancholically tinged melodies of the Finnish tangos and songs, the expression becomes very poignant. The trauma of the feeling of not really belonging to either country is narrated through music and story together. However, apart from music scenes, and despite the protagonist being a musician himself, it cannot be argued that music is 'a driving force' or is guiding formal or stylistic organisation. Narrative, editing and camera work do not cooperate with the music in any other way than as a kind of Greek tragedy choir, commenting on and explicating the story and the feelings. Still, without the songs much of the film's communication would have been lost.

Hence, in a strict sense it would be correct to label this film a music-film. However, the songs are expressing the feelings of the protagonist, and the orchestra could be regarded as some kind of substitute for him since Kai does not want to sing any more; to play Finnish rock made him finally only angry – he is not even 'a proper Finn', Kai says. This creates a parallel with *Kidz in da Hood*. He is as confined emotionally and in the same perspective of identity as Armina and Johan, and if we interpret the songs as emanating from Kai but channelled through the orchestra, the film could be labelled as a musical even if the numbers formally are performed on another narrative level. There are of course different ways to combine the musical and the documentary genres, and it seems to be a combination that is rather popular in Nordic cinema, last seen in the Academy Award-winning *Searching for Sugar Man* (Malik Bendjelloul, 2012). In the next example, another way of using the musical genre in connection with documentary will be discussed.

Song Power and Power Music

Finnish Blood Swedish Heart is also a road movie, a genre that is often connected with music. Features of that genre are also present in *Heftig og begeistret* (*Cool and Crazy*, Knut Erik Jensen, 2001), a 'docu-musical' about the male choir in the little northern Norwegian village Berlevåg (Iversen 2006: 181). Choral singing is very popular in the Nordic countries, and in that respect the film offers easy recognition for many audiences. Additionally, the film takes place in a small village haunted by depopulation and the closing down of the local fishing industry, which is a reality for many smaller villages in the North – hence, the film presents varying identification possibilities which in combination became a successful formula. Again, we see the focus on the social classes and life situations that are frequent in Nordic musicals, characteristics that differ from most American musicals. The representation of the funny and open-minded men in the choir, devoting so much time to singing together and living out so much of their lives in front of the audience, made them extremely popular after the film; they were even 'chased' by women who wanted to marry them (Sørenssen 2005). They are representatives of the so-called ordinary people, but are depicted as men with a never-failing joy of living as well as a fighting spirit, which seems to emanate from singing. In one scene, they are standing in a roaring snowstorm, with icicles hanging from their noses, and with hoarfrost in their eyebrows, singing an old Swedish religious song. Bjørn Sørenssen interprets this scene as an expression of the director's play with male Northern stereotypes (2005), but at the same time it can also be read as a sign that these men survive everything through collective singing.

The songs connect to narrative events discussed in the film and in this way illustrate and become ways of expression for the men and the themes they are concerned with, in the manner that musicals often do. In this way the songs function in relation to existential themes of life, death, love, but also to nature.

The numbers are generally performed in the context of nature, close to the sea, and sometimes sea waves pour over the camera, even drowning the voices. The roaring sea and the howling winds function as sound accompaniments to the numbers. The men singing together become intertwined with nature; song and sea, culture and nature become amalgamated. The editing and *mise-en-scène* are also clearly subordinated to some songs, for example in the song about dancing. Here the men are placed graphically in the picture, making patterns that are changing between shots. Together with the camera choreography it gives the impression of a still-standing dance. *Cool and Crazy* is powered by music in a multi-layered way: the choir exhibits a convincing song power, which is at the same time empowering for the men and a driving force for the narrative. Even if the film does not function as an ordinary musical, in a remodelled way it exhibits many genre characteristics: music emanates from the characters, it comments and drives the narrative and the whole film and narrative is imbued by music. For the common man in a lonely place in northernmost Scandinavia, as well as for the people in the suburban Stockholm in *Kidz in da Hood*, singing and music become the force on which to rely when life gets tough.

In most of the films discussed here, ordinary sounds and natural elements sometimes become a foundation for music in that they are transformed to rhythm and music. This practice forms the basis for another film where music in a strict sense is a story element, and at the same time a formal and stylistic element that rules the unfolding narrative, the editing, characters and *mise-en-scène*. The film is the Swedish *Sound of Noise* (2010) by Johannes Stjärne Nilsson and Ola Simonsson, an experimental comedy criminal musical film (!) about a group of activists against sound pollution, who are tired of all the haphazard noise that exists around us and strive to organise the sounds in the world. They do this through a musical composition taking place in different spots in a city which is used as an orchestra. Totally unexpected items function as instruments in rhythmic arrangements, such as operating utensils in an operating theatre, stamps and counters in a bank office, crushers and asphalt drills outside a concert hall, and electric lines in a power station. The grand finale in the power station influences the whole city when the 'playing' on the electric lines shuts off the lighting in the city. A superintendent who hates music is chasing the activists and finds metronomes as clues where they have carried out their actions. The film connects to a futuristic experimental tradition, where for example Fernand Léger in *Ballet Mécanique* from 1924 used ordinary items in a visually structured pattern. The idea was to transform the ordinary function and surrounding of the objects, and arrange them in an aesthetic order. All the artists in this tradition used items for visual patterning, whereas *Sound of Noise* uses them for auditory structuring, transferring the objects' sounds to music. To my knowledge this is completely original and innovative.

If Selma in *Dancer in the Dark* gets transferred to her dream world through natural sounds, Amina in *Kidz in da Hood* finds a rhythmic construction in everyday sounds, and sounds from nature are accompanying the choir in *Cool and Crazy*, then for *Sound of Noise* music is equal to natural sounds. Thus, the film can even be considered as a discussion about the relation between sounds, natural sounds and music. The title of the film is of course a parody on *The Sound of Music*, a musical that pops up in different Nordic films as reference, and here the use of actual sounds is carried to an extreme. The film does not contain songs or dance, but the whole organisation is driven by music, and in some scenes the narrative *is* music in the sense that *all* stylistic and formal elements on every level are dictated by music: editing, movements by objects and actors, *mise-en-scène*, camera work etc. are shaped rhythmically, temporally, tonally, melodically. Some would probably say that *Sound of Noise* is not a musical because of the absence of song and dance. However, I would definitely label it an experimental musical film, transgressing the genre restrictions into a new kind of musical.

Concluding Remarks: Characteristics of Nordic Musicals

The way music nowadays is deployed in many films transgresses the uses and functions of ordinary non-diegetic or diegetic music, lending the music a much more foregrounded role and more prominent functions and places in the narrative. Perhaps the musical genre is becoming more and more absorbed into other genres, making the genres fuse in an unprecedented way. The connotations of the musical as a genre have become floating notions, especially in cultural transfers where we can see that genre elements are freely used in a kind of cinematic play.

The films discussed here are all driven or powered by music, as the characters in the narratives get their power from music: from the more uncertain genre designation in *Finnish Blood Swedish Heart*, to a kind of backstage musical in *Kidz in da Hood*, from music as power in *Dancer in the Dark* and *Cool and Crazy*, to a complete musical organisation in *Sound of Noise*, where the 'power of music' takes on several connotations, both materialistic and psychological. Music is both a stylistic organisational element and a narrative active part; music often carries these dual functions on the level of narration, as well as on the level of the characters. It is simultaneously a non-diegetic cinematic component and a diegetic plot agent. And it is often used as an expression for the 'ordinary people' or lower social classes, or people in some kind of underdog position who often feel they are being left outside: unemployed fishermen in a faraway village, European migrants in the US or African migrants in Sweden, Finns who have problems with their migratory identity and feelings of not being properly appreciated as guest workers in Sweden, people living in worn-out suburbs, or, for that matter, people tired of sound pollution in the cities. Migration, multiculturalism and connected identity negotiations are themes that are recurrent in Nordic musicals. Traumatic or at least troublesome life situations provide the narrative basis in these films. Through the natural sounds that surround them, they find channels into other worlds that give them new power, and in the films discussed here, music is often triggered by everyday objects, sometimes to a degree that amalgamates the sounds of nature and music, as in *Cool and Crazy*, or makes music of all objects around us, as in *Sound of Noise*. All these factors are characteristic for Nordic musicals, but this does not imply that they are exclusively Nordic. Still, there is a discernible generic pattern which carries some societal motifs that at present are very much on the agenda in the Nordic countries.

To audiences that perhaps presuppose that Nordic musicals only have two manifestations, that is to say a tribute to Swedish popular music culture in *Abba: The Movie* (Lasse Hallström, 1977), which Altman suggests is the only example of a Scandinavian musical (1996), or *Dancer in the Dark*, which is an auteur discussion of the genre on an almost theoretical level, this discussion of Nordic musicals can demonstrate that musical gems are hiding in films with stories and characters which are traditionally not regarded as typical for the genre musical in a Hollywood sense.

References

Altman, Rick (1987), *The American Film Musical*, Bloomington: Indiana University Press.
Altman, Rick (1996), 'The Musical'. In Geoffrey Nowell-Smith (ed.), *The Oxford History of World Cinema*, Oxford: Oxford University Press, pp. 294–303.
Altman, Rick (1999), *Film/Genre*, London: British Film Institute.
Arroyo, José (2000), 'How do you solve a problem like von Trier?', *Sight & Sound* 10 (9): 14–16.
Austin-Smith, Brenda (2006), '"Mum's the Word": The Trial of Genre in *Dancer in the Dark*', *Post Script* 26 (10): 32–42.
Badley, Linda (2011), *Lars von Trier*, Urbana: University of Illinois Press.
Bainbridge, Caroline (2007), *The Cinema of Lars von Trier: Authenticity and Artifice*, London: Wallflower.
Bergström, Åsa and Anders Wilhelm Åberg (2012), 'Från rännsten till förort. Etnicitet, klass och könsroller i tre svenska barnfilmsmelodramer 1944–2006'. In Sara Kärrholm and Paul Tenngart (eds), *Barnlitteraturens världen och värderingar*, Lund: Studentlitteratur, pp. 289–322.
Bondebjerg, Ib (2005), 'The Danish Way: Danish Film Culture in a European and Global Perspective'. In Andrew Nestingen and Trevor G. Elkington (eds), *Transnational Cinema in a Global North: Nordic Cinema in Transition*, Detroit: Wayne State University Press, pp. 111–41.
Dyer, Richard (1981), 'Entertainment and utopia'. In Rick Altman (ed.), *Genre: The Musical: A Reader*, London: Routledge & Kegan Paul in association with the British Film Institute, pp. 175–88.

Dyer, Richard (2012), *In the Space of a Song: The Uses of Song in Film*, London: Routledge.
Feuer, Jane (1993), *The Hollywood Musical*, 2nd edn, Basingstoke: Macmillan
Grant, Barry Keith (2012), *The Hollywood Film Musical*, Chichester: Wiley-Blackwell.
Iversen, Gunnar (2006), 'The Old Wave: Material History in *Cool and Crazy* and the New Norwegian Documentary'. In C. Claire Thomson (ed.), *Northern Constellations: New Readings in Nordic Cinema*, Norwich: Norvik Press, pp. 175–92.
Martin, Adrian (2001), 'Musical Mutations: Before, Beyond and Against Hollywood'. In Philip Brophy (ed.), *Cinesonic: Experiencing the Soundtrack*, North Ryde, NSW: Australian Film, Television, and Radio School, pp. 67–103.
Nestingen, Andrew (2008), *Crime and Fantasy in Scandinavia: Fiction, Film, and Social Change*, Seattle: University of Washington Press.
Schepelern, Peter (2000), *Lars von Triers film: tvang og befrielse*, 2nd edn. København: Rosinante.
Smith, Susan (2005), *The Musical: Race, Gender and Performance*, London: Wallflower Press.
Sørenssen, Bjørn (2005), 'Heftig og begeistret/Cool and Crazy'. In Tytti Soila (ed.), *The Cinema of Scandinavia*, London: Wallflower Press, pp. 235–41.
Taylor, John Russell and Arthur Jackson (1971), *The Hollywood Musical*, New York: McGraw-Hill.
Wallengren, Ann-Kristin (2008), 'Hollywood in Sweden: Cinematic References Imagining America', *Film International* 6 (5): 42–50.
Yeoh, Gilbert (2011), '"What kind of magic is this? How come I can't help adore you?": Lars von Trier's *Dancer in the Dark* as a religious film', *Journal of Religion and Film* 15 (1), April, <http://www.unomaha.edu/jrf/Vol15.no1/Yeoh_DancerDark.html>.

PART IV
NORDIC HORRORS

13. SLASHER IN THE SNOW: THE RISE OF THE LOW-BUDGET NORDIC HORROR FILM

Tommy Gustafsson

Arguably, the horror film is the most frowned upon film genre, perhaps only surpassed by the porn film. Historically, the horror film has often been seen by Nordic film critics and film censors since the 1930s as something foreign or as yet another sign of unlawful Americanisation. Although the production of genre films has been prominent among all Nordic film industries ever since the silent film period, these genre films have mostly consisted of comedies and, especially in recent years, crime and detective films. The Nordic horror film in all its shapes and forms has been an anomaly in the Nordic countries, and this argument does not include the somewhat anachronistic genre labelling of films such as *The Phantom Chariot* (*Körkarlen*, Victor Sjöström, 1921) and *The Vampire* (*Vampyr*, Carl Theodore Dreyer, 1932).

This historic rejection can be explained by three interrelated factors: (1) a weak tradition of horror in Nordic film and literature; (2) an officially sanctioned aversion from depictions of horror which was seen as 'brutalizing, arousing, or creating confusion to law and order' (Skoglund 1971: 18) via the establishment of national film censorship boards in all the Nordic countries; (3) the difficulties of financing horror films as a consequence of this publicly sanctioned aversion. When state-funded film institutes were established in the Nordic countries between 1955 and 1972, they did not fund 'low-brow' horror films. This in turn created two outcomes. First, only a few feature horror films have been produced in all of the Nordic countries and, consequently, compiling a precise list to cover these is not the easiest task.[1] Nevertheless, all in all there have been approximately ninety feature films produced that could be labelled as horror films. These range from Iceland's two horror films, *The Reykjavik Whale Watching Massacre* (Júlíus Kemp, 2009) and *Frost* (Reynir Lyngdal, 2012) to the fifty or so horror films produced in Sweden. Second, and the main reason for the difficulty in compiling a list, is the fact that these feature horror films have been produced, almost without exception, with extremely low budgets and outside the regular film industry. Accordingly, the great majority of all Nordic horror films have never been available on the regular cinema circuit but have instead been screened on obscure occasions (mostly for family and friends), been released direct-to-DVD or not at all or, in the best of cases, been screened at special film festivals such as the Fantastic Film Festival in Lund, Sweden.

Recently there has been a noticeable upswing for the horror film genre, especially in Norway and Sweden but also in Finland with films such as *Rare Exports* (Jalmari Helander, 2010) and *Sauna* (Antti-Jussi Annila, 2008), and to a lesser degree in Denmark and Iceland. Although still in the low-budget area, the digital revolution has allowed young filmmakers to develop films that have the look of more expensive studio-funded films. The inspiration is also taken from horror films produced in the US, but often with distinct Nordic traits, themes and milieux. The 'Nordicness' of these films should not, however, be overstated as a selling point, either abroad or to neighbouring Nordic countries. As Jo Sondre Moseng and Håvard Andreas Vibeto make clear in an article on Nordicness in contemporary Norwegian cinema, most of these traits are '"lost in translation" at the level of international reception' (2011: 37).

The aim of this chapter is to analyse the rise of the low-budget Nordic horror film in the new millennium by discussing and comparing a sample

Figure 13.1 The Nordic version of the final girl. The resourceful and sexually experienced Jannicke (Ingrid Bolsø Berdal) finishes off the male monster in *Cold Prey* (2006). Image courtesy of Fantefilm.

of Norwegian and Swedish films. In order to analyse the position the genre holds today I will explore themes and subgenres that are noticeable in and perhaps specific to the Nordic Horror film, and how these themes relate to the international repertoire of contemporary horror films. The horror film has many subgenres and here I will simplify the selection by using Aristotle's basic division of genre into tragedy and comedy, leaving out comic and quirky horror films such as *Dead Snow* (*Død snø*, Tommy Wirkola, 2009), *Trollhunter* (*Trolljegeren*, André Øvredal, 2010) and *Frostbite* (*Frostbiten*, Anders Banke, 2006) and discusing only the 'tragic' ones intended to frighten their audiences. These include slasher/stalker films like *Cold Prey* (*Fritt vilt*, Roar Uthaug, 2006), torture porn films like *Detour* (*Snarveien*, Severin Eskeland, 2009) and zombie films like *Wither* (*Vittra*, Sonny Laguna, Tommy Wiklund, 2012).

Slasher in the Snow

Given the official position against horror and violent films in the Nordic countries it is no wonder that so many Nordic horror films included some sort of comic relief, for example *Rare Exports*' humorous take on Santa Claus or the Swedish *The Visitors* (*Besökarna*, Jack Ersgard, 1988), a haunted house film set in rural Sweden that served as a frontrunner for the genre since it actually made it to the regular cinema circuit and became a surprise hit. More hardcore and gorier horror films had always been exceptions (and often amateurishly made) up until the new millennium when a new generation of horror films were produced. These films did not shy away from the type of graphic images that would have been cut for sure in the previous millennium. Perhaps not surprisingly, this development coincided with the abolition of film censorship in the Nordic countries: Denmark in 1997,[2] Finland in 2001, Norway in 2004 and Sweden in 2011 (Sverige. Utredningen om översyn av filmgranskningslagen m.m. 2009: 38–9).

One of the most popular as well as scorned subgenres of the horror film is the slasher/stalker, which started with *Black Christmas* (Bob Clarke, 1974) and later had its heyday during the 1980s with films like *Halloween* (John Carpenter, 1978) and *Friday the 13th* (Sean S. Cunningham, 1980) and their multiple sequels. Many films in this subgenre were routinely heavily cut and even banned in the Nordic countries, for example *Halloween 5* (Dominique Othenin-Girard, 1989) in Sweden and *Friday the 13th* in Iceland. Although several of these slasher films were shown in cinemas, most of them were viewed as rented VHS-tapes, usually in cut versions. In that shape they became a part of the youth culture of the time, and subsequently many of the writers and directors of the new generation of horror films brought those viewing experiences with them into their film productions (see, for example, the interview with screenplay writer Thomas Moldestad (Ognjanovic 2010); for further examples, see Forsell 2004 and Strandberg 2012).

In Norway Roar Uthaug co-wrote (with Thomas Moldestad) and directed the slasher film *Cold Prey*. The film became a success, with 260,000 tickets sold in Norway, and received two sequels, *Cold Prey 2* (*Fritt vilt 2*, Mats Stenberg, 2008) and *Cold Prey 3* (*Fritt vilt 3*, Mikkel Brænne Sandemose, 2010). The series, although with different directors, writers and producers, follows, in many parts, the formula for initiating and prolonging a slasher film series in the classic sense. All three films are well produced with solid acting, professional photography, editing and special effects, and with suitable scores. The high production values can in part be explained by Norway's system of funding films where, if film producers muster up half of the budget, the Film Fund will support the other half.

The first film is about five friends who travel to a distant mountain top in Jotunheimen to snowboard. One of them breaks his leg and they take shelter in an abandoned and typical Norwegian mountain hotel, where a psychotic and deformed (but masked) maniac kills them off one by one until the final girl, Jannicke (Ingrid Bolsø Berdal), manages to kill the male monster. The characteristics of the five friends slavishly follow the classical formula and include: the promiscuous girl and her boyfriend, the stand-up guy, the male comic relief, and the final girl, all of whom are usually killed in this predictable order. The follow-up is a one-to-one replica of *Halloween 2* (Rick Rosenthal, 1981) where Jannicke is, as is Jamie Lee Curtis's character, brought to a hospital together with the corpse of the monster, who of course wakes up in the morgue and then goes on a rampage in the dark corridors and cellar of the hospital before the final girl kills him once again in a concluding stand-off. The third instalment is a prequel that reveals the monster's back story, but this film is only an echo of the first film's premise with the twist that none of the teenage victims survive.

Even if these films have unoriginal screenplays, they also deviate from their predecessors, most strikingly in their use of nature as an active part of the *mise-en-scène*. As Norwegian film scholar Gunnar Iversen has remarked, nature has always been a sign of a good and healthy life in Norwegian film history, but in *Cold Prey*, as well as in other Norwegian horror films, the beauty of nature becomes the opposite, that is, death and evil (2011: 304). But as Pietari Kääpä points out in an ecological analysis of the same film, 'nature [also] presents a means of survival for the final girl' as Jannicke 'uses tree branches, snow, wind and ditches' in order to combat the monster (Kääpä 2014: 70).

Iversen also comments on the films' view of women and their sexuality, which differs from the classical trope of the final girl that Carol J. Clover pinpointed in the early 1990s (1993: 35–41). In *Cold Prey* the seemingly promiscuous girl refrains from having sex, but is nevertheless the one who gets killed first. On this basis Iversen points out that this girl should have been a candidate to be the final girl (2011: 305), but sexuality is not the only decisive factor. The final girl also needs to be observant and active in her resistance against the monster, and the promiscuous girl in *Cold Prey* does not fit that description. On the other hand, that description fits the film's actual final girl, Jannicke, with the addition that she is resourceful and experienced already from the start, unlike earlier final girls who often had to learn as they went along.[3] The difference between these Norwegian slashers' view of gender and Clover's findings could be attributed to the fact that some thirty to forty years had passed since Clover's main sample of films were made. Nonetheless, here the strong self-image of the Nordic countries as the most gender-equal region in the world shines through; a self-image that is supported by the annual *Global Gender Gap Report* where the Nordic countries hold the positions 1, 2, 3, 4 and 8 in the list of the world's most gender-equal countries (The Global Gender Gap Report 2013: 8).

A Gory Take on the Antagonism between the City and the Countryside

In Sweden, two slasher films were produced at approximately the same time. First out was *Camp Slaughter* (Martin Munthe, 2004), a low-budget film that is set 'somewhere in rural Scandinavia' but where the Swedish actors speak in broken English, the intent being to sell it on the 'American home video market', as director Martin Munthe claimed in an interview (Strandberg 2012). The film is strongly inspired by *The Texas Chain Saw Massacre* (Tobe Hooper, 1974), similarities including, among other things, claiming to be based on a true story, as well as telling the story of a deranged family whose son is an inbred, giant freak, masked with a hood and dressed in a woman's gown. The son, called Bunny, escapes captivity and he and his family then stalk and kill a group of teenagers who happen to pass by the family mansion.

Camp Slaughter does not have the production values of the *Cold Prey* series and the film is extremely violent, but the gore is created and cut in an amateurish way that borders on comedy. On the other hand, the low production value, especially the camera work, gives the film an eerie look not unlike its progenitor. The film was viewed by an audience of 15,989 people at the cinemas (SFI 2014) and it was largely reviled by Swedish reviewers who ironically wondered if the Swedish Film Institute could not issue a certificate of work prohibition for the film's director (Bråstedt 2004), a statement which was immediately used in advertisements for the film. However, it should be mentioned that among non-Swedish user reviewers at IMDb, *Camp Slaughter* is hailed as 'a tense and scary' homage to the campsite flicks of the 1980s (2014a).

The other Swedish slasher film, *Drowning Ghost* (*Strandvaskaren*, Mikael Håfström, 2004), was made with a considerably higher budget and with well-known actors. The film was based on an old screenplay that the director had written years before, which was put into production after Håfström's success with the Oscar-nominated *Evil* (*Ondskan*, Mikael Håfström, 2003). The film takes place at an elite boarding school, as does *Evil*, where the haunted ghost of a drowned farmer – who allegedly killed three students with a scythe and then drowned himself some hundred years ago – is said to visit the school on a given date every year. The film's premise is based on folklore, as drowned ghosts are part of Swedish mythology. However, using the dark, labyrinthine corridors of the old boarding school, the film soon turns into a whodunit that uses 'horror film clichés by the dozen to avoid having to make the effort to write a sufficiently clever script', according to the lukewarm reviews (Cramby 2004).[4]

Untamed nature does not play the same important part in these Swedish slashers as in the first two instalments of *Cold Prey*, despite the fact that nature is as important for Sweden's self-image as it is in Norway. Instead the cultural-historical landscape of the countryside and its inhabitants are more important in inducing feelings of uncertainty and fear, and this is also the setting for Norwegian *Cold Prey 3*. It should be noted here that the trope of antagonism between the city and the countryside has been a prominent film theme in all the Nordic countries since at least the 1920s, first often expressed as a criticism of the backward countryside and later as a romanticised portrayal of a lost world (Quist 1995: 222–49; Iversen 2011: 38–52). The deadly threat of the backward other has, of course, been part of the international horror tradition since *Deliverance* (John Boorman, 1972) and *The Texas Chainsaw Massacre*, and in recent years a large number of films have been produced in this tradition: *Wrong Turn* (Rob Schmidt, 2003), *The Hills Have Eyes* (Alexandre Aja, 2006), *Eden Lake* (James Watkins, 2008).

However, this subgenre combining the slasher film with the city/countryside opposition has also been closely connected to extreme depictions of violence and gore in a way that does not correspond with the Nordic slasher films discussed here, with the exception of *Camp Slaughter*. Although violence, of course, is conspicuous in both the *Cold Prey* franchise and *Drowning Ghost*, the great majority of all kills are either committed off-screen, or in a way that hides the stabbings and beheadings from view, and where gore is downplayed. This actually means that the Nordic slasher film deviates from its American counterpart in one important aspect since the thrill of the explicit kill, one of the slasher's most important entertaining elements (Nowell 2011: 50–5), is suppressed. This subtleness of gore can be understood as a balancing act between the historical submission before Nordic censorship and the need to indulge Nordic and international audiences alike, who certainly get most of their genre knowledge from the more violent American films. Accordingly, none of the reviewers complained that these Nordic films contained too much violence, rather the opposite (Nordgren 2004).

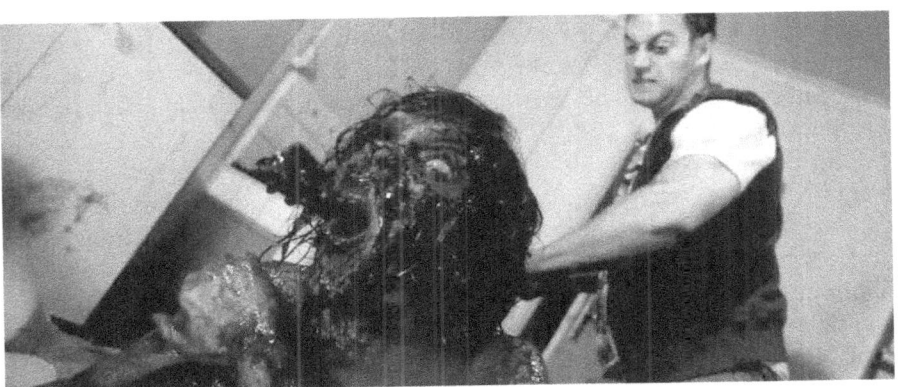

Figure 13.2   Extreme violence in *Wither* (2013), a gruesome and well-crafted gore extravaganza loosely based on Nordic folklore of the Vittra. Image courtesy of Stockholm Syndrome Film.

Iversen makes another observation about female gender in Norwegian horror films, in addition to the already mentioned final girl, that turns the idea of the sexually abstinent final girl upside-down. He notices that instead of being 'punished' for having sex, as in the classic and postmodern American slasher film (Hutchings 2004: 199, 216), the girls who do not have sex are being punished instead. That is, to survive, the final girl in Nordic films has to be both observant and active in her resistance, but she must also be sexually experienced. If you are a virgin, you die (Iversen 2011: 305–6). This trope actually fits with both the Norwegian and Swedish films discussed here. For example, the final girl in *Drowning Ghost*, Sara (Rebecka Hemse), has had sexual encounters and has even gone through an abortion, and in *Camp Slaughter* the sole survivor, Cindy (Christina Luoma), has had the only explicit sexual encounter in the film.

Torture Porn à la the North

A related and more niche subgenre to the slasher is the so called torture porn genre, that is, films that deliberately focus on graphic portrayals of gore and graphic violence in prolonged scenes where the impetus for fear comes from the physical destruction of the body, rather than from the unknown and supernatural beings as in mainstream horror films. Consequently, there is a greater emphasis on style, makeup and visual effects. And in addition to this, torture porn films have a strong tendency not to re-establish any social and moral order, but to end on a very bleak note. Prototypes for this controversial genre of films are *Saw* (James Wan, 2004) and *Hostel* (Eli Roth, 2005), and the subgenre has continued to be in the spotlight with films like *Martyrs* (Pascal

Laugier, 2008), *A Serbian Film* (*Srpski film*, Srdjan Spasojevic, 2010) and *The Human Centipede II* (*Full Sequence*) (Tom Six, 2011). The last two films were even censored in the UK before their DVD release by the British Board of Film Classification (BBFC 2010).

Considering the high levels of explicit violence in the torture porn genre, one would perhaps not expect to find that such films are produced in the Nordic countries, but they are, here exemplified by two similar productions made in Norway: *Manhunt* (*Rovdyr*, Patrik Syversen, 2008) and *Detour*. These films continue the city/countryside complex from the slasher but with a few additional Nordic twists. Both films are inspired by the 1970s low-budget American horror films (*Manhunt* even takes place in 1974, the same year as *The Texas Chainsaw Massacre* was made) and both films employ the concept of competent final girls who kill the rural attackers. However, the extreme display of violence in *Manhunt*, with its drawn-out scenes of torture, fear and death, stands out in comparison to other Nordic horror films.

As the title reveals, *Manhunt* is the story of four young men and women who venture out into Norwegian nature for a relaxing vacation but are instead attacked by the locals who hunt them down and kill them for sport, literally like animals. The final girl, Camilla (Henriette Bruusgaard), manages to ferociously kill all of the attackers, only to be caught by their mother in the end. Film scholar Pietari Kääpä makes the observation that *Manhunt*, bordering between the slasher and torture porn, blurs the distinction between humans and non-humans as the hunted final girl it forced to follow her basic instincts, becoming like an animal, turning on her attackers (Kääpä 2014: 71).

According to the director the film team was 'more or less forced to make a rough and dirty film in guerilla fashion', which explains the gritty look. The degree of violence, however, is attributed as a homage to the 'uncompromising, energetic and rough ... nihilistic horror film that thematically reflects the survival horror from the 1970s' (RSTVIDEO 2009), that is, violence for its own sake or as an expression of art. Not surprisingly, *Manhunt* did not receive as favourable reviews, or as large an audience, as *Cold Prey* did. The extreme violence is also commented on in negative ways by most reviewers who claimed that audiences would not get scared, only disgusted and bored by the lack of story (see, for example, Nyborg Eriksen 2008). Clearly, the historical mistrust of the horror film, in combination with the excess of violence in *Manhunt*, got an outlet here as it was deemed to be misplaced in a Nordic context.

Swedish ethnologist Jonas Danielsson has discussed the feelings of disgust as entertainment and pleasure in the horror film. Both the slasher and the torture porn film can be labelled as splatter films, a genre that borders on comedy and slapstick and where excessive gory scenes have a tendency to turn into comic relief (for habitual audiences). The repulsive elements can also, according to Danielsson, work towards forming an identity for hardcore horror fans. That is, repugnant images serve to provide the grounds that separate horror fans from mainstream film audiences. This means that the excess of visual effects is often perceived as more important than a film's plot and story (Danielsson 2006: 85–101). In other words, *Manhunt* obviously catered to a niche audience but it was received as a mainstream horror film, probably due to the fact that the film had theatrical release (with accompanying reviews) in Norway. In other markets it was distributed with straight-to-DVD release.

The second Norwegian torture porn film, *Detour*, follows a young Norwegian couple who have visited the border shops in Sweden and are now on their way back with the car packed with smuggled alcohol. The film blends themes from films like *Wrong Turn* and *My Little Eye* (Marc Evans, 2002) as the Norwegian couple are lured into the woods on a detour and captured by a twisted Swedish family who intend to torture and kill them in front of running cameras, streaming the whole thing to anonymous, paying customers on the Internet. However, one element separates this film from other films in the same genre in a conspicuous way. The extreme violence is toned down and is more suggestive than explicitly on display, as if the film adjusts its levels of violence according to Nordic conventions. This fact and the expectations of the genre are reflected in the reviews in which the film was hailed as a 'horror goodie bag' (Selås 2009), but where the absence of extreme violence was analysed accordingly: 'The gore scenes are simple ... In the end I sat just with one thought ... "when will it happen?" However, as the film ended I realized that this is a horror film for the faint hearted' (Goldielocks 2009). This could, in other words, be characterised as a breach of the genre contract since the expectations of the torture porn genre are not fulfilled.

Religion as an International Marker

The fact that the psycho-maniac family which the young Norwegian couple encounter in *Detour* is Swedish has, of course, mainly a local significance since Norway and Sweden are bordering countries with a historical neighbourliness comparable to Canada and the US. Nonetheless, the filmmakers use another universal trope to characterise the Swedish family, namely religion – and this religiousness is used to represent backwardness and craziness in general and not to make a political point as in *Red State* (Kevin Smith, 2011). The interesting point, though, is that it is the Swedes who are represented as religious, a surprising fact considering that Sweden is one of the most secular countries in the world. There is however an historical explanation for this paradox. In 2004 the so called Knutby Murder became front-page news for months in Scandinavian countries when the actions of a small and isolated Swedish Pentecostal congregation exploded into the media after one of its pastors convinced a female member to commit murder by sending her text messages, claiming them as being from God (Cristiansson 2012). These sensational events even spawned a documentary, *Skotten i Knutby* (Karin Svärd, Phil Poysti, 2005) and a television miniseries, *Vägen hem* (Karin Swärd, 2009), which were both distributed in Norway.

Even if *Detour*'s use of religion is quite shallow, this nevertheless works as an international marker, just as Ingmar Bergman's films often included religious themes that were shunned in secular Sweden but which gained appreciation and generated discussions in an international context (Söderbergh Widding 2008). Religion in the form of Christianity (usually versus the Devil) is also a common theme in the horror genre with films like *The Exorcist* (William Friedkin, 1973) and *The Rite* (Mikael Håfström, 2011).

In Swedish *Psalm 21* (Fredrik Hiller, 2009) religion and the religious sect, inspired by the Knutby Murder, are used again as the terrifying theme. The film is about a young nonspiritual priest who travels from the capital, Stockholm, to the rural north of Sweden to investigate the mysterious death of his father, also a priest but of the fire and brimstone type. Here the young priest encounters a strange and religious fundamentalist family. Throughout the film he is also haunted by several dead spirits/demons, including his mother and father, which test his faith. The filmmakers make an effort to validate the religious theme with references to *The Book of Psalms*; especially psalm 21 and the lines, 'Thou shalt make them like a fiery oven in time of thy wrath / the Lord shall destroy them in his displeasure, and the fire shall consume them.' Even so, the theological arguments never become more than a superficial critique of religion which, according to most Swedish reviewers, only disguised the fact that the film lacked a comprehensible screenplay (Tingbrand 2010). Still, several non-Swedish user reviews at IMDb praised *Psalm 21* for its treatment of religion, which demonstrates the greater interest for religion in an international perspective (see, for example, Trashgang 2012).

Conclusion

In 2012 arguably one of the goriest Nordic horror films was produced in Sweden. *Wither* was marketed as the first Swedish zombie film[5] and according to one of its directors, Sonny Laguna, the film was inspired by the new Norwegian horror film, especially the use of Nordic mythology in *Trollhunter* (Strandberg 2013). In *Wither*, then, the filmmakers loosely take advantage of Nordic folklore about the Vitter, a sometimes invisible species of nature spirits that look like humans and live underground, in order to produce a gory zombie film. The plot is shamelessly pinched from *The Evil Dead* (Sam Raimi, 1981) with a group of youngsters who go to a cabin in the woods where they first meet a stranger who warns them, and then are infected one by one by a zombielike virus from the Vitter, consequently killing each other in a gruesome and well-crafted gore extravaganza. Once again this abundance of blood and violence was rejected outright by Swedish reviews which claimed that the 'overdose of blood made *Wither* ridiculous' (Johnson 2013). In another short review the film was trashed on the basis that it did not contain 'anything that would change the world', and here the amount of blood was ironically mentioned no fewer than five times (Lumholdt 2013). Internationally the violence was criticised as well, but not routinely or without further analysis as in Sweden. In American magazine *Fangoria*, *Wither* was criticised for not being able to handle the violence realistically or ideologically:

> It seems the filmmakers have forgotten that while we've all seen *Evil Dead*, their characters haven't . . . Once the eyes of these young adults roll back, film over and blood spews from their orifices, their friends are just as quickly on top of them, brutally beating away with whichever blunt object is nearest. The group shares little in the way of shock, instead almost immediately smashing faces in, blowing holes in heads and impaling away. Being the majority of the principal cast is women and that's who falls prey first, *Wither* can't avoid taking on an unsettling atmosphere when their male counterparts start perpetrating such graphic business. (Zimmerman 2013)

There is no doubt that violence and gore are and have been anomalies in Nordic cinema, even in the modern horror film where violence is definitely restrained visually or downplayed by being presented in a comical context as in *Dead Snow*. Even a torture porn film like *Detour* broke with its own genre expectations by limiting the display of extreme gore in comparison with international films in the same subgenre. This restraint can be explained by historical factors such as censorship and a social distaste for audiovisual violence that ostracised the entire horror genre as inappropriate for financial support and, of course, as a sign of Americanisation of the Nordic film cultures. However, in an international spectrum these variations of violence and gore do not stand out as something that signifies Nordic horror. What, on the other hand, could be said to stand out as something that characterises 'Nordicness' is the quirkiness that typifies many of the comical Nordic horror films not discussed in this chapter. Also, the Nordic final girl stands out in comparison with international genre equivalents since the Nordic final girl is more prepared for action, and sexually active, in contrast to classical examples such as Jamie Lee Curtis's role in *Halloween*.

The filmmakers could definitely have elaborated on the history of the Vitter in *Wither* in order to flesh out the thin plot, but as in *Trollhunter*, *Drowning Ghost* and also in the Norwegian *Thale* (Aleksander L. Nordaas, 2012), where a Huldra is the main antagonist, the creatures of Nordic mythology are mostly there as a thinly disguised plot device that certainly exhibits 'Nordicness' but which, at the same time, as Moseng and Vibeto claimed, mostly is 'lost in translation' on an international market anyway; hence the shallow treatment of them. The same can be said for the cosmetic and often ignorant use of religion in Nordic horror films where the strong societal secularisation present in most Nordic countries and regions shines through.

Nature with its diverse settings has been a prominent part of Nordic film culture since the 1910s (Solia, Söderbergh Widding and Iversen 1998, passim), and nature is also conspicuous in the contemporary Nordic horror film. However, this comes with a twist. In most Nordic countries Nordic nature and its landscapes have functioned as a sort of national fetish of health since at least the nineteenth century. But as Gunnar Iversen has remarked, in Norwegian horror films nature is transformed from health to death. This could also be said for the Icelandic *The Reykjavik Whale Watching Massacre* (Kääpä 2014: 72–6). The display of nature is prominent in the *mise-en-scène* of other Norwegian and Swedish horror films as well, but not as the cause of death. Instead it is often the cultural landscape of the countryside and, in particular, its 'backward' inhabitants that causes death. This could be said to be a gory development of an older trope where antagonism between the city and the countryside has served as a melodramatic drive in numerous Nordic films since the 1920s.

At the moment the Nordic horror film is experiencing a creative, and in some cases also a commercial, peak. Many contemporary Nordic horror films have gained international recognition and distribution (at least on DVD), for example *Let the Right One In* (*Låt den rätte komma in*, Tomas Alfredson, 2008), winner of sixty-three international prizes (IMDb 2014b), and *Wither*, nominated for the Fangoria Annual Chainsaw Awards in the category Best Foreign Film in 2014. In spite of this, these often well-produced horror films seldom get cinema distribution in their neighbouring Nordic countries. This could conceivably depend on the lingering aversion against violence and gore, but a more likely reason is the fact that the closeness in language, behavior and geography renders these horror films to be perceived as less exotic and less scary than, for example, their American and Asian counterparts.

Notes

1. Denmark 16; Finland 7; Iceland 2; Norway 18; Sweden 51. The great majority of these films were produced between 2000 and 2013. This breakdown is based on searches for 'List of Swedish horror films' etc. on Wikipedia, and also by consulting specialist books such as Dellamorte 2003.
2. Denmark abolished film censorship for adults in 1969, but did not close down the censorship board until 1997.

3. In Norwegian reviews, Jannicke's character is constantly referred to as having 'pure agent Ripley characteristics' (Maaland 2006) or as 'Jotunheimen's Sigourney Weaver' (Ståle Nilsen 2008).
4. *Evil*, but not so much *Drowning Ghost*, was also Håfström's ticket to Hollywood, where he has directed several successful genre films, among them two cliché-packed but commercially successful horror films, *1408* (2007) and *The Rite* (2011).
5. *Wither* was not the first Swedish zombie film per se, but the first that got a decent distribution in Sweden. Before that short films like *The Resurrection of Michael Myers Part 2* (Richard Holm, Henrik Wadling, 1989) and *Zombie Psycho Sthlm* (Micke Engström, 2004) had been made, and in 2005 the feature film *Die Zombiejäger* (Jonas Wolcher, 2005) was produced, but without regular cinema distribution.

References

BBFC (2010), 'Srpski Film – A Serbian Film (2010)', <http://www.bbfc.co.uk/releases/srpski-film-serbian-film-2010>, accessed 26 January 2014.
Bråstedt, Mats (2004), 'Camp slaughter', *Expressen*, 16 January.
Clover, Carol J. (1993), *Men, Women and Chainsaws: Gender in the Modern Horror Film*, Princeton, NJ: Princeton University Press.
Cramby, Jonas (2004), 'Strandvaskaren', *Expressen*, 15 October.
Cristiansson, Therese (2012), *Himmel och helvete: Mord i Knutby*, Stockholm: Bokförlaget Forum.
Danielsson, Jonas (2006), *Skräckskönt: Om kärleken till groteska filmer – en etnografisk studie*, Umeå: Bokförlaget h:ström.
Dellamorte, Daniel (2003), *Svensk sensationsfilm: en ocensurerad guide till den fördolda svenska filmen, 1951–1993*, Malmö: Tamara Press.
Forsell, Mikael (2004), 'Rebecka Hemse jagar "Strandvaskaren"', *Ystads allehanda*, 13 October.
Global Gender Gap Report, The (2013), World Economic Forum, <http://www.weforum.org/reports/global-gender-gap-report-2013>, accessed 5 March 2014.
Goldielocks (2009), 'Lesernes anmeldelser', *Verdens gang*, <http://www.vg.no/film/film.php?id=10557>, accessed 29 January 2014.
Hutchings, Peter (2004), *The Horror Film*, Harlow: Pearson Education.
IMDb (2014a), User reviews Camp Slaughter, <http://www.imdb.com/title/tt0337910/reviews?start=0>, accessed 21 January 2014.
IMDb (2014b), Låt den rätte komma in, Awards, <http://www.imdb.com/title/tt1139797/awards?ref_=tt_awd>, accessed 6 February 2014.
Iversen, Gunnar (2011), *Norsk filmhistorie: Spillefilmen 1911–2011*, Oslo: Universitetsforlaget.
Johnson, Mats (2013), 'Vittra', *Göteborgs-Posten*, 9 August.
Kääpä, Pietari (2014), *Ecology and Contemporary Nordic Cinemas: From Nation-building to Ecocosmopolitanism*, London: Bloomsbury.
Lumholdt, Jan (2013), 'Hinkvis med blod räcker inte', *Svenska Dagbladet*, 9 August.
Maaland, Borghild (2006), 'Blodsprutende grøss', *Verdens gang*, 12 October.
Moseng, Jo Sondre and Håvard Vibeto (2011), 'Hunting High and Low: Notes on Nazi Zombies, Francophiles and National Cinema(s)', *Film International* 9 (2): 30–41.
Nordgren, Nils (2004), 'Få ljuspunkter i allt för lite skrämmande historia', *Svenska Dagbladet*, 15 October.
Nowell, Richard (2011), *Blood Money: A History of the First Teen Slasher Film Cycle*, London and New York: Continuum.

Nyborg Eriksen, Elise (2008), 'Skummelt i skauen', *ABC Nyheter*, 10 January.
Ognjanovic, Dejan (2010), 'Interview with Thomas Moldestad ('Fritt vilt')', *The Temple of Ghoul*, <http://templeofghoul.blogspot.se/2010/02/interview-with-thomas-moldestad-fritt.html>, accessed 19 January 2014.
Qvist, Per Olov (1995), *Folkhemmets bilder: Modernisering, motstånd och mentalitet i den svenska 30-talsfilmen*, Lund: Arkiv förlag.
RSTVIDEO (2009), 'Rstvideo.com intervjuar Patrik Syversen (Rovdyr)', <http://rstvideo.com/rstvideo-com-intervjuar-patrik-syversen-rovdyr/>, accessed 26 January 2014.
Selås, Jon (2009), 'Skrekkelig godtepose', *Verdens gang*, 30 July.
SFI (2014), The Swedish Film Institute, <http://www.sfi.se/sv/statistik/>, accessed 21 January 2014.
Skoglund, Erik (1971), *Filmcensuren*, Stockholm: Pan/Norstedts.
Söderbergh Widding, Astrid (2008), 'What Should We Believe?: Religious Motifs in Ingmar Bergman's Films'. In Maaret Koskinen (ed.), *Ingmar Bergman Revisited: Performance, Cinema and the Arts*, London and New York: Wallflower Press, pp. 194–209.
Soila, Tytti, Astrid Söderbergh Widding and Gunnar Iversen (1998), *Nordic National Cinemas*, London and New York: Routledge.
Ståle Nilsen, Morten (2008), 'Oppfølgernerver', *Verdens gang*, 9 October.
Strandberg, Jonas (2012), 'Martin Munthe om film', *Popkultur*, <http://popkultur.nu/2012/07/11/martin-munthe-om-film/>, accessed 20 January 2014.
Strandberg, Jonas (2013), 'Smutsig och klaustrofobisk skräckfilm på svenska', *Popkultur*, <http://popkultur.nu/2013/08/07/smutsig-och-klaustrofobisk-skrackfilm-pa-svenska/>, accessed 1 February 2014.
Sverige. Utredningen om översyn av filmgranskningslagen m.m. (2009), Avskaffande av filmcensuren för vuxna: men förstärkt skydd för barn och unga mot skadlig mediepåverkan: betänkande, Stockholm, <http://www.regeringen.se/content/1/c6/12/79/25/16fd1b8a.pdf>, accessed 17 January 2014.
Tingbrand, Teresa (2010), 'Svensk skräck som är mer fniss än rys', *Aftonbladet*, 5 November.
Trashgang (2012), 'Criticism towards religion', IMDb, <http://www.imdb.com/title/tt1322355/reviews?ref_=tt_ov_rt>, accessed 31 January 2014.
Zimmerman, Samuel (2013), 'WITHER (Movie Review)', *Fangoria*, <http://www.fangoria.com/new/wither-movie-review/>, accessed 2 February 2014.

14. NORDIC VAMPIRES: STORIES OF SOCIAL EXCLUSION IN NORDIC WELFARE STATES

Outi Hakola

Nordic vampire films, comprising films produced in Denmark, Sweden and Finland, are not a coherent or regular phenomenon. Although they are familiar with and even borrow the conventions of Anglo-American vampire lore, their features often differ from the international horror mainstream in specifically Nordic ways. Rochelle Wright (2010: 56, 67) describes Nordic cases as being characterised by a fusion or hybridity of genres, including both the Anglo-American horror genre and Nordic socio-psychological drama, and argues that as a consequence, in Nordic vampire films the supernatural merges with realism. Internationally most vampires are social outcasts whose blood-desire and unnatural relationship with death mark them as evil, yet the Nordic vampires are not necessarily evil, but sympathetic characters whose social exclusion is often unrelated and prior to their vampirism (Wright 2010: 59).

In the Nordic films, and especially in recent Swedish films such as Anders Banke's *Frostbite* (*Frostbiten*, Sweden, 2006), Peter Pontikis's *Not Like Others* (*Vampyrer*, Sweden, 2008), Tomas Alfredson's *Let the Right One In* (*Låt den rätta komma in*, Sweden, 2008), and Josef Elias's *Sun Shadows: Faithful Kiss* (Sweden, 2011), vampires are excluded characters who have lost their right to social care. For example, the child vampire Eli in *Let the Right One In*, and the vampire sisters Vanja and Vera in *Not Like Others*, are detached from society and community, and they are deprived of the benefits of the Nordic welfare state – such as education and health care. Instead, they hide from others and avoid any social contact. For them, as for many other Nordic vampires, vampirism is a curse which causes them to mourn the lack of social cohesion and social support. In these films, the marginalisation leaves these characters no other choice but to turn against society by feeding on its members.

The Nordic welfare states, Sweden, Norway, Finland, Denmark and Iceland, are small countries with similar social structures; they have relatively high tax rates, as well as a strong emphasis on social cohesion, social responsibility and gender equality. Jon Kvist, Johan Fritzell, Bjorn Hvinden and Olli Kangas suggest that in the Nordic welfare state, wealth is constantly redistributed through taxes and benefits. However, redistribution of cash and social security benefits are instruments of the welfare state, whereas the uniqueness of the model is founded on active labour market policies, including social services, childcare, education, and healthcare and rehabilitation services. The aim of socially oriented economic policies is to offer a certain standard of life and equal opportunities to everyone (Kvist et al. 2012: 3–9). However, vampire films expose outcast characters who have either stepped or been forced outside the social safety nets and from their marginalised position they cause a threat to the existing society.

As social outcasts they represent a domesticated form of the supernatural. Instead of hiding behind any mythical sense of evil or wickedness, they remain socially responsible for their actions, and their acts focus more on social norms than moral ones. Thus, instead of seeking inspiration from the ongoing battle between good and evil (as many Anglo-American vampire films do), Nordic vampire films focus on the socio-cultural context of the Nordic welfare model that promotes social belonging. In these films, the aims of the welfare state have failed, and the existence of the vampires is proof of this. This specific cultural context gives Nordic vampires unique cinematic features among international vampire lore. In this chapter, I will explore how Nordic vampires reveal the underlying vulnerabilities within the Nordic welfare model.

Vampires and the Crisis of the Welfare State

Nordic welfare states were developed during the early twentieth century, and many important developments took place after the Second World War (Greve 2007: 44). Although the Nordic vampire films tend to be a recent phenomenon, already some earlier films address the challenges to the construction of the welfare state. First of all, a French–German co-production *Vampyr: The Strange Adventure of David Gray* (*Vampyr: Der Traum des Allan Gray Dreyer*, 1932) was directed by the Danish filmmaker, Carl Theodor Dreyer. Although the film is not Nordic as such, and the story takes place in a small French village, the questions about modern society raised in the film resonate with those that inspired the Nordic countries to develop the welfare state. In the film an occultist researcher, Allan Gray, arrives at a village cursed by a female vampire, Marguerite Chopin. An embodiment of death that threatens to consume others, she is being helped to capture her victims by a local (and male) doctor. By assisting the vampire, the doctor, who comes to function as a key authority in the welfare state, fails to provide care-giving (see also Peirse 2008: 165). In this film, the use of a small village in a rural region exposes how an isolated location can challenge the realisation of social equality and how abuse on the part of the authorities can threaten social cohesion. Later on, similar themes come to play an important role in the Nordic vampire films, because these themes challenge the sufficiency of the welfare model which values fair distribution of social justice and universality of both membership and allocation of the benefits (Kildal and Kuhnle 2005: 14–29).

Indeed, within the first Nordic vampire film similar questions of social equality and access to care-giving are emphasised. Erik Blomberg's film *White Reindeer* (*Valkoinen peura*, Finland, 1952) takes place in secluded Finnish Lapland, and combines themes of a mythical Lapland, animal transformations and vampirism. In this film, the newly-wed Pirita fails to find a socially acceptable way to adjust to her new village and marital status and feels forced to seek help from a shaman. Her aim is to make her absent husband, a reindeer herder, stay at home with her. A spell cast by a shaman changes her into a white reindeer – an animal irresistible to any reindeer herder. However, the spell has a crucial side effect: the white reindeer is not only a beauty, but a vampire too and in her reindeer form Pirita ends up feeding on the herders. While she initially hopes to gain social belonging and care, she ends up even more excluded from society and disconnected from her husband. In the end, her husband chases the white reindeer, not knowing that this is his wife in animal form, and kills her. Only after she transforms back into her human form is Pirita's tragic fate revealed to her husband. In this film, Pirita seeks help for her feelings of exclusion, but fails to get social support and is left to deal with her problems alone.

White Reindeer addresses the challenges of access to and equality of social services. These questions were topical considering the film's background – both the building of the welfare state and the aftermath of international conflict. Although all the Nordic countries introduced widespread welfare legislation after the Second World War, in Finland achieving the ideals of a welfare state was subject to disruption, notably caused by the Winter War and the Continuation War with the Soviet Union and the Lapland War with Germany. These wars led to large-scale evacuations and the resettlement of refugees as well as massive physical destruction of Lapland. The challenges of rebuilding strengthened the values of the welfare model, but they also delayed the equal execution of social rights. When the film was released, Lapland was still recovering and the outsiders' positions were especially difficult, just as in the case of Pirita who was not allowed to gain similar social status to local people.

The recent vampire films highlight the fears associated with the breakdown of the traditional welfare model. Films such as *Frostbite, Not Like Others, Let the Right One In* and *Sun Shadows* were released between 2006 and 2011, during the reorganisation of the Nordic welfare model, and these films draw their power from the collective concerns about how welfare is produced in the Nordic countries. It is no surprise that these films are Swedish, as Sweden was the first Nordic country to introduce new demands of cost-efficiency and productivity. The changes started in the 1990s and since then public services have become partly privatised, not only in Sweden but in other Nordic countries as well (Greve 2007). Although the values of the welfare model still exist, the clear focus on public services is not as predominant as it used to be (Greve 2011: 111). Several studies have been conducted on changed practices and experiences. For example, the research of Gun-Britt Trydegård (2012: 119–21, 127) shows that care workers have experienced a decline in opportunities to provide good quality care. The recent vampire films address these experiences and fears of decline in equal rights to social care. These films have an overarching atmosphere of a sense of social neglect, and the films focusing on the rearrangement of welfare state practices narrate the fear of what happens if the public services become marginalised and inaccessible and people are left alone to face the challenges of life.

Frostbite was the first Swedish vampire production, and it exploits typical horror features familiar from international vampire traditions. In this film, the genetically enhanced vampires are monstrous figures who cause bloody havoc in a small northern town. However, already in this film a sadder undertone and references to consequences of bad care-giving can be detected. The story centres on the hospital, one of the centres of care-giving, where, once again, a doctor becomes a source of abuse and mistreatment. Professor Gerhard Beckert keeps a girl he has taken with him from Germany in a coma and studies her body in a Swedish hospital up north. The girl is a vampire who is not represented as evil, but as a lost child without her parents. Instead of helping the girl, he is studying her vampire genes in order to create a perfect monster. Later, blood drugs created by Beckert end up in the wrong hands, turning most of the town's teenagers into bloodsucking vampires. In this film, a lack of medical responsibility and surveillance causes reckless and unethical medical research. As a consequence, the whole town becomes threatened by uncontrollable death, a concrete example of failure in care-giving and undesired social disorder.

Let the Right One In was released two years later, but in this film, the conventions of drama are more important than those of horror. The film is based on the vampire novel *Låt den rätte komma in* (2004) by John Ajvide Lindqvist and it tells of an unlikely friendship between a 12-year-old boy Oskar and a vampire, Eli, who is trapped in a 12-year-old girl's body. The film engages the viewer with the socially excluded characters and from their perspective the welfare state appears inaccessible and unwelcoming. As a vampire, Eli is excluded from society and spends her time hiding from the world. Eli is a tragic character who is sadly excluded from the world of childhood, characterised by birthday presents, candy, games and friends. Oskar is also a lonely figure, who is bullied at school. Although the aim of the welfare state has been thought to have several positive impacts, such as solidarity, collaboration, engagement and responsibility for the common good, negative impacts, such as a heavy tax burden, lack of innovation and dynamism, and lack of public responsibility for people's private arrangements, have been recognised (Kvist et al. 2012: 9). In *Let the Right One In*, the lack of public responsibility is visible. Both Eli and Oscar are left alone to face their problems while the adults and authority figures close their eyes.

For example, in the film, both the bullies and Oscar are incapable of breaking the circle of violence which consumes them. Thus, the bullying is something waiting to be revealed and rehabilitated, although the school, authorities and parents fail to recognise this. Because of it, Oskar falls outside the safety net and he is never directed to the social services. The dynamism of the welfare state fails. Instead, he develops worrying (violent) behaviour models. Oskar collects a scrapbook of violent crimes and practises stabbing. When Eli first sees Oskar, he stabs a tree with his knife: 'What are you staring at? Are you scared? Squeal!' Oskar's tendency to violence interests Eli and later on she claims that they are alike. To Oskar's objection, 'But I don't kill people', Eli responds, 'But you'd like to, if you could. To get revenge, right? I do it because I have to.'

The boy's problematic situation opens the door for an alternative lifestyle. He falls outside the welfare state which has failed him and turns to another rejected character, Eli, and embraces a life filled with the survival of the fittest, violence, revenge and death. John Calhoun (2009: 31) sees their reciprocal relationship as a necessity for their survival. The boy's openness to alternative relationships invites the vampire in, and, in a way, Eli even encourages Oskar's violent characteristics by demanding Oskar to respond to violence. In other words, Eli is more or less a reflection of Oskar's rage. Calhoun argues that *Let the Right One In* addresses society's fears about monstrous children and the adults' failure to protect them from monstrosities. He argues that the film is about failed community where the lack of communal feeling leaves everyone to fend for themselves (Calhoun 2009: 27, 31). In the film, Oskar abandons his life as a full member of the welfare state. In return, he is given protection and companionship, the elements of the good life that the Nordic Welfare model failed to provide him. *Let the Right One In* proposes that unless children (and other people who need social care) are looked after, they will fall outside those social networks that have taken decades to build in Nordic societies, and from their outsider positions they become a threat to the rest of society. Thus, the film indicates the danger of what might happen if welfare state practices deteriorate.

The same discussion concerning abandoned children who have fallen outside the care-giving models and social responsibility continues in *Not Like Others* which was released only a month after *Let the Right One In*. It tells the story of two young sisters over the course of one night in Stockholm. The movie never mentions the word vampire, but the Swedish title of the film, *Vampires*, contextualises the events. Although the girls live off blood, they never bite anyone, instead using a knife to open their victims' throats. The girls appear to be homeless outcasts with no place in the welfare society. In this sense, the film articulates the collapse of social safety nets: without parental guidance the girls are forced to survive on their own and they don't know how to do it by socially accepted norms. The film pictures their last night together, as Vanja wants to leave the vampire lifestyle behind and try to live like 'the others'. Although Vera is suspicious of the plan, Vanja is optimistic: 'I've heard that others managed it. Finally they just blended in.' In a way, *Not Like Others* depicts the possibility of restoring social positions, if only the girls are willing to actively take part in the society.

The theme of social exclusion continues in Josef Elias's film *Sun Shadows: Faithful Kiss* (2011). The film itself is an online version of raw material as it remains unfinished due to financial difficulties. The story follows, more or less, the events of the *Twilight* saga (2008–12), but with the genders swapped. In this story, we have a male vampire hunter who falls in love with a girl vampire. Especially at the beginning of the film, the girl, Caroline, emphasises her involuntary exclusion from society. She was murdered and turned into a vampire, and as a consequence, she has to suffer the role of the outcast, non-belonging, liminality and unwelcomed feelings of blood-lust and aggression. She is trying to make the best of a bad situation, but the real threat is that she will never find a peaceful co-existence with the rest of the society. The attempted relationship with the vampire hunter is her chance of getting social recognition for her existence.

Sense of Detachment

In all these films, vampires are trying to survive and they have become painfully aware of their social exclusion and non-belonging. In this way they are not depicted as monsters as such, but as victims of circumstances that are not in their control. Similarly Rochelle Wright argues that vampirism is used as a metaphor for otherness and exclusion. She argues that in *Frostbite*, *Let the Right One In* and *Not Like Others* the marginalised vampires (the girl vampire taken from Germany to Sweden, a gypsy-styled Eli, and probably Eastern Europeans Vanja and Vera) are also framed as immigrants as they have darker features than is typical for Swedish heritage (Wright 2010: 57–62). Just as Pirita in *White Reindeer* is an outsider in her new village, these vampires are outsiders to the welfare state that fails to open its borders to new residents.

The vampire films' emphasis on distanced social feelings is supported by the visual imagery. In particular, elements of darkness and wild nature are visible in the use of long and dark winter nights. Fascinatingly, while in some recent Anglo-American films, such as the *Twilight* saga, vampires can tolerate sunshine and light, most Nordic vampires are still limited by darkness. They remain either hiding or hidden from everyday life with nightfall and shadows reinforcing their separation from mainstream society. Yvonne Leffler (2010: 46–8) argues that the darkness, nature and wildness are typical of Nordic horror in general. Darkness raises questions over society's dark undertones, and in addition, snow and coldness bring forward a sense of detachment and the 'impression that there is "no way out of here"' (Bruhn, Gjelsvik and Thune 2011: 4). In *Frostbite*, the dark-loving vampires can overwhelm the northern village during the polar nights when there is no sunlight to bring rescue for local residents. Similarly, in *Let the Right One In*, the depressing scenery of grey and concrete suburban buildings in Stockholm is complemented with constant images of wintry landscapes which highlight the feeling of outsiderness, detachment and society's cold relations with its citizens.

Furthermore, exclusion and marginalisation are manifested visually through repetitious images of looking through windows. In *Not Like Others*, the vampire girl Vera is constantly left outside. The church doors will not open to her and she has to settle for looking through the windows into spaces where she is unwelcome. Similarly, in *White Reindeer*, Pirita is left outside in the winter night banging the doors and peering in through the windows when she is trying to seek help for her curse. The image of the onlooking vampire, separated from social spaces by a plane of glass, captures the dynamic between the desire to belong and societal inaccessibility. In *Let the Right One In*, both the vampire and the boy deal with reflective surfaces, the repetitious images of windows, doors and walls. Here, these surfaces are used to exclude and marginalise both characters from the rest of the society, but in addition, they are used to create a theme of parallel worlds – the vampire's life and the life of ordinary people. Jørgen Bruhn, Anne Gjelsvik and Henriette Thune argue that the constant use of windows and other transparent and reflective surfaces in *Let the Right One In* highlights the questions of threshold, liminality, borders, limits and transgression. Although windows can be used as a meeting point between two worlds, mostly they highlight the sense of detachment as a physical boundary (Bruhn et al. 2011: 3–7, 10–12).

Andrew Kaplan, interestingly, sees the window as both a contrast and connection between an interior and an exterior world. The window both opens a view and reflects the image. In other words, the window frames either the inside or the outside, depending on the point of view: 'The window can coordinate the external world of places and events with the internal world of thought and feeling' (Kaplan 2002: 162–6.) Similarly, in one scene in *Let the Right One In* windows are used to highlight the difference between Oskar's and Eli's worlds. The scene starts with a shot of the house where the two windows are contrasted. From a distant point of view the viewer can see the half-naked Oskar in a brightly lit window whereas next door Eli's shadow is barely visible through a covered window. At this point, Oskar's life is still transparent and connected to the society, whereas Eli's access to society is forbidden and her window is blocked. The question of parallel worlds is that of the welfare state and the marginalised existence outside that model. A similar argument can be made with other Nordic vampire films, where the constant gazing through windows highlights how social ostracisation pushes characters into the position of a desiring onlooker. In addition, constant gazing through windows highlights how out of the place the characters feel, how they do not belong to society.

Sexuality and Gender Equality

Vampires' transformation into undead monsters is always more than a physical process, because they transcend categorical definitions of life and death in decidedly social ways. In the international vampire film market the transformation often emphasises the possibility for eternal life and liberation from social norms. Liberation concerns individual freedom, such as unlimited desire and sexual empowerment, all of which become threats to existing social structures and need to be re-controlled by destroying the vampires (see, also, Wood 1996: 369–70, 378). In this tradition, which is heavily determined by Anglo-American productions, we have, on the one hand, evil sexual predators such as Dracula, in love with death, possession and destruction. On the other hand, the romantic vampire tradition, with tragic lovers, such as Louis from *Interview with the Vampire: The Vampire Chronicles* (1994) or Edward from *Twilight* (2008), emphasises sexual intimacy and empowerment. Both types address the questions of sexuality, a theme characteristic for vampire stories.

Also in Nordic films, sexuality plays some role, but it rarely has liberating effects. Instead of being sexual predators, the Nordic vampires often appear as victims. In *Not Like Others*, Vera attacks and drains two men during one night. However, in both cases Vera responds defensively, as the men try to sexually abuse and rape her. Killing provides a way to protect and avenge herself. In *Frostbite*, the events start during the Second World War when a soldier encounters a girl vampire whose mother he had to kill. The girl is left alone and the soldier, who is revealed as a doctor later in the film, takes the girl with him. As an adult, authority figure and care-giver, he is supposed to help the girl, but instead he starts to abuse her body in order to create a perfect monster. In this story, the child vampire appears not as a deadly creature, but as an abused girl in the hands of an older man. While keeping her body in a coma, the doctor continues to bring roses to her and makes other romantic gestures as well. In this way, the film hints at a paedophiliac relationship between the girl and the doctor.

Similarly, in *Let the Right One In*, a paedophiliac relationship is hinted at. In the original novel, *Låt den rätta komma in*, Eli's guardian, Håkan, is a paedophile and as such an outcast from society. In the film Håkan's background is bypassed, but even here, although Eli is technically older than Håkan, the man can be seen as a paedophile as the relationship between the 12-year-old body and the adult male body is a cultural taboo. Håkan appears to adore Eli and he kills out of love. Once, when Håkan is interrupted during his draining process and he fails to provide the blood for Eli, the vampire accuses him: 'You're supposed to help me! Do I really have to take care of this myself?' After killing her own victim Eli cries while hugging the body. Clearly, killing does not come naturally to her, although it is her means of survival. Thus, for Håkan, the violent sacrifice to Eli is not only to keep the vampire alive, but also to protect the vampire from the need to kill. At one point in the film, he is caught in the act, but he refuses to expose the vampire and instead invites Eli to feed on him. So far, he has sacrificed his social and moral status for the solitary companionship with the vampire, but now he sacrifices his life as well. This sacrifice is the ultimate gift from a vampire's perspective, but a problematic act, an avoidance of criminal liability, from society's perspective, especially when his fate seems to set the example for Oskar's future fate as the film hints that Eli replaces her old provider with a younger version. Similarly, the delicate sexual tension that emerges from Eli and Oskar's relationship invokes questions of paedophilia, with any clear answer obfuscated by Eli's confusing mismatch of age and body.

All in all, Nordic vampire films complicate the roles of seducer and seduced, concentrating on the vulnerability of marginalised people. These films also question the roles of victims and monsters as they have often been addressed in the (Anglo-American) horror films. In these films, those who act monstrously are also victims of circumstances, especially in the case of Eli, Oskar or the girl vampire in *Frostbite*, who still belong to the category of children and should not be called to account for their actions like the adults, but who should be protected by the welfare state.

The sexual victimisation of the many Nordic vampires illuminates the consequences of neglect and failure in public care, and these themes are further emphasised by questioning the equality of gender roles, another important aim in the Nordic welfare model. Unlike in the international mainstream, mistreated Nordic vampires are often women and girls. In *White Reindeer*, a lonely bride is transformed into a vampire reindeer. *Let the Right One In* revolves around the child vampire Eli whose gender identity is blurred. Eli is a 'boy' who has been castrated at the moment of vampire transformation and after that he has become socially recognisable as a girl. *Not Like Others* tells the story of two young women without any parental guidance. In *Frostbite*, a girl vampire is mistreated in a hospital and *Sun Shadows* narrates the love story of the vampire girl Caroline. These women and girls are victims who do not celebrate their vampire conditions, which often arise through tragically unfulfilled desires to belong. They yearn for love and attention, but men in these films fail to see their need for support, instead opting to threaten and abuse them.

The abusing men represent a society that values individual goals, power and control – values antithetical to the welfare model. Indeed, as Christina Bergqvist argues, gender equality plays an important role in the Nordic model which guarantees social and political citizenship to both men and women. In order to achieve this goal many institutional solutions, such as accessible public child care, have been created to support equal opportunities. However, the inclusion of women in the public and political processes has been ambiguous; for example, men continue to govern the top positions and have stronger public voices (Bergqvist 1999: 1–6). Thus, even in the Nordic countries women tend to represent values such as care-giving and social concern whose voice may threaten the productivity of society. Similarly, the unfortunate fates of the Nordic women vampires reveal the weaknesses in the remodelling of the welfare state. These women represent the necessity for continuing social care and reveal the consequences of following (male) individualistic goals.

Conclusions

A couple of recent films, Danish *Angel of the Night* (1998) and the Finnish film *The Book of Fate* (2003), play more with Anglo-American horror genre rules than with drama-inspired Nordic vampire films. They portray their vampires more or less as evil predators. *The Book of Fate* is a parody of Hollywood's violent genres and it contains scenes from westerns, war and action films, as well as from science fiction in addition to the vampire scene which opens and closes the film. Similarly, *Angel of the Night* is an action-filled horror flick where typical scenes of vampire hunting and sexual possession are repeated. Both films exaggerate well-known international genre conventions, yet even these films share some Nordic features. For example, in both films, gender roles continue to play an important role and women have strong and important parts in the stories. Furthermore, they both refer to paganism and centuries-old beliefs, thus playing on the Nordic tendency to utilise paganism and borrow nature-related pre-Christian folk-beliefs and religious practices (see Leffler 2010). These themes are visible also in *White Reindeer* where paganism is strongly present through shaman beliefs. Even in the recent Swedish films which rather address modern society, the vampires are left out from the Christian sphere of society – for example when Vera longs to enter the church but is left outside. Here religion marks the inaccessible mainstream and homogeneous society for the outcast.

In general, Nordic vampire films tend to concentrate on a lack of intersubjective responsibility, telling stories of neglectful, dysfunctional or abusive care-providers. They narrate what happens if people are left to face their problems without social safety nets. When the newly transformed vampires have their social right to public services removed, they are forced to find their own means of survival, which in their case leads to the consumption of human blood. As such, they serve as warnings of what might happen if Nordic welfare states fail to provide adequate social services for people in need. These films reveal a Nordic fear of what may happen if productivity and individualism replace equality and public responsibility as central social values. In this way, Nordic vampire films reveal the fractures and weaknesses in the Nordic welfare model. Instead of using vampirism to expound the joys of individual freedom, Nordic vampire films fixate on social exclusion and loneliness. The Nordic vampire's relationship to death is not a victorious one, but about the scariness of eternal social exclusion.

Despite these characteristics that can be recognised from the Nordic vampire films, neither the films nor the 'brand' of Nordic welfare states are coherent phenomena. These countries have different historical, geographical and political characteristics and their film industries have unique traditions. For example, so far vampires have not been popular in Norway or Iceland, whose filmmakers have instead run with different undead characters, such as zombies. Also, in the Nordic tradition, Swedish vampire films have been the recent dominant trend, whereas Finnish and Danish films have remained curiosities. Yet, in all these films the Nordic background is visible, setting them at the margins of or apart from the international mainstream.

References

Bergqvist, Christina (1999), 'Introduction'. In Christina Bergqvist (ed.), *Equal Democracies?: Gender and Politics in the Nordic Countries*, Oslo: Scandinavian University Press, pp. 1–16.

Bruhn, Jørgen, Anne Gjelsvik and Henriette Thune (2011), 'Parallel Worlds of Possible Meetings in *Let The Right One In*', *Word & Image: A Journal of Verbal/Visual Enquiry* 27 (1): 2–14.

Calhoun, John (2009), 'Childhood's End: *Let the Right One In* and Other Deaths of Innocence', *Cineaste* 35 (1): 27–31.

Greve, Bent (2007), 'What Characterises the Nordic Welfare State Model', *Journal of Social Sciences* 3(2): 43–51.

Greve, Bent (2011), 'Editorial Introduction: The Nordic Welfare States – Revisited', *Social Policy & Administration* 45 (2): 111–13.

Kaplan, Andrew (2002), 'Windows: A Meditation on Modernity', *Word & Image: A Journal of Verbal/Visual Enquiry* 18 (3): 162–72.

Kildal, Nanna and Stein Kuhnle (2005), 'The Nordic Welfare Model and the Idea of Universalism'. In Nanna Kildal and Stein Kuhnle (eds), *Normative Foundations of the Welfare State: The Nordic Experience*, Abingdon and New York: Routledge, pp. 13–33.

Kvist, Jon, Johan Fritzell, Bjorn Hvinden and Olli Kangas (2012), 'Changing Social Inequality and the Nordic Welfare Model'. In Jon Kvist, Johan Fritzell, Bjorn Hvinden and Olli Kangas (eds), *Changing Social Equality. The Nordic Welfare Model in the 21st Century*, Bristol and Chicago: The Policy Press, pp. 1–22.

Leffler, Yvonne (2010), 'The Gothic Topography in Scandinavian Horror Fiction'. In Mikko Canini (ed.), *The Domination of Fear*, Amsterdam: Rodopi, pp. 43–52.

Peirse, Alison (2008), 'The Impossibility of Vision: Vampirism, Formlessness and Horror in *Vampyr*', *Studies in European Cinema* 5 (3): 161–70.

Trydegård, Gun-Britt (2012), 'Care Work in changing Welfare States: Nordic Care Workers' Experiences', *European Journal of Ageing* 9: 119–29.

Wood, Robin (1996), 'Burying the Undead: The Use and Obsolescensce of Count Dracula'. In Barry Keith Grant (ed.), *The Dread of Difference: Gender and Horror Film*, Austin: University of Texas Press, pp. 364–78.

Wright, Rochelle (2010), 'Vampire in the Stockholm Suburbs: *Let the Right One In* and Genre Hybridity', *Journal of Scandinavian Cinema* 1 (1): 55–70.

PART V

GENRE BENDERS

15. A NATIONAL/ TRANSNATIONAL GENRE: PORNOGRAPHY IN TRANSITION

Mariah Larsson

The most (in)famous Swedish pornographic film from the 1970s is perhaps *Fäbodjäntan* (*Come and Blow the Horn*, 1978). In the national imagination, it has become not only iconic of an era clouded by myth and legend of Swedish sin and a golden age of porn and erotic cult movies, but also of a half-jokingly celebrated Swedishness as well. Partly this has to do with the title and the setting, as Mats Björkin notes in his essay on the film '*Fäbodjäntan*: Sex, Communication, and Cultural Heritage' (2005): the *fäbod* is a place away from farming villages where, historically, farmers brought their animals for summer pasturage. Women followed the herds to the *fäbod* to watch them. Although *Come and Blow the Horn* takes place in contemporary times, it still plays upon this national historical image, and it is shot in the county of Dalecarlia (Dalarna) which is particularly associated with the *fäbod* practice. Although perhaps not the ideal of Sweden, through its director's use of national iconography – summer, the *fäbod*, an alleged Viking artifact (the horn itself), skinny-dipping – and more or less unintentional comedy, the film has through the years become a part of the 'imagined community' (Anderson 1983) of Sweden.

However, and as Björkin also points out in his essay, *Come and Blow the Horn* is directed by an American, namely sexploitation and porn director Joe Sarno (Björkin 2005), under one of his many pseudonyms, Lawrence Henning. It is produced by Joe Sarno Productions – probably created only to produce *Come and Blow the Horn* and one other Sarno film, *Kärleksön* ('Love Island', 1977), with the same female star, Leena Hiltunen – and GeBe Film AB, a

Swedish distribution company that sometimes also ventured into production (Larsson 2010). Paradoxically, although *Come and Blow the Horn* exists in the national imagination as an iconic example of 'Swedish sin', it has not made a corresponding impression abroad. In that manner, it differs from other, similar enterprises, like Sarno's sexploitation *Inga* from ten years earlier (*Jag – en oskuld*, 1968), also shot in Sweden with Swedish actresses and actors, and claimed to be one of the films that propelled the notion of Sweden as a particularly sinful or sexually liberated country.

The Scandinavian, or rather, Swedish and Danish, stereotype is one of several national and/or ethnic stereotypes that populate the sexual imagery. It may be that it is one of the less insidious stereotypes if compared to the conception of Asian women as submissive, black men as primitive or Latina women as fond of anal sex – it is, for instance, constructed out of an ideal of whiteness, with tall, blonde, buxom women who are both elegant and sexually emancipated at the same time (see Bernardi 2006; Capino 2006; Williams 2004). However, it is nevertheless a stereotype that for many years functioned as a brand name: the German expression *Schwedenfilm* which stood for any blue movie, not necessarily one coming from Sweden; the American label Swedish Erotica that first produced 8 mm and eventually video films of hardcore porn; the 'Swedish Marriage Manual' that Travis Bickle takes his date Betsy to see in *Taxi Driver* (Martin Scorsese, 1976);[1] 'Inga from Schweden' that Jamie Lee Curtis impersonates in *Trading Places* (John Landis, 1983) and 'Ulla from Sweden' played by Uma Thurman in *The Producers* (Susan Stroman, 2005); or even the Swedish bikini team featured in the Old Milwaukee beer commercials from the 1990s.

Several scholars have analysed and discussed this conception of Sweden (e.g. Arnberg 2009; Glover and Marklund 2009; Lennerhed 1994; Schaefer 2014). In this chapter, however, the purpose is rather to show how a national stereotype has functioned as a facilitator of a transnational cinema – which sexploitation and pornography had already become in the 1960s (if not earlier) – and additionally, how this process has worked the other way around: how the transnational endeavours of the sexploitation, softcore and hardcore film industries reproduced and came to further reinforce ideas of the national in these films. If, in the 1960s and 1970s, films were produced by several, often small, companies that were formed and abandoned or transformed in an endeavour to cash in on the legalisation of pornography and the liberalisation of obscenity laws (Larsson 2010), much pornography today is produced and distributed by subsidiaries of large conglomerate networks such as Private Media Group or Beate Uhse AG. If, in the 1960s and 1970s, sexually explicit material was most often viewed in public or semi-public spaces (cinema theatres, clubs, stores), today it is most often watched at home on the computer. Nevertheless, the national still functions as a marker, evident through the 'tags' used to classify material on the Internet.

Transnationality and Sexually Explicit Films

The discussion of transnational cinema often focuses on transnational cinema's political potential. Accordingly, it would, ideally, indicate a cinema that brings the national into question, even as it brings people together, potentially both in the production and reception of a film by having nationally diverse audiences, or audiences with backgrounds that span more than one national or cultural identity. It would be a cinema that not only crosses borders, but dissolves them as well: 'Because of the intimacy and communal dynamic in which films are usually experienced, cinema has a singular capacity to foster bonds of recognition between different groups' (Ezra and Rowden 2006: 4).

However, as a general term, transnational means simply 'across nations'. As Ezra and Rowden observe, the 'transnational comprises both globalization – in cinematic terms, Hollywood's domination of world film markets – and the counterhegemonic responses of filmmakers from former colonial and Third World countries' (2006: 1). Although Ezra and Rowden move on to emphasise the latter of the two, the counterhegemonic responses, the original meaning of the term cannot be completely erased. As Pietari Kääpä points out, seeing transnational cinema as 'non-English language films with culturally specific, "difficult" content, as distinctly other from mainstream European or Hollywood cinema' leads to an incomplete picture (Kääpä 2013: 26).

So on the one hand, the transnational is made out as a kind of utopian space of communication. On the other hand, nationality is still the significant identifier that makes the transnational or even postnational possible (Hedetoft and Hjort 2002). At the same time, there is an increasing alarmism surrounding the transnational and global movements which pinpoints in particular the dissolving national border as a problem – it may relate to drugs or weapons or the trafficking of humans for sexual or other purposes, it may relate to ideas that spread via social media, and it may also relate to images and networks of, for instance, child pornography users. The need to cooperate across national boundaries and form international agreements on how to combat transnational crime has become increasingly urgent (e.g. Albanese 2011).

These issues are important in relation to a genre that has become progressively more bound to the Internet and thus potentially less nation-bound – although it was never very nation-bound to begin with. In a global marketplace, one could argue that nationality – and especially in relation to the comparatively anonymous bodies of pornography – has become moot and the only things that are of significance are the looks of these bodies and the acts that they perform.[2] However, national (and ethnic) stereotypes are frequently tagged on streaming sites for porn and thus become a signifier which separates one blow-job or double penetration from another.

Somewhat contradictorily, pornographic film is rarely discussed in studies of European popular cinema or transnational cinema. For instance, in *Cinema of the Other Europe* (Iordanova 2003), the porn industry in Budapest is not discussed at all. In other studies of popular cinema or transnational cinema, the same absence is also evident, as in *Transnational Cinema: The Film Reader* (Ezra and Rowden 2006) or *European Cinema in Motion* (Berghahn and Sternberg 2010).

This is not stated in order to criticise scholars of transnational or popular film. Rather, the point is that although pornography is sometimes described as popular culture or even as male popular culture, pornography may very well be consumed to an extent that makes it quite pervasive but 'popular' connotes a sense of acceptance and enjoyment by a general public that is usually not associated with porn. In addition, since much porn has moved onto the Internet, where it is now watched in clips rather than in entire films, discussions of 'cinema' do not really include the particular medium of streamed clips on the Internet which is now the dominant one for consumption of pornographic moving images. Pornography as a moving-image genre falls between the definitions and is therefore – perhaps conveniently – left out of cinema studies, although some particular film scholars do specialise in porn research.

Nor is pornography considered art. Many studies of transnational film focus on artistic or political films, the 'counterhegemonic responses' (Ezra and Rowden) to global Hollywood, and here, too, porn falls between definitions. It is not Hollywood, but it is not art cinema either. Although pornography to a large extent is transnational, both through the ease with which it travels across borders and because it is often co-produced, it does not in general evoke aesthetic or political sentiments. One important exception to this is the alternative, activist (queer, feminist, lesbian) pornography which has political and aesthetic purposes. Furthermore, one might ask whether, in fact, pornography is a genre at all, or rather simply a particular function of a text or image – the function being that of sexually arousing the consumer. However, this function itself might be said to be the defining feature of the genre (see Williams 1991). As the horror film evokes fear, the pornographic film (or clip or image or text) evokes sexual arousal. This does not exclude other intentions, like aesthetic or political, or other effects, like laughter or disgust. Due to its morally, politically and (historically) legally ambiguous status, porn has, however, developed its own production practices, its own distribution networks, its own venues of exhibition, its own codes of behaviour surrounding consumption. As a genre, then, pornography exists outside the usual dichotomies associated with film studies. It is neither Hollywood cinema (although it is market-driven and commercial) nor European cinema (although it may very well be produced in Europe); it is neither popular in the sense that comedies or action movies are popular, nor is it artistically valuable in accordance with various subsidy systems or prestigious film awards (the adult industry has several award occasions of its own). Furthermore, pornography's ambiguous status is one reason that it, as stated before, combines the local or regional and the global or transnational: the combination is born out of its own particular conditions for existence.

The legalisation of pornography happened in sequence in several Western nation-states (1969 in Denmark, 1971 in Sweden, 1973 in West Germany, for instance), but in many of these countries, the production of pornography increased even before legalisation occurred (e.g. Arnberg 2010; Kutchinsky and Snare 1999). In an 'industry' consisting of small-scale entrepreneurs, 8 mm films and magazines could be produced comparatively cheaply but sold expensively and discreetly to a large audience at home and, perhaps more importantly, abroad. The magazine *Private*, started by Berth Milton Sr in Sweden in the mid-1960s, had articles in Swedish, English and German (Arnberg 2010). Milton is a case in point – according to his biographer, he started the business on a small scale, publishing from his apartment, and the buyer simply sent the money for an issue to him and he put the magazine in an envelope and sent it back. Consequently, Milton had large black trash bags with currency from all over the world in his home (Sjöberg 2009).

In a similar manner, the back covers of the 8 mm films by, for instance, Danish Color Climax Corporation, had texts in English, French and German. Since images were the main selling point, written text functioned to supplement the pictures or to entice potential viewers into buying or renting the film (Larsson forthcoming a). In comparison with 35 mm, feature-length films, these 8 mm productions could quite easily be put into a padded envelope and sent by regular mail.

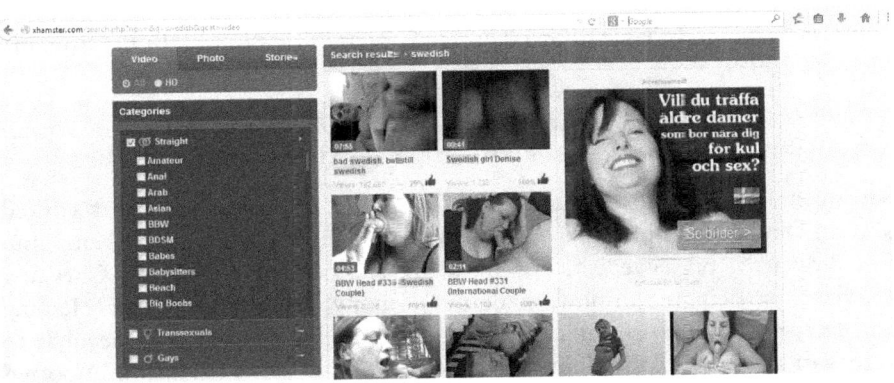

Figure 15.1 'Bad Swedish but still Swedish': National designations are very much alive as a part of the tagging of film clips.

The somewhat dubious circumstances surrounding these early instances of enterprising porn pioneers – operating in both legal and financial grey zones – make finding any definite research results difficult. However, by looking at what was submitted to the National Board of Film Censors in Sweden, one can observe that the majority of 8 mm hardcore porn during the period 1971–9 was produced in Denmark and West Germany (Larsson forthcoming a). Nonetheless, according to the adult loop database, companies such as Color Climax and the American label Swedish Erotica sometimes released the same films under their respective labels, exchanging footage with one another (Adultloop 2014).

The more costly and less explicit sex films – sex comedies, sex educational films, social problem films – that were produced during this time demanded larger machinery for distribution than magazines and 8 mm films. Their advantage was that they were rarely as illegitimate or socially unacceptable as hardcore porn (Arnberg and Larsson 2013). Several of these were made as co-productions, dubbed into English, brought together performers (and sometimes directors) from different countries, and were loose adaptations of internationally known literary works like the Mac Ahlberg/Inge Ivarson productions *Flossie* (1974) based on an anonymously published novella from 1897, *Justine and Juliette* (1975) based on two of the Marquis de Sade's novels from the eighteenth century, and *Molly* (1977) based on Daniel Defoe's 1722 *The Fortunes and Misfortunes of the Famous Moll Flanders* (Hedling and Larsson 2010; Larsson and Hedling 2009). At the same time, both magazines and films played on the national stereotype of Swedish sexuality and Swedish women. *Private* headlined on the cover with 'Svenska flickor, Schwedische Mädchen, Swedish girls' (Arnberg 2009: 481) and the films emphasised the Swedish female leads – Marie Forså, with the more internationally marketable pseudonym Maria Lynn, Christina Lindberg or Marie Ekorre – on their posters. When the films were exported, they received titles that sometimes contained some reference to Sweden (Hedling and Larsson 2010; Larsson and Hedling 2009).

Pornography as Tourism and the National as Signifier

Several stars of both sex film and porn films in the 1970s travelled and worked abroad. Some examples are American porn performers Harry Reems and Eric Edwards, but Swedish, non-hardcore stars Marie Forså and Christina Lindberg participated in films made in Germany, Japan and France (Hedling and Larsson 2010; Larsson and Hedling 2009). This is in no way peculiar to actors of sexually explicit films. Hollywood has since its inception imported talent from abroad, but in contrast to European stars in Hollywood films, the origin of the porn performer or sex film star, or the fact that he or she has travelled, is often emphasised in some way. One of Lindberg's two Japanese films was accordingly titled *Journey to Japan* or *Poruno no joô: Nippon sex ryokô* (Sadao Nakajima, 1973).

Contemporary examples would be the Swedish-Finnish porn performer Johanna Jussinniemi, known as her star alias Puma Swede (Swede 2012), or Camilla Svensson, known as Ingrid Swede, of a slightly older generation. Puma Swede operates out of the US, whereas Ingrid Swede used to work within the European porn industry, but both have utilised the signifier of nationality in creating their own star brand.

These are examples of porn stars or sex stars who have left their home country to work somewhere else, and who underline their own origins as something to be noted or in order to differentiate themselves. However, conversely, there are also situations in which the filmmakers (often men) themselves travel and make films with 'local' stars (often women) in a discourse of exploration, conquest and tourism. Within the subgenre of gonzo porn, it is not unusual to bring the camera to a country or a city in order to shoot porn scenes there (for instance, *Buttman Goes to Rio* (1990) or *Rocco Ravishes the Czech Republic* (2009)), but even a softcore classic like the French *Emanuelle* (Just Jaeckin, 1974) evokes location and difference as important elements in the construction of the erotic (in this particular case Thailand). Similarly, when Joe Sarno made *Inga* in the late 1960s, the fact that the film was shot in Sweden served to underscore its 'sinful' character. The national can thus be said to be a strong signifier within pornography, both suggesting various stereotypes and providing differentiation.

FEMINIST PORN AS TRANSNATIONAL FILM

As mentioned earlier, one kind of pornography that does have aesthetic and political purposes is activist porn. In her dissertation on queer, feminist and lesbian pornography, film scholar Ingrid Ryberg discusses how the queer, feminist and lesbian activist movement provides a 'transnational film culture' that 'includes a wide range of productions, discussions and articulations of notions and categories such as queer porn, feminist porn, female erotica, lesbian erotica, dyke porn, female to male trans porn, BDSM and fetish porn, post porn, meta porn, art porn, sex ed, indie porn and alt porn' (Ryberg 2012a: 14–15). It is manifested in film festivals and feminist porn awards in places such as Berlin, San Francisco and Toronto (Ryberg 2012a: 14).

One of the case studies in Ryberg's dissertation is *Dirty Diaries*, a collection of short feminist porn films released in 2009. The production of *Dirty Diaries* was financed by the Swedish Film Institute. The production company, Story AB, is Stockholm-based and consists of several filmmakers and producers (Story.se 2014), and the producer and artistic leader of the project was

Mia Engberg, part of the Story AB group. Looking simply at the production of *Dirty Diaries*, there is no way it can be described as a transnational film project.

Nevertheless, the project came out of a felt political need to make feminist porn that would subvert the ideological grounds for mainstream pornography, redefine pornography and explore the female gaze. According to the Swedish film database, 'the project aims to redefine porn and make it queer, feminist, and innovative' (SFI 2014). The Swedishness of *Dirty Diaries* is, consequently, on the one hand indisputable – funded as it is by the Swedish Film Institute, produced by a Swedish production company and led by a Swedish producer and artistic leader. On the other hand, *Dirty Diaries* has connections abroad and has its starting point in discussions about sexuality, gender and representation that have been held in a transnational community (Ryberg 2012a: 15, 18).

Furthermore, the project was easily marketable abroad. Outside Sweden, *Dirty Diaries* had been sold to eleven countries: Belgium, Denmark, France, Finland, Germany, Holland, Hong Kong, Luxembourg, Norway, Spain and the USA (Ryberg 2012a). Nonetheless, at least in the US, the Swedishness of the project was underscored by its reception – the fact that it was funded by the Swedish Film Institute (understood as the Swedish state) and that it was feminist was an important part of the understanding of the film. The Conan O'Brien show featured a spot interpreting Swedish feminist porn in a comedic way, showing a blonde woman having her feet massaged by a delivery man, both speaking in English with a kind of made-up Swedish accent (Ryberg 2012b).[3]

Both the transnational, albeit subcultural, audience of queer, lesbian and feminist movements, for which transnational exchanges have been a vital part, and the national stereotype of Sweden as a nation associated with sex as well as a strong welfare state, presumably came together in the reception of *Dirty Diaries*.

Domestic and Global Markets

Contemporary Nordic pornography suffers to a large extent from the same problem that is plaguing the porn industry in general: with the wide assortment of pornography available for free on the Internet, it has become increasingly difficult to make money from porn production (Andersson 2005, Larsson forthcoming b, Nowak). In addition, the way consumers watch porn today, in clips ranging from a few minutes to half an hour, continues the development since the introduction of the VCR towards abandoning narratives in favour of sex scenes focusing on the sex act itself. However, the use of narratives in pornographic films can be said to be a brief parenthesis, or, in Eric Schaefer's words, an 'entr'acte' (Schaefer 2004: 371), and mainly reserved for those feature-length pornographic films that were screened in cinemas in the 1970s.

Before that, porn was illegal and moving-image porn consisted of short films – 'stag films' – with a rudimentary or anecdotal story or simply a set-up of the situation in which sex could occur. After the 1970s, the transition to video meant that narrative became less central and films could very well consist of a compilation of scenes bound together by a theme, a director/producer or a starring performer. Nonetheless, even during that parenthesis, pornographic moving images were consumed in short 8 mm films as well as in outtakes consisting of sex scenes from longer, narrative films (Larsson forthcoming a). Narrative, as Peter Lehman points out, has never been the most significant attraction in a pornographic film (Lehman 2006).

That porn today is to a large extent consumed in short clips does not mean that narrative porn films are not made any more, only that they have become less common than in the 1970s. One example is the Swedish 2007 remake of the classic *Deep Throat* (Gerard Damiano, 1972). It was titled *Svenska långt ner i halsen* or *Swedish Deep Throat* (Mike Beck), evoking its difference from the original not through its more recent production – like the remake of the Swedish classic *The Language of Love* (Torgny Wickman, 1969) that was called, upon its release in 2004, *Kärlekens språk 2000/The Language of Love 2000* (Anders Lennberg) – but rather through a national designation. The film was produced by German Tabu Entertainment and Swedish MAX's video, which had been acquired by German Beate Uhse AG in 2001. It was released in Germany under the title *Gaaantz tief drin . . .* ('Deeep inside . . .'). From this example, it might seem that although Germany provides a significant market for several Swedish cultural products such as crime fiction and Astrid Lindgren stories, using 'schwedisch' in the title for this production would not associate with a particular sexual stereotype adding any value to the film. Rather, the use of the national designation in the Swedish title indicates an interest with the domestic audience for a domestic product. Not surprisingly perhaps, Swedish-produced porn is sought after in Sweden – as evidenced, for instance, by several threads on the Swedish discussion forum Flashback (2014), but also by the large section of Swedish material on Maxshop.se (2014). On the one hand, it might be a question of a sense of accessibility (this female performer might be my neighbour or a friend of a friend), but also, the Swedishness of Swedish porn might also associate with the same kind of 'imagined community' as *Come and Blow the Horn*. Thus, it might be read as more egalitarian, more natural and more 'free-spirited'.

However, on sites such as Xhamster, Youporn, Xtube etc. national designations are very much alive as a part of the tagging of film clips. Tags thus do not only include 'anal sex', 'hairy', 'mature' or 'blow job', but nationalities as well. The search for 'Swedish' on xhamster yielded more than 600 hits and 'Danish' around 1,000, whereas 'Norwegian' and 'Finnish' yielded less (100+ and 24 respectively) (Xhamster 2014).

These national designations are evidently not restricted to the Nordic countries. For instance, both 'French' and 'Italian' get many hits, whereas 'Lebanese' only gets a few. Nonetheless, it is very clear that certain ideas about looks and practices go together with the stereotypes of nationality, so that 'Swedish', 'Danish' and 'Norwegian' are associated with blonde women (whereas 'Finnish' seems to be associated either with very blonde hair or dark hair). A few instances are described as 'Swedish Arabian girl' or 'Swedish black girl'. The material in the search result for 'Swedish' contained vintage material from the 1970s – including Swedish Erotica clips and porn classics like *Come and Blow the Horn*; so-called tributes to Swedish celebrities (a man jerking off to a picture of the celebrity in question); 'upskirt' footage and other clandestinely shot material; cross-national couplings; Swedish porn stars; and also material where 'Swedish' functioned very simply as part of a general description like 'Swedish teen giving blowjob', 'Mature Swede gangbanged', 'Young Swedish man masturbating'. The national designation of Swedish thus functions in some cases to supply factual information for the viewer, be it as part of a description of who someone is, like 'Swedish Princess Madeleine', or in order to explain what a particular material is (from the label Swedish Erotica or a Swedish classic porn film). However, in other cases, it locates something geographically or describes a person nationally. Whether the blonde busty MILF or skinny teen actually is Swedish is another question, but it provides the performer with something of an identity, even a sense of authenticity as he or she can be attached to certain conceptions of the nation in question.

Conclusion: Transnational/National Pornography

As the venues for watching pornography changed with the advent of the Internet, the conditions for porn's existence changed as well. In a way, it moved even further away from traditional concepts of cinema and is today even more firmly settled as something other than both Hollywood and Europe. As a genre, then, one might say that pornography has become more stable. Yet, at the same time it has also proliferated and become more differentiated – homemade and cottage-industry porn as well as feminist and queer porn exist side by side with professionally produced porn from commercial companies (see McNair 2013).

On the one hand, the national still draws enough attention to function as a tag on porn sites, and as such, responds to stereotypes of nationality and ethnicity. On the other hand, the production and distribution of pornography has expanded across borders – as the consumer sits at home, looking for allegedly Swedish, Brazilian or Greek performers, the producers and distributors of porn are located as subsidiaries of large conglomerate networks like Beate Uhse AG (offices in sixteen European countries, according to Beate Uhse 2014) or

Private Media Group (offices in Barcelona and Las Vegas, according to Private 2014), and the films produced in such diverse places as Budapest, Hungary or Malmö, Sweden.

As the various examples in this chapter demonstrate, nationality still plays an important role in the distribution and consumption of pornographic material. One can say that there has been both continuity and change in the development since the late 1960s and early 1970s. Stereotypes are similar, with blonde females still being associated with the Scandinavian (or rather, the Danish and Swedish). The flow of sexually explicit images across borders is probably larger today, but it seems, too, that national designations can be used to market a material domestically as well, evoking a sense of the 'imagined community' of *Come and Blow the Horn*. As the example of *Dirty Diaries* shows, transnationality plays an important role in feminist, queer and lesbian pornography as well, but even in this case, the national may be a focus of interest in the reception.

One can also note that the plethora of small companies of the early years have given way to fewer and larger companies selling the material. The hands-on production and distribution of 8 mm films and magazines (with mail-order lists and catalogues) might be said to be continued in the cottage-industry porn that is distributed directly on the Internet. However, some of the companies from the early years still exist but have transformed. Private started out as a one-man enterprise and became listed on NASDAQ in 1999. Beate Uhse began as a one-woman enterprise in Germany after the Second World War, providing information on birth-control and selling condoms, and Beate Uhse AG is now listed on the Frankfurt Stock Exchange. MAX's video is owned by Beate Uhse AG but sells domestically in Sweden as Maxsshop.se. One of the dominating companies of the 1970s, Color Climax, is now only a distribution company.

On the Internet, the national designation is but one of several markers of content. That it is still used, however, demonstrates that even in the transnational world of sexually explicit images, nationality functions as a signifier of difference.

Notes

1. Actually, as Elisabet Björklund has demonstrated, the scenes shown in *Taxi Driver* during this visit to the cinema are from the American film *Sexual Freedom in Denmark* (John Lamb, 1970) with an unidentified Swedish soundtrack; see Björklund 2011.
2. Whether porn bodies really are anonymous is a debatable question, however. The star culture within porn has been very strong (see e.g. Lehman 2006) – at least as long as pornography remained a sellable commodity in the forms of theatre-exhibited films, videos or DVDs. On streaming sites for porn, there are several stars featuring but also a large number of non-named performers.
3. The Conan O'Brien show featured a brief film clip, in which a delivery man calls at a woman's home with ice cream. Then, the woman is shown writhing and moaning

with pleasure, and the clip cuts to the man massaging her feet. The notion of 'porn for women' thus excludes sex and focuses instead on other kinds of pleasures – probably both in accordance with television regulations and with gendered stereotypes of sexuality.

References

Adultloop (2014), <http://adultloopdb.nl/swedish-erotica>, accessed 13 February 2014.
Albanese, Jay S. (2011), *Transnational Crime and the 21st Century: Criminal Enterprise, Corruption, and Opportunity*, New York and Oxford: Oxford University Press.
Anderson, Benedict (1983), *Imagined Communities: Reflections on the Origin and Spread of Nationalism*, London: Verso.
Andersson, Mattias (2005), *Porr: en bästsäljande historia*, Stockholm: Prisma.
Arnberg, Klara (2009), 'Synd på export: 1960-talets pornografiska press och den svenska synden,' *Historisk tidskrift* 129 (3): 467–86.
Arnberg, Klara (2010), *Motsättningarnas marknad: den pornografiska pressens kommersiella genombrott och regleringen av pornografi i Sverige 1950–1980*, Lund: Sekel bokförlag.
Arnberg, Klara and Mariah Larsson (2014), 'Benefits of the In-Between: Swedish Men's Magazines and Sex Films 1965–1975', *Sexuality & Culture*, 18 (2): 310–30.
Beate Uhse (2014), <http://www.beate-uhse.ag/>, accessed 13 February 2014.
Berghahn, Daniela and Claudia Sternberg (2010), *European Cinema in Motion: Migrant and Diasporic Film in Europe*, Basingstoke: Palgrave Macmillan.
Bernardi, Daniel (2006), 'Interracial Joysticks: Pornography's Web of Racist Attractions'. In Peter Lehman (ed.), *Pornography: Film and Culture*, New Brunswick, NJ: Rutgers University Press, pp. 220–43.
Björkin, Mats (2005), 'Fäbodjäntan: Sex, Communication and Cultural Heritage', *Frispel: festskrift till Olle Edström*, Göteborg, pp. 165–73
Björklund, Elisabet (2011), '"This is a Dirty Movie" – *Taxi Driver* and "Swedish Sin"', *Journal of Scandinavian Cinema* 1 (2): 163–76.
Capino, José B. (2006), 'Asian College Girls and Oriental Men with Bamboo Poles'. In Peter Lehman (ed.), *Pornography: Film and Culture*, New Brunswick, NJ: Rutgers University Press, pp. 206–19.
Ezra, Elisabeth and Terry Rowden (2006), *Transnational Cinema: The Film Reader*, London: Routledge.
Flashback (2014), <https://www.flashback.org/>, accessed 13 February 2014.
Glover, Nic and Carl Marklund (2009), 'Arabian Nights in the Midnight Sun? Exploring the Temporal Structure of Sexual Geographies', *Historisk Tidskrift* 129 (3): 487–510.
Hedetoft, Ulf and Mette Hjort (eds) (2002), *The Postnational Self: Belonging and Identity*, Minneapolis: University of Minnesota Press.
Hedling, Olof and Mariah Larsson (2010), 'National Boundaries? Pornographic Films in Sweden in the 1970s'. In Savas Arslan et al. (eds), *Media, Culture and Identity in Europe*, Bahcesehir: Bahcesehir University Press, pp. 271–9.
Iordanova, Dina (2003), *Cinema of the Other Europe: The Industry and Artistry of East Central European Film*, London: Wallflower.
Kääpä, Pietari (2013) 'Transnational Approaches to Ecocinema: Charting an Expansive Field'. In Tommy Gustafsson and Pietari Kääpä (eds), *Transnational Ecocinema: Film Culture in an Era of Ecological Transformation*, Bristol and Chicago: Intellect, pp. 21–43.
Kutchinsky, Berl and Annika Snare (eds) (1999), *Scandinavian Studies in Criminology*, vol. 16: *Law, Pornography and Crime: The Danish Experience*, Oslo: Univ.-forl.

Larsson, Mariah (2010), 'Practice Makes Perfect? The Production of the Swedish Sex Film in the 1970s', *Film International* 8 (6): 40–9.
Larsson, Mariah (forthcoming a), The Exhibition of Pornographic Films in Malmö 1971–6.
Larsson, Mariah (forthcoming b), 'The Death of Porn? An Autopsy of "Scandinavian Sin" in the 21st Century'. In Mette Hjort and Ursula Lindqvist (eds), *Companion to Nordic Cinema*, Oxford: Wiley-Blackwell.
Larsson, Mariah and Olof Hedling (2009), 'Skandinavische Lust und europäisches Kino. Eine schwedische Filmografie', *Montage/AV* 18 (2): 137–48.
Lehman, Peter (2006) 'Revelations About Pornography'. In Peter Lehman (ed.), *Pornography: Film and Culture*, New Brunswick, NJ: Rutgers University Press, pp. 87–98.
Lennerhed, Lena (1994) *Frihet att njuta: Sexualdebatten i Sverige på 1960-talet*, Stockholm: Norstedts.
Maxshop.se (2014), <http://www.maxsshop.se/>, accessed 13 February 2014.
McNair, Brian (2013). *Porno? Chic! How Pornography Changed the World and Made it a Better Place*. London: Routledge.
Nowak, Peter (year unknown), 'The Death of Porn', Askmen.com, <http://www.askmen.com/entertainment/special_feature_3700/3785_the-death-of-porn.html>, acessed 13 February 2014.
Private (2014), <http://www.prvt.com>, accessed 13 February 2014.
Ryberg, Ingrid (2012a), 'Imagining Safe Space: The Politics of Queer, Feminist and Lesbian Pornography', Dissertation, Stockholm University.
Ryberg, Ingrid (2012b), 'Swedish Porn Discourse Reloaded: Dirty Diaries: Twelve Shorts of Feminist Porn', paper presented at the FilmForum, Udine-Gorizia, 20–9 March.
Schaefer, Eric (2004), 'Gauging a Revolution: 16mm and the Rise of the Pornographic Feature'. In Linda Williams (ed.), *Porn Studies*, Durham, NC: Duke University Press, pp. 370–400.
Schaefer, Eric (2014), '"I'll Take Sweden": The Shifting Discourse of the "Sexy Nation" in Sexploitation Films'. In Eric Schaefer (ed.), *Sex Scene: Media and the Sexual Revolution*, Durham, NC: Duke University Press, pp. 207–34.
SFI (2014), Swedish Film Institute, <www.sfi.se/sv/svensk-filmdatabas.se>, accessed 13 February 2014.
Sjöberg, Thomas (2009), *Private med Milton och Milton: den osannolika historien om ett svenskt porrimperium*, new edn., Stockholm: Fischer & Co.
Story.se (2014), <www.story.se>, accessed 13 February 2014.
Swede, Puma (2012), *Mitt liv som porrstjärna*, Stockholm: Lind & Co.
Williams, Linda (1991), 'Film Bodies: Gender, Genre, and Excess', *Film Quarterly* 44, (4): 2–13.
Williams, Linda (2004), 'Skinflicks on the Racial Border: Pornography, Exploitation, and Interracial Lust'. In Linda Williams (ed.), *Porn Studies*, Durham, NC: Duke University Press, pp. 271–308.
Xhamster (2014), <http://xhamster.com/>, accessed 13 February 2014.

16. GOING HOLLYWOOD: NORDIC DIRECTORS IN AMERICAN CINEMA

Arne Lunde

Starting with a historical overview of the presence of Nordic directors in Hollywood, this chapter aims to explore the critical mass of Nordic directorial talents in contemporary American cinema. It interrogates their importance for the transnational dynamism of Nordic cinema outside its normative national borders and reveals how vitally Nordic directors have contributed to an increasingly globalised Hollywood. By configuring Nordic directors within different temporal and categorical groupings, this study charts differences and similarities of 'Nordic' stylistic and thematic traits when migrating into Hollywood cinema.

1920s Hollywood's Scandinavian Colony

Until the 1990s, only the 1920s featured any sustained collective presence of Nordic directors in Hollywood. Three of European silent cinema's greatest artists, Victor Sjöström, Mauritz Stiller and Benjamin Christensen, immigrated to Hollywood during a decade in which the American film industry first actively courted competing talent from overseas. The Scandinavian film colony in Los Angeles would at its height in the mid- to late 1920s also include actors such as Stiller's protégée Greta Garbo, Einar Hanson, Lars Hanson, Nils Asther, Anna Q. Nilsson, Warner Oland, Jean Hersholt, Anders Randolph and Greta Nissen.

The most ambitiously productive and successful of the Nordic directors in silent Hollywood was Victor Sjöström, renamed Seastrom in Hollywood, who directed ten features in all at Goldwyn/MGM between 1923 and 1930, including three masterworks, *He Who Gets Slapped* (1924), *The Scarlet Letter* (1926) and *The Wind* (1928). Those three films in particular retain much of the naturalistic power and vision of the director's Swedish masterworks. As Bo Florin has argued, Sjöström successfully reintegrated many of his Swedish cinema stylistic visual elements (most prominently, his evocative dissolve transitions) into new contexts and narrative conventions. But Florin also states that 'Although he was regarded as alien and exotic at the beginning, his last works seemed to have turned him into just another Hollywood director' (Florin 2013: 136). After directing one talkie, *A Lady to Love* (in both English- and German-language versions) in 1930, Sjöström returned permanently to Sweden.

It is difficult to assess how well Mauritz Stiller might or might not have assimilated into Hollywood filmmaking in the long run, because of his truncated career there. Stiller and Garbo arrived in Hollywood from Berlin in 1925. Stiller was fired and replaced by MGM five weeks into the shooting of *The Torrent* (1926) and nothing of his film footage survives (although production stills do). Stiller's artisanal, unorthodox methods of shooting and editing ran into MGM's more corporate, assembly-line demands. Moving to Paramount and closer to Hollywood's German-speaking film colony, Stiller worked seamlessly with German émigré producer Eric Pommer and star Pola Negri on the First World War espionage feature *Hotel Imperial* (1927). His increasingly poor health from lung and respiratory ailments forced him to leave several successive Paramount productions during shooting. The terminally ill Stiller returned to Sweden and died in a Stockholm hospital in November 1928.

Most famous for his notorious 1922 Swedish–Danish *Häxan* (aka *Witchcraft through the Ages*), Danish director Benjamin Christensen struggled at the producer-driven MGM to retain his artistic freedom as a European film stylist. His three projects there were all compromised and formulaic. Christensen then reinvented his industry persona at First National in Burbank. Aggressively countering his reputation from the MGM period as a dour, painstakingly slow and unproductive European director, he became 'Ben' Christensen at First National, a speedy, energetic, budget-conscious and efficient American-style craftsman. Forming his own production unit, Christensen directed four films within a single year. Only *Seven Footprints to Satan* (1929) has survived, but Christensen's gifts for eroticised fantasy and horror, crime and the occult, sudden narrative twists, surrealism, comic irony and expressionist camerawork (with cinematographer Sol Polito) were given much freer imaginative rein than at MGM. Failing to find backing as an independent producer–director in Hollywood in the early 1930s, he returned to Copenhagen in 1935.

Interim Period: 1930s–1970s

Between the repatriation of these four silent-era directors during the 1920s and 1930s and the arrival of a new wave in the 1980s, Scandinavian directors were largely absent from Hollywood. The lone Nordic director working steadily there during this period was Swedish actor-turned-director Alf Kjellin, who had played the young lead in Alf Sjöberg's *Hets/Torment* (1944). Kjellin was brought to Hollywood by MGM, where he appeared under the pseudonym Christopher Kent in Vincente Minelli's *Madame Bovary* (1949). He resumed his Swedish career but returned to Hollywood in 1959 as an actor and television director. His prolific work directing TV series in the 1960s–80s included multiple episodes of *Alfred Hitchcock Presents, Doctor Kildare, I Spy, The Man from UNCLE, Mission Impossible, Gunsmoke, Hawaii Five-0, The Waltons, Columbo, Barnaby Jones, Vega$* and *Dynasty*, among scores of other programmes. Kjellin died in 1988 at the age of 68 in Los Angeles of a heart attack.

The first major film director to make the move to Hollywood since the 1920s was Sweden's Jan Troell. His international breakthroughs were two film adaptations of Vilhelm Moberg's immigrant novels *The Emigrants* (*Utvandrarna*, 1971) and *The New Land* (*Nybyggarna*, 1973), both co-starring Max von Sydow and Liv Ullmann as Swedish immigrants to Minnesota in the 1850s. *The Emigrants* earned Troell Oscar nominations for best director and best adapted screenplay. Invited to Hollywood by Warner Bros, Troell made the period western *Zandy's Bride* in 1974. Pairing Gene Hackman as a struggling California rancher with Liv Ullmann as his Swedish immigrant mail-order bride from Minneapolis, *Zandy's Bride* was a New Hollywood naturalistic, downbeat western shot on location in and around Big Sur on the central California coast. In retrospect, the film seems a thematic continuation of Troell's Swedish immigrant saga. Troell's second Hollywood production, *Hurricane* in 1979 (a partial remake of the 1937 John Ford classic *The Hurricane*), was far more artistically compromised. The 70 mm epic film starred Mia Farrow, Max von Sydow and Jason Robards, with legendary Swedish cinematographer Sven Nykvist as Director of Photography. Producer Dino de Laurentis had originally hired Roman Polanski to direct *The Hurricane* but was forced to turn to Troell when Polanski fled the country on his notorious statutory rape charge. After the highly troubled production of this 1970s disaster film, Troell resumed his successful career in Scandinavia.

1980s to the Present: Three Groupings

The major focus of this chapter is on more contemporary Nordic directors in Hollywood of the 1980s and beyond. By charting the adaptive or resistant stances of this cluster of Nordic directors in Hollywood, one can divide them into several distinct groups. The first group here is comprised of Nordic directors (Renny Harlin, Ole Bornedal and Mikael Håfström) who have assimilated into more straightforward popular genre filmmaking. The second group (Lasse Hallström, Thomas Vinterberg, Susanne Bier and Nicolas Winding Refn) have taken a less flexible, more resistant stance towards Hollywood genres and have maintained 'independent' stylistic identities within Hollywood cinema. The members of the third group (Norwegian directors Nils Gaup, Erik Skjoldbjærg, Petter Naess and Bent Hamer) have each made a single film with Hollywood funding, more often than not under artistically compromised circumstances.

Hollywood assimilations and popular genres

As Pietari Kääpä has explored in his definitive article 'Born American?: Renny Harlin and Global Hollywood' (2011), Renny Harlin has negotiated a hesitant path between his Finnish homeland identity and the commercial career opportunities beyond Finnish cinema's borders. *Born American/Jäätävä Polte* (1985) was a Reaganite anti-Soviet Cold War thriller designed as a calling card to Hollywood. Harlin's early success with the tent-pole franchise entries *Nightmare on Elm Street 4: The Dream Master* (1988) and *Die Hard 2: Die Harder* (1990) allowed him in the 1990s to become 'the king of action flicks'. The production-plagued *Cutthroat Island* (1995) is most famous as a notorious flop that nearly bankrupted Carolco Entertainment. That ill-fated pirate spectacle and the espionage/amnesia thriller *The Long Kiss Goodnight* (1996), both starring Harlin's then-wife Geena Davis in the lead roles, retrospectively read as feminist texts. As Kääpä argues, 'Harlin's emphasis on gender equality and aggressive femininity can be viewed as a sort of Nordic trope, harkening back to widely publicized notions of gender emancipation amongst the Nordic states' (2011: 65). Harlin's technical skills for staging and delivering pyrotechnic spectacle are unparalleled. Critical accusations of the 'empty content' of his narratives seem inextricably linked with their awesome Wagnerian explosions and jettisoned bodies in flight. Nonetheless, few émigré directors have engaged Hollywood action genre conventions and pre-CGI special effects with such formal confidence, ironic wit and comic-book pulp pleasure.

Ole Bornedal wrote and directed the 1994 Danish horror-thriller *Nightwatch/ Nattevagten*, which starred Nicolaj Coster Waldau, Sofie Gråbøl and Kim Bodnia. The film won a prize at the Cannes film festival and was picked up for distribution by Miramax. Bob and Harvey Weinstein subsequently hired Bornedal to work at Miramax/Dimension in New York and Los Angeles for a year and half. As part of that contract, Bornedal remade *Nightwatch* in Hollywood in 1997, co-writing the screenplay with Steven Soderbergh and casting Ewan MacGregor, Nick Nolte, Josh Brolin and Patricia Arquette. In an interview with Mette Hjort, Bornedal related that 'the actual shooting of *Nightwatch* was terrific, everything was totally wonderful, and I was free to do as I pleased, but everything suddenly became extremely complicated during the post-production phase' (Hjort and Redvall 2010: 236). The American remake of *Nightwatch* had only moderate success and lost much of the specific milieu that made the Danish original much more creepily effective. While the Hollywood remake opens immediately with a gratuitously gruesome murder, the 1994 Danish version builds its eerie mood much more slowly and is only a pure thriller in its last third. Bornedal's original has a Copenhagen urban specificity and satirical wit that flaunts Danish social taboos, with scenes of near-fellatio in a fancy restaurant, vomiting in church during communion and a vertical sex scene against a morgue wall. At such moments, *Nattevagten* (which came out the same year as Lars von Trier's *The Kingdom*) anticipates some of the generational cultural rebellion against the Danish bourgeoisie we see in the Dogme movement's *The Idiots* and *The Celebration*. Yet the film ends in a church wedding scene with Bach being played and the four young leads being reintegrated into social collective wholeness. By comparison, the Hollywood version ends in a dark post-trauma scene of emergency medical attention and the bare survival of the principals. As part of the Miramax deal, Bornedal also produced *Mimic*, the 1997 sci-fi/horror film directed by Guillermo del Toro. The Danish director has mostly worked as a director and screenwriter in Scandinavia since then, except for a brief return with *The Possession*, a 2012 American supernatural horror film produced by Sam Raimi and dealing with a haunted dybbuk box.

Mikael Håfström started in Sweden in television as a writer–director and co-wrote the screenplay for Josef Fares's *Kopps* (2003). His directorial breakthrough was *Evil/Onskan* (2003), based on Jan Guillou's semi-autobiographical novel about bullying at an elite Swedish boys' school in the 1950s. That film and his Swedish horror film *Drowning Ghost/Strandvaskaren* (2004) led to Hollywood work on thrillers and horror films: *Derailed* (2005) with Clive Owen and Jennifer Aniston, *1408* (2007) with John Cusack and Samuel L. Jackson and based on Stephen King short story, *The Rite* (2011) an exorcism thriller with Anthony Hopkins, and *Escape Plan* (2013) co-starring Sylvester Stallone and Arnold Schwarzenegger as prisoners plotting an escape from the highest-tech maximum security prison ever devised. Reigning motifs of Håfström's films from *Evil* onwards have tended to be 'escape thrillers', in which rebels trapped in prison-like spaces and no-way-out situations outwit their captors against extreme odds.

Like Harlin, Håfström appears to have fully assimilated into Hollywood-genre filmmaking for the long haul. Both directors have respectively mastered action-oriented, effects-driven popular genres and both have increasingly been absorbed into 'American/Hollywood' personae largely unconnected to their

Nordic origins. Bornedal is more difficult to place, having chosen to return to Scandinavia after the disappointing Miramax interlude. Arguably, Bornedal's remaking of his own Danish classic thriller inside the Hollywood system factors into a looming sense of falling below expectations. In comparison, Harlin and Håfström were unencumbered by any parallel requirements to transplant a Nordic hit into Hollywood soil.

Oppositional stances beyond genre boundaries

The second group under consideration is comprised of Swedish director Lasse Hallström and Danish filmmakers Thomas Vinterberg, Susanne Bier and Nicolas Winding Refn. Compared to Harlin, Bornedal and Håfström, these four have taken a less flexible and more resistant stance towards Hollywood genres. And each has managed to carve out more independent and individualistic stylistic identities within the Hollywood system than the first group explored.

Lasse Hallström's early films include music videos for the Swedish pop band ABBA. He also made the feature-length pseudo-documentary *ABBA: The Movie* in 1977. Hallström also made several successful romantic comedies in the 1970s in contemporary Swedish urban settings. The success of *My Life as a Dog/Mitt liv som hund* (1985), his poignant coming-of-age film set in late 1950s Sweden, ultimately brought the director to Hollywood. Largely specialising in character-centred dramas adapted from popular fiction, Hallström has forged an elegant, measured 'European' style within larger-budget, star-driven Hollywood projects. He has, for example, worked with Richard Dreyfuss and Holly Hunter in *Once Around* (1991), Johnny Depp in *What's Eating Gilbert Grape* (1993) and *Chocolat* (2000), Julia Roberts in *Something to Talk About* (1995), Michael Caine in *The Cider House Rules* (1999), Kevin Spacey and Julianne Moore in *The Shipping News* (2001) and Richard Gere in *Hatchi: A Dog's Tale* (2009). Hallström returned to Swedish cinema for *The Hypnotist* (*Hyponistören*, 2012) and has directed the Disney film *The Hundred-Foot Journey* (2014). While his American films have veered towards a middle-brow literary bent, they are usually elevated by the same kind of rich ensembles of actors and emotional poignancy that launched his international career through *My Life a as Dog*.

Thomas Vinterberg had his international breakthrough with Dogme film no. 1, *The Celebration/Festen* (1998). Lured by a mixture of international financing sources and near-complete freedom, Vinterberg embarked on his next project which was *It's All About Love* (2003), an English-language feature with a cast that included American stars Joaquin Phoenix, Claire Danes and Sean Penn. Vinterberg spent five years on the project. Made for $10 million, this science-fiction paranoid thriller is set in 2021 as Earth is descending into a new ice age. While visually stunning and poetic throughout, the film suffers from a convoluted and, at times, nonsensical plot. Vinterberg himself preferred to call it 'a dream'. *It's All About Love* was judged a colossal folly at its Sundance premiere in 2003. It became the most-anticipated and then most-reviled film by a Danish filmmaker since the disastrous premiere of Carl Th. Dreyer's *Gertrud* in Paris in 1964. The film's American distributor, Universal's Focus Features, sat on it for a year and finally dumped it on the market in October 2004, where it quickly sank. The experimental eclecticism of *It's All About Love* reads at moments as a kind of love-letter homage to both the studio-system Hollywood cinema of the 1940s and 1950s and to the New Hollywood of the 1970s. It is a futurist film with a retro style, with set design, costuming and lighting that more echo post-Second World War America than an imagined 2021. Noir as a genre seems a touchstone for the film. Against an image of total blackness, John's disembodied voiceover opens the narrative proper with the lines: 'My name is John Marczewski. I want to tell you the story about the last seven days of my life.' Immediately, as in classic noirs such as *Double Indemnity* (1944) and *D.O.A.* (1950), you know you have a doomed narrator who will die before the film is over. The corporate crime and ruthless syndicates of fifties Hollywood noir are echoed in the hierarchical structure of Ice International.

Yet, *It's All About Love* seems equally influenced by the New Hollywood aesthetics and pessimism of the late 1960s and the 1970s – the era of Vietnam and Watergate. *It's All About Love*'s paradoxical negotiations with Hollywood style, genre, artifice and cultural imperialism reveal Vinterberg's and co-writer Mogens Rukov's tremendous ambivalence towards Hollywood cinema. Heartfelt homage and savage critique weave together nearly indivisibly. Vinterberg embraces the glories of Hollywood studio stylistics while replicating a sinister, dystopian 'New York City', nearly all of which is achieved inside Denmark's Filmbyen studios in Hvidøvre outside Copenhagen. Aesthetically, *It's All About Love* poetically meditates on the kinds of synergistic fusions of entertainment and art cinema that his personal pantheon (Hitchcock, Polanski, Kubrick and Coppola) had earlier negotiated. Yet ideologically, the film interrogates genres like the suspense thriller, science fiction and even horror, as weapons in a merciless exposure of Hollywood (and America) as craven, dehumanising cultural–economic forces. Just as Vinterberg used a prominent Danish family in *The Celebration* to skewer an entire nation's worst qualities (hypocrisy, racism, conformity and smugness among them), that stinging invective went international in his much-anticipated, much-reviled follow-up. Despite the darkness and bite of Vinterberg's films, there's also a beguiling lyricism and tactile immediacy at work in them. And *It's All About Love* seems to wear its own title as a badge of honour.

Susanne Bier's early filmmaking career began in Sweden, but her Danish breakthrough was the romantic comedy *The One and Only/Det eneste Ene*

(1999), one of the top box-office successes in Danish film history. Bier became part of the Dogme movement with *Open Hearts/Elsker dig for evigt* (2002), a Copenhagen marital melodrama that experimented with infrared photography and stylised abstraction at the edges of its Dogme über-realism. Bier's Danish film *Brothers/Brødre* (2004), about a Danish/NATO war vet's trauma from his capture and torture in Afghanistan, was remade in Hollywood as *Brothers* in 2009 with Jim Sheridan directing. Bier's *After the Wedding/Efter Bryllupet* (2006) further explored Danish transnational links to the larger world through the compelled return to Copenhagen of a Danish expat working at a children's orphanage in India. The film's success abroad and its nomination for a Best Foreign Language Film Oscar helped lead to Bier's first Hollywood project, *Things We Lost in the Fire* (2007), a Paramount film co-starring Halle Berry, Benicio Del Toro and David Duchovny. Another Bier romantic melodrama about emotionally wounded survivors, *Things We Lost in the Fire*, revealed that Bier could successfully transfer her Danish signature style to a Hollywood production. Here, as in nearly all her films, she uses extreme close-ups (often parts of faces, eyes, hands) and a shoulder-mounted mobile camera, to create intensely personal family melodramas about surviving great trauma and loss. Bier returned to Denmark to make *In a Better World/Haevnen*. As with Bier's *Brothers* and *After the Wedding*, this 2010 drama (starring Mikael Persbrandt, Trine Dyrholm and Ulrich Thomsen) aims at a global vision, straddling locations between a refugee camp in a hellish, warlord-controlled Sudan and the violence and bullying just under the surface of a tranquil small town in Denmark. The film won the 2011 Golden Globe Award for Best Foreign Language Film. It also earned the Best Foreign Language Film at the Oscars, becoming only the third Danish film to win, after *Pelle the Conqueror* and *Babette's Feast* in the late 1980s. In 2012, Bier directed the mostly English-language *All You Need is Love/Den skaldede frisør* set in Italy's Tuscany region and romantically pairing Pierce Brosnan with Trine Dyrholm. The literal Danish translation of this film, 'The Bald Hairdresser', was too culturally specific and strange for a global market perhaps, just as *In a Better World* re-brands the downbeat literal meaning of the Danish original title 'Vengeance' with a more upbeat kind of utopian hopefulness. Returning to Hollywood, Bier recently completed *Serena* (2014), starring Hollywood A-listers Bradley Cooper and Jennifer Lawrence (plus the often-menacing Danish actor Kim Bodnia), which is set in 1930s Depression-era North Carolina.

Although Nicolas Winding Refn was born in Copenhagen, he grew up in New York City between the ages of 8 and 17, living with his mother and stepfather. Like Victor Sjöström before him, Refn had the unusual experience of an American childhood and youth, a return to Scandinavia as a teenager, and a subsequent re-immigration to Hollywood as an established Nordic filmmaker. Refn's *Pusher* in 1996 and *Bleeder* in 1999 announced the arrival of a

Danish cinema artist of von Trier-like talent and ambition (including his name in prominent banner-like letters over the film titles in the opening credits, à la 'LARS VON TRIER'). In *Bleeder*, Refn's screenplay showcases a Tarantino-like erudition inside a Copenhagen video store, as Mads Mikkelsen's clerk Lenny recites to a new customer the massive, cinephilia-laden list of international film directors on the shelves, followed by Zlatko Buric's Kitko reeling off the store's stunning variety of porn variations by section. *Bleeder* and the *Pusher* trilogy (*With Blood on My Hands: Pusher II* in 2004 and *I'm the Angel of Death: Pusher III* from 2005) all share a kinetic, collective vision of the Copenhagen criminal drug world. Compared to Refn's subsequent films, they have a stylised but reality-based naturalism, a high-octane authenticity grounded in the mean streets of the Danish capital.

Refn has subsequently taken genre movies with commercial qualities and twisted them into stream-of-consciousness fictions wedded to the psychological fantasy worlds of the central character. His first Hollywood film *Fear X* (2003), with John Turturro (as a grieving security cop at a mall whose wife has been murdered), is an experimental departure from the realism of *Pusher*. *Fear X* is a down-a-rabbit-hole mystery story that withholds clarity or closure. This cryptic, dream-like meditation on surveillance culture, mass consumerism and ultimate unknowability stylistically cites *Blow-Up*, *Point Blank* and *Barton Fink* among its myriad visual references. In the UK, Refn made the radically experimental prison film *Bronson* in 2008 in Nottingham. But his most American star-driven vehicles have been *Drive* (2011) and *Only God Forgives* (2013), both starring Ryan Gosling. *Drive*, which won Refn the best director prize at Cannes, is a clear example of a European art film director's vision being protected by a major star. Refn has cited the John Boorman–Lee Marvin collaboration *Point Blank* and the Peter Yates–Steve McQueen *Bullitt* as models for his own relationship with Gosling. Refn is an unconventional Hollywood director in numerous senses. The architect of one of the great modern car-chase movies – *Drive* – doesn't drive a car himself, and he also insists that all the actors come to his house in LA to audition, as well as to rehearse there. Refn claims that the genesis of *Only God Forgives* was an image in his mind of a man looking at his hand. The film's symbolist *leitmotif* of 'hands' is as important to Refn as the genre plot about drug dealers using a Bangkok boxing club as a front. Perhaps with a nod to the drug-world aesthetics of his *Pusher* films, Refn has said that if *Drive* is like good cocaine, *Only God Forgives* is acid. In his post-Danish career, Refn's films have drawn increasingly on mythology and Brothers Grimm-like fairy tales for inspiration, and he has made intensely personal, Bergman-like philosophical meditations cloaked within star-driven, popular genre films.

While the members of this second grouping of Hallström, Vinterberg, Bier and Refn have all taken more oppostional stances towards Hollywood genres and retained aspects of their Nordic stylistic identities in Hollywood, all four have achieved this in distinct and individualistic ways. For example, what may be most striking about Hallström's signature as a European director in America is his interest in exploring regional identities, not just New York City and Los Angeles per the more normative formulas. Hallström's post-Sweden films are collectively set in distinct places, not generic 'anywhere' but specific sites with their own regional markings and diversity. His Hollywood career is a kind of cinematic travel/tourism by choice. *What's Eating Gilbert Grape* is set in Iowa but shot in Texas; *Once Around* shot in Boston and the Caribbean; *Something to Talk About* (1995) set in the American South; *Cider House Rules* in Maine in 1943; *The Shipping News* in Newfoundland; *Chocolat* in France; *Casanova* (2005) in eighteenth-century Venice; and so on. Even *ABBA: The Movie* is a concert film shot in Australia. While Hallström's more classical, almost 'invisible' narrative style is less showy and self-conscious than that of the other three directors, beneath his middle-brow literary adaptations seems an enormous curiosity about places and spaces at the margins and the specific grain of the rural, the local and the regional. By comparison, Susanne Bier's original screenplays (often co-written with Anders Thomas Jensen) consistently remain romantic melodramas about emotionally wounded survivors, and Bier's signature style of extreme (and oddly truncated) body and facial close-ups has been a hallmark of both her Danish and Hollywood productions to date. At their best Hallström and Bier both communicate rare emotional power in their respective works and both effectively mine the melodramatic affect within their familial sagas. The Thomas Vinterberg of *It's All About Love* and the entire post-Danish career of Nicolas Winding Refn, on the other hand, appear to eschew any particular fixed genre at all but rather reveal formal experiments and hybridic art films, cleverly citing myriad directorial influences. Of the four directors discussed here, Refn as a stylist may be the most original and visionary, his stance in each successive film the most oppositional and independent (not unlike his fellow Dane Lars von Trier).

Hollywood one-shots from Norwegian directors

This third grouping is comprised of Norwegian filmmakers Nils Gaup, Erik Skjoldbjærg, Petter Naess and Bent Hamer. Each director made a single film with Hollywood funding, under artistically compromised circumstances and with varying levels of success.

Nils Gaup wrote and directed the first feature film ever to be shot in the Sami language, *Pathfinder/Veiviseren* (1987), based on a twelfth-century legend. It received Norway's second Academy Award nomination for best foreign language film (the first being Arne Skouen's *Nine Lives/Ni liv* from 1957). The success of *Pathfinder* led to Gaup working for the Disney studio on

Shipwrecked (1990), adapted from Oluf Falck-Ytter's 1873 Norwegian boys' adventure novel *Haakon Haakonsen: en norsk Robinson*, and starring Stian Smestad as Haakon and Irish actor Gabriel Byrne as the chief pirate villain. Disney, however, had a strict corporate view of filmmaking and insisted on master coverage shots so that they could edit and select shots as they wished, contrary to Gaup's usual practice of story-boarding and editing in the camera. The result looked more like a family-friendly echo of Disney's *Treasure Island* (1950) than a Gaup signature project.

Erik Skjoldbjærg grew up heavily influenced by American thrillers of the 1970s as well as European art house films. His 1997 mystery thriller *Insomnia* starred Swedish actor Stellan Skarsgård as a sleep-deprived Stockholm homicide detective on the edge. A kind of *film blanc* set in northern Norway during the nightless summer, this neo-noir was remade by director Christopher Nolan and starred Al Pacino as a corrupt LA detective, with Alaska substituting for northern Norway. Skjoldbjærg's lone Hollywood film to date is *Prozac Nation* (2001), a US–German co-production featuring Christina Ricci, Jason Biggs, Anne Heche, Michelle Williams, Jonathan Rhys-Meyers and Jessica Lange. Adapted from Elizabeth Wurtzel's memoir *Prozac Nation: Young and Depressed in America* (and set in the mid-1980s), the film chronicles a Harvard student's spiral into drugs and clinical depression. Skjoldbjærg's *Insomnia* eerily conveyed the altered states and slow mental crack-up of its detective protagonist. It thus shares several thematic links with *Prozac Nation*, not only in Ricci's steady mental/emotional disintegration but in the casting of Lange as her disturbed mother (the actress having played the unstable and tragically lobotomised actress Frances Farmer in *Frances* in the 1982 Hollywood biopic). Despite its excellent cast of young actors, *Prozac Nation* remains a fairly conventional film by committee. When Skjoldbjærg returned from Hollywood to Norwegian cinema in 2004, he co-wrote and directed a radically updated version of Henrik Ibsen's 1882 play *An Enemy of the People/En folkefiende*. Potentially, Skjoldbjærg's recycling of Ibsen's tragicomedy about a lone idealist and a town nearly crushed by corrupt businessmen, industrial poisons and lies and cover-ups may reflect his own Hollywood experience.

Petter Naess has also directed only one Hollywood film, *Mozart and the Whale* (2006). Filmed on location in Spokane, Washington, the film focuses on a community centre for adults with various forms of autism. The film co-starred Josh Hartnett and Radha Mitchell as an offbeat romantic pair who share high-functioning conditions of Asperger Syndrome. The film's odd title is based on the respective Halloween costumes that the couple wear early in the film. Naess had earlier earned international success with *Elling* (2000), which received Norway's fourth Oscar nomination for Best Foreign Language Film. Based on a novel by Ingvar Ambjørnsen, *Elling* was an odd-couple comedy drama about Elling and Kjell-Bjarne, two quirky middle-aged roommates released from a state mental institution and provided with a state-funded allowance and apartment in Oslo. (*Elling* even spawned two sequels in Norway and inspired a 2010 Broadway stage production starring Brendan Fraser.) Josh Hartnett's star power and interest in the project got *Mozart and the Whale* made, and he most likely handpicked Naess to direct. *Elling* made autism, OCD, paranoia and other mental health conditions seem charmingly and hilariously quirky and it also portrayed a beguiling surrogate family of eccentrics and outsiders, qualities shared by *Elling* and *Mozart and the Whale*.

Bent Hamer appears to have fully retained his unique Nordic aesthetic with little compromise in his lone American venture. Hamer is best known for *Kitchen Stories/Psalmer fra kjøkkenet* (2003), which wryly observed the absurdity of a team of Swedish efficiency experts surveying the kitchen habits of Norwegian bachelor farmers in 1950s Norway. He followed up *Kitchen Stories* with his American indie film *Factotum* (2005), produced by Jim Stark and starring Matt Dillon, Marisa Tomei, Lili Taylor and Fisher Stevens. Adapted by Hamer from several Charles Bukowski novels all set in Los Angeles, *Factotum* was shot on location in Minneapolis. Hamer's deadpan style, evocative long silences, stylised colour tableaux and loner eccentrics all travelled extremely well to urban Minnesota. Hamer's subsequent film in Norway, *O'Horten* (2007), with Baard Owe as an elderly, newly retired train engineer experiencing a surreal, transformative night in Oslo, seems fully part of Hamer's larger frieze of sublimely understated oddball humanism.

Why each of these Hollywood one-shots was a Norwegian remains an open question. Although Norwegian cinema has achieved enormous breakthroughs in international visibility and viability over the past twenty years, for decades it lived under the shadow of the far larger Swedish and Danish national cinemas. And unlike its Nordic neighbours, Norway has (so far at least) not produced an international 'name' director, for example a Sjöström, Stiller, Dreyer, Bergman or Kaurismäki. The experiences of Nils Gaup, Erik Skjoldbjærg and Petter Naess in Hollywood arguably reveal directors mismatched to projects largely controlled by studio overlords. Bent Hamer's low-key and ironic Bukowski-in-Minneapolis indie project seems the lone film here to have survived Hollywood inteference and the dilution of Norwegian film talent abroad.

Conclusion

For Nordic directors in Hollywood, adopting, resisting or manipulating the reigning American popular genres of the period has always been a particular challenge. In the silent era, Sjöström assimilated most seamlessly into MGM's producer-dominant system and its factory-system adapations of popular novels and prestige plays. Yet it was really the power and clout of star Lillian Gish at MGM in the mid-1920s that protected Sjöström enough to make *The Scarlet*

Letter and *The Wind* between more compromised, routine projects assigned him by Thalberg and Mayer. While Stiller and Christensen failed to succeed in the MGM system, both reinvented themselves at rival studios, Stiller with continental melodramas at Paramount (with star-muse Pola Negri headlining) and Christensen at First National with so-called 'mystery-comedies' (in the vein of Universal's hit *The Cat and the Canary*). In both cases, Stiller and Christensen found their commercially revived identities within identifiable popular genres and more permissive studio house styles. It is interesting that the only Nordic director for several decades in their wake is Alf Kjellin, whose work in episodic television in the 1950s–70s is the most rigidly genre-specific of all of the émigrés under consideration in this chapter. With much tighter budgets and shooting schedules allowed than in feature films, Kjellin mastered the one-hour TV format, initially in the dark-humoured and macabre *Alfred Hitchcock Presents* (arguably not too unlike Benjamin Christensen's mystery–comedy features of 1928–9). Kjellin's multi-genre abilities excelled in Cold War espionage shows (*The Man from UNCLE*, *I Spy*, *Mission Impossible*), westerns (*Gunsmoke*), hospital dramas (*Doctor Kildare*), cop/detective programmes (*Hawaii Five-0*, *Columbo*, *Barnaby Jones*) and family sagas (*The Waltons*, *Dynasty*), among scores of other TV-directing credits. Kjellin was so successful as a hyper-efficient journeyman TV director that he became a kind of prisoner of that success. Despite his desire to do so, he was unable to move up within the more highly stratified Hollywood system of that period from the weekly TV grind into feature films with more prestige, artistic freedom and time.

In more contemporary contexts, genre has also remained a decisive factor in the assmilation and resistance experiences of Nordic directors in Hollywood cinema. Renny Harlin and Mikael Håfström are most emblematic of the émigrés who have used technical command of dominant American popular genres and narrative formulas as an express ticket to steady work in Hollywood. In this sense they are the most assimilated, their 'Nordicness' virtually invisible and unremarked on. Ole Bornedal might have taken this same path at Miramax had he chosen to do so. Yet, Bornedal appears more linked to the Norwegian one-shot directors, each of whom braved a single Hollywood-funded project and then chose to return to Europe. As we saw with the initial failures and reiventions of Stiller and Christensen, persistence, drive and perhaps even luck are not inconsiderable factors in this process of negotiating oneself into the Hollywood system for a longer term. Despite landing in the comparatively writer-/director-friendly New Hollywood of the 1970s, Jan Troell ranked at its restraints compared to his more artisanal career in Sweden (where union rules did not forbid him operating his own camera, for example). Arriving in Hollywood two decades later, Lasse Hallström carved out a long career niche in Hollywood projects that transcend hard-and-fast genre limits. His literate, character-driven vehicles seem more akin to the indie movement in tone, his Swedish outsider position always part of his wide-roving fascination with the regionally specific versus the nationally generic. Thomas Vinterberg used funding from Universal's Focus Features to interrogate an eclectic mix of Hollywood genres and styles while filming an ersatz New York mostly on Danish sound stages. Nicolas Winding Refn mastered the mean streets gangster film in Denmark and his English-language projects abroad have never strayed far from his obsessions about masculine codes of violence and vengeance. Part of Winding Refn's elegant illusionism is his hiding of metafilmic art cinema tropes within male action thriller genre trappings. Meanwhile, Susanne Bier is closer in sensibility to Hallström than her fellow Danes here, embracing genre conventions (especially those of melodrama and romantic comedy-drama) with a deeper emotionalism than the more self-conscious and genre-hybridic stylistics of Vinterberg and Winding Refn allow. As this chapter has tried to examine and at times problematise, the historical process of Nordic directors adapting to Hollywood cinema has never quite been a zero-sum game of either total assimilation or resistance. Rather, the reality of each director's experience can be fixed within a more subtle spectral continuum, one highly influenced by genre yet nuanced by a range of other factors.

References

Florin, Bo (2013), *Transition and Transformation: Victor Sjöström in Hollywood, 1923–1930*, Amsterdam: Amsterdam University Press.

Hjort, Mette, Eva Jørholt and Eva Novrup Redvall (2010), *The Danish Directors 2: Dialogues in the New Danish Fiction Cinema*, Bristol: Intellect.

Kääpä, Pietari (2011), 'Born American? Renny Harlin and Global Hollywood', *Film International* 9 (2): 55–70.

Lunde, Arne (2010), *Nordic Exposures: Scandinavian Identities in Classical Hollywood Cinema*, Seattle: University of Washington Press.

Lunde, Arne (2011a), 'After *The Celebration*: Thomas Vinterberg's *It's All About Love*', *Film International* 9 (2): 20–9.

Lunde, Arne (2011b), 'Scandinavian Auteur as Chameleon: How Benjamin Christensen Reinvented himself in Hollywood, 1925–29', *Journal of Scandinavian Cinema* 1 (1): 7–23.

17. A CULTURE OF RECIPROCITY: THE POLITICS OF CULTURAL EXCHANGE IN CONTEMPORARY NORDIC GENRE FILM

Pietari Kääpä

> Right now, the region is one of the most robust places for cool films and since we've been supporting genre film from the region, we've built a great relationship with Norwegian Film Institute. Traditionally, they've dealt with more high-minded films, but they've definitely seen the potential in genre film in the last few years.
>
> Tim League in Calore (2012)

Tim League, the founder of Austin's Alamo Drafthouse Cinema chain, and a key figure in distributing genre cinema in the US, outlines several significant developments in the international profile of Nordic film culture. His comments touch on the context where a range of genre films like *Iron Sky* (Vuorensola, 2012), *Død snø/Dead Snow* (Wirkola, 2008), *The Reykjavik Whale Watching Massacre* (Kemp, 2010) and *Kommandør Treholt og Ninja troppen/Norwegian Ninja* (Malling, 2010) have broken the perception of a bleak sense of Nordic miserabilism of the Bergman or the Kaurismäki variety. Instead, cinemas of the Nordic countries are now 'cool' and receive blessing from both high-minded arts institutions and geeky fans alike. Furthermore, it seems genre has a substantial role to play here with both producers and creative institutions from the Nordic countries embracing its commercial and creative potential. In addition, League's comments were published in *Wired* magazine, a venue for tech-savvy media connoisseurs, which reports on the very latest in the intersection of technology and communications. The combination of genre and new media culture clearly provides Nordic film producers with a novel take on infiltrating what is, in reality, still very much a global niche market.

From where do the inspiration and incentives for such productions emanate? How does the often quirky genre-related content of these films fit in with the parameters of national cinema culture in the Nordic context? The quirkiness prevalent in the above productions is not entirely surprising, as Nordic film productions have a history of featuring odd comic behaviour including works by well-known auteurs such as Lars von Trier, Aki Kaurismäki, Nicolas Winding Refn and Bent Hamer. Yet, the works of Vuoresola, Malling and others are distinct from these more experimental auteurs (even if the films of the art auteurs also display playful uses of commercial genre conventions). Rather, films like *Iron Sky* and *Norwegian Ninja* owe as much to early Sam Raimi and Peter Jackson as they do to their respective national cultural and cinematic histories. As the above comments suggest, these films are premised on combining elements as well as utilising identifiable genre patterns and domestic norms for productions that are able to differentiate themselves in the global marketplace.

Effectively, these are 'fan' films but done on an extravagant, professional scale, combining strategies that amount to the sort of 'textual poaching' identified by Henry Jenkins (1992; Nazis, ninjas as narrative material) with the use of professional crews and industrial backing to realise films that lie somewhere in between affective homages and large-scale blockbusters. Furthermore, the ways these films use genre position them as exemplary cases of 'reactive globalization'. The term, used first by Mette Hjort (2006) to discuss the variety of strategies used by Danish filmmakers in dealing with transnational movements of film culture, puts emphasis on the agency of small national filmmakers to enter the often very competitive international marketplace, in which, of

Figure 17.1 Action in the fjords: *Norwegian Ninja* (Thomas Cappelen Malling, 2011). Image courtesy of Torden Films.

course, even their own national film markets are involved. Genre emerges as a key tactic in such reactive strategies, where producers use their knowledge of global mainstream culture (in this case Global Hollywood) in ways that simultaneously subvert and affirm the connotations of those cultural products. As they do this, they also bolster the cultural industries of their respective small nations, using both domestic resources and reputations as cultural capital. I characterise this form of cultural and economic exchange as a form of cultural reciprocity, meaning that both the national and international 'sides' of this production matrix can benefit considerably from utilising not only production resources but also perceptions about the types of culture they are producing to considerable effect.

To explore the implications of such reactive strategies, I focus on two case studies, *Norwegian Ninja* and *Iron Sky*. Instead of a traditional academic discussion, I base much of this chapter on interviews conducted with the filmmakers of both ventures. Erik Vogel, the producer of *Norwegian Ninja*, illustrates the cultural and industrial politics of small nation film cultures which operate within the realities of a marketplace governed as much by Hollywood as by domestic protectionist film policy. Timo Vuorensola, the director of *Iron Sky*, provides a discussion of network culture from a small nation perspective, discussing both new media technologies and various forms of crowdsourcing in this context. Both producers are able to shed light on the changing practices of film production in the Nordic countries and especially the central role genre plays in these transformations – as well as how their productions fit in with this cultural reciprocity.

Rethinking the Parameters of National Cinema

As many of the chapters in this collection attest, Nordic cinema often comes with certain art cinema associations. This is not only to do with the tradition of international distribution for films that focus on bleak social realities or emphasise artistic experimentation, but it also concerns the various traditions of 'quality cinema' delineated by the respective film institutes of the Nordic countries (see Soila, Iversen and Söderbergh 1998). In contexts of small film cultures, the role of organisations such as the Finnish Film Foundation and the Norwegian Film Institute are of key importance. They dictate the central tenets of policy and impose substantial influence over what gets produced and distributed in domestic theatres. While institutes continue to play the role of gate keepers, Tero Kaukomaa, the producer of *Iron Sky*, notes that the impetus for the existence of films like *Iron Sky* comes from a wider transformation in film culture. According to him, 'In Finland, we have a new generation of directors that are willing to do features that authentically want to connect with the audiences. Simultaneously we have a new generation of producers that have professionalized film production' (Kaukomaa in Vuorensola et al. 2012: 25). The professionalisation of film production and the increasing role of genre are also noted by Vogel, who states that 'the 1990s were the dark ages' in Norway, but recent transformations in policy mean that embracing genre has resulted in an impetus to 'start making more commercial films' (Marcus 2010). Vogel's arguments could be applied to the Finnish context with little variation (see Pantti 2000 and Kääpä 2012 for more discussion on this, as could those of Kaukomaa to Norway.

Timo Vuorensola inspects the dynamics of genre from an alternative angle: 'Finnish mentality – whatever it may be – brings its own flair to genre film and brings Finnishness into theatres not in an emphasized way, but as more of a background radiation' (Vuorensola 2012). In this reciprocal conceptualisation, nation and genre combine in unusual ways that benefit both areas of film culture. Interestingly, Vuorensola's perspective is shared by the Finnish Film Foundation, which funded the project with 800,000 EUR, the maximum available to domestic productions. This financial production support has a more symbolic role to play as well, as without it the project would not have been taken seriously by the German and Australian producers, Vuorensola states. The budget of *Iron Sky* is a complex piecemeal of sources, and includes 1 million EUR from fans. The rest comes from more traditional sources such as Hessen Film Invest, Eurimages, Nordisk Film & TV Fond, Screen Queensland, several pre-sales and spending-related financing bodies like DFFF in Germany and Australian tax-offsets. To be able to consolidate interest from potential international participants as well as from domestic sources, *Iron Sky* had to be able to stand out from the normative conceptions of 'Hollywoodised' or 'Finnish' film. One of the ways it was able to do this, according to Kaukomaa, was by establishing a 'reputation in the visual effects area' and by producing a film which would showcase these efficiently. Another area for this 'concerns marketing and community knowledge' (Kaukomaa 2012). In both instances, the production company was able to offer something unusual by conventional Finnish standards as well as maintain the key impression of being an international standard commercial production.

A similar argument applies to *Norwegian Ninja*'s production history, where domestic and international cultural influences exist in a dynamic relationship. While *Norwegian Ninja* is not the same sort of multinational production as *Iron Sky*, its funding structure includes both domestic and Nordic funds. The 17.9 million NOK (1.8 million GBP approximately) production received 10 million NOK from the Norwegian Film Institute, development money from the Nordic Film & TV fund, with Film Fund FUZZ (Western Norway) providing equity funding. The considerable percentage of domestic funds is reflected in its narrative which focuses on a much more localised theme, reinventing the story of disgraced former minister Arne Treholt as the tale of a covert spy protecting his country from vested foreign threats. Much as was the case with Vuorensola, the director of the film reveals a reciprocal understanding of cultural exchange beneath its seemingly local theme and production history:

> In 1982 I was 12 years old. I was grounded for a while and my bedroom became my world. I spent a lot of time watching Star Wars and Ninja movies on my VCR. The now-famous Arne Treholt case remains a mystery today, 28 years later. Unable to believe the government's and the media's 'true story' of his pro-Soviet espionage, I still prefer the video-game-novel-news mash-up that seduced my mind back in '82: Arne Treholt was neither traitor nor spy – he was a Ninja Master working for the King, defending the Norwegian Way. (Tordenfilm 2011)

The dynamics of exchange underlying both *Norwegian Ninja* and *Iron Sky* showcase how cultural affiliation enables producers to position their work in ways that take advantage of global cultural flow and the specifics of small nation film cultures, as well as of traditional production structures and new production methodologies. To illustrate these dynamics of cultural reciprocity, the chapter now focuses on interviews with Erik Vogel and Timo Vuorensola to debate, firstly, reciprocal forms of globalisation and national cinema, and secondly, the role of new media platforms in these reciprocal transformations.

An Interview with Eric Vogel (*Norwegian Ninja*)

Pietari Kääpä: What role do genre structures play in your work?

Erik Vogel: They are important but never the reason for making a film. To put it another way: genre is a means to an end, to tell a specific story, but never an end in itself. In that sense, I am a producer, not a specialist in, for example, horror or thriller films, but rather focused on exploring various storytelling options for a given project, and finding the best tools (genre-wise) for the job.

PK: Can you tell me more about the financing of *Norwegian Ninja*? What role do national film institutes, from your perspective, play in consolidating a production such as this?

EV: In order to produce *Norwegian Ninja* at a budget level high enough to realise Thomas's script and directorial vision, we were dependent on securing support from one of the commissioning editors at the Norwegian Film Institute. They decide on projects through a number of factors, but they are mainly considering the artistic merits of the project, as opposed to another funding scheme at the Institute where the main emphasis is on commerciality.

Thankfully, we found a great deal of enthusiasm with our commissioning editor, and received development support, followed by production support. So, for our project – which I will categorise as perhaps being 'art house action' – the role of the Institute was critical to be able to make the film.

The budget level we had for production was approximately 3 million USD [2010 exchange rate]. This was a mid-range budget level for a Norwegian theatrical film at the time, meaning a regular, full crew and a typical shooting period of seven to eight weeks. But since you can shoot a drama film at that budget level, it also implies you can't shoot a VFX-heavy action extravaganza unless you are very creative about it. We had visual effects, action scenes, animals, vehicles and other expensive things to fit into that financial frame. But with a very experienced crew and a truly open-minded and innovative director, we were able to make do with those resources.

Note that with some more mainstream and/or lower budgeted films, it is possible here to sidestep an artistic or commercial 'pre-approval' from the Institute. You do this by raising private equity on the promise of automatic box office support from the Institute upon the release. This still means you are dependent on public funding (in the back end), even if you work with very commercial projects and private investors. The market is simply too small to sustain films made solely on private financing and risk.

But, as mentioned, *Norwegian Ninja* was financed in a pretty traditional way for Norwegian drama or arthouse films, where the public funding comes first, and is subsequently used as leverage to attract the private funding. A government supported, satirical ninja movie is a very rare bird though . . .

PK: Would you characterise your film as a Norwegian film? Or is it more internationally oriented (you often discuss the potential of audiences missing specific references)?

EV: Definitely a Norwegian film first and foremost. At least I view it that way, as the story and characters are specifically Norwegian, the film was produced and financed in Norway, and created by a Norwegian crew.

But the ninja and cult film elements, *Star Wars*/other film references and overall early 1980s aesthetic are of course international elements. The writer/director and I both grew up watching all those things on imported VHS films. They have been assimilated by our culture, and in our film put to use to serve our Norwegian outlook. I do however mainly see these elements as 'form', and not 'content', where the actual themes and content are definitely Norwegian. Sometimes exaggeratedly so.

PK: Your film has received substantial international interest – could you talk a bit about how this gels with a production that takes an inherently Norwegian subject but frames it in unexpected ways?

EV: Frankly, I was surprised that the very specific, historical context for the film (the Treholt espionage case and subsequent trial) actually worked pretty well abroad. I remember asking our sales agent why, and the answer was: it works because there's a specific, historical context. If the film's story and ideas had stopped short at 'a film about some Norwegian ninjas', it wouldn't have worked.

The expression I've used in the past to describe the 'category' of the film is: international genre with a local twist. This approach has worked for many films in the later years, including *Iron Sky*, *Låt den rätte komma in*/*Let The Right One In* and many others.

Another (and more) successful Norwegian example is *Trollhunter*, which came out at the same time as our film.

PK: Do you see crowdfunding as a significant aspect of your film – or even the whole future of cinema?

EV: No to the first part of the question. We crowdsourced some development work through the portal Wreck-A-Movie, which was a real help in the beginning of the project. But we quickly saw that you can't really get more out of this activity than you put in. A lot of dedication is needed to build up and maintain a significant community of fans. And with no real resources to set aside for it, our crowdsourcing activities were limited to what the director and myself were able to do. As production started to draw near, we had to devote ourselves more and more to the filmmaking, and eventually the effort faded away.

It was a good learning experience though. And we did get some great practical help and ideas from the followers/fans of the film. But it wasn't a significant part of the big picture. We spent four years working on the film, and had crowdsourcing efforts going for maybe half a year, actively.

Crowdfunding was something we didn't launch a campaign for. As mentioned above, the financing was pretty traditional, with the sources of funding all residing within the film industry (distributor, regional fund, television channels, sales agent, equipment rental house, etc.).

To the second part of the question: Crowdfunding is already a great tool for filmmakers, and will continue to be so. However, I believe this is true only for a subset of projects that can attain a critical mass of interest, and with substantial efforts from the filmmakers to make the campaign work. The bulk of projects around the world are still funded in 'older', more established ways.

I don't feel qualified to say whether crowdfunding will be significant to the whole future of cinema. That's a prediction which is hard to make. But I can say it will be significant for some of the future of cinema. It won't go away, and still has huge potential to grow as a financing approach.

PK: How do you see Norwegian cultural institutes responding to crowdsourcing and fan culture?

EV: They are not very cutting edge in this sense on an institutional level, but I don't find that surprising. They are institutions working to reach politically decided goals, and don't have a need to be cutting edge in their approach to crowdsourcing and fan culture. But there are persons in the 'system' that are definitely in tune, and who are interested. Through a current, increased focus on the marketing and distribution of films, there is definitely a shift in attitude in the actual institutions as well, though.

PK: Do you see any correlations between you and other projects such as *Iron Sky*, beyond the use of similar platforms for production, a film production ethos?

EV: Definitely. When I met the *Iron Sky* gang, it was back in 2007. In the early days of that project, and ours. And it was an instant, mutual connection through shared sensibilities. Over the years we've kept in touch, and I count them as friends. I've also met many other like-minded filmmakers and projects through bringing *Norwegian Ninja* to genre film markets and festivals.

I see this phenomenon partly as generational and cultural, with a shared set of inspirations implanted in people who were born in the West sometime in the 1970s and had our childhood in the 1980s. This generation has since then come into positions of being able to make films. We share cultural touchstones like Lucas/Spielberg/Amblin Entertainment films, certain comic books, VHS culture, the Cold War etc. that were important in our youth. Secondly, there is a technological aspect – the power of advanced digital effects and cinematographic equipment is within reach for filmmakers today even on very low budgets.

PK: Any plans for similar ventures that combine traditional resources with emerging ones?

EV: Yes. The very slow-moving, institution-dependent and traditional way of making films here in Norway takes its toll. It's very time-consuming, and there is a high chance of investing a lot of energy into projects that end up dying a very slow death in the financing and development stages, for one or several of a million reasons. So I'm considering a couple of new projects that will allow for a lower-risk (financially) but also freer mode of production. Harnessing a fan-base and doing it together with them is one way of doing this, but not the only one. With advanced equipment and experienced filmmakers readily available, it's possible to go quicker from script to screen than before, if the content (which necessarily will be front and centre, instead of high production values) is strong enough. There's nothing to announce just yet, but a couple of projects like this are being explored.

PK: What do you think about the audience response to your film domestically as well as at international festivals?

EV: It definitely had a mixed reception at home. There was a clear tendency for the film to be better received in the big cities than in more rural areas. We saw this both in the reviews and the ticket sales. The bigger, urban media were generally very favourable. In a qualitative sense, the film played best to a grown-up audience, while we probably bored many teenagers and other younger people who didn't recognise a lot of the references.

Internationally, the film played excellently on the genre film circuit, beginning with an international premiere at Fantastic Fest in Austin which both led to a US sale of distribution rights and garnered two awards (best director and best actor in the Next Wave competition). From there, it went on to Sitges, AFI Fest and many other major festivals. The festival audiences were generally very positive.

PK: Is Nordic film about quirkiness? This seems to be a label that enables many of these productions to penetrate the markets.

EV: I think that's correct, from the outside point of view. At least, it's possible to say it's true for a certain strand of Nordic films, with a humorous or genre-informed bent. The more serious-minded wave of so-called Nordic Noir films is more about 'moodiness' and 'bleakness' though. Not very quirky.

PK: Is there a Nordic film culture or are all the countries distinct in terms of their cultural heritage, contemporary modes and so on?

EV: From a bird's eye view or from abroad, it's easy to put all films in a basket bearing exactly that moniker: Nordic films. This is also how the market lumps together the region, business wise (it's often considered to be a single territory when it comes to the buying and selling of distribution rights).

But from the ground level there are huge differences between the individual countries in my opinion. Also, in the genres that are made. Sweden had Bergman and has Moodysson, plus a slew of up-and-coming filmmakers breaking out now. The Danes have von Trier, Vinterberg and many others. The Finns have the Kaurismäkis. These and other internationally high-profile directors influence their local industries, the repertoire of films that get made. The distinct 'moods', culture and histories of each country also inform this.

We have a more fluid field in Norway, where only a few truly strong voices reach international audiences right now, like Joakim Trier on the art house side and a few, strong genre film makers led by Tommy Wirkola (*Dead Snow*, *Hansel & Gretel Witch Hunters*, 2012), Morten Tyldum (*Headhunters*, 2011) and the duo of Rønning/Sandberg (*Max Manus*, 2008, *Kon-Tiki*, 2012) and they will direct the next *Pirates of the Caribbean* film.

PK: Could you tell us a bit about your inspirations and influences in producing your film?

EV: Certainly, it is a combination of many things. The project originated with the writer/director who presented the idea to me at an early stage. I was immediately struck by the pure originality of the idea, the subversiveness that comes from the irreverent treatment of recent historical events, and the playfulness in the storytelling.

Building from there, the influences in filmmaking terms which are most clearly evident in the film itself are personal favorites like *The Life Aquatic with Steve Zissou* (2008), *Brazil* (1985), the 1975 Norwegian puppet animation film *Pinchcliffe Grand Prix*, *Star Wars* and many Cold War era action and ninja B-movies, but especially the Swedish classic *The Ninja Mission* from 1984. These are shared influences by both director Thomas and myself. He also brought many, many other inspirations and influences to the film, which in some cases, are evident in such subtle ways that it takes two or more viewings to spot them.

When it comes to producing, I was mainly inspired by the project itself, which was so rich and challenging. It was an attempt to do something no-one had seen before – mixing many styles of filmmaking, and trying out wild effects work, martial arts, creative use of archive materials, animals, vehicles and much more. And all this to explore underlying themes of who writes historical truth, who defines what makes a hero or a villain. This was perhaps the leading intellectual pursuit of the film for me, and actually refers back to how I feel about genres: they are the means to the ultimate end. Which is to first and foremost make the viewer engage emotionally with your story, and then to make them think.

Towards an Iron Sky

For Vogel, the correlations between genre cinema and national culture feature centrally in understanding the place of small nation cinema in a globalised marketplace. Similar views have been expressed above by Timo Vuorensola and Tero Kaukomaa in the Finnish context. For them, the integration of national themes and funding structures is entirely essential for operating internationally, much as these international aspirations are also essential for contemporary Finnish cinema. Above, Vogel has outlined some of the industrial and organisational reasons for such perspectives to emerge, but we now turn to the use of new media platforms in the production of *Iron Sky* to illustrate alternative ways in which reactive globalisations operate.

The impetus for producing *Iron Sky* was largely reliant on the success of *Star Wreck*, a series of fan-made productions starting from 1992 that follow the adventures of Captain Pirk and his crew. Evolving from crudely animated early short films to a large-scale feature-length film, the series was an essential stepping stone for both Samuli Torssonen (the producer) and Vuorensola to expand their operations. Key to this success was the fan following established by *Star Wreck*, which would function as a resource base for the various forms of crowdsourced operations essential to the production. The project used a variety of digital platforms to get its fans involved in the design, the production, the marketing and the distribution of the film. Fans would be able to crowdfund the early stages of the film with small donations, they could offer substantial investments in return for profit participation, they would help with getting the word of mouth round, and finally, the very fact that they were interested would be key to persuading official organisations like the Finnish Film Founation and commercial participants to see the potential market for the product. As Vuorensola and Kaukomaa state regarding the fans, 'the best way to market your film is to get a lot of people to watch it for free' (Alonso 2007). While *Iron Sky* was conceptualised on the premise of open participation, this was a 7.5 million EUR production, resulting in a combination of open culture and official commercial production.

At stake in these film politics are also considerations over the dynamics of small nation film production going global and of a large international production utilising its localised connotations. An apt comparison for, at least, the aspirations of the production is the Linux model, that is, Linus Torvall's development of an open source operating system to compete with Microsoft and others, offered freely available online. To support this assertion of an independent competitor challenging dominant media systems, Vuorensola and Kaukomaa frequently discuss their need to challenge the established parameters of global film culture (Svanbäck, 2010). But both producers are entirely aware that *Iron Sky* is also a commercial venture, a fact that complicates its role in this reciprocal exchange. To best illustrate these concerns, we now turn to an interview with Timo Vuorensola that explains many of his key concerns regarding the ways new media platforms and established film production and distribution structures operate. Through this, we also get a good sense of how national production parameters change with the increasing incorporation of online platforms.

An Interview with Timo Vuorensola

Pietari Kääpä: How do net cultures and crowdsourcing change the patterns of production and distribution of Finnish film? How do the cultural institutions, such as film institutes, respond to them?

Timo Vuorensola: Net culture, the use of social media, crowdsourcing, -funding and -investing are all areas that are here to stay. Their main role is to support independent film – which applies automatically to every Finnish film, as well as the majority of European ones – and make them more competitive in relation to Hollywood cinema. The Internet can simply contribute more resources for films in terms of marketing, production and finance.

The changes facilitated by the Internet were still widely considered somewhat irrelevant in 2008, or even met with contempt, but slowly the attitudes have become more favourable, and what we had discussed in seminars and festivals all around the world since the release of *Star Wreck* is now considered pioneering work. Many professionals in the film industry are turning to us to consult on the impact of these changes.

PK: Have the film producers in Finland taken Internet culture seriously enough?

TV: No, they have not, but that is to be expected. The film industry is slow to change – producers are hesitant unless a well-known name is pushing progress forward – but once irrefutable evidence of success starts to materialise, heads turn.

PK: You open up your productions to user participation with crowdsourcing etc. Is the role of the director changing and would it be better if this role became more user related?

TV: The director is – and will be – a dictator, and democracy plays no role in participant creative production on the Internet or outside it. The role of the director will eventually change, but more in the direction of a marketer, a motivator or a creative dictator.

PK: Commercialisation has an ever-increasing presence in film culture and its production funding. What role does economic logic play in comparison to independent or grassroots ideology?

YV: Commercialism is and will be a major part of film production. Economic thinking can complicate or guide both large-scale Hollywood productions as well as indie and grassroots work. Smart producers will understand this and will try to navigate their productions through the problems of commercialism and art. If someone does not understand the simple correlation between film production and commercialism, they are working in the wrong field.

PK: How would you contextualise *Iron Sky* in relation to mainstream production (Finnish, European, universal)?

TV: As a kick starter, inspiration and a way forth that will encourage Finnish, European and universal film production to combat the overpowering presence of the US film industry.

PK: Online distribution and production operate across borders. What is the role of national culture in a changing media culture environment?

TV: Cultural context is inevitably central in constructing these productions – we are not able to avoid the influence of our roots. The shoddiest quality comes from a producer trying to eradicate their cultural roots. A film can inspect any topic, it can be in any language, it can be shot anywhere, and actors can be from anywhere, but the roots of the director have to be visible in the production. Rootless productions are the most pitiful cases – they seem to be from nowhere.

Iron Sky has been successful in combining traditional production culture – that is, traditional sources comprise 90 per cent of its budget, the distribution is predominantly theatrical, and not based on online channels, and so on – and cultural implications of the Internet – that is, the use of community building, remixing material, the use of alternative copy and distribution rights etc. We work hard to combine these areas to ensure that we use the best qualities of both worlds.

PK: Do we need to situate *Star Wreck* and *Iron Sky* in the scale of Finnish film culture or are these cases of productions using new and external forms of cultural heritage?

TV: *Star Wreck* and *Iron Sky* are certainly reflections of and contributions to Finnish film culture but they can also be situated productively within a global network-based production culture.

PK: Is integration of production resources important for transforming the parameters of Nordic film (thinking about your cooperation with inhouse visual effects house Energia VFX)?

TV: In our case certainly. We set out to do a Hollywood-scale effects film – more than 700 shots which is in the same realm as *Transformers* – but with a twentieth of the budget. It was very important that we were able to use a production house that had the will to go all out so we could get the production organised no matter what. I think production houses like Energia, which are both ambitious and of extremely high quality, but also innovative and affordable, will be more and more essential for the production of independent films.

PK: Is integration an important term for your form of production, meaning that the production, realisation, distribution and even the coordination of reception is increasingly in the hands of the producers?

TV: The distribution, production, financing and franchising of Internet-led productions will demand more and more creative productionship, and the role of the producers will in this case be even more central.

The Changing Norms of National Cinema

The complex production history of *Iron Sky* plays out as a dynamic example of small nation film culture using its peculiar smallness to appeal to global financiers and audiences. In turn, the global also filters to Finland as the crowdsourcing initiatives and explicit genre material of the film bring new perspectives to this particular small nation film culture. When taken in tandem with Vogel's perspectives on *Norwegian Ninja*, Vuorensola's words note some of the main considerations in producing genre cinema in contemporary small nations. The dynamics are characterised by a similar set of push-and-pull strategies as the conceptualisation of reactive globalisation. By this we mean that national and international concerns in production, funding, distribution and marketing are comprehensively integrated – there is no point in even trying to set them apart, at least in terms of genre productions such as these which are inherently about cultural exchange and adaptation. Intriguingly, the integration of traditional production and distribution modes with advances in online collaboration is increasingly pointing to mutual reciprocity between these two areas, not competition between them. While one could question the logic of prioritising international success, as many critics have done, gaining such recognition is essential for productions such as *Norwegian Ninja*, and even more so, *Iron Sky*. And even as these successes often filter back to an increased profile in the domestic marketplace, the pervasive transnational logic of Internet culture makes global integration and connectivity the norm.

Conclusion

Iron Sky and *Norwegian Ninja* are only two of the more explicit examples of innovation in Nordic cinema. As many of the more recent Nordic genre productions show, emphasis on novel production and marketing strategies is increasingly central to breaking into the international marketplace. While these productions are anomalies, being as they are enabled by histories of transnational flow and contemporary integration of different media systems, they point to a set of emerging strategies in global integration. From the more traditional heritage films to the uses of popular genre idioms imported from the global mainstream, Nordic cinema producers clearly position themselves as competitive players able to navigate the demands of the markets. Yet, we also need to ask whether the strategies adopted in these contexts ultimately amount to some unique take on the methods of positioning their competitiveness. After all, we can note similar patterns in many other small nation contexts. Taking a snapshot of some key small-film cultures from *The Cinema of Small Nations*, it is not difficult to identify similar strategic patterns. Out of the nations identified by the volume's contributors, Hong Kong and New Zealand stand out for their embrace of commercial genre productions. Hong Kong, of course, has a long history of producing fantasy and action films that have also penetrated and considerably influenced the global mainstream. Similarly, New Zealand's *Lord of the Rings*-propelled industry has produced indigenous comedies such as *Black Sheep* (Jonathan King, 2006) that rely on a mixture of imported genre conventions and local references.

While some of the small nations, including Cuba, struggle with domestic political control often suspicious, to say the least, of consciously commercial genre production, the closest comparison points to Nordic film come, unsurprisingly, from two small nations in Western Europe, Scotland and Ireland. These nations are part of a wider regional network of UK-wide institutions across the UK and Ireland, including close collaboration with the British Film Institute. Yet, indigenous organisations, such as the Irish Film Board and Creative Scotland, manage the day-to-day operations of domestic film production. This makes sense, as while the productions from these nations are often identified as part of British cinema, they maintain very distinct national lineages. For example, Ireland's output for 2012, the year of release for *Iron Sky*, showcases serious drama (*What Richard Did*, Lenny Abrahamsson), gritty social realism (*King of the Travellers*, Mark O'Connor), children's television film (*Eliot and Me*, Fintan Connoly), documentary linking the nation with a global scale (*When Ali Came to Ireland*, Ross Whitaker) and, interestingly, a

CGI-heavy horror comedy (*Grabbers*, Jon Wright) and killer clown extravaganza *Stitches* (Conor McMahon, 2012). The first four categories fall in line with 'typical' state-sponsored small nation films, touching on the sort of 'valuable' cultural production that wins prizes domestically and garners festival distribution abroad. *Stitches* and *Grabbers*, however, are clear indicators of the types of reciprocal strategies emerging as vital aspects of most contemporary small film industries. The latter especially has much in common with *Iron Sky* and *Norwegian Ninja* as it uses both genre conventions – big monsters and quirky main characters – with elements that could be described as either excessive stereotypes or banal nationalist indicators – in this case, excessive alcohol and uilleann pipes on the soundtrack.

Yet, even as excessive alcohol consumption is not only a particularly Irish facet – indeed, it is often identified as a specific Nordic trope – so it is clear that quirky genre productions are not the sole property of the Nordic countries. This logic also extends to the institutional context of these productions as the role of organisations like the Irish Film Board and Creative Scotland is not that much different from the various Nordic film institutes. This certainly raises the question whether there is something unique about the cultural politics of the Nordic countries and if the many calls to 'exceptionalism' posed here have such merit. These suggestions need to be carefully considered as, on the level of small nations, the Nordic film cultures come across as sharing as much with key comparative cases as they differ from other potential comparisons. While it is certainly clear that Nordicness is both a cultural value system – whether this is to do with language, cultural references, political frameworks or specific lineages or genre production – and an industrial context, we should be careful not to homogenise a 'Nordic effort', even as we must be mindful of similarities these cultures share not only with one another but also with other (inter)national film cultures.

Instead of continuing to persist with designations of exceptionalism, perhaps it is more productive to fully acknowledge these similarities and differences and place the strategies adopted by Nordic 'creatives' in their full context. Accordingly, as the chapters of this collection show, these films are produced in a reciprocal context where the specific forms adopted by the films are part of international film culture. In many ways they continue to exemplify the centrality of a culture of reciprocity at the heart of Nordic film culture – that is, the vitality of the multidirectional flow of international influences to and from the Nordic region. While these strategies are more obvious in the case of horror films, popular comedy, for one, would seem to contradict this reciprocal rhetoric. It is often a genre identified as 'inexportable' because of its excessive reliance on cultural references that do not travel to foreign audiences; yet when we focus on 'indigenous' comedies, we can see that their narrative constructions and thematic considerations tend to follow similar patterns in international genre cinema. And while it remains true that their audiences are mostly domestic, these levels of similarity require much more incisive interrogation.

The discussion above largely omits the looming elephant in the room – the role of Hollywood in setting the patterns to be followed. Certainly, it would make little sense to ignore this considerable influence. Yet, simultaneously, the infrastructural mix of private and public resources, highlighted, for example, by the adoption of 50/50 financing schemes in most of the Nordic countries, and the combination of genre patterns with social considerations specific to the region, demonstrate the distinctiveness of these national cinemas. As many of the chapters in this collection show, the combination of egalitarian principles with individualistic aspirations, of the ethos of the welfare state with extreme forms of neoliberal practice, exemplifies Nordic film culture. At the same time, contemporary strategies in digital creativity and infrastructural connectivity continue to reformulate how the industries as well as the organisations in charge of policy conceptualise the relevance and role of national cinema. Productions such as *Iron Sky* and *Norwegian Ninja* continue to challenge the traditional parameters in which national cinema is understood, and thus continue to expand its parameters. It is clear that the means of delineating such parameters must now account for the increasingly global networks that underlie these ventures, a process that in many ways continues the ongoing dialogue between domestic and imported content, albeit in ways where such distinctions are increasingly blurred. As part of these cultures of reciprocity – defined by dialogue and interconnectivity – these definitions ought to be considered not as competitive categories but rather as mutually beneficial forms of cultural production. And genre production, both as a form of content and as a creative strategy, seems to be very much at the forefront of these contemporary cultures of reciprocity.

References

Alonso, Eduardo (2007), 'An open source adventure from outer space', *Free!*, February.
Calore, Michael (2012), 'Iron Sky's Moon Nazis: Shock Troops in Nordic Genre Film Invasion', *Wired*, <http://www.wired.com/underwire/2012/03/iron-sky-nordic-genre-films/>, accessed 4 October 2014.
Hjort, Mette (2006), *Small Nation, Global Cinema: The New Danish Cinema*, Minneapolis: University of Minnesota Press.
Jenkins, Henry (1992), *Textual Poachers: Television Fans and Participatory Culture*, London: Routledge.
Kääpä, Pietari (2012), *Directory of World Cinema: Finland*, Bristol: Intellect.
Kaukomaa, Tero (2012), Interview with Pietari Kääpä, 30 November.
Marcus, J. S. (2010), 'Norway in Action', *The Wall Street Journal*, 22 October.
Pantti, Mervi (2000), *Kansallinen Elokuva On Pelastettava*, Helsinki: SKS.
Soila, Tytti, Astrid Söderbergh Widding and Gunnar Iversen (1998), *Nordic National Cinemas*, London and New York: Routledge.

Svänback, Andrea (2010), 'Finsk films skarpaste vildhjärna anfaller', *Hufvudstadsbladet*, 18 July.
Tordenfilm (2011), 'Norwegian Ninja Production Notes'.
Vuorensola, Timo (2012), Interview with Pietari Kääpä, 11 October.
Vuorensola, Timo, Tero Kaukomaa, Samuli Torssonen, Jarmo Puskala, Pekka Ollula and Janos Honkonen (2012), *Näin tehtiin Iron Sky*, Helsinki: Docendo.
Vogel, Erik (2014), Interview with Pietari Kääpä, 8 January.

INDEX

9 Millimeter (1997), 105
21 Ways to Ruin a Marriage (*21 tapaa pilata avioliitto*, 2012), 161
42nd Street (1933), 176
101 Reykjavík (2000), 2

A Funny Man (*Dirch*, 2011), 25
Abba: The Movie (1977), 184, 235
Abbott, George, 177
Åberg, Anders, 179
Abrahamsson, Lenny, 258
Abyss, The (*Afgrunden*, 1910), 2
After the Wedding (*Efter bryllupet*, 2007), 237, 239
Aghed, Jan, 42
Ahlberg, Mac, 222
Aja, Alexandre, 194
Aknestik, 137
Alanen, Antti, 161
Alfredson, Tomas, 203
Alger, Horatio, 104
Alien Vs. Predators: Requiem (2010), 77
All You Need Is Love (*Den skaldede frisør*, 2012), 237
Allen, Woody, 158
Åmark, Klas, 34–6, 39, 44
Almodovar, Pedro, 147
Altman, Rick, 173, 178, 184, 187

Amadeus (1984), 26
Ambjørnsen, Ingvar, 6, 240
Ambush (*Rukajärven tie*, 1998), 13
Amelie (2001), 147
American Graffiti (1973), 174
An Enemy to Die For (*En fiende att dö för*, 2011), 50, 245
Andersen, Benedict, 150
Anderson, Paul Thomas, 148
Anderson, Wes, 148
Andersson, Mattias, 224
Angel of the Night (1998), 212
Annila, Antti-Jussi, 191
Aniston, Jennifer, 234
Antell, Love, 141
Arcel, Nikolaj, 52–3
Arctic Heat (1985), 11–12
Army of Shadows (*L'armée des ombres*, 1969), 39, 42
Arn: The Kingdom at Road's End (*Arn: Riket vid vägens slut*, 2008), 50–3, 56–7
Arn: The Knight Templar (*Arn: Tempelriddaren*, 2007), 50–3, 56–7
Arnberg, Klara, 218
Arquette, Patricia, 233
Arroyo, Jose, 176
As Good As It Gets (1997), 158

INDEX

As It Is in Heaven (*Så som i himmelen*, 2004), 3
Åsbrink, Elisabeth, 44
Asther, Nils, 230
Auge, Marc, 135, 145
August, Pernilla, 145
Aunimo, Rane, 167
Ausonius, John, 107
Austen, Jane, 165
Austin-Smith, 176
AVP: Alien Versus Predator (2004), 77
Axel, Gabriel, 149, 154

Babette's Feast (*Babettes gæstebud*, 1987), 149, 154
Bacon, Lloyd, 176
Badding (2000), 23
Badley, Linda, 176
Ballet Mecanique (1924), 182
Bamberg, Rolf, 127
Banke, Anders, 203
Banks, Leslie, 77
Barton Fink (1967), 238
Battle Royale (2000), 78
Beast, The (*Odjuret*, novel, 2004), 107
Beck, Mike, 225
Bendjelloul, Malik, 181
Benny and Joon (1993), 158
Beowulf & Grendel (2005), 49
Berdal, Ingrid Bolsø, 191
Berghahn, Daniela, 220
Bergman, Ingmar, 1, 3, 10, 48, 56, 95, 97, 198, 238, 241, 244, 253
Bergman, Ingrid, 3
Bergqvist, Christina, 212
Bergström, Åsa, 179
Bergting, Peter, 113
Berkel, Christian, 40
Berkeley, Busby, 177
Bernadotte, Folke, 35
Bernardi, Daniel, 218
Berry, Halle, 235
Best Man's Wedding, The (*Jalla! Jalla!*, 2000), 149
Beyond (*Svinalängorna*, 2010), 145
Beyond the Border (*Gränsen*, 2011), 50
Bier, Susanne, 5, 43, 233, 235–9, 243
Big Heat, The (1953), 68
Biggs, Jason, 240
Bildt, Carl, 106
Billig, Michael, 21, 96
Björk, 152, 157

Björkin, Mats, 217
Björklund, Elizabeth, 227
Black Christmas (1974), 191
Black's Game (*Svartur á leik*, 2012), 71
Blade Runner (1982), 13
Blomberg, Erik, 205
Bodnia, Kim, 233
Body Fat Index of Love, The (*Rakkauden rasvaprosentti*, 2012), 161
Bohwim, Knut, 8
Bondebjerg, Ib, 175
Boorman, John, 194, 238
Booth, Wayne C., 164
Bordwell, David, 63
Bornedal, Ole, 233–5, 242–3
Bowen, Chuck, 101
Box 21 (novel, 2005), 107
Brannagh, Kenneth, 9
Breaking the Waves (1996), 149
Bridge, The (2013–), 93, 100–1
Bridge, The (*Bron/Broen*, 2011–), 1, 61, 91–101
Bridget Jones's Diary (2001), 7
Bringing Up Baby (1938), 160, 170
Britton, Andrew, 160
Broch, Nicolai Cleve, 38
Brødre i blodet (novel, 1996), 6
Brolin, Josh, 233
Bronson (2008), 238
Brooks, James, 158
Brosnan, Pierce, 237
Brothers (*Brødre*, 2004), 237
Bruhn, Jorgen, 209
Buckingham, David, 2
Buckowski, Charles, 241
Buric, Zlatko, 238
Buried Dogs (*Begravde hunder*, 2008), 67
Burton, Tim, 149
Buttman Goes to Rio (1990), 223
Byrne, Gabriel, 240

Cabaret (1972), 176
Caine, Michael, 235
Calhoun, John, 207
Camp Slaughter (2004), 193
Capino, Jose, 218
Captain Grogg animations (1916–21), 3
Carlsson, Ing-Marie, 152
Caroline Mathilde (Queen), 52–3

INDEX

Carpenter, John, 191
Cassuto, Leonard, 67
Causey, Ann, 81, 84, 87
Cavell, Stanley, 162, 164
Celebration, The (*Festen*, 1998), 154, 234
Chan, Felicia, 157
Chandler, Raymond, 63, 67
Chechik, Jeremy, 158
Children of Nature (*Börn natturunar*, 1991), 149, 152–3
Chocolat (2000), 235, 239
Christensen, Benjamin, 230, 242
Christian VII, 53
Cider House Rules The (2000), 235, 239
Cimino, Michael, 81
City State (*Borgríki*, 2011), 70–2
Clarke, Bob, 191
Cliffhanger (1993), 12
Cockpit (2012), 162
Cohan, Steven, 134, 137, 142, 145
Cold Fever (*A köldum klaka*, 1995), 149, 152
Cold Prey (*Fritt Vilt*, 2006), 6, 190–4, 196
Cold Prey 2 (*Fritt Vilt 2*, 2008), 192
Cold Trail (*Köld slóð*, 2006), 70
Collins, Suzanne, 78
Come and Blow the Horn (*Fäbodjäntan*, 1978), 217, 225
Connell, Richard, 77, 84, 88
Contraband (2012), 71
Cool and Crazy (*Heftig og begeistret*, 2001), 149, 181–4
Cooper, Bradley, 237
Cornelis (2010), 24–6, 28
Coster-Waldau, Nikolaj, 65, 82
Cramby, Jonas, 194
Cukic, Dejan, 111
Cunningham, Sean S. 191
Curtis, Jamie Lee, 218
Custen, George F., 22–7, 126
Cutthroat Island (1995), 233

Dahl, Christer, 107
Dahl, Knud, 155
Damiano, Gerard, 225
Dancer in the Dark (2000), 175–9, 183
Danielsson, Jonas, 196–7
Davis, Geena, 233
Day of Wrath (*Vredens dag*, 1943), 48
de Laurentis, Dino, 232

Dead Snow (*Død snø*, 2013), 5, 14–15, 191, 199, 244, 253
Dead Snow 2 (*Død snø 2*, 2014), 15
Deal, The, (2003), 120
Death Kiss, The (*Dödskyssen*, 1916), 3
Deep Throat (1972), 225
Deer Hunter, The (1978), 81
Deerslayer, The (novel, 1841), 84
Defoe, Daniel, 222
Del Toro, Benicio, 235
Del Toro, Guillermo, 234
Deleyto, Celestino, 162
Deliverance (1972), 194
Demy, Jacques, 173, 176
Den perfekta stöten (2014), 9
Den usynlige hær (1945), 34
Deneuve, Catherine, 176
Depp, Johnny, 235
Derailed (2005), 234
Detour (*Snarveien*, 2009), 191
Diderot, Denis, 53
Die Hard 2: Die Harder (1990), 12, 233
Dillon, Matt, 241
Dog's Tale, The (2009), 235
Donen, Stanley, 177
Double Indemnity (1944), 236
Downfall (*Der Untergang*, 2004), 40
Dragomir, Mrsic, 111–12
Drengene fra Sankt Petri (1991), 34
Dreyer, Carl Theodore, 1, 48, 189, 204, 236, 241
Dreyfus, Richard, 235
Drive (2011), 238–9
Drowning Ghost (*Strandvaskaren*, 2004), 193, 200, 234, 245
Duchovny, David, 237
Duken, Ken, 36
Dunham, Lena, 93
Dyer, Richard, 174, 178
Dyrholm, Trine, 237

Easy Money – Life Deluxe (*Snabba cash – Livet deluxe*, 2013), 114
Easy Money (*Snabba Cash*, 2010), 9, 109–15
Easy Money (*Snabba cash*, novel, 2006), 104–9
Easy Money II (*Snabba Cash II*, 2012), 111–12
Easy Rider (1969), 144
Ebbe The Movie (2009), 120

Eco, Umberto, 48
Edelmann, Samuli, 135, 142
Eden Lake (2008), 194
Eden Pastora – Commandant 'Zero (2006), 120
Edfelt, Catti, 179
Edward Scissorhands (1990), 148
Edwards, Eric, 222
Eklund, Bernt, 121
Ekman, Gösta, 8
Ekorre, Marie, 222
Elias, Josef, 203
Eliot and Me (2012), 258
Elkington, Trevor G., 7, 14
Ellfsen, Per Christian, 155
Elling (aka *Me, My Friend and I*, 2001), 6–7, 149, 155, 240–1
Elsaesser, Thomas, 156–7
Emannuele (1974), 223
Emigrants, The (*Utvandrarna*, 1971), 232
Enemy of the People, The (*En folkefiende*, 2004), 240
Engström, Emma, 121
Erlendsdóttir, Ágústa Eva, 71
Eronen, Tommi, 55
Ersgard, Jack, 191
Escape Plan (2013), 234
Espinosa, Daniel, 111, 113
Eternal Sunshine of the Spotless Mind (2004), 148
European Union MEDIA, 93
Evans, Marc, 197
Evans, Peter, 162
Everlasting Moments (*Maria Larssons eviga ögonblick*, 2008), 24
Evil (*Ondskan*, 2003), 194
Evil Dead, The (1982), 198
Eyerman, Ron, 145
Ezra, Elizabeth, 219–20

Factotum (2005), 241
Fagervall, Markus, 141
Falck-Ytter, Oluf, 240
Falling Angels (*Putoavia Enkeleitä*, 2008), 23
False Trail (*Jägarna 2*, 2011), 76, 80, 86, 88
Fares, Josef, 149, 234
Farrow, Mia, 232
Farschou-Hviid, Bent, 39

Fast Five (2011), 114
Father's Old and New (*Isän vanha ja uusi*, 1955), 163–5
Fear X (2003), 238
Fehmer, Siegfried, 36
Fenimore Cooper, James, 84
Feuer, Jane, 2, 5, 174, 176
Finnish Blood, Swedish Heart (*Laulu koti-ikävästä*, 2012), 133–45, 178–83
Finnish Film Foundation, 4, 10, 12, 14, 22, 246–7
Finnish Film Institute, 12
Flame & Citron (*Flammen og citronen*, 2008), 33–4, 39–45, 50
Floberg, Bjørn, 64, 67
Florin, Bo, 231
Flossie (1974), 222
Fogelstrøm, Lasse, 80
Følsgaard, Mikkel Boe, 53
Ford, John, 232
Foreign Fields (*På fremmed mark*, 2000), 78
Forman, Milos, 7, 180
Forrest Gump (1994), 148
Forså, Marie, 222
Fortunes and the Misfortunes of the Famous Moll Flanders, The (novel, 1722), 222
Fosse, Bob, 176
Frances (1982), 240
Franzén, Peter, 66, 68
Frears, Stephen, 129
Freedman, Carl, 104
Friday the 13th, The (1980), 191
Friðriksson, Friðrik Thor, 149, 152–3
Friedman, Milton, 109–10
Fritzell, Johan, 205
Frost (2012), 190
Frost, Vicky, 96–7
Frostbite (*Frostbiten*, 2006), 203–8, 212–14
Fukuyama, Francis, 106

Gainsborough, Serge, 142
Galbraith, James K., 109
Galbraith, John Kenneth, 109
Gallen-Kallela, Akseli, 23, 29–30
Game of Thrones (2011–), 93
Gängkrig 145 (graphic novel, 2009), 113
Gangsterfilmen (1974), 105
Garbo, Greta, 230

Garter Snake (Vares – Sukkanauhakäärme, 2011), 68
Gaup, Nils, 233, 239, 241, 245
Geijerstam, Eva af, 42
Gere, Richard, 235
Gertrud (1964), 236
Gibson, James J., 83
Girl with the Dragon Tattoo, The (2011), 3
Girl with the Dragon Tattoo, The (Män som hatar kvinnor, 2009), 3
Girls (2012–), 93
Gjelsvik, Anne, 209
Glanzelius, Anton, 151
Glover, Nic, 218
Goodman, Irwin, 23
Gondry, Michel, 148
Gosling, Ryan, 238
Gotta Run! (Ajolähtö, 1982), 145
Grabbers (2012), 259
Gråbøl, Sofia, 233
Grant, Barry Keith, 173–4, 178
Greve, Bent, 206
Grieg, Edvard, 22
Grundbulten (novel, 1974), 107
Guillou, Jan, 50, 52, 234
Gulager, Clu, 105
Gustavasson, Ylva, 179

H:r Landshövding (2008), 120
Haagen Schmidt, Jørgen, 39
Hackman, Gene, 232
Håfström, Mikael, 193, 233–5
Hair (1979) 180
Halloween (1978), 191
Halloween 2 (1981), 192
Hallström, Lasse, 149, 158, 233, 235, 245
Hamer, Bent, 12, 233, 239, 241, 245
Hamilton (Hamilton: I nationens intresse, 2012), 13–14
Hammerich, Rumle, 82
Hammett, Dashiell, 63
Hamsun (1996), 24
Hamsun, Knut, 24
Hannah and her Sisters (1986), 158
Hans Christian Andersen (1952), 22
Hansel & Gretel Witch Hunters (2012), 253
Hanson, Einar, 230
Hanson, Lars, 230
Haraldsson, Björn Hlynur, 70

Hard Target (1993), 77, 80, 84
Hark, Ina Rae, 134, 145
Harlin, Renny, 3, 11–12, 156, 233–5, 242
Harry Potter and the Philosopher's Stone (2001), 7
Hartnett, Josh, 240–1
Hawks, Howard, 160
Hayes, Will H., 104
He Who Gets Slapped (1924), 231
Headhunters (Hodejegerne, 2011), 61–2, 65–7, 72, 76, 80, 82, 87–99, 253
Hedetoft, Ulf, 219
Hedling, Olof, 222
Helander, Jalmari, 191
Helge (Olsson), Mats, 11
Helin, Sofia, 51
Helismaa, Reino, 23
Hella W (2011), 23
Hellström, Börge, 107, 115
Helstad, Benjamin, 54
Henni, Lisa, 111
Hennie, Aksel, 8, 41, 62, 65, 82
Hepburn, Katherine, 170
Here, Beneath the North Star (Täällä Pohjantähden alla, 2009–10), 26
Hersholt, Jean, 230
Heyerdahl, Thor, 22
Higbee, Will, 94, 136
Higson, Andrew, 24, 30, 94
Hills Have Eyes, The (2004), 194
Hiltunen, Leena, 217
Hirschbiegel, Oliver, 40
Hjort, Mette, 96, 98, 137, 145, 147, 154, 234, 245
Hobbes, Thomas, 104, 108
Hoffmann, Karl Heinz, 40
Hokus Pokus Alfons Åberg (2013), 5
Holst, Marius, 54–5
Homeland (2011–), 93
Hooper, Tobe, 193
Hostel (2005), 194
Hotel Imperial (1927), 231
Hour of the Wolf (Vargtimmen, 1968), 10
House of Angels (Änglagård, 1992), 149
Human Centipede II, The (2011), 196
Hundred Foot Journey, The (2013), 235
Hunger Games, The (2012), 78, 80
Hunger Games: Catching Fire, The (2013), 78

Hunt, The (*Jagten*, 2012), 76, 80–2, 85, 88–9
Hunters, The (*Jägarna*, 1996), 76, 80, 84–6, 88
Hurricane (1979), 232
Hurricane, The (1937), 232
Hutchings, Peter, 194
Hvinden, Peter, 204
Hypnotist, The (*Hypnotistören*, 2013), 235

I Am Curious – Yellow (*Jag är nyfiken – en film I gult*, 1967), 148
Ibsen, Henrik, 240
Idiots, The (*Idioterne*, 1998), 153, 234
Ikonen, Ansa, 2
In a Better World (*Hævnen*, 2010), 5, 237
Indriðason, Arnaldur, 69
Inga (*Jag – en oskuld*, 1968), 218, 223
Insomnia (1997), 62, 64–6, 72, 240
Insomnia (2002), 64
Iordinova, Dina, 157, 220
Iron Sky (2012), 5, 14–15, 244–8, 250–1, 254–60
It Happened One Night (1934), 154
Italian for Beginners (*Italiensk for begyndere*, 2000), 147, 154, 157
It's All About Love (2004), 235, 239
Ivarson, Inge, 222
Iversen, Gunnar, 7–8, 13, 36, 192, 195, 200

Jäättenmäki, Anneli, 119–28
Jackson, Peter, 245
Jaeckin, Just, 223
Jähkel, Lennart, 86
Jar City (*Mýrin*, 2006), 61, 69–70, 72
Järnefelt, Jonna, 120, 127
Järvinen, Anna, 141
Jenkins, Henry, 245
Jensen, Knut Erik, 149, 181
Jensen, Sara Indrio, 154
Jeunet, Jean-Pierre, 147
Johansson, Alf W., 42
Johansson, Ingmar, 151
Johnsen, Sara, 149
Johnson, Mats, 199
Joner, Kristoffer, 54
Jonsson, Jens, 114
Jönsson, Reidar, 151
Jönssonligan dyker upp igen (1986), 8

Journey to Japan (1973), 223
Junk Mail (*Budbringeren*, 1997), 149
Jussinniemi, Johanna, 223
Justine and Juliette (1975), 222

Kääpä, Pietari, 135, 142, 192, 196, 200, 219, 233
Kajanus, Robert, 25, 30
Kalde spor (1962), 34
Kampen om tungtvannet (1948), 34
Kamprad, Ingvar, 44
Kanal (1957), 42
Kangas, Olli, 204
Kaplan, Andrew, 210
Karkama, Pentti, 134, 145
Kassila, Matti, 163
Kaukomaa, Tero, 14, 246–7, 254
Kaurismäki, Aki, 1, 12, 241, 244, 251, 253
Kaurismäki, Mika, 136, 142, 149, 155–7, 253
Kemp, Julian, 190, 244
Keynes, John Maynard, 109
Kidz in da Hood (*Förortsungar*, 2006), 179, 181
Killing, The (2011–), 94
Killing, The (*Forbrydelsen*, 2007–), 1, 64, 94
King, Roger, 79
King, Stephen, 234
King of Devil's Island (*Kongen av Bastøy*, 2010), 54–7
King of the Travelers (2012), 258
Kilpeläinen, Tuure, 145
Kinnaman, Joel, 110, 114
Kinnaman, Melinda, 152
Kitchen Stories (*Psalmer fra kjøkkenet*, 2003), 241
Kittelsen, Agnes, 37
Kivi, Aleksis, 23
Kjellin, Alf, 232, 242
Knithilä, Elina, 142
Koivunen, Anu, 155, 161, 164
Koivusalo, Timo, 21, 26–7
Kolker, Philip, 138, 145
Kon-Tiki (2012), 22, 253
Kopps (2003), 234
Korkiasaari, Jouni, 135, 146
Kragh-Jacobsen, Sören, 153
Krickic, Zlatko, 70
Kristin Lavransdatter (1995), 49

INDEX

Krugman, Paul, 110
Kukkonen, Ada, 142
Kuparinen, Mikko, 161, 170
Kvist, Jon, 204

Laakso, Kimmo, 160
Laderman, David, 139, 145
Lady to Love, A (1930), 231
Lagerström, Louise, 42
Laguna, Sonny, 191
Lake of the Dead (*De dødes tjern*, 1958), 9–10
Lamb, John, 227
Landis, John, 218
Landy, Marica, 21, 28
Lange, Jessica, 240
Langhelle, Jörgen, 155
Langlete, Magnus, 54
Language of Love, The (1969), 225
Lapidus, Jens, 104, 107, 111–13, 115
Larsen, Thomas Bo, 81
Larsmo, Ola, 38, 41
Larsson, Matti, 115
Larsson, Stieg, 1, 61, 94, 115
Lasch, Christopher, 112
Lasermannen – en berättelse om Sverige (novel, 2002), 107
Last Wedding, The (*Kivenpyörittäjän kylä*, 1995), 145
Latvalehto, Kai 134
Laugier, Pascal, 195
Lawrence, Jennifer, 237
League, Tim, 244
Leffler, Yvonne, 209
Leger, Fernand, 182
Lehman, Peter, 225
Lehtisalo, Anneli, 22
Leifer, Vilhelm, 40
Leino, Eino, 23
Lennerhed, Lena, 218
Lepage, Henri, 106
Let the Right One In (*Låt den rätte komma in*, 2008), 200, 203, 205, 208, 210, 212, 214, 252
Life Aquatic with Steve Zissou (2008), 253
Life Deluxe (*Livet deluxe*, novel, 2011), 113
Life of Aleksis Kivi, The (*Aleksis Kiven elämä*, 2002), 23–4
Lilla Jönssonligan och cornflakeskuppen (1996), 8

Lim, Song Whee, 94
Lindberg, Christina, 222
Lindblad, Helena, 121
Lindhardt, Thure, 39
Lindley, Arthur, 56
Lindström, Anders, 97
Linna, Väinö, 26
Lipkin, Steven, 122, 127
Lipponen, Paavo, 119
Lipton Cockton in the Shadows of Sodoma (1995), 13
Little Caesar (1931), 104, 109
Little Caesar (novel, 1929), 104
Löfgren, Orvar, 145
Loiri, Vesa-Matti, 135
Long Kiss Goodnight, The (1996), 233
Looking for Fidel (2004), 120
Love Actually (2003), 170
Love and Journalism (*Kärlek och journalistik*, 1916), 3
Love and Lemons (*Små citronen gula*, 2013), 163
Love Island (*Kärleksön*, 1977), 217
Love Mates (*Änglar, finns dom?*, 1961), 2
Lowenthal, Leo, 24
Lucas, George, 174
Lyftet (1978), 107
Lyftet (novel, 1976), 107
Lyngdal, Reynir, 191
Lynn, Marie, 222

McCoy, Horace, 63
McCrea, Joel, 77
Macdonald, Dwight, 27
MacDonald, Ross, 67
MacDowell, James, 148, 164
McGregor, Ewan, 233
McNair, Brian, 226
Macody Lund, Synnøve, 65
McQueen, Steve, 238
McTiernan, John, 77
Madame Bovary (1949), 232
Magnusson, Peter, 163
Mäkelä, Aleksi, 67
Mäkelä, Taru, 159–65
Mäki, Reijo, 67
Maksimainen, Jaana, 161
Man Who Could Not Laugh, The (*Mannen som ikke kunne le*, 1968), 2

Man Without a Past (*Mies vailla menneisyyttä*, 2002), 149, 155–7
Manhunt (*Rovdyr*, 2008), 196
Mankell, Henning, 1, 61, 64, 94–5, 105, 107
Mannerheim, Carl Gustaf Emil, 23
Mansfield, Jayne, 165
Mänty, Harri, 141
Manus, Max, 36, 38–40
Margaret (2009), 120
Marin, Adrian, 174
Marklund, Carl, 218
Mårlind, Måns, 93
Martyrs (2008), 194
Marvin, Garry, 81
Marvin, Lee, 238
Marx, Karl, 104
Mary Poppins (1964), 173
Matti (2006), 23
Matti Nykänen, 23
Max Manus: Man of War (*Max Manus*, 2008), 33–4, 36–44, 50
Melville, Jean-Pierre, 39, 42
Meriluoto, Aila, 24
Midsummer of Love (*Sommaren med Göran*, 2009), 162–3
Mifune (*Mifune's sidste sang*, 1998), 153
Mikkelsen, Mads, 39, 53, 80, 85, 238
Miller, Daniel, 139, 146
Miller, Laura, 95
Mills, Katie, 141, 146
Milton, Berth, Sr. 221
Mimic (1997), 234
Minelli, Vincent, 232
Mitchell, Radha, 240
Moldestad, Thomas, 192
Möller, Olle, 107
Molly (1977), 222
Monica Z (2013), 22, 24–5, 29
Monroe, Marilyn, 14
Montand, Yves, 145
Moodyson, Lukas, 149
Moonlight Sonata, The (*Kuutamosonaatti*, 1988), 10
Moonlight Sonata II: Street Sweepers, The (*Kuutamosonaatti 2: Kadunlakaisijat*, 1991), 10
Moore, Julianne, 235
Mortimer, Claire, 160–1
Moseng, Jo Sondre, 191
Most Dangerous Game, The (1932), 77, 80

Motion Picture Producers and Distributors of America (MPPDA), 104
Mozart and the Whale (2006), 240
Munthe, Martin, 193
My Life as a Dog (*Mitt liv som hund*, 1985), 149, 151–2, 157, 235
My Little Eye (2002), 197
Mygind, Peter, 39
Mysterud, Ivar, 87

Naficy, Hamid, 135, 146
Nakajima, Sadao, 223
Næss, Arne, 79–80, 87
Næss, Peter, 149, 155, 233
Najafi, Babak, 113
Nattbuss 807 (1997), 105
Nätterqvist, Joakim, 51
Neale, Steve, 24
Negri, Pola, 231, 242
Nell, Victor, 79
Nesbø, Jo, 61, 66–7
Nestingen, Andrew, 3, 5, 7, 12, 112, 145, 149–50, 156, 175
Never Fuck Up (*Aldrig fucka upp*, novel, 2008), 113
New Land, The (*Nybyggarna*, 173), 232
Nichols, Bill, 121, 156
Nightmare on Elm Street 4: The Dream Master (1988), 233
Nightwatch (*Nattevagten*, 1994), 233–5
Nightwatch (1997), 233–5
Nilssen, Trond, 54
Nilsson, Anna Q., 230
Nilsson, Johannes, Stjärne, 182
Nine Lives (*Ni liv*, 1957), 239
Ninja Mission, The (1984), 11–12, 253
Nissen, Greta, 230
No Thank You (*Ei kiitos*, 2014), 162, 170
Nolte, Nick, 233
Nordaas, Alexander L. 199
Nordic Film and Television Fund, 14
Nordin, Sven, 155
Nordisk Films Kompagni, 2
Nordgren, Nils, 194
Norén, Lars, 97
Norsk Filmfond, 4, 14
Northern Exposure (1990–3), 158
Norwegian Film Institute, 4, 244, 246–8

269

Norwegian Ninja (Kommander Trehjolt og ninjatroppen, 2010), 14, 244–51, 257–60
Not Like Others (*Vampyrer*, 2008), 203–14
Nowell, Richard, 194
Nurmi, Paavo, 135
Nutley, Colin, 149
Nyborg Erikssen, 196
Nykänen, Matti, 23

O'Donovan, Gerard, 101
O'Horten (2007), 241
Of Mice and Men (novel, 1937), 7, 25
Ojanen, Sofia, 167
Oland, Warner, 230
Olofsson, Clark, 107
Olsen Banden Junior (2001), 9
Olsen Gang series (*Olsen Banden*, 1968–98), 2, 8–9
Olsen-banden (1968), 8
Olsen-banden (1969), 8
Olsen-banden deruda' (1977), 8
Olsen-banden går i krig (1978), 8
Olsenbanden jr. (2003), 9
Olsen-banden ser rødt (1976), 8
Omberg, Kjetil, 14
One Man's War (*Yhden miehen sota*, 1973), 145
Once Around (1991), 235, 239
Once Upon a Time in Phuket (*En gang I Phuket*, 2011), 162
One Flew Over the Cuckoo's Nest (1975), 7
Open Hearts (*Elsker dig for evigt*, 2002), 237
Organisation for Economic Co-operation and Development (OECD), 106
Orion's Belt (*Orions Belte*, 1985), 10
Ottosson, Paul N. J., 3
Outinen, Kati, 156
Outlaw, Saga of Gisli, The (*Utlaginn*, 1981), 49
Ovid, 83
Owe, Baard, 241
Owen, Clive, 234

Päätalo (2008), 23
Päätalo, Kalle, 23
Pacino, Al, 240
Paget, Derek, 121–8
Pajama Game, The (1957), 177

Paju, Anna, 170
Pakarinen, Darya, 141
Palin, Michael, 148
Palme (2012), 119–27
Palo, Tauno, 2
Pantti, Mervi, 247
Passer, Dirch, 25
Pathfinder (*Veiviseren*, 1987), 239
Patterson, Floyd, 151
Paul, Adolf, 30
Peeping Tom (1960), 68
Pelle the Conqueror (1988), 237
Peltola, Markku, 155
Penn, Sean, 235
Persbrandt, Mikael, 237
Persson, Fredrik, 43
Petersen, Kjeld, 25
Phantom Chariot, The (*Körkarlen*, 1921), 3, 189
Phoenix, Joaquin, 235
Pichel, Irving, 77
Pillai, Nicholas, 160
Pinchcliffe Grand Prix (1975), 253
Pitko, Matti, 127
Polanski, Roman, 232
Pommer, Eric, 231
Pontikis, Peter, 203
Portes de la Nuit, Les (1946), 145
Poussu, Tarmo, 142, 146
Predator (1987), 77, 80, 84
Predator 2 (1990), 77, 80
Predators (2010), 77, 80
Press (*Pressa*, 2007–), 69
Priest of Evil (*Harjunpää ja pahan pappi*, 2010), 66, 68–9
Prime Minister (*Pääministeri*, 2009), 119–28
Producers, The (2006), 218
Pryce, Jonathan, 71
Punch-Drunk Love (2002)
Pusher trilogy (1996–2005), 13, 112, 238

Quick, Thomas, 106
Qvist, Per Olov, 194

Raimi, Sam, 245
Rais-Nordentoft, Aage, 78
Rambo: First Blood Part II (1985), 11
Randolph, Anders, 230
Ranthe, Lars, 81
Rare Exports (2010), 6, 190–1

Rask, Markus, 152
Rautavaara, Tapio, 23
Red State (2011), 197
Redvall, Eva, 234
Reems, Harry, 222
Reiner, Rob, 158
Reini, Antti, 67
Reykjavik Rotterdam (2008), 71
Reykjavik Whale Watching Massacre, The (2009), 190, 200, 244, 245
Rhys-Meyers, Jonathan, 240
Ricci, Christina, 240
Ritchie, Guy, 114
Road North (*Tie pohjoiseen*, 2012), 133–45
Roberts, Julia, 235
Rocco Ravishes the Czech Republic (2009), 223
Rome, Open City (*Roma, città aperta*, 1945), 42
Ronkainen, Mika, 180
Rose of the Rascal, The (*Rentun ruusu*, 2001), 23, 26
Roseanna (novel, 1965), 107
Rosenfeldt, Hans, 61, 93
Rosenqvist, Juha, 167
Rosenstone, Robert A., 47
Roslund, Anders, 107, 115
Ross, Kristin, 139, 146
Rossellini, Roberto, 42
Roth, Eli, 194
Rousseau, Jean-Jacques, 53
Rowden, Terry, 219
Royal Affair, A (*En kongelig affære*, 2012), 52–4, 56–7
Royal Tennenbaums, The (2001), 148
Ryberg, Ingrid, 223
Ryti, Risto, 23

Saladin, 51–2
Salmi, Hannu, 28
Salminen, Arto, 159, 164
Sandemose, Mikkel Braenne, 192
Sarno, Joe, 217, 223
Sauna (2008), 55–7, 190
Saw (2005), 194
Scarface (1932), 109
Scarface (1983), 105, 115
Scarlet Letter, The (1926), 231
Schaefer, Eric, 218, 224
Schenk, Ernst-Günther, 40
Schepelern, Peter, 176

Scherfig, Lone, 147, 153
Schmidt, Rob, 194
Schoedsack, Ernest B., 77
Schwarzenegger, Arnold, 234
Scorsese, Martin, 218
Se7en (1995), 68
Searching for Sugar Man (2012), 181
Segerstedt, Torgny, 24
Seiling, Charlotte, 93
Seims, Trond Espen, 67
Seinfeld (1989–98), 158
Selås, 197
Selin, Markus, 11–12
Selmer, Ketty, 40–1
Seppälä, Jaakko, 167
Serbian Film, A (*Srpski film*, 2010), 196
Seventh Seal, The (*Det sjunde inseglet*, 1957), 48, 56
Sexual Freedom in Denmark (1970), 227
Shipping News, The (2001), 235, 239
Shipwrecked (1990), 240
Shove, Elizabeth, 139, 146
Sibelius (2003), 21–31
Sibelius, Aino, 25–6, 28
Sibelius, Jean, 21–31
Sigurðardóttir, Yrsa, 69
Sigurðsson, Ingvar, 69, 71
Sigurjónsson, Sigurður, 70–1
Silence, The (*Tystnaden*, 1963), 3
Six, Tom, 196
Simonsson, Ola, 182
Sjöman, Vilgot, 148
Sjöström, Victor, 230, 237
Sjöwall, Maj, 61, 63–4, 94, 107
Skarsgård, Stellan, 54, 62, 64, 240
Skjoldbjærg, Erik, 64, 233, 239, 241
Skouen, Arne, 239
Sletaune, Pål, 149
Smith, Kevin, 197
Smith, Susan, 176
Soderbergh, Steven, 233
Söderbergh Widding, Astrid, 7, 200, 245, 258
Soila, Tytti, 7, 200, 245, 259
Sökarna (1993), 105
Solum, Ove, 36
Soman, Milind, 51
Something To Talk About (1995), 235
Song of Norway (1970), 22
Sørenssen, Björn, 181
Sorlin, Pierre, 29, 31

INDEX

Sound of Music, The (1965), 173, 178
Sound of Noise, The (2010), 182–3
Spacey, Kevin, 235
Spasojevic, Srdjan, 196
Spencer, Neil, 142, 146
Spielberg, Steven, 251
Spira, Joel, 111
Springer, Julian, 144, 146
Staalesen, Gunnar, 67
Stables, Kate, 39
Stalker (1979), 56
Stallone, Sylvester, 234
Star Wars (1977), 247–8
Star Wreck, 257, 260
Stein, Björn, 93
Steinbeck, John, 7, 25
Stenberg, Mats, 192
Stengade, Stine, 40
Stevens, Fisher, 241
Stiches (2012), 259
Stigsdotter, Ingrid, 95
Stiller, Mauritz, 230, 241
Stone, Oliver, 108
Storage, The (*Varasto*, 2011), 159–65
Stormare, Peter, 86
Stringer, Julian, 134, 144
Stroman, Susan, 218
Strömstedt, Lasse, 107
Struensee, Johan, 53
Substitute, The (*Vikaren*, 2007), 13–14
Substitute Wife (*Vaimoke*, 1936), 163–5
Summer by the River, A (*Kuningasjätkä*, 1998), 22
Summer Rebellion (*Kesäkapina*, 1970), 145
Sun Shadows: Faithful Kiss (2011), 203–8, 212
Sundbärg, Gustav, 99
Sundholm, John, 2
Sundvall, Kjell, 76, 84
Surviving the Game (1994), 78
Susman, Warren I., 50
Suvakci, Mahmut, 111
Svensk Filmindustri (SF), 5
Svensson, Camilla, 223
Swan and the Wanderer, The (*Kulkuri ja Joutsen*, 1999), 22–3, 26
Swede, Ingrid, 223
Swede, Puma, 223
Swedish Censorship Board, 11
Swedish Deep Throat (*Svenska långt när i halsen*, 2007), 225

Swedish Film Institute, 4–5, 11, 42, 193, 223–4
Syversen, Patrik, 196

Tähti, Annikki, 156
Tamas, Gellert, 107
Tapper, Mikael, 127
Tarantino, Quentin, 114
Tarkovsky, Andrej, 56
Taxi Driver, (1976), 218
Taylor, John Russell, 174
Taylor, Lili, 241
Texas Chain Saw Massacre, The (1974), 10, 193
Thale (2012), 199
Thatcher, Margaret, 106
Things We Lost in the Fire (2007), 237
Third Man, The (1949), 65
This Life (*Hvidstengruppen*, 2012), 50
Thompson, Jim, 63
Thomsen, Ulrich, 237
Thörnell, Olof, 39
Thors, Björn, 71
Three Seconds (*Tre sekunder*, novel, 2009), 115
Thune, Henriette, 209
Thurman, Uma, 218
Time of Roses (*Ruusujen aika*, 1968), 10
Together (*Tillsammans*, 2000), 149
Tomei, Marisa, 241
Tönnies, Ferdinand, 105
Torment (*Hets*, 1944), 232
Torrent, The (1926), 231
Tough Ones, The (*Häjyt*, 1999), 22
Trading Places (1983), 218
Treasure Island (1950), 240
Treholt, Arne, 247–8
Trier, Joakim, 253
Troell, Jan, 24, 232, 242
Troll Hunter (*Trolljegeren*, 2010), 192, 200
Trydegård, Gun-Britt, 206
Tunnel, The (2013–), 91, 93, 100–1
Turner, Bryan, 141, 146
Turturro, John, 238
Twilight Saga, The (2008–12), 208–9
Two Soldiers (*Två soldater*, novel, 2012), 115
Tyldum, Morten, 253

Uhse, Beate, 227
Ullmann, Liv, 49, 95, 232

Umbrellas of Cherbourg, The (Les parapluies de Cherbourg, 1964), 173
Upperdog (2009), 149
Uthaug, Roar, 192
Uuno Turhapuro films (1973–2004), 4

V2: Dead Angel (V2: Jäätynyt enkeli, 2007), 67
Vaala, Valentin, 161, 163
Valhalla Rising (2009), 49
Valkyrie (2008), 40
Vampire (Vampyr, 1932), 189, 204
Varela, Matias, 111
Vares: Private Eye (Vares: yksityisetsivä, 2004), 67
Varning för Jönssonligan (1981), 8
Veijonen, Juha, 67
Vibeto, Håvard Andreas, 191
Viita, Lauri, 24
Vikander, Alice, 52
Vinterberg, Thomas, 12, 76, 80, 85, 154, 233, 235–6, 238–9, 243, 253
Virratvuori, Jussi, 164
Virta, Olavi, 23
Virtanen, Ville, 55
Visitors, The (Besökarna, 1988), 191
Vogel, Erik, 247, 257–9
Von Brömssen, Thomas, 152
von Quirnheim, Mertz, 40
von Sydow, Max, 232
von Trier, Lars, 12, 149, 154, 157, 175, 177–8, 234, 238–9, 245, 253
Vreeswijk, Cornelis, 25–6
Vuoksenmaa, Johanna, 161
Vuorensola, Timo, 244–7, 254–9

Wahlöö, Per, 61, 63–4, 94, 107
Wajda, Andrzej, 42
Wall Street (1987), 108
Wallström, Martin, 114
Wan, James, 194
Watkins, James, 194
Watson, Keith, 91, 100
Watson, Stephanie, 146
Wedderkopp, Annika, 80
Wenders, Wim, 152
Westwell, Guy, 36–7
What Richard Did (2012), 258
What's Eating Gilbert Grape? (1993), 158, 235
When Ali Came to Ireland (2012), 258

When Harry Met Sally (1989), 158
When the Raven Flies (Hrafninn flygur, 1984), 49
Whitaker, Ross, 258
White Reindeer, The (Valkoinen Peura, (1954), 9, 205, 209, 211, 213
White Slave Trade, The (Den hvide slavehandel, 1910), 2
White, Hayden, 27
Wickman, Torgny, 225
Wierup, Lasse, 115
Wiklund, Tommy, 191
Wilderness (Villmark, 2002), 10
Williams, Linda Ruth, 218, 220
Williams, Michelle, 240
Wind, The (1928), 231
Winding Refn, Nicolas, 3, 13, 49, 112, 233, 235, 237, 239, 243, 245
Winge, Victora, 36
Wings of Desire (Der himmel uber Berlin, 1987), 152
Winston, Brian, 121
Winter War, The (Talvisota, 1989), 2
Wirkola, Tommy, 192, 244, 253, 257
Witchcraft through the Ages (Häxan, 1922), 48, 231
Wither (Vittra, 2013), 6, 191, 195, 198–200
Within Limits (2009), 120
Wold, Susse, 80
Wollen, Peter, 139, 146
Woo, John, 77
Wood, 210
Wood, James, 170
Wray, Fay, 77
Wright, Rochelle, 203, 208
Wrong Turn (2003), 194
Wuolijoki, Hella, 23

Yates, Peter, 238
Yeoh, Gilbert, 173
Young Girls of Rochefort, The (Les demoiselles de Rochefort, 1967), 173
Yours until Death (novel, 2010), 67
Yrjänä, Joensuu, Matti, 68

Zander, Ulf, 40, 42–4
Zandy's Bride (1974), 232
Zemeckis, Robert, 149
Zetterlund, Monica, 25
Zwart, Harald, 156

EU representative:
Easy Access System Europe
Mustamäe tee 50, 10621 Tallinn, Estonia
Gpsr.requests@easproject.com